America's
TEST KITCHEN

ALSO BY THE EDITORS OF COOK'S ILLUSTRATED
HOME OF AMERICA'S TEST KITCHEN

The Best Recipe
The Best Recipe: American Classics
The Best Recipe: Grilling and Barbecue
The Best Recipe: Italian Classics
The Best Recipe: Soups and Stews
Perfect Vegetables
The Quick Recipe
Restaurant Favorites at Home

The America's Test Kitchen Cookbook
Here in America's Test Kitchen

The Best Kitchen Quick Tips

The Complete Book of Pasta and Noodles
The Cook's Illustrated Complete Book of Poultry

How to Barbecue and Roast on the Grill
How to Cook Chicken Breasts
How to Cook Chinese Favorites
How to Cook Garden Vegetables
How to Cook Shrimp and Other Shellfish
How to Grill
How to Make an American Layer Cake
How to Make Cookie Jar Favorites
How to Make Ice Cream
How to Make Muffins, Biscuits, and Scones
How to Make Pasta Sauces
How to Make Pot Pies and Casseroles
How to Make Salad
How to Make Sauces and Gravies
How to Make Simple Fruit Desserts
How to Make Soup
How to Make Stew
How to Sauté

To order any of our books,
visit us at http://www.cooksillustrated.com
or http://www.americastestkitchen.com
or call us at 800-611-0759

INSIDE AMERICA'S TEST KITCHEN

# INSIDE
# AMERICA'S TEST KITCHEN

BY THE ·EDITORS OF
## COOK'S ILLUSTRATED

ILLUSTRATIONS
John Burgoyne

PHOTOGRAPHY
Carl Tremblay
Daniel Van Ackere

AMERICA'S TEST KITCHEN
BROOKLINE, MASSACHUSETTS

America's Test Kitchen
17 Station Street
Brookline, MA 02445

ISBN 0-936184-71-X
Library of Congress Cataloging-in-Publication Data
The Editors of *Cook's Illustrated*

Inside America's Test Kitchen: New Recipes and Product Ratings from Public Television's Favorite Cooking Show
1st Edition

ISBN 0-936184-71-X (hardback): $29.95
1. Cooking. 1. Title
2003

Manufactured in the United States of America

Distributed by America's Test Kitchen, 17 Station Street, Brookline, MA 02445
Editor: Jack Bishop
Series Designer: Amy Klee
Director of Editorial Operations: Barbara Bourassa
Art Director: Robin Gilmore-Barnes
Graphic Designer: Nina Madjid
Jacket Designer: Julia Sedykh
Photographers: Carl Tremblay (color and documentary photography);
Daniel Van Ackere (silhouette photography)
Illustrator: John Burgoyne
Production Manager: Jessica Lindheimer Quirk
Associate Editor: Rebecca Hays
Copy Editor: India Koopman
Proofreader: Amy Monaghan
Indexer: Cathy Dorsey

# CONTENTS

PREFACE BY CHRISTOPHER KIMBALL  ix

INSIDE AMERICA'S TEST KITCHEN  xi

INDEX  337

CHAPTER 1
Salad 101  3

CHAPTER 2
Summer Tomatoes  13

CHAPTER 3
One-Pot Wonders  29

CHAPTER 4
East Coast Seafood  39

CHAPTER 5
New Orleans Menu  53

CHAPTER 6
Freedom from Red Sauce  63

CHAPTER 7
Quick Pasta  75

CHAPTER 8
Pot Roast  99

CHAPTER 9
Maple-Glazed Pork Roast  111

CHAPTER 10
Truck Stop Favorites  121

CHAPTER 11
Chicken in a Skillet  131

CHAPTER 12
Chicken in a Pot  141

CHAPTER 13
Steak and Potatoes  155

CHAPTER 14
Steak Tips  169

CHAPTER 15
Stir-Fry 101  179

CHAPTER 16
Asian Noodles  191

CHAPTER 17
Italian Classics  205

CHAPTER 18
French Food in a Flash  217

CHAPTER 19
Teatime  243

CHAPTER 20
Sunday Brunch  255

CHAPTER 21
The Pancake Show  269

CHAPTER 22
Cookie Jar Favorites  281

CHAPTER 23
Summer Berry Desserts  293

CHAPTER 24
Easy Sheet Cakes  303

CHAPTER 25
Lemon Cheesecake  313

CHAPTER 26
Showstopper Desserts  323

# PREFACE

ARE YOUR "BLIND" TASTE TESTS REALLY BLIND? DO YOU really test a recipe 30 or 40 times? Is the "bad" food at the beginning of the show really that bad? Does the "good" food really taste as good as it looks? Do you ever make mistakes on camera that viewers don't see? Are you really having fun during filming?

The short answer to all of these questions is "Yes!" The tastings really are blind (I have no idea which brands are which when I taste them on camera), we do test recipes for weeks at a time, the "bad" food really is that bad, the "good" food really does taste good (in some cases so good that we keep eating after the camera is turned off), we make our share of mistakes on and off camera, and, yes, we really do have a lot of fun filming *America's Test Kitchen*.

*Inside America's Test Kitchen* not only brings you the recipes, taste tests, cookware ratings, and food science from our public television show, it also brings you *inside* our test kitchen, the place where we test recipes for *Cook's Illustrated* magazine and also film *America's Test Kitchen*. You get a front-row seat, watching the series unfold as we prep, sauté, bake, grill, taste, and test our way through another 26 episodes. It is indeed as much fun as it appears to be on television, and we hope that *Inside America's Test Kitchen* will become your behind-the-scenes guide to the show, the recipes, and the people who make it all work.

Cooking and music have a lot in common. I recently met a banjo player who loves old-time music—fiddle tunes that predate bluegrass and were popular at a time when most households could lay claim to a $5 banjo. One night last summer, I played along with her band in a house lit only by candles at the end of a long dirt road not far from our Vermont farm. We worked through some of the classic repertoire: "Shady Grove," "Waterbound," and "Barlow Knife." Like cooking, making old-time music seems like a hard thing to do, especially the fiddling, but also like cooking, it's easier to learn by watching other people do it. Once you see it done, the underlying structure of the tunes becomes clearer and you can really start to play.

What does this have to do with a cooking show? Well, watching *America's Test Kitchen* is a bit like watching a bunch of old-time fiddlers. The cast has played the old favorites hundreds, if not thousands, of times and is eager to share them with you, the viewer. You can just sit back and watch or sit up and pay really close attention and start to learn what makes these classic recipes tick. If nothing else, a good time should be had by all, fiddling away in the kitchen, trying to make a little magic with a few basic ingredients and more than our share of enthusiasm.

Thanks for watching *America's Test Kitchen*. We hope that you find the time to get into the kitchen to make a little music.

Christopher Kimball
Founder and editor, *Cook's Illustrated* magazine
Host, *America's Test Kitchen*
Brookline, Massachusetts, 2003

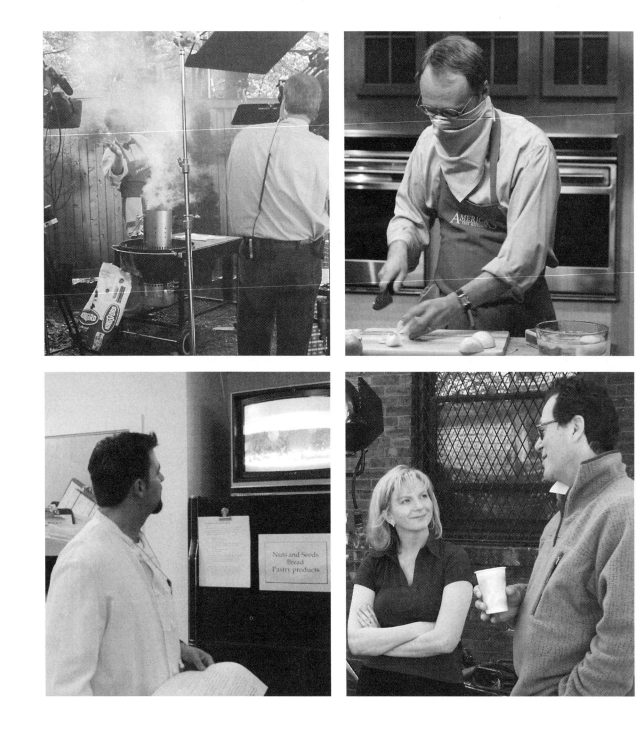

# INSIDE AMERICA'S TEST KITCHEN

AMERICA'S TEST KITCHEN IS A GROUP OF EDITORS, RECIPE developers, test cooks, art directors, photographers, tasters, equipment testers, and scientists all working in pursuit of a single goal—foolproof versions of favorite recipes. We cook in a real kitchen located in Brookline, Massachusetts. This kitchen is home to *Cook's Illustrated* magazine, numerous cookbooks, including *The Best Recipe,* as well as our public television show, *America's Test Kitchen.* We are dedicated to—some might say, obsessed with—helping Americans to cook better.

What, exactly, happens in America's Test Kitchen? We start with favorite American recipes. This means old-fashioned comfort food like coconut cream pie, grilled steak, mashed potatoes, and chocolate chip cookies. It also means "new" classics—often from other cuisines—such as pad Thai, tarte Tatin, and strawberries with balsamic vinegar. We begin the recipe development process by talking about the problems we have encountered when preparing these dishes in the past. We draw up a list of common pitfalls with a particular recipe—say, sticky noodles when making pad Thai, or soggy crust when preparing coconut cream pie— and then we start researching possible solutions. We comb through dozens of cookbooks and magazines, looking for interesting or unusual strategies. We search the Internet and get on the phone with experts in the field.

After compiling a lengthy list of kitchen tests, we start cooking. We usually make about a half-dozen versions of a particular recipe to refine our goals and sort out the problems. After this diagnostic phase, we start testing the variables, one by one. Which types of potatoes are best for mashing—russets, Yukon Gold, all-purpose, or red? Should we boil the potatoes in their skins, or should we peel them and cut them into chunks? What's the best tool for mashing the potatoes—a food mill, ricer, or potato masher? Should we add milk, half-and-half, or cream, and how much dairy is the right amount?

As we answer these questions, our recipe begins to take shape. Along the way, other questions—usually regarding equipment, ingredients, or science—often present themselves. Does it matter which kind of vegetable peeler you use to peel the potatoes? Is salted or unsalted butter better? Why do some potato varieties become soupy when dairy is added to them while others turn fluffy and smooth?

When we have a recipe that we all agree is the best it can be, we test it again (and again) on different stoves, with different pots and pans, until we know that it will work for every cook in every kitchen.

## The Cast

OUR TELEVISION SHOW HIGHLIGHTS THE BEST RECIPES developed in the test kitchen during the year—those recipes that our test kitchen staff makes at home over and over again. These recipes are accompanied by our most exhaustive equipment tests, our most shocking food-tasting results, and our most informative science experiments. These four elements—recipes, equipment tests, food tastings, and science experiments—are blended together to create television episodes that we hope are engaging and entertaining.

Christopher Kimball, the founder and editor of *Cook's Illustrated* magazine, is the ringmaster. He directs the presentation of these tests, tastings, and experiments. He is the host of the show and asks the questions you might ask. Why does sugar make beaten egg whites more stable? Which unsweetened chocolate makes the best brownies? What separates a great omelet from a mediocre one?

It's the job of our two executive chefs, Julia Collin Davison and Bridget Lancaster, to demonstrate our recipes. They show Chris what works, what doesn't, and explain why. In the process, they discuss (and show us) the best and worst examples from our development process—the cookies that burned, the cake that fell, and the chicken that was rubbery. As they cook, they reveal the findings from our exhaustive

kitchen work. They teach Chris (and the audience) the right way to mince an onion, why browning makes a tastier stew, and how to make salad.

Adam Ried, our equipment guru, shares the highlights from our detailed testing process in the Equipment Corner segments. He brings with him our favorite (and least favorite) gadgets and tools. He tells you which saucepan performed best in a dozen kitchen tests and shows why most grill brushes are nearly worthless. (Although he did find one unusual gem that makes cleaning the grill grate a pleasure—well, almost.) You learn why most vegetable choppers don't work and why every kitchen should be stocked with at least one kind of vegetable peeler.

Jack Bishop is our ingredient expert. He has Chris taste our favorite (and least favorite) brands of common food products—everything from canned tomatoes and olive oil to milk chocolate and mayonnaise. Chris may not always enjoy these exercises (it's not much fun tasting balsamic vinegar straight up), but he usually learns something as Jack explains what makes one brand superior to another. Good cooking starts with the right ingredients, and our Tasting Lab segments will help you shop efficiently.

## The Crew

ONLY FIVE COOKS AND EDITORS APPEAR ON THE TELEVISION show, but another 50 people work to make the show a reality. During filming, executive chefs Erin McMurrer and Dawn Yanagihara ran the "back kitchen," where all the food that appeared on camera originated. Along with the on-air crew, Erin and Dawn also planned and organized the 26 television episodes shot in May 2003. India Koopman helped develop equipment segments, Keri Fisher organized tastings, John Olson wrote many of the science segments, and Melissa Baldino researched all of the "Food Facts."

During filming, chefs Erika Bruce, Matthew Card, Garth Clingingsmith, Keith Dresser, Sean Lawler, and Diane Unger-Mahoney were in the kitchen from early in the morning to late at night helping Erin and Dawn cook all of the food needed on the set. Nina West was charged with the Herculean task of making sure all of the ingredients we needed were on hand. Kitchen assistants Judy Davis, Laura Courtemanche, and Greg Wislocki also worked long hours peeling potatoes, making pies, and baking cookies. Keri Fisher, Rebecca Hays, and Susan Light helped coordinate the efforts of the kitchen with the activities on the set by readying props, equipment, and food.

Jim McCormack, vice president for operations and technology, and Rich Cassidy, systems administrator, supervised the building of the test kitchen and helped turn the kitchen into a shooting set. They made sure all of the wiring, computers, and ovens were ready to go. Barbara Bourassa, director of editorial operations, staffed the kitchen and made sure all of the resources we needed were in place.

The staff of A La Carte Communications turned our recipes, tastings, equipment tests, and science experiments into a lively television show. Special thanks to executive producer Geof Drummond; director and editor Herb Sevush; director of photography Dean Gaskill; camera operators Stephen Hussar and Michael McEachern; jib camera operator Peter Dingle; audio engineer Gilles Morin; video engineer Eliat Goldman; script supervisor/makeup specialist Brenda Coffey; second camera operator/gaffer Thomas Hamilton; gaffers Patrick Ruth and Jack McPhee; grips Robert Ouzounian and Aaron Frutman; production manager Elena Battista; and production assistant Yale Miller.

We also would like to thank Hope Reed, who handles station relations, and co-executive producer Nat Katzman. Sur La Table and Vendange Wines helped to underwrite the show, and we thank them for their support. Props for the show were supplied by Olga Russo at A. Russo & Sons; Mahoney's Garden Center of Cambridge, Massachusetts; and Sur La Table.

We hope this book gives you an inside look at the fun, the chaos, and the food that make *America's Test Kitchen* unique. We are passionate about our work, and we hope you enjoy making (and eating) our recipes as well as reading about the process by which they were created. Our mission is pretty simple. We want to help make you a better cook. We hope that our television show and this book will do just that. If you have comments or questions about the show or the book, contact us at www.americastestkitchen.com. Visit www.cooksillustrated.com for more information about *Cook's Illustrated* magazine.

INSIDE AMERICA'S TEST KITCHEN

Keri readies 14 red wine vinegars for an on-camera tasting.

# SALAD 101

## CHAPTER I

IN THIS CHAPTER

**THE RECIPES**
Greek Salad
Country-Style Greek Salad

Wilted Spinach Salad with Warm
    Bacon Dressing
Foolproof Hard-Cooked Eggs

**TASTING LAB**
Jarred Roasted Red Peppers
Supermarket Red Wine Vinegars
Gourmet Red Wine Vinegars

Salad seems so easy. Just dress some leafy greens and serve, right? Well, as with most simple kitchen tasks, success depends on the details. Here's how we make a basic leafy green salad with a vinaigrette dressing in the test kitchen.

1. Tear the greens into bite-size pieces.

2. Soak the greens in a bowl of cold water. (We use the bowl of a salad spinner.)

3. Spin the greens dry, adding paper towels to the spinner to blot up excess moisture. (The greens can be refrigerated in a spinner lined with paper towels for a day or so.)

4. Use good oil in the dressing, which usually means extra-virgin olive oil.

5. Use the right ratio of oil to vinegar in the dressing. In most cases, 3 parts oil to 1 part vinegar works best.

6. Whisk the vinegar and salt and pepper together and then whisk in the oil to emulsify the dressing.

7. Dress the greens in a large bowl—at least 50 percent larger than the amount of greens—so there's plenty of room for tossing.

8. Toss gently. You want to fluff the greens, not bruise them.

# GREEK SALAD

**WHAT WE WANTED:** A salad with crisp ingredients and bold flavors, highlighted by briny olives and tangy feta, all married together with a bright-tasting dressing infused with fresh herbs.

Most pizza-parlor versions of Greek salad consist of iceberg lettuce, chunks of green pepper, and a few pale wedges of tomato, sparsely dotted with cubes of feta and garnished with one forlorn olive of questionable heritage. The accompanying dressing is loaded with musty dried herbs. How could we make this pizzeria staple worthy of the dinner table?

We started by testing different vinaigrette recipes, with ingredients ranging from vinegar and lemon juice to yogurt and mustard. Tasters thought that the yogurt-based dressing overwhelmed the salad and that the mustard and cider vinegar versions were just "wrong." Lemon juice was harsh and white wine vinegar was dull, but a dressing that combined lemon juice and red wine vinegar had the balanced flavor we were looking for. There was no place for dried herbs in this salad. Fresh herbs typically used in Greek cuisine include dill, oregano, parsley, mint, and basil. Tasters loved the idea of mint and parsley, but they lost their zip when mixed with the vinaigrette. Oregano's bold flavor stood up well to the vinegar and lemon juice and was the clear favorite. Pure olive oil and extra-virgin olive oil worked equally well, and the addition of a small amount of garlic gave the dressing the final kick it needed.

The next ingredients up for scrutiny were the vegetables. Although lettuce is not commonly found in traditional Greek salad, it is a main ingredient in the American version. The iceberg lettuce had to go. Romaine, which has the body and crunch of iceberg but also more color and flavor, was the natural choice. Tomatoes were also essential, and only the ripest ones would do. Green bell pepper got a unanimous thumbs-down. Everyone preferred the sweeter red variety, which was improved even further by being roasted. In the interest of saving time, we also tried jarred roasted red peppers, which tasters liked even better. The jarred peppers are packaged in a vinegary brine and have more depth of flavor than freshly roasted peppers do (for more information, see the Tasting Lab on page 6).

Onion was next. When the pungency of the raw onion sent some tasters running for breath mints, someone suggested soaking the onion in water to eliminate its caustic bite. We took that idea one step further: Why not marinate the onion in the vinaigrette? On a whim, we included some cucumber as well. The results were striking. The cucumber, which had been watery and bland just minutes before, was bright and flavorful, and the onion had lost its unpleasant potency.

Now the vinaigrette recipe was finalized and the vegetables selected, but something was still missing. We returned to the mint and parsley that had been eliminated from the vinaigrette. Instead, we simply mixed them with the vegetables, tossed this mixture together with the onion and cucumber that had been marinating in the vinaigrette, generously sprinkled the salad with feta and kalamata olives, and offered it to tasters. It was a hit. This was a Greek salad worthy of being served on china—not in an aluminum takeout container.

**WHAT WE LEARNED:** Use a combination of lemon juice and red wine vinegar in the dressing. Marinate the onion in this dressing to reduce its sting; marinate the cucumber in the dressing to flavor it. Use fresh herbs rather than dried, and replace dull iceberg lettuce with crisp, flavorful romaine.

## GREEK SALAD  Serves 6 to 8

Marinating the onion and cucumber in the vinaigrette tones down the onion's harshness and flavors the cucumber. For efficiency, prepare the other salad ingredients while the onion and cucumber marinate. Use a salad spinner to dry the lettuce thoroughly after washing; any water left clinging to the leaves will dilute the dressing.

### vinaigrette

| | |
|---|---|
| 3 | tablespoons red wine vinegar |
| 1½ | teaspoons juice from 1 lemon |
| 2 | teaspoons minced fresh oregano leaves |
| ½ | teaspoon salt |
| ⅛ | teaspoon ground black pepper |
| 1 | medium clove garlic, minced or pressed through a garlic press (about 1 teaspoon) |
| 6 | tablespoons olive oil |

### salad

| | |
|---|---|
| ½ | medium red onion, sliced thin (about ¾ cup) |
| 1 | medium cucumber, peeled, halved lengthwise, seeded (see the illustration at right), and cut into ⅛-inch-thick slices (about 2 cups) |
| 2 | romaine hearts, washed, dried thoroughly, and torn into 1½-inch pieces (about 8 cups) |
| 2 | large vine-ripened tomatoes (10 ounces total), each tomato cored, seeded, and cut into 12 wedges |
| ¼ | cup loosely packed torn fresh parsley leaves |
| ¼ | cup loosely packed torn fresh mint leaves |
| 6 | ounces jarred roasted red bell peppers, cut into ½ by 2-inch strips (about 1 cup) |
| 20 | large kalamata olives, each olive pitted and quartered lengthwise |
| 5 | ounces feta cheese, crumbled (1 cup) |

**1.** Whisk the vinaigrette ingredients in a large bowl until combined. Add the onion and cucumber and toss; let stand to blend flavors, about 20 minutes.

**2.** Add the romaine, tomatoes, parsley, mint, and peppers to the bowl with the onions and cucumbers; toss to coat with the dressing.

**3.** Transfer the salad to a wide, shallow serving bowl or platter; sprinkle the olives and feta over the salad. Serve immediately.

### VARIATION
### COUNTRY-STYLE GREEK SALAD

This salad, made without lettuce, is served throughout Greece, where it is known as country or peasant salad. It is excellent with garden-ripe summer tomatoes.

Follow the recipe for Greek Salad, reducing the red wine vinegar to 1½ tablespoons and the lemon juice to 1 teaspoon in the vinaigrette. Omit the lettuce and use 2 medium cucumbers, peeled, halved lengthwise, seeded, and cut into ⅛-inch-thick slices (about 4 cups) and 6 large tomatoes (about 2 pounds), each tomato cored, seeded, and cut into 12 wedges.

### TECHNIQUE: Seeding Cucumbers

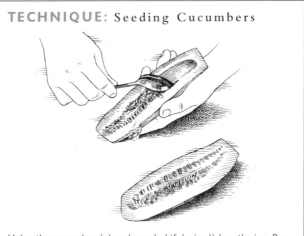

Halve the cucumber (already peeled if desired) lengthwise. Run a small spoon inside each cucumber half to scoop out the seeds and surrounding liquid.

## TASTING LAB:
### Jarred Roasted Red Peppers

JARRED PEPPERS ARE CONVENIENT, BUT ARE ALL BRANDS created equal? To find out, we collected five brands from local supermarkets. The contenders were Divina Roasted Sweet Peppers, Greek Gourmet Roasted Sweet Red Peppers, Lapas Sweet Roasted Peppers, Gaea Flame Roasted Red Peppers, and Peloponnese Roasted Florina Whole Sweet Peppers. Three of these brands identified the type of pepper used (Divina, Gaea, and Peloponnese all use Florina peppers), and we wondered if a company's willingness to identify the variety of pepper it was selling would be an indicator of the quality of the pepper. In other words, would tasters prefer the clearly identified Florina peppers over the generics (whose main ingredient was identified only as "peppers")? To identify their preferences, tasters tried the peppers "as is," straight from the jar.

What we found was that tasters did not necessarily prefer the peppers labeled Florina. What counted was the flavor and texture of the pepper itself as well as the flavor of the brine. The top two brands, Divina (roasted Florina pimento red peppers) and Greek Gourmet (fire-roasted peppers), were preferred for their "soft and tender texture" (the Divinas) and "refreshing," "piquant," "smoky" flavor (the Greek Gourmets). The other brands were marked down for their lack of "roasty flavor" and for the unpleasantly overpowering flavor of the brines. These peppers were described as having a "pepperoncini-like sourness" or a "sweet and acidic aftertaste"; one person said they tasted as if they'd been "buried under brine and acid."

The conclusion? Tasters preferred peppers with a full smoky, roasted flavor, a spicy but not too sweet brine, and a tender-to-the-tooth texture.

**BEST JARRED ROASTED RED PEPPERS**
Divina peppers (left) were the top choice of tasters. Greek Gourmet peppers (right) were a close second.

## TASTING LAB:
### Supermarket Red Wine Vinegars

THE SOURCE OF THAT NOTABLE EDGE YOU TASTE WHEN sampling any red wine vinegar is acetic acid, the chief flavor component in all vinegar and the byproduct of the bacterium *Acetobacter aceti*, which feeds on the alcohol in wine. The process of converting red wine to vinegar once took months, if not years, but now, with the help of an acetator (a machine that speeds the metabolism of the *Acetobacter aceti*), red wine vinegar can be made in less than 24 hours.

Does this faster, cheaper method—the one used to make most supermarket brands—produce inferior red wine vinegar? Or is this a case in which modern technology trumps Old World craftsmanship, which is still employed by makers of the more expensive red wine vinegars? To find out, we included in our tasting vinegars made using the fast process (acetator) and the slow process (often called the Orleans method, after the city in France where it was developed).

We first tasted 10 nationally available supermarket brands in two ways: by dipping sugar cubes in each brand and sucking out the vinegar (a method professionals use to cut down on palate fatigue) and by making a simple vinaigrette with each and tasting it on iceberg lettuce. We then pitted the winners of the supermarket tasting against four high-end red wine vinegars (see Tasting Lab: Gourmet Red Wine Vinegars, page 9).

Although no single grape variety is thought to make the best red wine vinegar, we were curious to find out if our tasters were unwittingly fond of vinegars made from the same grape. We sent the vinegars to a food lab for an anthocyanin pigment profile, a test that can detect the 10 common pigments found in red grapes. Although the lab was unable to distinguish specific grape varieties (Cabernet, Merlot, Pinot Noir, Zinfandel, and the like), it did provide us with an interesting piece of information: Some of the vinegars weren't made with wine grapes (known as *Vitus vinifera*) but with less expensive Concord-

type grapes, the kind used to make Welch's grape juice.

Did the vinegars made with grape juice fair poorly, as might be expected? Far from it. The taste-test results were both shocking and unambiguous: Concord-type grapes not only do just fine when it comes to making vinegar, they may be a key element in the success of the top-rated brands in our tasting. Spectrum, our overall winner, is made from a mix of wine grapes and Concord grapes. Pompeian, which came in second among the supermarket brands, is made entirely of Concord-type grapes.

What else might contribute to the flavor of these vinegars? One possibility, we thought, was the way in which the acetic acid is developed. Manufacturers that mass-produce vinegar generally prefer not to use the Orleans method

# Rating Supermarket Red Wine Vinegars

TWENTY STAFF MEMBERS OF *COOK'S ILLUSTRATED* TASTED THE VINEGARS USING TWO METHODS. FIRST, WE DIPPED slow-dissolving sugar cubes into the vinegars before tasting—this method cuts down on palate fatigue. Next, we made simple vinaigrettes and sampled them with lettuce. The vinegars are listed in order of preference. All vinegars are available in supermarkets nationwide.

### HIGHLY RECOMMENDED
### Spectrum Organic Red Wine Vinegar
**$4.49 for 16.9 ounces**

This peppery, sweet, "full-bodied" vinegar won first place in the vinaigrette tasting and had the highest score overall. It was liked for its fruity flavors, which reminded tasters of lemons, berries, cherries, and grapes.

### HIGHLY RECOMMENDED
### Pompeian Red Wine Vinegar
**$2.29 for 16 ounces**

Tasters liked this fruity, "bright and tangy" vinegar with grape and cherry highlights, giving it first place in the plain tasting. Some tasters thought the vinaigrette made with this vinegar was "lackluster," while others liked its mild flavors.

### RECOMMENDED
### Eden Selected Red Wine Vinegar
**$2.59 for 16 ounces**

This vinegar placed third in the vinaigrette tasting. It was praised for its mild, berry-like flavor. Tasters put it in eighth place in the plain tasting, calling it weak and "not strong or fruity enough."

### RECOMMENDED
### Whole Foods Red Wine Vinegar
**$4.69 for 12.7 ounces**

Tasters could easily detect the Concord grapes in this vinegar, along with blackberry and cherry flavors. Tasters were split on the vinaigrette, with comments ranging from "it's the only one worth eating" to "tastes like rancid Concord grapes."

### RECOMMENDED
### Star Red Wine Vinegar
**$2.19 for 12 ounces**

Tasters gave this vinegar second place in the vinaigrette tasting. It was liked it for its "bright but mild" flavor, though some tasters though it was "one-dimensional." It didn't do so well in the plain tasting, where it was described as rough.

### RECOMMENDED
### Heinz Gourmet Red Wine Vinegar
**$2.79 for 12 ounces**

While some tasters liked this vinegar's mellow flavor, others disliked its "insipid aroma" and lack of acidity and fruit flavors. Comments about the vinaigrette were divided, ranging from "not very complex" to "well seasoned."

### RECOMMENDED
### Four Monks Red Wine Vinegar
**$2.69 for 12.7 ounces**

Tasters liked this vinegar's subtle, light flavor and gave it second place in the plain tasting. These subtle characteristics were lost in the vinaigrette, which tasters found acidic and oily.

### RECOMMENDED WITH RESERVATIONS
### Colavita Red Wine Vinegar
**$2.95 for 16.9 ounces**

This vinegar placed in the bottom half of both taste tests. Tasters thought it had a fruity flavor, though most of them couldn't decide what fruit it tasted like, calling it "Kool-Aidy."

### RECOMMENDED WITH RESERVATIONS
### Progresso Red Wine Vinegar
**$3.49 for 25 ounces**

The mellow flavors of this vinegar reminded some tasters of apples and berries, though some thought it had a weak aroma and little flavor. Comments about the vinaigrette were uniformly negative.

### RECOMMENDED WITH RESERVATIONS
### Regina Red Wine Vinegar
**$1.99 for 12 ounces**

This vinegar placed next-to-last in the plain tasting and last in the vinaigrette tasting. Tasters disliked its sourness and "biting aftertaste," calling it "very harsh and unbalanced."

because it's slow and expensive. Spectrum red wine vinegar is produced with the Orleans method, but Pompeian is made in an acetator in less than 24 hours.

What, then, can explain why Spectrum and Pompeian won the supermarket tasting and beat the other gourmet vinegars? Oddly enough, for a food that defines sourness, the answer seems to lie in its sweetness. It turns out that Americans like their vinegar sweet (think balsamic vinegar).

The production of Spectrum is outsourced to a small manufacturer in Modena, Italy, that makes generous use of the Trebbiano grape, the same grape used to make balsamic vinegar. The Trebbiano, which is a white wine grape, gives Spectrum the sweetness our tasters admired. Pompeian vinegar is finished with a touch of sherry vinegar, added to give the red vinegar a more fruity, well-rounded flavor. Also significant to our results may be that both Spectrum and Pompeian start with wines containing Concord grapes, which are sweet enough to be a common choice when making jams and jellies.

When pitted against gourmet vinegars, Spectrum and Pompeian still came out on top. Which red wine vinegar should you buy? Skip the specialty shop and head to the supermarket.

## TASTING LAB:
### Gourmet Red Wine Vinegars

DURING OUR SEARCH FOR RED WINE VINEGARS, WE found gourmet vinegars made from a single grape variety (such as Zinfandel) that cost up to eight times as much as mass-market vinegars. Wondering if the difference in taste would match the difference in cost, we tasted four gourmet vinegars: "O" Zinfandel Vinegar ($7.99 for 6.8 ounces), Sparrow Lane Cabernet Sauvignon Vinegar ($11.95 for 12.75 ounces), Vinaigre de Banyuls ($29.95 for 25.5 ounces), and Martin Pouret Cabernet Franc Vinegar ($9.95 for 17.66 ounces). We tasted the vinegars plain and in a vinaigrette and then included the supermarket vinegar that had won each of these tests (Pompeian and Spectrum, respectively).

"O" Zinfandel's distinct earthy, fruity flavor made it the clear winner of the plain tasting. Surprisingly, Pompeian placed second. Tasters thought it had a more balanced flavor than the other three gourmet vinegars.

In the vinaigrette test, Spectrum's "bright, sweet" flavors soundly beat out the gourmet brands. "O" Zinfandel placed second; tasters described it as "round and fully flavored" with a "lovely sweet-tart balance." The three remaining gourmet vinegars were called bland, harsh, and unremarkable.

# SPINACH SALAD

**WHAT WE WANTED:** A rich but well-balanced salad that has plenty of bacon without being greasy.

We can't think of a better way to enjoy fresh spinach than to toss it with a rich, warm, sweet-tart dressing and then cover the lot with plenty of crisp bacon. Yet ordering a wilted spinach salad in a restaurant is a move we usually regret. The spinach, which is often drowned in an oily, bland dressing and sprinkled with minuscule bacon bits, leaves us perplexed—and still hungry. This salad can be made with a simple method and a short list of ingredients. Why, then, was a good one so hard to find?

The first hurdle—having to wash, dry, and trim mature curly spinach—was easily overcome. Kitchen tests determined that prewashed, bagged baby spinach works best in this salad, as it is both more tender and sweeter than the mature variety.

Aside from the spinach, bacon is the central ingredient, with the potential to provide plenty of smoky, salty flavor. We chose thick-cut bacon, finding that it offered more presence and textural interest than thin-cut. (Slab bacon can also be used, but it fries up chewy, not crispy.) The easiest way to achieve substantial, uniform pieces (and avoid tiny Baco-style bacon bits) was to cut the strips before frying them rather than crumbling them afterward. At this point, we also confirmed that hard-cooked egg wedges (a common ingredient) belonged in this salad. Their creamy yolks and cool whites formed a natural partnership with the bacon.

With plenty of mouthwatering bacon fat at the ready, we were loath to use another type of oil in the dressing, though some recipes call for either vegetable or olive oil. Happily, tests bolstered our conviction that dressing made solely with bacon grease not only had a lush texture but a hearty flavor; oil-based dressings tasted flat.

We found eight types of vinegar in the test kitchen cabinets and tested all of them, as well as lemon juice. Tasters criticized many of the choices, calling them boring and one-dimensional. Rice vinegar showed promise—its sweetness played well against the rich bacon fat—but it wasn't acidic enough and seemed a bit out of place for such an American recipe. More traditional cider vinegar, which is quite sharp, brightened the dressing considerably. A little sugar added a pleasing sweet element.

Most recipes for this salad call for a generous amount of fat (or oil) and a small amount of acid (vinegar). Typical ratios are 2, 3, or even 4 parts fat to 1 part acid, a standard formula for vinaigrette. We mixed up bacon fat and cider vinegar dressings using each proportion and were disappointed with all of them. To avoid being saddled with a fatty, lifeless mixture, we'd have to throw convention by the wayside. This meant cutting back on the bacon fat and elevating the vinegar level to counterbalance the fat and richness contributed by the fried bacon and egg yolks. After fiddling with the ratio, we settled on a dressing made with 3 tablespoons each of fat and vinegar.

We now had a great-tasting salad, but tasters asserted that it wasn't wilted enough. Because adding more dressing would only result in an overdressed, swampy salad, we weren't sure how to proceed. Luckily, the issue resolved itself when we sautéed a half-cup of onions and mixed them into the dressing. They added enough volume and heat to wilt the spinach perfectly after a few tosses. Wondering if yellow onions were the best choice, we also tested sautéed scallions, shallots, red onions, and garlic. Tasters preferred red onions and garlic, so we opted to use both.

**WHAT WE LEARNED:** For the best results, use baby spinach and thick-cut bacon. Cider vinegar tastes best with the bacon fat, and you need to use a lot more vinegar than you would in other salads. Finally, cook some onions and garlic in the bacon fat, which will add flavor to the dressing and help wilt the spinach properly.

## WILTED SPINACH SALAD WITH WARM BACON DRESSING Serves 4 to 6 as a first course

This salad comes together quickly, so have the ingredients ready before you begin cooking. When adding the vinegar mixture to the skillet, step back from the stovetop—the aroma is quite potent.

- 6 ounces baby spinach (about 8 cups)
- 3 tablespoons cider vinegar
- ½ teaspoon sugar
- ¼ teaspoon ground black pepper
  Pinch salt
- 10 ounces (about 8 slices) thick-cut bacon, cut into ½-inch pieces
- ½ medium red onion, chopped medium (about ½ cup)
- 1 small clove garlic, minced or pressed through a garlic press (about ½ teaspoon)
- 3 hard-cooked eggs (recipe follows), peeled and quartered lengthwise

**1.** Place the spinach in a large bowl. Stir the vinegar, sugar, pepper, and salt together in a small bowl until the sugar dissolves; set aside.

**2.** Fry the bacon in a medium skillet over medium-high heat, stirring occasionally, until crisp, about 10 minutes. Using a slotted spoon, transfer the bacon to a paper towel–lined plate. Pour the bacon fat into a bowl, then return 3 tablespoons bacon fat to the skillet. Add the onion to the skillet and cook over medium heat, stirring frequently, until softened, about 3 minutes. Stir in the garlic and cook until fragrant, about 15 seconds. Add the vinegar mixture, then remove the skillet from the heat. Working quickly, scrape the bottom of the skillet with a wooden spoon to loosen the browned bits. Pour the hot dressing over the spinach, add the bacon, and toss gently until the spinach is slightly wilted. Divide the salad among individual plates, arrange the egg quarters over each, and serve immediately.

## FOOLPROOF HARD-COOKED EGGS Makes 3

We have always considered hard-cooking an egg to be a crapshoot. One cook's simmer might be another cook's boil, and the eggs can cook faster or slower depending on the water temperature. Because there's no way to watch the proteins cook under the brittle shell of an uncracked egg, this often leads to overcooked eggs with rubbery whites and chalky yolks. After trying various methods, we decided on this one, which is foolproof as long as you can recognize when water is at a boil and can time 10 minutes. You can double or triple this recipe as long as you use a pot large enough to hold the eggs in a single layer, covered by an inch of water.

- 3 large eggs

**1.** Place the eggs in a medium saucepan, cover with 1 inch of water, and bring to a boil over high heat. Remove the pan from the heat, cover, and let sit for 10 minutes. Meanwhile, fill a medium bowl with 1 quart of water and 1 tray of ice cubes (or equivalent).

**2.** Transfer the eggs to the ice bath with a slotted spoon and let sit 5 minutes. Peel the eggs.

Matt brushes puff pastry with beaten eggs—
to help form a barrier against moisture from
the tomatoes—before baking the tart shell.

# SUMMER tomatoes

CHAPTER 2

## IN THIS CHAPTER

### THE RECIPES

Classic Gazpacho
Quick Food Processor Gazpacho
Spicy Gazpacho with Chipotle
    Chiles and Lime

Tomato and Mozzarella Tart
Tomato and Mozzarella Tart with
    Prosciutto
Tomato and Smoked Mozzarella
    Tart

### SCIENCE DESK

Why Does Cold Food Require
    More Seasoning?

### TASTING LAB

Puff Pastry
Supermarket Mozzarella
Fresh Mozzarella

It's feast or famine when it comes to good tomatoes. For most of the year, supermarkets stock pretty red orbs that have almost no flavor and are either mealy or rock-hard. The situation completely changes during the summer, when local tomatoes are available at farmers markets and roadside stands. These tomatoes may not always look perfect, but they are sweet and tangy, ripe and juicy—in short, everything a tomato should be.

What's the best way to enjoy summer tomatoes? It's hard to argue with a recipe that goes something like this: Slice, salt, and serve. Still, there are times when you want to use tomatoes in more elaborate dishes, and gazpacho and a cheesy tart are two of our favorite uses for summer tomatoes.

While these two recipes sound easy, we've had plenty of thick, bland gazpacho and soggy tomato tarts. Our goals when developing these summer recipes were simple: Keep the focus on the tomato flavor, and make sure the texture is correct. We wanted the soup to be chunky, not thick or porridge-like, and we wanted the tomato tart to be crisp, not watery or squishy.

# GAZPACHO

**WHAT WE WANTED**: A chilled soup with clearly flavored, distinct pieces of vegetable in a bracing tomato broth.

Gazpacho is high summer in a bowl. Popular on both sides of the Atlantic, this ice-cold, uncooked vegetable soup, made principally of tomatoes (whole and juice), cucumbers, bell peppers, and onions and seasoned with olive oil and vinegar, is sometimes referred to as liquid salad in its native Spain. That slang name may be more apt on these shores, though, as many American gazpacho recipes simply instruct the cook to puree all the vegetables together in the blender. Needless to say, the resulting mixture is more a thin vegetable porridge with an anonymous vegetal flavor.

It's little wonder, then, that texture is one key to a great gazpacho. As you might imagine, philosophies about what is the right texture and how to achieve it vary considerably. Traditionally, gazpacho was thickened with water-soaked bread for extra body, but a number of the recipes we looked at skipped the bread altogether. Some recipes dictate that the mixture be put through a mesh strainer to create a silky smooth texture, while others leave it chunky. With gorgeous summer produce and ingredients that remained constant from recipe to recipe, we knew that the basic flavor profile would not be a problem here. That left thickening, method of manufacture as it related to texture and flavor both, and the seasonings as the most important questions to explore.

In deference to tradition, we started by trying a number of bread-thickened gazpachos. No matter what kind of bread was used or how long it was soaked, tasters consistently favored breadless brews. The consensus among our palates was that the bread-thickened soups had a subtle but inescapable pastiness. It was the same with the gazpachos that were passed—rather laboriously, we might add—through a strainer. Their texture was too uniform for a soup that featured fresh vegetables.

With our preference for a chunky-style soup established, we had to figure out the best method for preparing the vegetables. Although it was a breeze to use, the blender broke the vegetables down beyond recognition, which was not at all what we wanted. The food processor fared somewhat better, especially when we processed each vegetable separately. This method had distinct pros and cons. On the pro side were ease and the fact that the vegetables released some juice as they broke down, which helped to flavor the soup. The cons were that no matter how we finessed the pulse feature, the vegetable pieces were neither neatly chopped nor consistently sized. This was especially true of the tomatoes, which broke down to a pulp. The texture of the resulting soup was more along the lines of a vegetable slushy, which might be acceptable, given the ease of preparation, but was still not ideal. On balance, the food processor is a decent option, especially if you favor speed and convenience, so we've included a recipe based on its use.

Needless to say, we pressed on to the old-fashioned, purist method of hand chopping the vegetables. It does involve some extra work, but it went much more swiftly than we'd imagined, and the benefits to the gazpacho's texture were dazzling. Because the pieces were consistent in size and shape, they not only retained their individual flavors but also set off the tomato broth beautifully, adding immeasurably to the whole. This was just what we were after.

One last procedural issue we investigated was the resting time. Gazpacho is best served ice cold, and the chilling time also allows the flavors to develop and meld. We tasted every hour on the hour for eight hours and found that four hours was the minimum time required for the soup to chill and the flavors to blossom.

Several of the key ingredients and seasonings also bore some exploration. Tomatoes are a star player here, and we preferred beefsteak over plum because they were larger, juicier, and easier to chop. Gazpacho is truly a dish to make only when local tomatoes are plentiful. We made several batches using handsome supermarket tomatoes, but the flavor paled in comparison with those batches made with perfectly ripe, local farm-stand tomatoes. We considered skinning and seeding them, but not a single taster complained when we didn't, so we skipped the extra steps.

When it came to peppers, we preferred red over green for their sweeter flavor. But red was less popular in the onion department; tasters rejected red onions, as well as plain yellow, as too sharp. Instead, they favored sweet onions—such as Vidalia or Maui—and shallots equally. We did note, however, that any onion was overpowering if used in the quantities recommended in most recipes (especially in the leftovers the next day), and the same was true of garlic, so we

dramatically reduced the quantity of both. To ensure thorough seasoning of the whole mixture, we marinated the vegetables briefly in the garlic, salt, pepper, and vinegar before adding the bulk of the liquid. These batches had more balanced flavors than the batches that were seasoned after all the ingredients were combined.

The liquid component was also critical. Most recipes called for tomato juice, which we sampled both straight and mixed in various amounts with water and low-sodium chicken broth. The winning ratio was 5 cups of tomato juice thinned with 1 cup of water to make the 6-cup total we needed. The water cut the viscosity of the juice just enough to make it brothy and light but not downright thin. Given our preference for ice-cold gazpacho, we decided to add ice cubes instead of straight water. The ice cubes helped to chill the soup and then provided water as they melted. We also conducted a blind tasting of tomato juices in which Welch's and Fresh Samantha's showed very well.

Finally, a word about the two primary seasonings, vinegar and olive oil. Spain is a noted producer of sherry, so it follows that sherry vinegar is a popular choice for gazpacho. When we tasted it, along with champagne, red wine, and white wine vinegars, the sherry vinegar was our favorite by far, adding not only acidity but also richness and depth. If you find that your stock of sherry vinegar has run dry, white wine vinegar was the runner-up and can be substituted. The oil contributes both flavor and a lush texture to this simple soup, and, in a word, only extra-virgin will do. Liquid or not, would you dress a beautiful summer salad with anything less?

---

WHAT WE LEARNED: For the best texture, chop the vegetables by hand. If you want to speed up the process, use a food processor, but never a blender, which turns the vegetables to slush. Save the bread for croutons rather than for thickening the soup.

## CLASSIC GAZPACHO Serves 8 to 10

Welch's and Fresh Samantha's are our favorite brands of tomato juice for this recipe—not too thick, with a bright, lively flavor. This recipe makes a large quantity because the leftovers are so good, but it can be halved if you prefer. Traditionally, diners garnish their own bowls with more of the same diced vegetables that are in the soup. If that appeals to you, cut some extra vegetables while you prepare those called for in the recipe. Additional garnish possibilities include croutons (see page 17), chopped pitted black olives, chopped hard-cooked eggs (page 11), and finely diced avocado.

- 3 ripe medium beefsteak tomatoes (about 1½ pounds), cored and cut into ¼-inch dice, following the illustrations on page 19 (about 4 cups)
- 2 medium red bell peppers (about 1 pound), cored, seeded, and cut into ¼-inch dice, following the illustrations on page 19 (about 2 cups)
- 2 small cucumbers (about 1 pound), one peeled and the other with skin on, both seeded and cut into ¼-inch dice, following the illustrations on page 19 (about 2 cups)
- ½ small sweet onion (such as Vidalia, Maui, or Walla Walla) or 2 large shallots, peeled and minced (about ½ cup)
- 2 medium cloves garlic, minced or pressed through a garlic press (about 2 teaspoons)
- 2 teaspoons salt
- ⅓ cup sherry vinegar
  Ground black pepper
- 5 cups tomato juice
- 1 teaspoon hot pepper sauce, such as Tabasco (optional)
- 8 ice cubes
  Extra-virgin olive oil for serving

**1.** Combine the tomatoes, bell peppers, cucumbers, onion, garlic, salt, vinegar, and pepper to taste in a large (at least 4-quart) nonreactive bowl. Let stand until the vegetables just begin to release their juices, about 5 minutes. Stir in the tomato juice, hot pepper sauce, if using, and ice cubes. Cover tightly and refrigerate to blend flavors, at least 4 hours and up to 2 days.

**2.** Adjust the seasonings with salt and pepper and remove and discard any unmelted ice cubes. Serve cold, drizzling each portion with about 1 teaspoon extra-virgin olive oil and topping with the desired garnishes (see note).

### VARIATIONS

### QUICK FOOD PROCESSOR GAZPACHO

Using the same ingredients and quantities as for Classic Gazpacho, core and quarter the tomatoes and process them in the workbowl of a food processor fitted with a steel blade until broken down into ¼- to 1-inch pieces, about twelve 1-second pulses; transfer to a large bowl. Cut the cored and seeded peppers and seeded cucumbers into rough 1-inch pieces and process them separately until broken down into ¼- to 1-inch pieces, about twelve 1-second pulses; add to the bowl with the tomatoes. Add the onion, garlic, salt, vinegar, and ground black pepper to taste; continue with the recipe as directed.

### SPICY GAZPACHO WITH CHIPOTLE CHILES AND LIME

A garnish of finely diced ripe avocado is a must with this variation.

Follow the recipe for Classic or Quick Food Processor Gazpacho, omitting optional hot pepper sauce and adding 2½ tablespoons minced chipotle chiles in adobo sauce, ¼ cup minced fresh cilantro leaves, and 6 tablespoons lime juice and 2 teaspoons grated lime zest along with the tomato juice and ice cubes.

## GARLIC CROUTONS Makes about 3 cups
These croutons can be stored in an airtight container at room temperature for a day or so.

- 3 medium cloves garlic, minced or pressed through a garlic press (about 1 tablespoon)
- ¼ teaspoon salt
- 3 tablespoons extra-virgin olive oil
- 3 cups ½-inch white bread cubes (from a baguette or country white loaf)

Adjust an oven rack to the middle position and heat the oven to 350 degrees. Combine the garlic, salt, and oil in a small bowl; let stand 20 minutes, then pour through a fine-mesh strainer into a medium bowl. Discard the garlic. Add the bread cubes to the bowl with the garlic oil and toss to coat. Spread the bread cubes in an even layer on a rimmed baking sheet and bake, stirring occasionally, until golden, about 15 minutes. Cool on the baking sheet to room temperature.

## SCIENCE DESK: Why Does Cold Food Require More Seasoning?

FLAVOR IS PERCEIVED BY OUR BRAINS PREDOMINANTLY BY the combined effort of our senses of taste and smell. The human ability to detect odor is outstanding; we recognize thousands of them. Our keen sense of smell makes good biological sense because we depend on it when we are hunting for food—be it in a forest or in the produce section at the grocery store. Taste is a much less complex sensation because it tells us the quality of what we have already selected and put in our mouth. There are just four fundamental tastes: sweet, salty, bitter, and sour. (Some experts argue for a fifth taste called *umami*, which is perceived as savory.) The way a food smells accounts for the vast majority of the flavor we perceive, probably more than 70 percent.

A problem occurs when we eat cold food. Smell needs volatile compounds to reach our nasal cavity. When the temperature of food drops, very little vapor is released; consequently, a cold food does not have much odor. This is a stroke of good fortune because if the corollary were true our refrigerators would stink. Unfortunately, without the

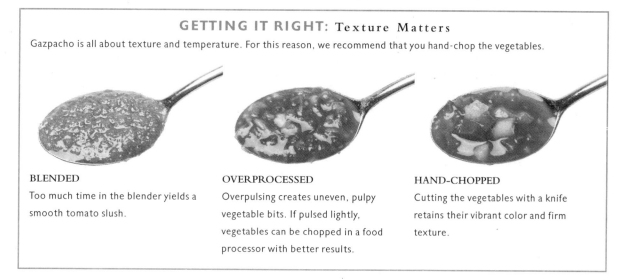

### GETTING IT RIGHT: Texture Matters
Gazpacho is all about texture and temperature. For this reason, we recommend that you hand-chop the vegetables.

**BLENDED**
Too much time in the blender yields a smooth tomato slush.

**OVERPROCESSED**
Overpulsing creates uneven, pulpy vegetable bits. If pulsed lightly, vegetables can be chopped in a food processor with better results.

**HAND-CHOPPED**
Cutting the vegetables with a knife retains their vibrant color and firm texture.

odor component the flavor of cold food is dramatically reduced. How do we keep cold food interesting?

One solution is to use flavorings that are particularly pungent. These might include garlic or citrus. The other is to focus on the sensation in our mouths, considering sweet, salty, bitter, and sour as the predominant flavorings. Vinegar is often found in cold recipes such as pickles, soups, and dressings because its acidity can be detected even at a low temperature. Sugar is commonly added in large quantities to cold desserts such as ice cream. Our sensitivity to salt is relatively uniform throughout the temperature spectrum, so we add similar quantities to both cold and warm foods. That said, it's always a good idea to check cold foods just before serving to see if they require more salt. An additional measure can be used to heighten sensation at low temperatures— the introduction of contrasting flavors. Try sprinkling salt on cold pineapple to emphasize the sweetness by providing a counterpoint. In short, to make that cold dish interesting, select strong-smelling seasonings and, when tasting, focus on the flavors sweet, sour, bitter, and/or salty.

## TECHNIQUE:
### Keeping a Cutting Board Stable

Chefs often use a no-skid mat beneath a cutting board to keep it from slipping all over the counter. If you don't own a mat, place a damp paper towel on the counter, then put the cutting board on top. The damp towel holds the board in place and can be used to wipe down the counter when you're done.

# TECHNIQUE: Cutting Vegetables into Perfect Dice

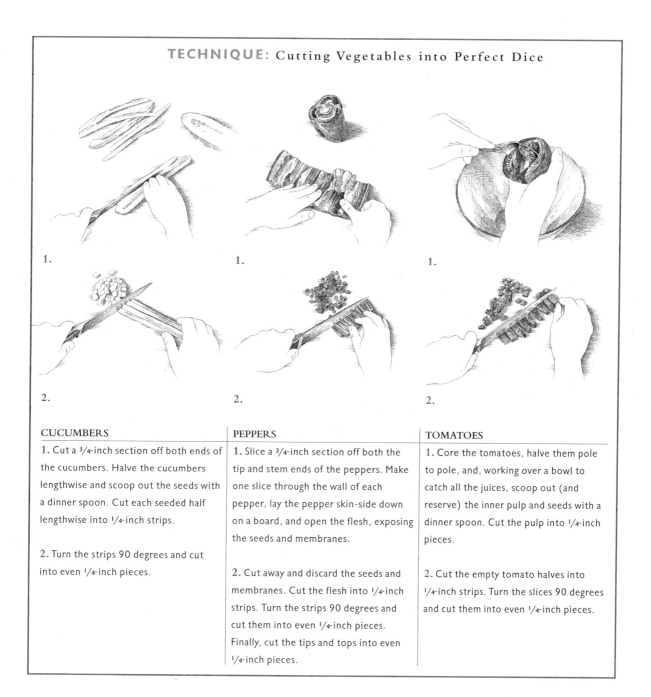

1.

2.

| CUCUMBERS | PEPPERS | TOMATOES |
|---|---|---|
| 1. Cut a ¾-inch section off both ends of the cucumbers. Halve the cucumbers lengthwise and scoop out the seeds with a dinner spoon. Cut each seeded half lengthwise into ¼-inch strips. | 1. Slice a ¾-inch section off both the tip and stem ends of the peppers. Make one slice through the wall of each pepper, lay the pepper skin-side down on a board, and open the flesh, exposing the seeds and membranes. | 1. Core the tomatoes, halve them pole to pole, and, working over a bowl to catch all the juices, scoop out (and reserve) the inner pulp and seeds with a dinner spoon. Cut the pulp into ¼-inch pieces. |
| 2. Turn the strips 90 degrees and cut into even ¼-inch pieces. | 2. Cut away and discard the seeds and membranes. Cut the flesh into ¼-inch strips. Turn the strips 90 degrees and cut them into even ¼-inch pieces. Finally, cut the tips and tops into even ¼-inch pieces. | 2. Cut the empty tomato halves into ¼-inch strips. Turn the slices 90 degrees and cut them into even ¼-inch pieces. |

# TOMATO TART

**WHAT WE WANTED**: A recipe we could easily make at home with a solid (not soggy) bottom crust and great vine-ripened flavor.

Falling someplace in between pizza and quiche, tomato and mozzarella tart shares the flavors of both but features problems unique unto itself. For starters, this is not fast food, as some sort of pastry crust is required. Second, the moisture in the tomatoes almost guarantees a soggy crust. Third, tomato tarts are often tasteless, their spectacular open faces offering false promises. We wanted something foolproof and simple.

The first thing we learned is that tomato and mozzarella tarts come in all shapes and sizes—everything from overwrought custardy pies resembling quiche to stripped-down, minimalist models that are more like pizza. A test kitchen sampling of these various styles delivered dismal results—sodden bottoms and tired toppings across the board—but we did agree that one recipe stood out: a simple construction of tomatoes and cheese shingled across a plain, prebaked sheet of puff pastry. Unwilling to make puff pastry from scratch (who is?), we grabbed some store-bought puff pastry and started cooking.

The winning recipe from the taste test consisted of a flat sheet of puff pastry with a thin border to contain the topping (tomatoes easily slip off a flat sheet of anything) and a thick glaze of egg wash to seal the dough tightly against the seeping tomatoes. From a single rectangular sheet of pastry dough (we found Pepperidge Farm to be the most available; two pieces of dough come in a single box), we trimmed thin strips of dough from the edges and cemented them with egg wash to the top of the sheet to create a uniform 1-inch border. This single tart shell looked large enough for two to three servings. With scarcely any more effort, we found we could serve twice as many by joining the two pieces of dough that came in the box (we sealed the seam tightly with egg wash and rolled it flat) and making a long rectangular version (roughly 16 by 8 inches). Once assembled, the tart got a heavy brushing with beaten egg.

From the initial test results, we knew that prebaking the crust would be essential to give it a fighting chance against the moisture from the tomatoes. Following the recipe on the back of the Pepperidge Farm box, we baked the enlarged tart shell at 400 degrees until it was light, airy, and golden brown. Now we ran into our first problem. The shell was too frail to support a heavy, wet filling. Baked at 350 degrees, the shell was noticeably squatter—and thus better suited to a heavy filling—but it was also unpleasantly tough and chewy. We wondered if a two-step baking method might be more successful: a high temperature for initial lift and browning, then a lower temperature to dry out the shell for maximum sturdiness. When started at 425 degrees (and held there until puffed and light golden, about 15 minutes) and finished at 350 degrees (and held there until well browned, 15 minutes longer), the crust was flaky yet rigid enough for a test cook to hold it aloft while holding onto just one end.

Now we had half-solved the problem of the soggy crust, but there was still work to do. The egg wash coating had proven only deflective, not impermeable. Liquid soaked through to the puff pastry, albeit at a slower rate than uncoated pastry. Egg wash was part of, but not the whole, solution.

Our next thought was that a layer of cheese might help. We gathered up a trio of mozzarellas for a tasting: fresh cow's milk, low-moisture part-skim cheese from the supermarket, and low-moisture whole milk cheese, also shrink-wrapped and from the supermarket. Fresh mozzarella won accolades for flavor, but its high moisture content rendered the crust mushy (even after pressing the cheese to extrude excess moisture). Part-skim mozzarella was deemed "a little bland," though its dry constitution fit the tart's needs. Whole milk mozzarella packed a fuller, creamier flavor and most pleased tasters; it was clearly the best choice. A scant half pound of grated cheese melted into a smooth, seemingly watertight layer across the tart's bottom. When the entire tart was assembled and baked, the bottom crust was vastly improved, but the tomatoes still gave off too much water, affecting the texture of the crust and the overall flavor of the tart.

Our first thought was to use tomatoes with a relatively low water content. We limited our tests to standard beefsteak (round) and Roma (plum) tomatoes as they are the two most readily available. A quick side-by-side test ruled out beefsteaks as excessively high in liquid. As we had suspected, Romas were the better choice for this recipe.

As for extracting the tomatoes' juices, roasting was an obvious choice, but we ruled it out as too time- and labor-intensive. Besides, we wanted the brighter flavor of lightly cooked tomatoes. Salting worked well but not perfectly. We sprinkled sliced tomatoes with salt and left them to drain on paper towels for 30 minutes. The underlying toweling was soaked through, but the tomatoes were still juicy to the touch. Increasing the amount of salt and time accomplished frustratingly little. A little gentle force, however, worked magic: We sandwiched the salted slices between paper towels and pressed down with enough force to extrude any remaining juices (and the seeds) but not enough to squish the slices flat. They were as dry as could be, yet still very flavorful.

Baked quick and hot to melt the cheese and preserve the tomatoes' meaty texture (425 degrees turned out to be the best temperature), the tart looked ready for the cover of a magazine, especially when slicked with a garlic-infused olive oil and strewn with fresh basil leaves. But just a few minutes from the oven, the horrible truth revealed itself: The crust was soggy. Despite the egg wash, the melted mozzarella, and the drained and pressed tomatoes, the tart continued to suffer the ills of moisture.

Discouraged but not undone, we kept turning the same image over in our mind: bits of hard-baked Parmesan cheese on bread sticks or those dreadful prebaked "pizza crusts." We wondered if a solid layer of crisply baked Parmesan, on top of the egg wash but beneath the mozzarella, would seal the base more permanently. We sprinkled finely grated Parmesan over the tart shell for the prebake and crossed our fingers. The cheese melted to such a solid (and deliciously nutty tasting) layer that liquid rolled right off, like rain off a duck's back.

We assembled a whole tart and were stunned by the results: Slices could be lifted freely and consumed like pizza, even hours from the oven. Rich in flavor and sturdy in form, this tart had character to match its good looks—and we could make it pretty quickly, too. Ready-made dough and minimal ingredients kept preparation brief, and total cooking time was less than an hour and a half. Not only was this tart better than we expected, it was also simpler.

---

**WHAT WE LEARNED:** Prebake the puff pastry crust, sealing it first with an egg wash and then grated Parmesan cheese to keep out the moisture from the tomatoes. Salt the sliced tomatoes and press them lightly to remove as much liquid as possible.

**TOMATO AND MOZZARELLA TART** Serves 4 to 6

The baked tart is best eaten warm within two hours of baking. If you prefer to do some advance preparation, the tart shell can be prebaked through step 1, cooled to room temperature, wrapped in plastic wrap, and kept at room temperature for up to two days before being topped and baked with the mozzarella and tomatoes. Use a low-moisture, shrink-wrapped supermarket cheese rather than fresh mozzarella. To keep the frozen dough from cracking, it's best to let it thaw slowly in the refrigerator overnight.

    Flour for the work surface
1   (1.1-pound) box frozen puff pastry (Pepperidge Farm), thawed in its box in the refrigerator overnight
1   large egg, beaten
2   ounces Parmesan cheese, finely grated (1 cup)
1   pound Roma tomatoes (about 3 to 4 medium), cored and cut crosswise into ¼-inch-thick slices
    Salt
2   medium cloves garlic, minced or pressed through a garlic press (about 2 teaspoons)
2   tablespoons extra-virgin olive oil
    Ground black pepper
8   ounces low-moisture whole milk mozzarella, shredded (2 cups)
2   tablespoons coarsely chopped fresh basil leaves

**1.** Adjust an oven rack to the lower-middle position and heat the oven to 425 degrees. Dust the work surface with flour and unfold both pieces of puff pastry onto the work surface. Following the illustrations on page 24, form 1 large sheet with a border, using the beaten egg as directed. Sprinkle the Parmesan evenly over the bottom of the shell. Using a fork, uniformly and thoroughly poke holes in the bottom. Bake 15 minutes, then reduce the oven temperature to 350 degrees. Continue to bake until golden brown and crisp, 15 to 17 minutes longer. Transfer the baking sheet to a wire rack. Increase the oven temperature to 425 degrees.

**2.** While shell bakes, place the tomato slices in a single layer on a double layer of paper towels and sprinkle them evenly with ½ teaspoon salt; let stand 30 minutes. Place a second double layer of paper towels on top of the tomatoes and press firmly to dry the tomatoes. Combine the garlic, olive oil, and a pinch each of salt and pepper in a small bowl; set aside.

**3.** Sprinkle the mozzarella evenly over the bottom of the warm (or cool, if made ahead) baked shell. Shingle the tomato slices widthwise on top of the cheese (about 4 slices per row). Brush the tomatoes with the garlic oil.

**4.** Bake until the shell is deep golden brown and the cheese is melted, 15 to 17 minutes. Cool on a wire rack 5 minutes, sprinkle with the basil, slide onto a cutting board or serving platter, cut into pieces, and serve.

**GETTING IT RIGHT:** Good Tart, Bad Tart

If you neglect to salt the tomatoes and fail to brush the dough with egg wash, the baked tart will be soggy and limp (top right). If you take both of these precautions *and* add a layer of grated Parmesan, individual slices will be firm and dry, having enough structural integrity to hold their shape (bottom left).

## TECHNIQUE:
### Shredding Semisoft Cheese Neatly

Semisoft cheeses such as cheddar and mozzarella can stick to a box grater and cause a real mess. To keep the holes from becoming clogged, coat the box grater with a light film of nonstick cooking spray. The cooking spray will keep the cheese from sticking to the surface of the grater.

### VARIATIONS

### TOMATO AND MOZZARELLA TART WITH PROSCIUTTO

Follow the recipe for the Tomato and Mozzarella Tart, placing 2 ounces of thinly sliced prosciutto in a single layer on top of the mozzarella before arranging the tomato slices.

### TOMATO AND SMOKED MOZZARELLA TART

Follow the recipe for the Tomato and Mozzarella Tart, substituting 6 ounces smoked mozzarella for the whole milk mozzarella.

## TASTING LAB: Puff Pastry

PUFF PASTRY IS A SUPERFLAKY DOUGH WITH HUNDREDS of buttery layers. It is made by wrapping a simple pastry dough around a stick of cold butter, rolling the dough, folding the dough over itself at least four times, and chilling the dough for at least one hour between each fold. When baked, the water in the butter creates steam, which causes the dough to puff into flaky, delicate layers.

Almost no one—not even chefs at fine restaurants—makes puff pastry. Home cooks have one, maybe two commercial options in the freezer case. Pepperidge Farm Puff Pastry Sheets (made with vegetable oil, not butter) are available in almost every supermarket. Better supermarkets and gourmet shops might carry Classic Puff Pastry from Dufour Pastry Kitchens. When pitted in the test kitchen against Pepperidge Farm, the all-butter pastry was easy to pick out and was the clear favorite. That said, tasters felt that Pepperidge Farm was pretty good. Each brand has different size sheets, so we decided to use the more widely available Pepperidge Farm puff pastry to develop our tart recipe.

## TASTING LAB: Supermarket Mozzarella

MOST HOME COOKS MAKE PIZZA OR LASAGNA EVERY NOW and then, and the array of baked pasta dishes and casseroles served under a blanket of melted mozzarella certainly doesn't end there. They are, in fact, almost as numerous as the seemingly endless mozzarella choices in most supermarkets, which typically include whole blocks and pouches of preshredded cheeses, both of which can be made from whole milk or skim milk (hence the moniker "part skim"). In addition, some supermarket (and most gourmet shops) sell fresh cheese floating in liquid. Like many of you, we've been warned about the pitfalls of using preshredded cheese, but unlike many of you, we have the time and inclination to put those warnings to the test. So we organized a blind tasting of 13 nationally available mozzarellas covering each of the four main variables—part-skim, whole milk, preshredded, and block—as well as three "fresh" mozzarellas (see pages 26 and 27) and tasted each one raw and melted on pizza.

All mozzarella, be it the supermarket variety or fresh cheese purchased at a specialty shop, falls into a cheese category called *pasta filata*. This means the cheese is made by stretching (or pulling, spinning, or "stringing"—the translation of *filata*) the curds to give the final product a fine layered effect and elastic texture. This process, according to Bill Wendorff, professor and chair of the food science department at the University of Wisconsin, Madison, aligns the proteins into long chains. The result is multiple layers of curd and a stringy texture; when you peel back a layer of the cheese, it resembles a cooked chicken breast.

The technical designation for fresh mozzarella sold floating in liquid (usually water or brine, opaque from whey that leaches out of the cheese) is "high moisture," which the U.S. Food and Drug Administration (FDA) defines as having a moisture content of at least 52 percent but not more than 60 percent by weight. Fresh, high-moisture mozzarella, however, is highly perishable and therefore poorly suited to long storage times and lengthy supermarket stays.

That brings us to the mozzarella typically found in supermarkets, melted on takeout pizza, and tasted in this test—a second variety designated "low moisture," with an

---

## TECHNIQUE: Assembling the Tart Shell

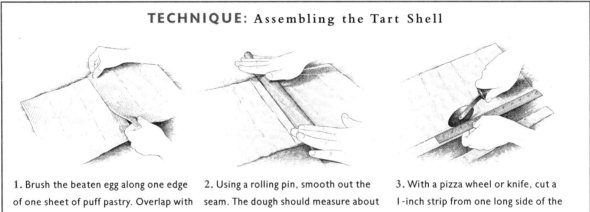

1. Brush the beaten egg along one edge of one sheet of puff pastry. Overlap with a second piece of dough by 1 inch and press down to seal the pieces together.

2. Using a rolling pin, smooth out the seam. The dough should measure about 18 by 9 inches. Use a pizza wheel or knife to trim the edges straight.

3. With a pizza wheel or knife, cut a 1-inch strip from one long side of the dough. Cut another 1-inch strip from the same side.

4. Cut a 1-inch strip from one short side of the dough. Cut another 1-inch strip from the same side. Transfer the large piece of dough to a parchment-lined baking sheet and brush with the beaten egg.

5. Gently press the long strips of dough onto each long edge of the dough and brush the strips with egg. Gently press the short strips of the dough onto each short edge and brush the strips with egg.

6. With a pizza wheel or knife, trim the excess dough from the corners.

FDA-mandated moisture content of 45 percent to 52 percent. This drier cheese is less perishable than the fresh version and therefore better suited to wide distribution and commercial uses. Many of the experts we contacted referred to low-moisture mozzarella as "pizza cheese," though that is not an official, FDA-recognized designation. They also mentioned that it is a uniquely American product, developed for the burgeoning U.S. pizza industry.

If only the differences in mozzarella ended with moisture. But they don't. Milk fat content also varies. We limited our tasting to whole milk mozzarella, which the FDA states must have a minimum milk fat content of 45 percent of the weight of the solids, and part-skim mozzarella, in which the milk fat content must be between 30 and 45 percent.

We broke our tasting into four parts. The first three were dedicated to low-moisture mozzarella: first the preshredded cheeses, then the block cheeses, and, finally, a face-off between the winners in each of these categories. In every case, we tasted the products both raw and melted (on our thin-crust pizza), and we included both part-skim and whole milk cheeses in each stage of the game. A fourth tasting included three types of fresh mozzarella and our favorite low-moisture cheese from the supermarket.

The tasters' impressions confirmed what anyone who has ever eaten a pizza already knows about mozzarella: It's pretty bland stuff. All of our samples had almost the same short ingredient list: pasteurized milk (and/or part-skim milk), cheese cultures, salt, and enzymes (as well as vinegar, in the case of the Polly-O cheeses and the Sorrento block cheeses). We found that these ingredients do indeed result in a neutral product. Don't count on finding much complexity or depth of flavor in any mozzarella. As a matter of fact, a quick glance at the charts on pages 26 and 27 reveals that none of the cheeses were met with much enthusiasm by tasters. "Mild," "milky," and "creamy" were the highest praises mustered for the winners.

That said, we were shocked to find that preshredded cheeses scored on par with their counterparts in block form. On a scale of 1 (worst) to 10 (best), the overall scores

of the shredded cheeses varied from a high of 6.9 to a low of 4.24. These numbers were closely mirrored by the block cheese ratings—a high of 6.73 and a low of 4.08. In our tests, the experts' warnings about the horrors of preshredded cheese turned out to be for naught—as long as you choose the right brand. Tasters found cheeses in both categories— shredded and block—that they liked and disliked.

Tasters' comments indicated that the shredded cheeses' reasonably good showing was due more to their texture when melted than to any particularly positive flavor characteristics. All of the shredded cheeses were packed with anti-caking agents, usually potato or rice starch and/or powdered cellulose. Cheese expert Barry Swanson, a professor in the department of food science and human nutrition at Washington State University, explained that the starches and cellulose, an indigestible glucose fiber that gives most plant tissues their structure, bind moisture in the cheese, helping to keep the shreds separate in the package. The anti-caking agents were a disadvantage for the shredded cheeses when tasted raw, however, causing tasters to make frequent use of the adjectives "chalky," "powdery," and "dusty." Honestly, though, no one we know would eat preshredded cheese raw anyway, so this factor is negligible.

The winning shredded cheese was Kraft part-skim, which beat out brands with Italian-sounding names as well as three samples made with whole milk. But for this surprising exception, our tasters generally ruled in favor of whole milk cheeses, at least when compared with the part-skim cheese made by the same company. Again, excepting Kraft, tasters found that the whole milk cheeses were creamier and less bland than their part-skim counterparts. Many whole milk mozzarellas contain an extra 10 calories and just 1 gram of fat per serving, so we'll take any flavor advantage we can get, especially if the alternative saves so few calories.

Among the block cheeses we considered, Dragone rose as the overall champ. It also won the whole shebang when we pitted it against Kraft, the winner of the preshredded competition. If you don't mind shredding a block of cheese yourself, we think you'll get the very best flavor and texture

# Rating Shredded Mozzarella

WE SELECTED FIVE WIDELY AVAILABLE BRANDS OF "SUPERMARKET," OR LOW-MOISTURE, MOZZARELLA AND SAMPLED those made with part-skim or whole milk. Because the most common use for this type of cheese is quick and convenient melting, we decided to include both preshredded and block forms (see right). Fifteen *Cook's Illustrated* staff members tasted these cheeses both raw and melted on pizza. Separate tests were performed in this manner, one for the category of shredded cheeses, and the other for block cheeses. The cheeses are listed below in order of preference, based on the combined scores of the raw and the pizza tests.

**RECOMMENDED**
### Kraft Shredded Low Moisture Part-Skim Mozzarella
**$2.50 for 8 ounces**

This cheese was the clear winner in both the raw and the pizza tests. When tasted raw, it was found to be "rich" and "tangy," with only a "slight chalkiness." On pizza, tasters found it to be "mild and lean," yet "tasty," "fresh," and "flavorful."

**RECOMMENDED WITH RESERVATIONS**
### Polly-O Shredded Low Moisture Whole Milk Mozzarella
**$3.29 for 8 ounces**

While this cheese rated overall as the tasters' second favorite, eaten raw it was found to be "nondescript" and "a little boring." But on pizza its true character came through: It was seen as having a "nice melted texture" with a "sharp flavor like cheddar."

**RECOMMENDED WITH RESERVATIONS**
### Sargento Chef Style Natural Low Moisture Whole Milk Mozzarella
**$2.50 for 8 ounces**

Considered "quite salty" but with a "nice chewiness" raw, this shredded cheese was a little "greasy" and "slightly acidic" when melted on pizza.

**RECOMMENDED WITH RESERVATIONS**
### Sorrento Shredded Low Moisture Whole Milk Mozzarella (known west of the Mississippi as Precious)
**$2.39 for 8 ounces**

This cheese was "soft and mild" and "non-chalky." It was considered to have a "nice texture" but "very little flavor" on pizza.

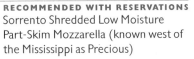

**RECOMMENDED WITH RESERVATIONS**
### Sorrento Shredded Low Moisture Part-Skim Mozzarella (known west of the Mississippi as Precious)
**$2.39 for 8 ounces**

"Holy powder" was one taster's comment when eating this cheese raw; others called it "pasty" and "artificial tasting." The cheese was better on pizza—one taster remarked on its "full cheesy flavor"—but it was nonetheless "a bit greasy" with "spotty melting characteristics."

**NOT RECOMMENDED**
### Sargento Chef Style Natural Low Moisture Part-Skim Mozzarella
**$2.50 for 8 ounces**

This shredded mozzarella was rejected because of its "sour," "tangy" flavor. It tasted "almost lemony" on pizza. The texture was described as "pasty" and "rubbery."

**NOT RECOMMENDED**
### Polly-O Shredded Low Moisture Part-Skim Mozzarella
**$3.29 for 8 ounces**

We found it interesting that this cheese took last place considering the high marks its whole milk counterpart received. The one redeeming quality was the thickness of the individual shreds of cheese, but the texture was "plasticky" and "gummy" with an "innocuous flavor."

## Rating Block Mozzarella

THE CHEESES ARE LISTED IN ORDER OF PREFERENCE based on scores from tasting the samples raw and on pizza.

**RECOMMENDED**
### Dragone Low Moisture Mozzarella Cheese (Whole Milk) $3.79 for 16 ounces
"Rich and creamy" and "tangy and briny" were some of the comments that caused this cheese to rate number one. On pizza it was described as "milky" and "creamy."

**RECOMMENDED WITH RESERVATIONS**
### Polly-O Part Skim Mozzarella
**$4.79 for 16 ounces**
Although tasters did not seem overly impressed by this cheese, they did find it to be very familiar and not offensive in any way. Tasters praised its "nice, mild flavor."

**RECOMMENDED WITH RESERVATIONS**
### Polly-O Whole Milk Mozzarella
**$4.79 for 16 ounces**
This cheese rated just below the part-skim version, but the differences were slight. On pizza it was thought to be "mediocre."

**NOT RECOMMENDED**
### Sorrento Whole Milk Mozzarella Cheese
**$3.49 for 16 ounces**
Off flavors were detected in both the raw and the pizza tasting. Tasters described it as "plasticky" and "slightly vinegarish."

**NOT RECOMMENDED**
### Sorrento Part Skim Mozzarella Cheese
**$3.49 for 16 ounces**
This cheese fared even worse than the whole milk version, although a few tasters found the salt level to "accentuate the pizza well."

**NOT RECOMMENDED**
### Dragone Low Moisture Part-Skim Mozzarella Cheese $3.79 for 16 ounces
This fell into last place and inspired comments such as "tasteless," with a "chemical aftertaste." It was "clumpy and thick" on pizza.

from a block of Dragone whole milk mozzarella. But if you are pressed for time, you'll do fine with a bag of Kraft preshredded, low-moisture part-skim mozzarella.

## TASTING LAB: Fresh Mozzarella

IT'S PRETTY COMMON KNOWLEDGE THAT FRESH mozzarella is best in salads and sandwiches, being creamier, more tender, and more flavorful than low-moisture supermarket mozzarella. But what about on pizzas and tarts? Many experts say that fresh cheeses make these dishes watery and ruin crisp pizza crust. We wondered if this was true. The local pizza parlor certainly doesn't use fresh mozzarella.

To find out, we pitted the winner of our supermarket low-moisture mozzarella test (Dragone whole milk block cheese) against three brands of fresh mozzarella: BelGioioso (widely available in supermarkets, $3.29 for a 7-ounce container with 4 ounces of actual cheese), Calabro (made locally with Vermont cow's milk, $7.95 per pound), and mozzarella di bufala (made by Mandara from Italy, with water buffalo milk, as all mozzarellas were originally, and priced at $7.95 for an 8-ounce ball). All four cheeses were tested both raw and on pizza.

Not surprisingly, all three fresh mozzarellas were preferred over the Dragone whole milk block mozzarella when eaten raw. However, we were surprised by the results on the pizza test. Only one fresh cheese, the BelGioioso, made a poor showing on pizza. The Calabro and the mozzarella di bufala easily beat the supermarket cheese on pizza. Panelists thought they both tasted "real" and had the most "milk flavor." A few tasters objected to the gamy flavor of the mozzarella di bufala, so it finished in second place. Calabro was our favorite for flavor and texture, and it also was the least expensive of the three fresh cheeses we tasted. This cheese is not available nationally (no fresh cow's milk mozzarella is), but based on these results we suggest that you look for a high-quality, locally made fresh mozzarella. It will taste great in salads and sandwiches, and it may surprise you on pizza or a tart.

Dawn prepares pots (and pots) of chili in the back kitchen for the next day's shoot.

# ONE-POT wonders

## CHAPTER 3

IN THIS CHAPTER

**THE RECIPES**

Beef Chili with Kidney Beans
Beef Chili with Bacon and Black
    Beans

Indoor Clambake

**EQUIPMENT CORNER**

Slow Cookers

**TASTING LAB**

Tomato Puree

The notion of dinner made in a single pot is certainly alluring. Chili is probably America's favorite one-pot supper, but this dish can be plagued with problems. The meat can be tough, the beans are often either undercooked or mushy, the chili can be either much too spicy or boringly bland, and, more often than not, the whole thing is swimming in a pool of orange grease. The "experts" generally complicate matters by using a combination of meats and homemade chili powder (made by toasting, seeding, and grinding dried chiles). We wanted great chili, but it had to be simple. We wanted something all-American that would appeal to everyone in the family.

No one thinks of a clambake as a one-pot wonder. The traditional recipe requires a sandy beach and a pit that takes hours to dig. After you've gathered stones to hold in the heat and harvested seaweed from the ocean, you've still got a lot of cooking to do. Although a real clambake is a treat, we love the flavors of the seafood, sausage, corn, and potatoes too much to relegate this dish to a once-in-a-lifetime event. Could we make an indoor clambake simple enough to prepare even on a busy weeknight?

# BASIC CHILI

**WHAT WE WANTED:** A basic all-American chili made with supermarket staples—ground meat, tomatoes, chili powder, and canned beans—that was easy to make and delicious.

Like politics, chili provokes heated debate. Some purists insist that a chili that contains beans or tomatoes is just not chili. Others claim that homemade chili powder is essential or that ground meat is taboo. But there is one kind of chili that almost every American has eaten (or even made) at one time or another. It's the kind of chili you liked as a kid and still see being served at Super Bowl parties. Made with ground meat, tomatoes, and chili powder, this thick, fairly smooth chili is spiced but not spicy. It's basic grub (and it can be great grub) that's not intended to fuel impassioned exchanges over the merits of ancho versus New Mexico chiles.

Although this simple chili should come together easily, it should not taste as if it did. The flavors should be rich and balanced, the texture thick and lush. Unfortunately, many "basic" recipes yield a pot of underspiced, underflavored chili reminiscent of Sloppy Joes. Our goal was to develop a no-fuss chili that tasted far better than the sum of its common parts.

Most of the recipes for this plain-spoken chili begin by sautéing onions and garlic. Tasters liked red bell peppers added to these aromatics but rejected other options, including green bell peppers, celery, and carrots. After this first step, things became less clear. The most pressing concerns were the spices (how many and what kind) and the meat (how much ground beef and whether or not to add another meat). There were also the cooking liquid (what kind, if any) and the proportions of tomatoes and beans to consider.

Our first experiments with these ingredients followed a formula we had seen in lots of recipes: 2 pounds ground beef, 3 tablespoons chili powder, 2 teaspoons ground cumin, and 1 teaspoon each red pepper flakes and dried oregano. Many recipes add the spices after the beef has been browned, but we knew from work done in the test kitchen on curry that ground spices taste better when they have direct contact with hot cooking oil.

To see if these results would apply to chili, we set up a test with three pots of chili—one with the ground spices added before the beef, one with the spices added after the beef, and a third in which we toasted the spices in a separate skillet and added them to the pot after the beef. The batch made with untoasted spices added after the beef tasted weak. The batch made with the spices toasted in a separate pan was better, but the clear favorite was the batch made with spices added directly to the pot before the meat. In fact, subsequent testing revealed that the spices should be added at the outset—along with the aromatics—to develop their flavors fully.

Although we didn't want a chili with killer heat, we did want real warmth and depth of flavor. Commercial chili powder is typically 80 percent ground dried red chiles with the rest a mix of garlic powder, onion powder, oregano, ground cumin, and salt. To boost flavor, we increased the amount of chili powder from 3 to 4 tablespoons, added more cumin and oregano, and tossed in some cayenne for heat. We tried some more exotic spices, including cinnamon (which was deemed "awful"), allspice (which seemed "out of place"), and coriander (which "added some gentle warmth"). Only the coriander became part of our working recipe.

It was now time to consider the meat. The quantity (2 pounds) seemed ideal when paired with two 16-ounce cans of beans. Tests using 90 percent, 85 percent, and 80 percent lean ground beef showed that there is such a thing as too much fat. Pools of orange oil floated to the top of the chili made with ground chuck (80 percent lean beef). At the other end of the spectrum, the chili made with 90 percent lean beef was a tad bland—not bad, but not as full flavored as the chili made with 85 percent lean beef, which was our final choice.

We wondered if another type of meat should be used in place of some ground beef. After trying batches of chili made with ground pork, diced pork loin, sliced sausage, and sausage removed from its casing and crumbled, tasters preferred the hearty flavor and creamy texture of an all-beef chili. (The exception was one batch to which we added bacon; many tasters liked its smoky flavor, so we made a version with bacon and black beans as a variation on the master recipe.)

Some of us have always made chili with beer and been satisfied with the results. Nodding to the expertise of others, we tried batches made with water (too watery), chicken broth (too chickeny and dull), beef broth (too tinny), wine (too acidic), and no liquid at all except for that in the tomatoes (beefy tasting and by far the best). When we tried beer, we were surprised to find that it subdued that great beefy flavor. Keep the beer on ice for drinking with dinner.

Tomatoes were definitely going into the pot, but we had yet to decide on the type and amount. We first tried two small (14-ounce) cans of diced tomatoes. Clearly not enough tomatoes. What's more, the tomatoes were too chunky, and they were floating in a thin sauce. We tried two 28-ounce cans of diced tomatoes, pureeing the contents of one can in the blender to thicken the sauce. Although the chunkiness was reduced, the sauce was still watery. Next we paired one can of tomato puree with one can of diced tomatoes and, without exception, tasters preferred the thicker consistency. The test kitchen generally doesn't like the slightly cooked flavor of tomato puree, but this recipe needed the body it provided. In any case, after the long simmering time, any such flavor was hard to detect. (For more information about buying tomato puree, see the Tasting Lab on page 33. For more information about buying diced tomatoes, see the Tasting Lab on page 222.)

We tried cooking the chili with the lid on, with the lid off, and with the lid on in the beginning and off at the end. The chili cooked with the lid on was too soupy, that cooked with the lid off too dense. Keeping the lid on for half of the cooking time and then removing it was ideal—the consistency was rich but not too thick. Two hours of gentle simmering was sufficient to meld the flavors; shorter cooking times yielded chili that was soupy or bland—or both.

Most recipes add the beans toward the end of cooking, the idea being to let them heat through without causing them to fall apart. But this method often makes for very bland beans floating in a sea of highly flavorful chili. After testing several options, we found it best to add the beans with the tomatoes. The more time the beans spent in the pot, the better they tasted. In the end, we preferred dark red kidney beans or black beans because both keep their shape better than light red kidney beans, the other common choice.

With our recipe basically complete, it was time to try some of those offbeat additions to the pot that other cooks swear by, including cocoa powder, ground coffee beans, raisins, chickpeas, mushrooms, olives, and lima beans. Our conclusion? Each of these ingredients was either weird tasting or too subtle to make much difference. Lime wedges, passed separately at the table, both brightened the flavor of the chili and accentuated the heat of the spices. Our chili was now done. Although simple, it is, we hope, good enough to silence any debate.

WHAT WE LEARNED: Cook the spices before the meat to bring out their flavor, and use all ground beef. Don't add any stock, beer, or water—the liquid from the tomatoes should be sufficient. Add the beans early in the process (not just before serving, as directed in most recipes), so they can soak up the flavors of the chili.

## BEEF CHILI WITH KIDNEY BEANS

**Makes about 3 quarts, serving 8 to 10**

Good choices for condiments include diced fresh tomatoes, diced avocado, sliced scallions, chopped red onion, chopped cilantro leaves, sour cream, and shredded Monterey Jack or cheddar cheese. If you are a fan of spicy food, consider using a little more of the red pepper flakes or cayenne—or both. The flavor of the chili improves with age; if possible, make it a day or up to five days in advance and reheat before serving. Leftovers can be frozen for up to a month.

| | |
|---|---|
| 2 | tablespoons vegetable or corn oil |
| 2 | medium onions, chopped fine (about 2 cups) |
| 1 | medium red bell pepper, stemmed, seeded, cut into 1/2-inch dice |
| 6 | medium cloves garlic, minced or pressed through a garlic press (about 2 tablespoons) |
| 1/4 | cup chili powder |
| 1 | tablespoon ground cumin |
| 2 | teaspoons ground coriander |
| 1 | teaspoon red pepper flakes |
| 1 | teaspoon dried oregano |
| 1/2 | teaspoon cayenne pepper |
| 2 | pounds 85 percent lean ground beef |
| 2 | cans (15 ounces each) dark red kidney beans, drained and rinsed |
| 1 | can (28 ounces) diced tomatoes, with juice |
| 1 | can (28 ounces) tomato puree |
| | Salt |
| 2 | limes, cut into wedges |

**1.** Heat the oil in a large heavy-bottomed nonreactive Dutch oven over medium heat until shimmering but not smoking. Add the onions, bell pepper, garlic, chili powder, cumin, coriander, pepper flakes, oregano, and cayenne and cook, stirring occasionally, until the vegetables are softened and beginning to brown, about 10 minutes. Increase the heat to medium-high and add half the beef. Cook, breaking up pieces with a wooden spoon, until no longer pink and

just beginning to brown, 3 to 4 minutes. Add the remaining beef and cook, breaking up pieces with a wooden spoon, until no longer pink, 3 to 4 minutes.

**2.** Add the beans, tomatoes, tomato puree, and 1/2 teaspoon salt. Bring to a boil, then reduce the heat to low and simmer, covered, stirring occasionally, for 1 hour. Remove the lid and continue to simmer 1 hour longer, stirring occasionally (if the chili begins to stick to the bottom of the pot, stir in 1/2 cup water and continue to simmer), until the beef is tender and the chili is dark, rich, and slightly thickened. Adjust the seasoning with additional salt. Serve with lime wedges and condiments (see note), if desired.

### VARIATION

### BEEF CHILI WITH BACON AND BLACK BEANS

Cut 8 ounces bacon (about 8 strips) into 1/2-inch pieces. Fry the bacon in a large heavy-bottomed nonreactive Dutch oven over medium heat, stirring frequently, until browned, about 8 minutes. Pour off all but 2 tablespoons fat, leaving the bacon in the pot. Follow the recipe for Beef Chili with Kidney Beans, substituting the bacon fat in the Dutch oven for the vegetable oil and an equal amount of canned black beans for kidney beans.

## EQUIPMENT CORNER: Slow Cookers

SLOW COOKERS (BETTER KNOWN AS CROCK-POTS, A name trademarked by the Rival company) may be the only modern kitchen convenience that saves the cook time by using more of it rather than less. To see if these appliances could cook not just slowly but also well, we purchased five of them, all 6-quart oval cookers, a size and shape offering the most options in terms of the amount and type of food that can be prepared. The contestants included three "standard" cookers, the Rival Crock-Pot ($39.99), the Farberware Millennium Slow Cooker ($39.99), and the Hamilton Beach Portfolio Slow Cooker ($34.99); one with a new "programmable" feature, the Rival Smart-Pot ($49.99); and one with a completely revamped design, the West Bend Versatility Cooker ($54.99).

All five models had the standard slow cooker temperature settings of low, high, and keep warm. To test the functioning of each setting, we cooked the pot roast recipe (page 102) on low for eight hours and the chili recipe (page 32) on high for four hours; we then set each pot of chili on "keep warm" for two hours. All five cookers produced good renditions of the pot roast and the chili, and all five kept the chili plenty warm for two hours. (The lowest temperature reached during warming was a piping-hot 187 degrees, by the West Bend cooker; the other four cookers maintained the chili at close to 200 degrees.)

What do we recommend? In the "standard slow cooker with no fancy features" category, both the Farberware Millennium and the Rival Crock-Pot performed admirably. The Hamilton Beach cooker showed slight scorching of the chili in the bottom corners of the crockery pot and so was slightly downgraded.

How did the two novel cookers fare? Rival's Smart-Pot is the only cooker on the market that lets you select a specific time and heat setting and then automatically shifts to the warm setting when the cooking time is up. Theoretically, this buys you a couple more hours at the mall or at work before you have to come home and tend the pot. Two hours after switching from high to warm, however, the Smart-Pot had brought the temperature of the chili down by just 10 degrees, from 205 to 195. We're not sure this feature is worth the extra money.

West Bend's Versatility Cooker is a standout because its pot is made from aluminum with a nonstick interior coating, which means you can use it to cook foods on the stove-

top, just as you would any other conventional pot. Both our chili and pot roast recipes start out with instructions for browning on the stovetop, and it was nice to brown foods in the same pot we ultimately used for slow cooking. While a crockery-less crockery pot does seem a little odd, this expensive model does get the job done, and then some.

**BEST SLOW COOKERS**
The Farberware Millennium (left) and the Rival Crock-Pot (middle) were the best basic models tested. The West Bend Versatility Cooker (right) has a stovetop-worthy pot made of aluminum rather than the classic ceramic. See www.americastestkitchen.com for up-to-date prices and mail-order sources for these top-rated products.

## TASTING LAB: Tomato Puree

IN THE FAMILY OF CANNED TOMATO PRODUCTS, TOMATO puree is the neglected middle child, often overlooked in favor of its older sibling, whole peeled tomatoes, or its hotshot younger sibling, diced tomatoes. The reason is clear: While whole and diced tomatoes prove a passable substitute for fresh tomatoes (they are simply skinned and processed), tomato puree is cooked and strained, thereby removing all seeds and all allusions to freshness. That's not to say that tomato puree doesn't have a role in most kitchens, it's just that puree performs best in long-cooked dishes where the thick, even texture of puree is important and fresh tomato flavor is not.

Although we haven't developed many recipes using tomato puree, we did find it to be necessary to achieve full tomato flavor and a smooth richness in our Beef Chili with Kidney Beans. But which brand is best? We gathered eight popular brands of tomato puree and tasted them plain. We then

# Rating Tomato Purees

FIFTEEN MEMBERS OF THE *COOK'S ILLUSTRATED* STAFF TASTED ALL EIGHT PUREES STRAIGHT FROM THE CAN. WE ALSO tasted the winner and loser of this tasting in a slow-simmering chili and found the differences to be negligible. The purees are listed in order of preference based on their scores in the plain tomato puree tasting. Because differences between brands fade with prolonged cooking, all brands are recommended.

**RECOMMENDED**
### Progresso Tomato Puree
**$1.50 for 28 ounces**

Tied for first place, this puree was "thick" and "strong," with a "fresh," "mild" flavor.

**RECOMMENDED**
### Hunt's Tomatoes Puree
**$.99 for 29 ounces**

Hunt's, one of the two top-rated purees, was favored for its "nice and thick" texture and "tomatoey" flavor, though some tasters found it "too sweet."

**RECOMMENDED**
### Cento Tomato Puree
**$1.19 for 28 ounces**

Most tasters found this puree "balanced," with a "good flavor," though many found it "slightly bitter."

**RECOMMENDED**
### Muir Glen Organic Tomato Puree
**$2.59 for 28 ounces**

The lone organic sample in the tasting, this puree was deemed "thick and strong," with "good flavor."

**RECOMMENDED**
### Pastene Tomato Puree
**$1.69 for 28 ounces**

Though some found this brand "fresh tasting," many tasters thought it tasted slightly "tinny."

**RECOMMENDED**
### Redpack Tomato Puree
**$1.19 for 29 ounces**

Some praised its "velvety smooth texture," while others agreed with the one taster who deemed it "middle of the road in every aspect."

**RECOMMENDED**
### Contadina Tomato Puree
**$1.29 for 29 ounces**

"Where's the salt?" wrote one taster of this puree, which many found "thin" and "bland." Others, however, praised its "good balance."

**RECOMMENDED**
### Rienzi Tomato Puree
**$.99 for 28 ounces**

Though it had strong "vegetable flavor," most found it "a bit flat" and "very thin."

---

tasted the winner and loser of the plain tasting in our chili.

We had a tie in the straight puree tasting, with Progresso and Hunt's sharing top honors. Hunt's was praised for "layers of flavor," while Progresso won points for its "strong tomato flavor." Coming in last was Rienzi, unanimously criticized as too thin and watery, though a handful of tasters liked the "vegetal" flavor that one taster described as being like "wicked salty V-8."

For part two of our tasting, we pitted Progresso against Rienzi in our chili recipe. Although it was easy to judge the winners and losers of the straight puree tasting, we wondered how clear the differences would be once the puree had been simmered for two hours with a half-dozen spices. The answer: not very clear. While some tasters found the batch made with Progresso "thicker" and "more full-flavored" and some found the batch made with Rienzi "slightly meatier" and "fresher and sweeter," most agreed with the taster who wrote, "I would use either one." Given that most recipes calling for tomato puree involve long cooking times and lots of ingredients, it's safe to say that using one particular brand over another is not going to make much of a difference in the final dish.

# INDOOR CLAMBAKE

**WHAT WE WANTED**: We wanted to re-create the great flavors of a clambake without help from the sand or the sea.

A clambake is a rite of summer along the East Coast. At this festive beach party, loads of shellfish and a variety of vegetables are steamed in a wide, sandy pit using seaweed and rocks warmed from a nearby campfire. This feast usually takes a day or more to prepare—digging the pit is no small chore—and hours to cook. Though some may mock the idea of a kitchen clambake, it is nonetheless a simple and efficient way (taking a mere half-hour) to prepare a fantastic shellfish dinner—complete with corn, potatoes, and sausage—for a hungry crowd.

An indoor clambake is not a novel idea. We found dozens of recipes in our cookbook library. While the methods used to put one together vary dramatically, the ingredients, in keeping with tradition, are fairly consistent, including clams, mussels, lobsters, potatoes, corn, onions, and spicy sausage. Some recipes tell the cook to partially cook each ingredient separately and then finish things together on the grill, while others recommend specific systems for layering the ingredients in a stockpot. Some recipes use seaweed or corn husks for extra flavor, while others tout the importance of smoky bacon. The goal of all of these recipes, however, is to manage the process such that the various components are cooked perfectly and ready to serve at the same time. Taking note of these different clambake styles, we began our testing.

It soon became apparent which methods were worthwhile and which simply made a mess. Partially cooking the ingredients separately before combining them on the grill was time-consuming and produced a clambake without that authentic clambake flavor. Layering the various ingredients in a stockpot, on the other hand, was both easy to do and produced tasty results. With the stockpot set over high heat, the components steamed and infused one another with their flavors. This method was not without problems,

however, as the onions turned out slimy, and half of the ingredients wound up submerged in shellfish-flavored water. Using this one-pot method as a point of departure, we began to tinker with the technical details and the ingredients.

Although every recipe we read called for adding water to the pot to create steam for cooking, we found the shellfish released enough of their own liquid to make adequate steam. When placed over high heat, the shellfish took only a few minutes to release the moisture needed to steam the whole pot, with a cup or more left over to use as a broth for the clams and mussels. We took advantage of those first few minutes when the pot was dry by lining it with sliced sausage, giving it a chance to sear before the steam was unleashed. We tested several kinds of sausage, and tasters preferred mild kielbasa. The light smoke flavor of this sausage works well with seafood, and the sausage is fairly juicy and fatty, making it perfectly suited to this cooking method.

With the sausage layered on the bottom, we played with the order in which to add the remaining ingredients. We found it best to lay the clams and mussels right on top of the sausage because they provide most of the necessary liquid for the steam and needed to be close to the heat source. Wrapping them loosely in a cheesecloth sack makes them easy to remove when done. Although potatoes actually take the longest to cook, they were best laid on top of the clams and mussels, close to the heat source yet easily accessible with a prodding knife to test their doneness. We shortened their cooking time by cutting the potatoes into 1-inch pieces. Corn, with a layer of husk left on, was placed on top of the potatoes. The husk, we found, protects the delicate corn from becoming infused with too much shellfish flavor. The husk also protects the corn from any foam released by the lobsters, which we placed on top of the corn. We decided to omit the onions, which no one had eaten anyway; the bacon, which smoked out the delicate flavor of the shellfish; and the seaweed, which was hard to find and unnecessary for flavor.

Layered in this fashion, the clambake took just 17 to 20 minutes to cook through completely over high heat. Surprisingly, the shellfish liquid is quite salty and naturally seasons all the ingredients. After taking a couple of minutes to remove the ingredients from the pot and arrange them attractively on a platter, we had a feast that had been made from start to finish in half an hour.

---

**WHAT WE LEARNED:** Don't bother to precook ingredients—they can all go into the pot at the same time. Success depends on how you layer the ingredients in the pot. Line a large pot with sliced sausage, following with the clams and mussels, the potatoes, the corn, and, finally, the lobsters.

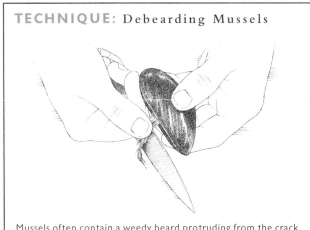

## TECHNIQUE: Debearding Mussels

Mussels often contain a weedy beard protruding from the crack between the two shells. It's fairly small and can be difficult to tug out of place. To remove it easily, trap the beard between the side of a small knife and your thumb and pull to remove it. The flat surface of the paring knife gives you some leverage to remove the beard.

### INDOOR CLAMBAKE Serves 4 to 6

Choose a large, narrow stockpot in which you can easily layer the ingredients. The recipe can be cut in half and layered in an 8-quart Dutch oven, but it should cook for the same amount of time. We prefer small littlenecks for this recipe. If your market carries larger clams, use 4 pounds.

- 2 pounds small littleneck or cherrystone clams, scrubbed (see the illustration on page 42)
- 2 pounds mussels, shells scrubbed and beards removed (see the illustration above)
- 1 pound kielbasa, sliced into ⅓-inch-thick rounds
- 1 pound small new or red potatoes, scrubbed and cut into 1-inch pieces
- 4 medium ears corn, silk and all but the last layer of husk removed (see the illustrations on page 37)
- 2 live lobsters (about 1½ pounds each)
- 8 tablespoons salted butter, melted

## TECHNIQUE:
### Preparing Corn for a Clambake

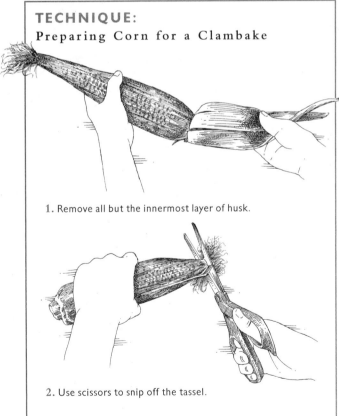

1. Remove all but the innermost layer of husk.

2. Use scissors to snip off the tassel.

**1.** Place the clams and mussels on a large piece of cheese-cloth and tie the ends together to secure; set aside. In a large, heavy-bottomed, 12-quart stockpot, layer the sliced kiel-basa, the sack of clams and mussels, the potatoes, the corn, and the lobsters on top of one another. Cover with the lid and place over high heat. Cook until the potatoes are ten-der (a paring knife can be slipped into and out of the cen-ter of a potato with little resistance), and the lobsters are bright red, 17 to 20 minutes.

**2.** Remove the pot from the heat and remove the lid (watch out for scalding steam). Remove the lobsters and set aside until cool enough to handle. Remove the corn from the pot and peel off the husks; arrange the ears on a large platter. Using a slotted spoon, remove the potatoes and arrange them on the platter with the corn. Transfer the clams and mussels to a large bowl and cut open the cheesecloth with scissors. Using a slotted spoon, remove the kielbasa from the pot and arrange it on the platter with the potatoes and corn. Pour the remaining steaming liquid in the pot over the clams and mussels. Using a kitchen towel to protect your hand, twist and remove the lobster tails, claws, and legs (if desired). Arrange the lobster parts on the platter. Serve immediately with melted butter and napkins.

Julia and Chris shape crab cakes into thick rounds, which will go into the refrigerator to firm up before they are pan-fried.

# EAST COAST *seafood*

## CHAPTER 4

IN THIS CHAPTER

**THE RECIPES**
New England Clam Chowder
Quick Pantry New England Clam
      Chowder

Maryland Crab Cakes
Tartar Sauce
Creamy Chipotle Chile Sauce

**EQUIPMENT CORNER**
Oyster Knives

**SCIENCE DESK**
Why Are Some Clams So Sandy?
Must Onions Make You Cry?

**TASTING LAB**
Mayonnaise

Clam chowder and crab cakes are available in most every seafood restaurant in the country. These dishes both have their origins along the East Coast and have been subjected to numerous changes (most not for the better) as they became more popular.

How many times have you ordered clam chowder in a restaurant only to be served a thin, runny soup? At the other end of the spectrum, many chowders are so thick that a spoon can stand up in the bowl.

Crab cakes can be mixed and shaped in a matter of minutes. But this simple recipe usually goes wrong long before that step, when the ingredients are chosen. Most restaurants use low-quality frozen or (gasp) imitation crabmeat. Better restaurants may use the real deal—fresh jumbo lump crabmeat—but they stretch this pricey ingredient with fillers, such as bread crumbs. Yes, the crab must be bound to form cohesive cakes, but in the end you want to taste the crab, not the binder.

We knew our test kitchen could get these simple dishes right. We also wanted to figure out the best tool and method for opening another East Coast favorite, oysters.

# NEW ENGLAND CLAM CHOWDER

WHAT WE WANTED: A delicious, traditional chowder that was economical, would not curdle, and could be prepared quickly.

We love homemade clam chowder almost as much as we love good chicken soup. After all, our test kitchen is located just outside of Boston, in the heart of chowder country. But we must confess that many cooks (including some that work in our test kitchen) don't make their own chowder. While they might never buy chicken soup, they seem willing to make this compromise. We wondered why.

Time certainly isn't the reason. You can prepare clam chowder much more quickly than you can a pot of good chicken soup. The reason why many cooks don't bother making their own clam chowder is the clams. First of all, clams can be expensive. Second, clams are not terribly forgiving—you must cook them soon after their purchase (chickens can be frozen), and then the chowder itself must be quickly consumed (again, chicken soup can be frozen or at least refrigerated for another day). Last, chowders are more fragile (and thus more fickle) than most soups. Unless the chowder is stabilized in some way, it's likely to curdle, especially when brought to a boil.

Before testing chowder recipes, we explored our clam options. Chowders are typically made with hard-shell clams (rather than soft-shell clams, such as steamers), so we purchased (from smallest to largest) cockles, littlenecks, cherrystones, and chowder clams, often called quahogs (pronounced ko-hogs).

Although they made delicious chowders, we eliminated littlenecks and cockles, both of which were just too expensive to toss into a chowder pot. Chowders made with the cheapest clams, however, weren't satisfactory. The quahogs we purchased for testing were large (4 to 5 inches in diameter), tough, and strong flavored. Their oversized bellies (and the contents therein) gave the chowder an overbearing mineral taste, detracting from its smooth, rich flavor.

Though only a little more expensive than quahogs, cherrystones offered good value and flavor. The chowder made from these slightly smaller clams was distinctly clam flavored, without an inky aftertaste. Because there are no industry sizing standards for each clam variety, you may find some small quahogs labeled cherrystones or large cherrystones labeled quahogs. Regardless of designation, clams much over 4 inches in diameter will deliver a distinctly metallic, inky-flavored chowder.

Some recipes suggest shucking raw clams and then adding the raw clam bellies to the pot. Other recipes steam the clams open. We tested both methods and found that steaming the clams open is far easier than shucking them. After seven to nine minutes over simmering water, the clams open as naturally as budding flowers. Ours did not toughen up as long as we pulled them from the pot as soon as they opened and didn't let them cook too long in the finished chowder.

Although many chowder recipes instruct the cook to soak the clams in salt water spiked with cornmeal or baking powder to remove grit, we found the extra step of purging or filtering hard-shell clams to be unnecessary (see the Science Desk on page 43 for more details). All of the hard-shells we tested were relatively clean, and what little sediment there was sank to the bottom of the steaming liquid. Getting rid of the grit was as simple as leaving the last few tablespoons of broth in the pan when pouring it from the pot. If you find that your clam broth is gritty, strain it through a coffee filter.

At this point, we turned our attention to texture. We wanted a chowder that was thick but still a soup rather than a stew. Older recipes call for thickening clam chowder with crumbled biscuits; bread crumbs and crackers are modern stand-ins.

Chowders thickened with bread crumbs failed to impress. We wanted a smooth, creamy soup base for the potatoes, onions, and clams, but no matter how long the chowder simmered, neither the bread crumbs nor crackers ever completely dissolved into the cooking liquid. Heavy cream alone, by contrast, did not give the chowder enough body. We discovered fairly quickly that flour was necessary not only as a thickener but also as a stabilizer; unthickened chowders separate and curdle.

Most recipes for chowder call for potatoes, some of them calling specifically for starchy baking potatoes, which tend to break down when boiled and so can double as a thickener. In our tests, these potatoes did not break down sufficiently but instead simply became soft and mushy. We found waxy red boiling potatoes to be best for creamy-style chowders. They have a firm but tender texture, and their red skins look appealing.

We now had two final questions to answer about

New England clam chowder. First, should it include salt pork or bacon, and, if the latter, did the bacon need to be blanched? Second, should the chowder be enriched with milk or cream?

Salt pork and bacon both come from the pig's belly. Salt pork is cured in salt, while bacon is smoked, and salt pork is generally fattier than bacon. Salt pork is the more traditional choice in chowder recipes, although bacon has become popular in recent decades, no doubt because of its availability. Jasper White writes in *Fifty Chowders* (Scribners, 2000), his definitive book on the subject, that chowders made years ago with salt pork often had a smoky flavor because they were also cooked over an open hearth. For modern cooks, bacon adds both the pork and the smoky flavor.

We made clam chowder with both salt pork and bacon, and tasters liked both versions. Frankly, we ended up using such small amounts of pork in our final recipe that either salt pork or bacon is fine. Bacon is more readily available and, once bought, easier to use up. Blanching the bacon makes it taste more like salt pork, but we rather liked the subtle smokiness of the chowder made with unblanched bacon.

As for the cream versus milk issue, we found that so much milk was required to make the chowder look and taste creamy that it began to lose its clam flavor and became more like mild bisque or the clam equivalent of oyster stew. Making the chowder with almost all clam broth (5 cups of the cooking liquid from the steaming clams), then finishing the stew with a cup of cream, gave us what we were looking for: a rich, creamy chowder that tasted distinctly of clams.

---

**WHAT WE LEARNED:** Use medium-size clams and then steam them open to create the liquid base for the chowder. Thicken the chowder with flour rather than potatoes; the flour also prevents the dairy from curdling. Use bacon rather than the traditional salt pork for a nice smoky flavor.

### NEW ENGLAND CLAM CHOWDER Serves 6

We like waxy potatoes (with red skins) in this recipe because they hold up much better than high-starch russets.

- 7 pounds medium-size hard-shell clams, such as cherrystones, washed and scrubbed clean (see the illustration at right)
- 4 slices thick-cut bacon (about 4 ounces), cut into ¼-inch pieces
- 1 large Spanish onion, chopped medium
- 2 tablespoons all-purpose flour
- 3 medium boiling potatoes (about 1½ pounds), scrubbed and cut into ½-inch dice
- 1 large bay leaf
- 1 teaspoon fresh thyme leaves or ¼ teaspoon dried thyme
- 1 cup heavy cream
- 2 tablespoons minced fresh parsley leaves
  Salt and ground black or white pepper

**1.** Bring 3 cups water to a boil in large stockpot or Dutch oven. Add the clams and cover with a tight-fitting lid. Cook for 5 minutes, uncover, and stir with a wooden spoon. Quickly cover the pot and steam until the clams just open, 2 to 4 minutes (see illustration 1 on page 43). Transfer the clams to a large bowl; cool slightly. Open the clams with a paring knife, holding the clams over a bowl to catch any juices (see illustration 2 on page 43). With the knife, sever the muscle that attaches the clam to the shell (see illustration 3 on page 43) and transfer the meat to a cutting board. Discard the shells. Mince the clams; set aside. Pour the clam broth into a 2-quart Pyrex measuring cup, holding back the last few tablespoons of broth in case of sediment; set the clam broth aside. (You should have about 5 cups. If not, add bottled clam juice or water to make this amount.) Rinse and dry the stockpot or Dutch oven, then return the pot to the burner.

**2.** Fry the bacon in the empty pot over medium-low heat until the fat renders and the bacon crisps, 5 to 7 minutes.

Add the onion and cook, stirring occasionally, until softened, about 5 minutes. Add the flour and stir until lightly colored, about 1 minute. Gradually whisk in the reserved clam broth. Add the potatoes, bay leaf, and thyme and simmer until potatoes are tender, about 10 minutes. Add the clams, cream, parsley, and salt (if necessary) and ground pepper to taste; bring to simmer. Remove from the heat, discard the bay leaf, and serve immediately.

VARIATION

### QUICK PANTRY NEW ENGLAND CLAM CHOWDER

From late summer through winter, when clams are plentiful, you'll probably want to make fresh clam chowder. But if you're short on time or find clams scarce and expensive, the right canned clams and bottled clam juice deliver a chowder that's at least three notches above canned chowder in quality. We

---

**TECHNIQUE: Scrubbing Clams**

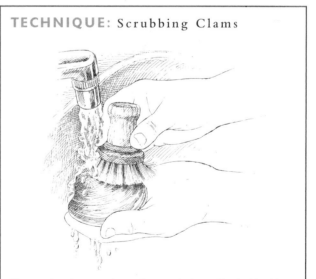

Many recipes instruct the cook to scrub clams. Don't skip this step; many clams have bits of sand embedded in their shells that can ruin a pot of chowder. We like to scrub clams under cold, running water using a soft brush, sometimes sold in kitchen shops as a vegetable brush.

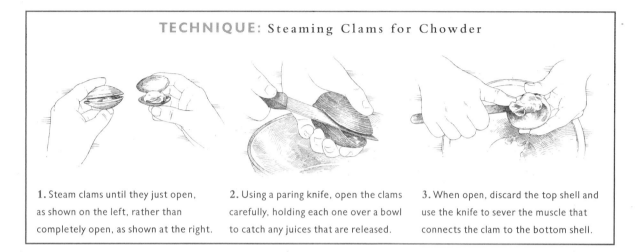

## TECHNIQUE: Steaming Clams for Chowder

**1.** Steam clams until they just open, as shown on the left, rather than completely open, as shown at the right.

**2.** Using a paring knife, open the clams carefully, holding each one over a bowl to catch any juices that are released.

**3.** When open, discard the top shell and use the knife to sever the muscle that connects the clam to the bottom shell.

tested seven brands of minced and small whole canned clams and preferred Doxsee Minced Clams teamed with Doxsee brand clam juice as well as Snow's clams and its clam juice. These clams were neither too tough nor too soft, and they had a decent natural clam flavor.

Follow the recipe for New England Clam Chowder, substituting for the fresh clams 4 cans (6½ ounces each) minced clams, juice drained and reserved and clam meat reserved in small bowl, along with 1 cup water and 2 bottles (8 ounces each) clam juice in medium bowl. Add reserved clam meat and juice at same points when fresh clam meat and broth would be added.

## SCIENCE DESK:
### Why Are Some Clams So Sandy?

CLAMS ARE EASY TO COOK. WHEN THEY OPEN, THEY are done. But perfectly cooked clams can be ruined by lingering sand. Straining the juices through cheesecloth after cooking will remove the grit, but it's a pain. Plus, you lose some of the juices to the cheesecloth. Worse still, straining will not remove bits of sand still clinging to the clam meat. Rinsing the cooked clams washes away flavor.

That's why so many clam recipes start by soaking clams in cold salted water for several hours. We tried various soaking regimens—such as soaking in water with flour, soaking in water with baking powder, soaking in water with cornmeal, and scrubbing and rinsing in five changes of water. If the clams were dirty at the outset, none of these techniques really worked. Even after soaking, many clams needed to be rinsed and the cooking liquid strained.

However, during the course of this testing, we noticed that some varieties of clams were extremely clean and free of grit at the outset. A quick scrub of the shell exterior and these clams were ready for the cooking pot, without any tedious soaking. The cooked clams were free of grit and the liquid was clean. If you want to make sure that your clams will be clean (and that your chowder will be free of grit), you must shop carefully.

Clams can be divided into two categories—hard-shell varieties (such as quahogs, cherrystones, and littlenecks) and soft-shell varieties (such as steamers and razor clams). Hard-shells live along sandy beaches and bays; soft-shells in muddy tidal flats. We have found that this modest difference in location makes all the difference in the kitchen.

When harvested, hard-shells remain tightly closed. In our tests, we found the meat inside to be sand-free. The exteriors should be scrubbed under cold running water to remove any caked-on mud, but otherwise these clams can be cooked without further worry about gritty broths.

Soft-shell clams gape when they are alive. We found that they almost always contain a lot of sand. While it's worthwhile to soak them in several batches of cold water to remove some of the sand, you can never get rid of it all. In the end, you must strain the cooking liquid (we find that a paper coffee filter works best). It's a good idea to rinse the cooked clams, too.

## SCIENCE DESK:
## Must Onions Make You Cry?

WHEN AN ONION IS CUT, THE CELLS THAT ARE DAMAGED in the process release sulfuric compounds as well as various enzymes, notably one called sulfoxide lyase. Those compounds and enzymes, which are separated when the onion's cell structure is intact, activate and mix to form the real culprit behind crying, a volatile new compound called thiopropanal sulfoxide. When thiopropanal sulfoxide evaporates in the air, it irritates the eyes, causing us to cry.

Over the years, we've collected more than 20 ideas from readers, books, and conversations with colleagues all aimed at reducing tears while cutting onions. We decided to put those ideas to the test. They ranged from the common sense (work underneath an exhaust fan or freeze onions for 30 minutes before slicing) to the comical (wear ski goggles or hold a toothpick in your teeth).

Overall, the methods that worked best were to protect our eyes by covering them with goggles or contact lenses or to introduce a flame near the cut onions. The flame, which can be produced by either a candle or a gas burner, changes the activity of the thiopropanal sulfoxide by completing its oxidization. Contact lenses and goggles form a physical barrier that the thiopropanal cannot penetrate. So if you want to keep tears at bay when handling onions, light a candle or gas burner or put on some ski goggles.

## EQUIPMENT CORNER: Oyster Knives

OYSTERS ARE A DELICACY ENJOYED UP AND DOWN THE East Coast, as well as along the Gulf and Pacific Coasts. Of course, fresh oysters must be shucked before eating, and this task inspires fear even among intrepid cooks. Most everyone we know worries that the process will take forever or that the knife will somehow end up cutting their hand. Keeping a folded dish towel between your hand and the oyster should keep you safe (see the illustrations on page 45), but what about speed? Does your choice of knife affect the rate and ease with which the oysters can be opened?

To find out, we rounded up 12 knives in various lengths and styles. We also included a church-key can opener, a household staple that some cooks swear by. The bad news first. We couldn't open a single oyster with the church-key opener. The good news is that we found three oyster knives that we liked quite a lot (even novice shuckers were impressed), and they have some common features.

Oyster knives tend to come in various styles named for cities along the East and Gulf Coast. A Boston-style oyster knife has a long blade that tapers to a roundish tip. A Providence-style knife has a wide, thin blade that ends in a pointed tip. A New Haven–style knife has a wide, thin blade with an angled, pointed tip. Finally, a Galveston-style knife has a long, wide blade with a rounded tip. Both the experienced and inexperienced shuckers in the test kitchen preferred the New Haven–style knife. Its angled, pointed tip easily penetrated the hinge between the bottom and top

shells and popped the oyster open. The flat or rounded tips on the other knives were less adept at this crucial task.

The other key factor in our ratings was the handle. Knives with contoured or textured handles consistently received high marks, while knives with slick or wooden handles were downgraded.

## TECHNIQUE: Shucking Oysters

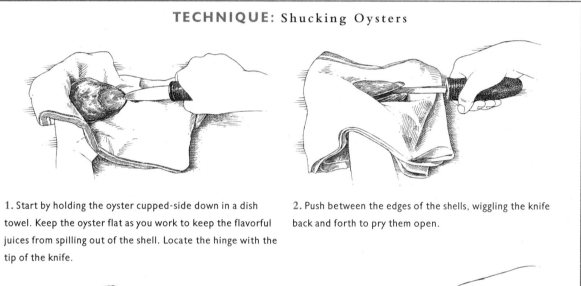

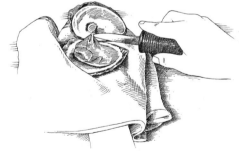

1. Start by holding the oyster cupped-side down in a dish towel. Keep the oyster flat as you work to keep the flavorful juices from spilling out of the shell. Locate the hinge with the tip of the knife.

2. Push between the edges of the shells, wiggling the knife back and forth to pry them open.

3. Detach the meat from the top shell and discard the shell.

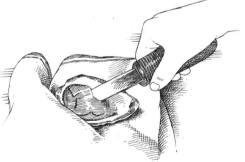

4. To make eating easier, sever the muscle that holds the meat of the oyster to the bottom shell. As you do all of this, work over a bowl to catch the precious oyster liquor that is released.

# Rating Oyster Knives

BOTH NOVICE AND EXPERIENCED SHUCKERS ATTEMPTED TO OPEN OYSTERS WITH 12 DIFFERENT BRANDS OF OYSTER knives plus a church-key can opener (which did not work—we couldn't open a single oyster with it). Models that opened the oysters easily, quickly, and safely received high marks. The knives are listed in order of preference. See www.americastestkitchen.com for up-to-date prices and mail-order sources for top-rated products.

**RECOMMENDED**
### Oxo Good Grips Oyster Knife
**$6.99**
Nonslip handle is comfortable, and the slightly angled blade and pointed tip were the easiest to work with.

**RECOMMENDED**
### Dexter-Russell S121 Oyster Knife
**$13.75**
This 2³/₄-inch New Haven–style knife has a slightly angled tip that makes opening oysters a breeze.

**RECOMMENDED**
### Mundial 5673 Oyster Knife
**$8.00**
Another good example of the New Haven style, with a slightly angled tip that we liked.

**RECOMMENDED WITH RESERVATIONS**
### Dexter-Russell S126 Oyster Knife
**$13.95**
Nice, firm grip, and blade has pointed tip that's the perfect length. If the tip were angled, this knife would be perfect.

**RECOMMENDED WITH RESERVATIONS**
### Mundial 5672 Oyster Knife
**$8.00**
Textured grip feels secure and the blade is thin and sharp. The tip on this Boston-style knife could be more pointed, though.

**RECOMMENDED WITH RESERVATIONS**
### Dexter-Russell S120 Oyster Knife
**$12.50**
This Boston-style knife has a nice handle, but the 4-inch blade seems too long, and the tip is blunt and thick.

**RECOMMENDED WITH RESERVATIONS**
### Dexter-Russell S137 Oyster Knife
**$14.60**
This Galveston-style knife has a good textured grip, but the 4-inch blade is thick and blunt.

**RECOMMENDED WITH RESERVATIONS**
### Mundial 5674 Oyster Knife
**$8.40**
This Galveston-style knife has an excellent contoured grip, but the blade is too long and too thick.

**RECOMMENDED WITH RESERVATIONS**
### Capco 3712 Oyster Knife
**$3.95**
This New Haven–style knife, with an angled tip, has a round wooden handle that testers found uncomfortable.

**RECOMMENDED WITH RESERVATIONS**
### Capco 3711 Oyster Knife
**$3.95**
Testers found the round wooden handle on this knife to be uncomfortable. The blade is thin but not as effective as others.

**NOT RECOMMENDED**
### Carlo Giannini Oyster Knife
**$11.00**
The slick handle is awkward to use, and the short, wide blade is not very effective.

**NOT RECOMMENDED**
### Wüsthof Oyster Knife
**$22.40**
Awkward finger guard severely limits maneuverability, and the blade is too short.

# MARYLAND CRAB CAKES

**WHAT WE WANTED:** A crab cake that tastes like the star ingredient, not the binder. The exterior would be crisp and brown, while the interior would be creamy and moist.

Good crab cakes taste first and foremost of sweet crabmeat. Too many restaurants serve crab-flecked dough balls. That's why the crab cake is especially suited to home cooking.

Great crab cakes begin with top-quality crabmeat. We tested all of the options and found the differences between them to be stark. Canned crabmeat is horrible; like canned tuna, it bears little resemblance to the fresh product. Frozen crabmeat is stringy and wet. Fresh pasteurized crabmeat is a bit watery but far better than the other options. Our top choice is fresh crabmeat, preferably "jumbo lump," which indicates the largest pieces and highest grade. This variety costs a couple of dollars more per pound than other types of fresh crab meat, but a 1-pound container is enough to make crab cakes for four; in our opinion, it's money well spent.

Fresh lump blue crab is available year-round but tends to be most expensive from December to March. The meat should never be rinsed, but it does need to be picked over to remove any shells or cartilage the processors may have missed.

Once we figured out what type of crab to use, our next task was to find the right binder. None of the usual suspects worked. Crushed saltines were a pain to smash into small-enough crumbs, potato chips added too much richness, and fresh bread crumbs blended into the crabmeat a little too well. We finally settled on fine dry bread crumbs. Their flavor is mild, and it's easy to mix them into the crabmeat. The trickiest part is knowing when to stop; crab cakes need just enough binder to hold them together but not so much that the filler overwhelms the seafood. We started out with ¾ cup crumbs but ended up reducing it down to just 2 tablespoons for our final recipe.

The other ingredients we adopted are also pretty basic.

Good, sturdy commercial mayonnaise (we like Hellmann's) keeps the crabmeat moist (a homemade blend can be too liquidy), and a whole egg, unbeaten, makes the crab, crumbs, and seasonings meld together both before and during cooking.

Classic recipes call for spiking crab cakes with everything from Tabasco to Worcestershire sauce, and those are both fine. But we've decided the best blend of tradition and trendiness is Old Bay seasoning combined with freshly ground white pepper and chopped fresh herbs.

Just as essential as careful seasoning is careful mixing. We found a rubber spatula works best, used in a folding motion rather than stirring. You want to end up with a chunky consistency. Those lumps aren't cheap.

We were pleased with our basic recipe on most fronts, but we still had trouble keeping the cakes together as they cooked. Our final breakthrough came when we tried chilling the shaped cakes before cooking. As little as half an hour in the refrigerator made an ocean of difference. The cold firmed up the cakes so that they fried into perfect plump rounds without falling apart. We found that formed cakes can be kept, refrigerated and tightly wrapped, for up to 24 hours.

We also tried different cooking methods. After baking, deep-frying, and broiling, we settled on pan-frying in a cast-iron skillet over medium-high heat. This method is fast and also gives the cook complete control over how brown and how crisp the cakes get. We first tried frying in butter, but it burned as it saturated the crab cakes. The ideal medium turned out to be plain old vegetable oil. It can be heated without burning and smoking, it creates a crisp crust, and it never gets in the way of the crab flavor.

**WHAT WE LEARNED:** Use fresh jumbo lump crabmeat, bind the crab with the minimum amount of dry bread crumbs, add mayonnaise for richness, and chill the shaped cakes thoroughly so they will hold their shape when cooked. Pan-frying in oil is the only way to cook crab cakes.

## MARYLAND CRAB CAKES Serves 4

The amount of bread crumbs you add will depend on the crabmeat's juiciness. Start with the smallest amount, adjust the seasonings, then add the egg. If the cakes won't bind at this point, add more bread crumbs, 1 tablespoon at a time. If you can't find fresh jumbo lump crabmeat, pasteurized crabmeat, though not as good, is a decent substitute.

    1   pound fresh jumbo lump crabmeat, picked over
        to remove cartilage or shell
    4   scallions, green part only, minced (about
        ½ cup)
    1   tablespoon chopped fresh herb, such as cilantro,
        dill, basil, or parsley
  1½    teaspoons Old Bay seasoning
  2–4   tablespoons plain dry bread crumbs
    ¼   cup mayonnaise
        Salt and ground white pepper
    1   large egg
    ¼   cup all-purpose flour
    ¼   cup vegetable oil
        Lemon wedges or dipping sauce (recipes follows)

**1.** Gently mix the crabmeat, scallions, herb, Old Bay, 2 tablespoons bread crumbs, and mayonnaise in a medium bowl, being careful not to break up the lumps of crab. Season with salt and white pepper to taste. Carefully fold in the egg with a rubber spatula until the mixture just clings together. Add more crumbs if necessary.

**2.** Divide the crab mixture into four portions and shape each into a fat, round cake, about 3 inches across and 1½ inches high. Arrange the cakes on a baking sheet lined with waxed or parchment paper; cover with plastic wrap and chill at least 30 minutes. (The crab cakes can be refrigerated up to 24 hours.)

**3.** Put the flour on a plate or in a pie tin. Lightly dredge the crab cakes in the flour. Heat the oil in a large, preferably non-stick skillet over medium-high heat until hot but not smoking. Gently place chilled crab cakes in the skillet; pan-fry until the outsides are crisp and browned, 4 to 5 minutes per side. Serve immediately with lemon wedges or dipping sauce.

## TARTAR SAUCE Makes generous ¾ cup

The classic sauce with seafood.

    ¾   cup mayonnaise
  1½    tablespoons minced cornichons (about 3 large),
        plus 1 teaspoon cornichon juice
    1   tablespoon minced scallion
    1   tablespoon minced red onion
    1   tablespoon capers, minced

Mix all of the ingredients in a small bowl. Cover and refrigerate until the flavors blend, at least 30 minutes. (The sauce can be refrigerated for several days.)

## CREAMY CHIPOTLE CHILE SAUCE

**Makes about ½ cup**

The addition of sour cream makes this sauce richer than traditional tartar sauce. The chipotles add smoky and spicy flavors. This sauce is our favorite with crab cakes.

- ¼ cup mayonnaise
- ¼ cup sour cream
- 2 teaspoons minced canned chipotle chiles in adobo sauce
- 1 small clove garlic, minced or pressed through a garlic press
- 2 teaspoons minced fresh cilantro leaves
- 1 teaspoon juice from 1 lime

Mix all of the ingredients in a small bowl. Cover and refrigerate until the flavors blend, about 30 minutes. (The sauce can be refrigerated for several days.)

---

## FOOD ANALYSIS: Mayonnaise

All eight brands that we tasted were also sent to a food lab and analyzed for oil, egg yolk, and total egg content, which are listed below as percentages of total weight. For comparison, the *Cook's* recipe for homemade mayo (with ¾ cup oil for each large egg yolk) contains 82.2 percent oil and 10.0 percent egg yolk (also 10.0 percent total egg).

| Mayonnaise | Oil Content (%) | Egg Yolk Content (%) | Total Egg Content (%) |
|---|---|---|---|
| Hellmann's | 78.8 | 2.9 | 8.8 |
| Kraft | 80.2 | 2.6 | 4.4 |
| Trader Joe's | 81.7 | 6.9 | 12.6 |
| Hain | 83.3 | 3.7 | 8.5 |
| Kraft Miracle Whip | 40.0 | 4.0 | 6.3 |
| 365 | 78.5 | 5.3 | 11.5 |
| Whole Foods | 85.3 | 5.7 | 11.5 |
| Spectrum | 81.8 | 2.0 | 9.6 |

---

## TASTING LAB: Mayonnaise

MAYONNAISE MIGHT NOT BE THE MOST EXCITING ITEM IN the refrigerator, but given that it is a $1 billion industry, one thing is for certain: Americans buy the creamy, white condiment on a regular basis. And chances are that the jar in most refrigerators is either Hellmann's (sold under the Best Foods label west of the Rockies) or Kraft mayonnaise. Together they account for 78 percent of mayonnaise sales. But a product that dominates the market isn't necessarily the best product. With the surge in popularity of preservative-free, unsweetened, and healthier mayos, we were curious to see if any of these newer spreads could challenge the favorites.

Our taste test included seven nationally available brands of mayonnaise along with Kraft Miracle Whip. Even though the U.S. Food and Drug Administration does not recognize Miracle Whip as a real mayonnaise, we included in our tasting because of its resounding popularity (Kraft sells more Miracle Whip than it does regular mayonnaise). Why is Miracle Whip considered a salad dressing and not a mayonnaise? The FDA defines mayonnaise as an emulsified semi-solid food that is at least 65 percent vegetable oil by weight, at least 2.5 percent acidifying ingredient (vinegar and/or lemon juice) by weight, and contains whole eggs or egg yolks. Miracle Whip, which is also sweeter than regular mayo, weighs in with only 40 percent soybean oil. (Water makes up the difference.)

When you make mayonnaise at home, you whisk together egg yolks and seasonings (lemon juice, salt, mustard, etc.), then slowly whisk in oil until the mixture is emulsified. The ingredients for commercial mayonnaise are premixed and then processed through a colloid mill, a machine that breaks the mixture down into tiny, uniform droplets and creates a stable emulsion with a light consistency. The biggest variations in brands of commercial mayonnaise concern the amount and type of oil, the amount and type of egg (both whole eggs and yolks are used in most products), and flavorings.

The results of our tasting mirrored the sales in America's grocery stores. Hellmann's placed first and Kraft finished second. No other brand was even close. What explains such a strong showing by Hellmann's and Kraft, given that there are few ingredients in mayonnaise and that most commercial mayonnaises are manufactured in similar fashion? We sent the mayonnaises to our food lab to test for oil, egg content (both whole eggs and yolks), acidity, and total fat.

The first suspect that we thought might explain our tasting results also happens to be the first item on the list of ingredients: oil. The oil content for the group ranged from 78.5 percent to 85.3 percent, well above the minimum 65 percent required by the FDA. The only exception, of course, was Kraft Miracle Whip, which has about half the oil of commercial mayonnaise. Oil level alone didn't yield any revealing information (Whole Foods had the most oil and 365 had the least oil, and they both scored poorly).

With that in mind, we went back to the lab results to see if we could find another trend, but the information was ambiguous. Acidity levels were similar (with the exception of tangy Miracle Whip), and total fat did not vary much. As we pored over the data, we noticed that Hellmann's and Kraft both had a very low egg yolk content, while Trader Joe's, our third-place finisher, had the highest egg yolk content (making it the most similar of all the contestants to the test kitchen recipe for homemade mayonnaise).

At this point we turned to tasters' comments on their tasting sheets. A good mayonnaise will have clear egg flavor and a touch of acidity to offset the significant amount of fat from the added oil. Hellmann's was liked for having that balance, and Kraft was thought to be "flavorful but not overpowering." Still, what tasters seemed to like most about these products was that they tasted like "what mayonnaise should taste like." Paul Rozin, a noted food psychologist from the University of Pennsylvania, wasn't surprised by our findings. "A blind taste test isn't blind to your past," he said. "The participant's first exposure to a food will usually become the standard to judge all others against. In the case of mayonnaise, many people grew up eating Hellmann's and Kraft. People like familiar tastes."

Well, if it's all about Hellmann's and Kraft, which one should you buy? In a bread tasting, Kraft beat out Hellmann's by a negligible margin, but in macaroni salad trials, Hellmann's placed second (behind Trader Joe's), while Kraft came in fifth. We recommend Hellmann's, but the difference between the two contenders is not overwhelming. If you are interested in a preservative-free, unsweetened brand, try Trader Joe's. Our tasters liked its bold egg flavor, and, what's more, it's the least expensive brand we tested.

Finally, is it possible for a light mayo to be as flavorful as the full-fat original? We put five brands to the test: Kraft Light Mayonnaise, Hellmann's Light Mayonnaise, Miracle Whip Light Salad Dressing, Spectrum Light Canola Mayonnaise, and Nayonaise (a soy-based sandwich spread), all with a fat content of 3 to 5 grams per serving. To see if our tasters could tell the difference, we also threw the winner of the full-fat tasting into the mix (Hellmann's Real Mayonnaise, 11 grams of fat per serving). As in the mayonnaise tasting, we sampled these products spread on bread and tossed in macaroni salad.

The results? Last place went to Nayonaise. Tasters were unanimous in thinking it bore no resemblance to mayonnaise. One taster said it tasted like "a cross between pureed cottage cheese and tofu." Miracle Whip ("overly sweet" and "pasty") and Spectrum ("bland" and "artificial") didn't fare much better. Tasters thought Kraft was too sweet but made a fairly decent macaroni salad. Hellmann's Light came in second place, very nearly beating out the winner, Hellmann's Real Mayonnaise. Although the light version had a pastier texture than regular Hellmann's, the bright, balanced flavors were similar when tasted on bread, and the two products were virtually identical in the macaroni salad. Even our most finicky taster admitted that the salad made with Hellmann's Light was "not bad."

# Rating Mayonnaises

NINETEEN MEMBERS OF THE *COOK'S ILLUSTRATED* STAFF TASTED THE MAYONNAISES TWO WAYS: SPREAD ONTO PLAIN white sandwich bread and tossed in a simple macaroni salad that contained only pasta, mayonnaise, onion, celery, parsley, and pickles. Mayonnaises are listed in order of preference based on their combined scores in the two tests. All mayonnaises are available in supermarkets nationwide.

### HIGHLY RECOMMENDED
## Hellmann's Real Mayonnaise (known west of the Rockies as Best Foods)
**$3.29 for 32 ounces**

The majority of tasters felt that Hellmann's was "what mayonnaise should taste like." It was liked for its bright, well-seasoned, and balanced flavors. Those classic flavors made macaroni salad that was mild, though some complained that it was "neutral tasting" and "not tangy enough."

### HIGHLY RECOMMENDED
## Kraft Real Mayonnaise
**$2.99 for 32 ounces**

This "flavorful but not overpowering" mayonnaise was another that panelists found to taste like "what you expect mayonnaise to taste like." Most liked its tangy, eggy flavors, while others called it "pleasant but bland" and "unremarkable."

### HIGHLY RECOMMENDED
## Trader Joe's Real Mayonnaise
**$1.79 for 32 ounces**

According to the label, this salty, tangy mayonnaise is "preservative free and unsweetened." It has bold egg and vinegar flavors that came through well in the macaroni salad. Tasters thought it had "a good mix of flavors" and "nicely balanced salt and vinegar."

### RECOMMENDED
## Hain Safflower Mayonnaise
**$3.69 for 24 ounces**

The only mayonnaise made with safflower oil, Hain was described as tart and sweet, with one taster calling it "clean and straightforward." Others thought it had "unbalanced sugar and vinegar."

### RECOMMENDED
## Kraft Miracle Whip Salad Dressing
**$3.39 for 32 ounces**

The panelists were divided into two distinctly different camps: Some thought this dressing had a nice, tangy flavor, while others said it tasted like "white BBQ sauce." Some liked it for making the macaroni salad taste "like store-bought salad"; others disliked it for the same reason. Everyone agreed on one thing: This brand was the sweetest of those tasted.

### RECOMMENDED WITH RESERVATIONS
## 365 Mayonnaise
**$1.99 for 32 ounces**

While some tasters liked its assertiveness, most thought this brand was too tart, with excessive egg flavor. Those dominating flavors were better received in the macaroni salad, which tasters thought had a nice, balanced flavor and was "pleasantly tangy."

### RECOMMENDED WITH RESERVATIONS
## Whole Foods Canola Mayonnaise
**$1.99 for 16 ounces**

Tasters thought that this mayonnaise was "faintly eggy," with a "sharp vinegar flavor." The macaroni salad was bland, and when tasted on bread the mayonnaise was described as "dull" and "boring."

### RECOMMENDED WITH RESERVATIONS
## Spectrum Canola Mayonnaise
**$2.99 for 16 ounces**

This mayonnaise was judged to be the blandest of the bunch. The macaroni salad "wasn't vinegary enough" and "needed sharper flavor." When tasted plain, this brand was thought to be too sweet; it also "lacked depth" and had an off, musty taste.

Bridget shows Chris the secret to great jambalaya—batch cooking the ingredients in a Dutch oven.

# NEW ORLEANS *menu*

## CHAPTER 5

IN THIS CHAPTER

**THE RECIPES**
Chicken and Shrimp Jambalaya

Bananas Foster

**EQUIPMENT CORNER**
Ice Cream Scoops

**TASTING LAB**
Pork Products
Vegetable Broth

Few cities are as much fun as New Orleans. The music is great, and the food is rightly famous. Jambalaya and bananas Foster are two of our favorite dishes from New Orleans. Although we've had delicious versions of both classics in New Orleans, our attempts to replicate these results in our Boston test kitchen have been less than successful.

Many jambalaya recipes yield soggy, sticky rice punctuated with dry pieces of chicken and rubbery shrimp. The dish demands a careful balance of flavor and attention to detail—as little as an extra quarter cup of liquid can ruin the rice.

Bananas Foster is high drama (the bananas and sauce are usually flambéed tableside in restaurants). That said, this dish has very few ingredients, and it seems like it should be easy to pull off at home (and it is). However, in our testing we found that most recipes are way too boozy. Yes, New Orleans is a party town, but we think you should be able to taste the fruit and the rich brown sugar sauce. We knew the test kitchen could figure out how to make this dish simply and safely at home.

# JAMBALAYA

**WHAT WE WANTED:** Most recipes ask a lot from the home cook and provide no more than mushy rice, rubbery shrimp, and dry chicken in return. We wanted to make great jambalaya in one hour.

With chicken, sausage, shrimp, rice, tomatoes, and a laundry list of herbs and spices, jambalaya may sound more like a weekend project than a weeknight dinner. But done right, jambalaya is a one-pot meal that can be on the table in about an hour. Like New Orleans, the city from which it came, jambalaya has a combination of sweet, spice, and smoke that makes it a standout. But when poorly executed, jambalaya is no better than the Vegas version of New Orleans: an imposter with gummy rice, overcooked shrimp, and tough, dry chicken.

We started by testing a half-dozen recipes, all of which followed the same protocol: In a large Dutch oven, brown the chicken and remove; brown the sausage and remove; sauté the vegetables; add the cooking liquid, tomatoes, seasonings, and rice; return the chicken and sausage to the pot; and, finally, add the shrimp when the rice is about half done. Our conclusion? We wanted fluffier rice, more succulent chicken, more delicate shrimp, a more modest amount of tomato, and fresher flavors. In addition, we wanted a streamlined method that would bring the dish together more easily.

Although most jambalaya recipes call for a whole chicken cut up into parts, we opted to use chicken thighs instead. We knew this would save us the time it takes to cut up a chicken, but we also thought that using thighs, which are composed of relatively fatty dark meat, might solve the problem of dry chicken, as white meat is more apt to dry out.

We started by searing both sides of the chicken (with the skin on to provide extra fat to flavor the dish) in just 2 teaspoons of hot vegetable oil, then removed it from the pot, set it aside to cool, and peeled off the skin (chicken skin becomes soggy and unappetizing when cooked in liquid).

Rice and liquid went into the pot, followed by the chicken, and, after just 25 minutes, the chicken and rice were perfectly cooked through. But there was something clumsy about eating the chicken off the bone. For our next test, we tried cooking the chicken in exactly the same way, but instead of serving the thighs whole, we shredded them. Now the dish looked and tasted much more appealing, offering a bite of chicken in every forkful.

Next we took on the sausage. After comparing the classic choice, andouille, with tasso, chorizo, and linguiça, we decided that nothing tastes like andouille—a Cajun sausage that infuses the other ingredients in the pot with spice and smoke (see Tasting Lab: Pork Products, on page 56). We browned ¼-inch pieces of andouille in the chicken fat and then set them aside, planning to add them back to the pot along with the liquid, rice, and chicken.

Vegetables were the next item on our roster. Because the trio of minced bell pepper, onion, and celery is key to Cajun cooking, we included all three in our recipe. However, after sampling bitter-tasting green peppers (the classic choice) side by side with sweet red peppers, we unabashedly chose the reds. We also decided to add 2 tablespoons of minced garlic to give the jambalaya more punch. Most recipes use artificial-tasting garlic powder or too little fresh garlic to make much of an impact.

Now approaching our tenth test, we began to dread the task of chopping and mincing the vegetables and garlic. So we took out the food processor and gave the vegetables a whirl. What a difference! Not only did the food processor get the job done in seconds, but the vegetables were cut into smaller pieces than when hand-chopped and so sautéed more quickly in the pan and contributed more flavor.

For the rice, we started with 2 cups of water to 1 cup of long-grain white rice, the liquid ratio recommended on the back of the rice box. But our rice turned out gummy, and there wasn't enough to serve four to six people. We decided to increase the rice to 1½ cups, using only 2¼ cups water instead of the traditional 3 cups. The rice was now too dry, so we bumped up the water to 2¾ cups. This rice was the perfect compromise between fluffy pilaf (too light for jambalaya) and sticky risotto (too heavy).

Most jambalaya recipes call for homemade chicken stock, but we found that canned chicken broth was fine given the other strong flavors in the dish. We also tried combining clam juice with the chicken broth, hoping that it might bring out the sweetness of the shrimp. Although the clam juice/chicken broth duo was pleasing, the rice needed more punch. To boost the flavor of the rice, we substituted ¼ cup of tomato juice (from a can of diced tomatoes) for an equal amount of water. Now the rice was perfect: flavorful and cohesive without being gummy, heavy, or sticky.

The next step was to find a way to keep the shrimp tender and sweet. We seared the shrimp in a hot pan, set them aside, and then added them back to the jambalaya when the chicken was halfway done. This batch was a failure. The shrimp were tough, and they took on a smoky flavor from the searing that provided little contrast with the andouille. For the next test, we added the raw shrimp just five minutes before the chicken and rice were finished. After removing the lid, we could see that the shrimp were perfectly cooked to a blushing pink, still tender and succulently sweet.

This jambalaya was smoky and sweet, spicy and savory, with perfectly tender shrimp, moist chicken, flavorful sausage, and rice cooked just so. You'd never have guessed we were eating it in our Boston test kitchen and not on Bourbon Street.

---

WHAT WE LEARNED: For the best flavor, use chicken thighs and andouille sausage. Cook the rice in a mixture of canned chicken broth, clam juice, and the juice from canned tomatoes. Add the shrimp once the rice is nearly done so that they don't overcook.

## CHICKEN AND SHRIMP JAMBALAYA
Serves 4 to 6

Because andouille varies in spiciness, we suggest tasting a piece of the cooked sausage and then adjusting the amount of cayenne in the jambalaya to suit your taste. If you can't find andouille, try tasso, chorizo, or linguiça; if using chorizo or linguiça, consider doubling the amount of cayenne. The onion, celery, bell pepper, and garlic can be chopped by hand instead of in the food processor. The shrimp don't need to be deveined, but you can do so if you prefer. If you're serving only four people, you may choose to skip the shredding step and serve each person one piece of chicken on the bone.

| | |
|---|---|
| 1 | medium onion, peeled, ends trimmed, and quartered lengthwise |
| 1 | medium rib celery, cut crosswise into quarters |
| 1 | medium red bell pepper, stem removed, seeded, and quartered lengthwise |
| 5 | medium cloves garlic, peeled |
| 2 | teaspoons vegetable oil |
| 4 | bone-in, skin-on chicken thighs |
| 8 | ounces andouille sausage, halved lengthwise and cut into ¼-inch pieces |
| 1½ | cups (10 ounces) long-grain white rice |
| 1 | teaspoon salt |
| ½ | teaspoon minced fresh thyme leaves |
| ¼ | teaspoon cayenne pepper (see note) |
| 1 | can (14.5 ounces) diced tomatoes, drained, ¼ cup juice reserved |
| 1 | cup bottled clam juice |
| 1½ | cups low-sodium chicken broth |
| 2 | large bay leaves |
| 1 | pound medium-large shrimp (31 to 35 shrimp per pound), shelled |
| 2 | tablespoons minced fresh parsley leaves |

**1.** In food processor, pulse the onion, celery, red pepper, and garlic until chopped fine, about six 1-second pulses, scraping down the sides of the bowl once or twice. Do not over-process; the vegetables should not be pureed (see the photo on page 58).

**2.** Heat the oil in a large heavy-bottomed Dutch oven over medium-high heat until shimmering but not smoking. Add the chicken, skin-side down, and cook until golden brown, about 5 minutes. Using tongs, turn the chicken and cook until golden brown on the second side, about 3 minutes longer. Transfer the chicken to a plate and set aside. Reduce the heat to medium and add the andouille; cook, stirring frequently, until browned, about 3 minutes. Using a slotted spoon, transfer the sausage to a paper towel–lined plate and set aside.

**3.** Reduce the heat to medium-low, add the vegetables, and cook, stirring occasionally and scraping the bottom of the pot with a wooden spoon, until the vegetables have softened, about 4 minutes. Add the rice, salt, thyme, and cayenne; cook, stirring frequently, until the rice is coated with fat, about 1 minute. Add the tomatoes, reserved tomato juice, clam juice, chicken broth, bay leaves, and browned sausage to the pot; stir to combine. Remove and discard the skin from the chicken; place the chicken, skinned-side down, on the rice. Bring to a boil, reduce the heat to low, cover, and simmer for 15 minutes. Stir once, keeping the chicken on top, skinned-side down. Replace the cover and continue to simmer until the chicken is no longer pink when cut into with a paring knife, about 10 minutes more; transfer the chicken to a clean plate and set aside. Scatter the shrimp over the rice, cover, and continue to cook until the rice is fully tender and the shrimp are opaque and cooked through, about 5 minutes more.

**4.** While the shrimp are cooking, shred chicken (see the illustration above). When the shrimp are cooked, discard the bay leaves; off heat, stir in the parsley and shredded chicken, and serve immediately.

## TECHNIQUE: Shredding Chicken

Hold one fork in each hand, with the prongs down and facing toward each other. Insert the prongs into the chicken meat and gently pull the forks away from each other, breaking the meat apart and into long, thin strands.

## TASTING LAB: Pork Products

ANDOUILLE, A SEASONED SMOKED SAUSAGE, IS THE MOST authentic choice for jambalaya, with tasso, also known as Cajun ham, a close second. (Tasso is a lean chunk of highly seasoned pork or sometimes beef that is cured and then smoked.) Because andouille and tasso can sometimes be hard to find in supermarkets, we tested the two against chorizo and linguiça (Spanish and Portuguese sausages, respectively), which are more widely available.

After making a batch of jambalaya with each sausage, tasters agreed there ain't nothing like the real thing. Andouille was perfection. It had intense heat and the bold flavor of garlic and herbs, and it imparted a noticeable yet manageable amount of smokiness to the dish. While well-seasoned and flavorful, tasso was ultrasmoky and had a strange, gristly texture that no one liked. Linguiça was bland and added little heat to the finished product; chorizo was slightly more piquant but still dull.

Andouille is clearly the best choice for jambalaya, but we wondered if all andouille were created equal. So we gathered five brands available nationally in supermarkets and by mail-order and put them to the test. Here are the results, with brands listed in order of preference:

Chef Paul's regular andouille (sometimes called "mild") took the crown, one vote shy of a sweep. Its "smoky," "rich," and "earthy" flavors and "balanced heat level" are the perfect accompaniment to the other big flavors in jambalaya.

Jacob's andouille was big, dark, and jerky-esque, with a strange muscled grain. Despite its aesthetic shortcomings, Jacob's andouille was our runner-up. It had a "deeply smoky," almost sweet flavor.

Chef Paul's hot andouille was so spicy it masked the sausage's other flavors.

Poche's andouille had little flavor to offer, and its texture was "chewy," "rubbery," and "tough."

North Country Smokehouse andouille was excessively spicy and had a strange "tinny" flavor.

The conclusion is clear: If you can find Chef Paul's regular andouille, buy it.

## GETTING IT RIGHT:
### The Best Pork for Jambalaya

Some traditional jambalaya recipes call for tasso, while others use andouille sausage. We tested both. Tasters thought tasso had great flavor, but they did not like its gristly texture and found its smokiness overpowering. Andouille is a better choice for jambalaya: spicy, bold, smoky, and perfectly textured.

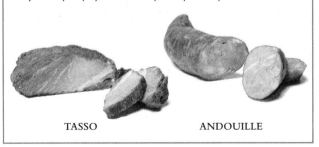

TASSO          ANDOUILLE

## TASTING LAB: Vegetable Broth

WE DON'T LIKE CANNED VEGETABLE BROTH. THAT WAS our assumption, at least, when we began this tasting. Usually thin, metallic, and overly sweet and/or salty, canned vegetable broth was a good idea in theory, we thought, but when it came time to prepare vegetable soups, sauces, and risottos (as well as dishes such as jambalaya), we instinctively reached for canned chicken broth.

But after one too many arguments around the editorial table about making vegetable dishes completely meat-free, we decided to review our preconceptions. We gathered nine popular brands of packaged vegetable broth and tasted them in three different applications: warmed, in an enriched vegetable soup stock, and in asparagus risotto.

The winner of the straight broth tasting, Swanson, was praised for its "nice sweet-sour-salty balance," though some tasters noted the "barely perceptible vegetable flavor." Second-place Better than Bouillon was deemed "good, nicely flavored," and "very tasty," but many found it "very sour," with "strong metallic flavors." Coming in at the bottom of the tasting was Kitchen Basics, which lost points for a sweet molasses flavor that one taster likened to "honey tea." It's no surprise that top-ranked Swanson had one of the highest sodium levels, with 970 milligrams per cup, compared with 330 milligrams per cup for Kitchen Basics, the lowest sodium level. Salt is perceived as flavorful, whereas the less salty broths were deemed bland and flavorless.

Our winning vegetable broth had a mean score of 5.3 out of 10—perfectly average, but not exactly high praise. That's OK—we're not advocating drinking straight vegetable broth. But how would canned vegetable broth fare in a recipe where it was not the leading lady but instead a strong supporting character?

For the second test, we enriched the canned vegetable broth with roasted vegetables and garlic. We pitted the winner, Swanson, and the loser, Kitchen Basics, of our straight broth tasting against each other. Swanson eked out a win,

with a saltier flavor that most tasters preferred. Kitchen Basics was praised by some as "flowery," "earthy," and "more vegetal," though it was those same qualities that some tasters listed as negatives in the plain broth tasting. Neither soup was bad; each had different flavor characteristics that worked in this application.

In the asparagus risotto, the results were surprising. We threw in what we thought would be a ringer—Swanson reduced-sodium chicken broth, the winner of our canned chicken broth tasting—to compete against Swanson and Kitchen Basics vegetable broths. Swanson vegetable broth was the tasters' favorite, praised as "well balanced," with "round, full flavors." The darkest colored of all the original broths in the tasting, Kitchen Basics, was liked by some for its "rich and hearty" flavor, though most tasters found the "muddy" color distracting, giving this broth a last-place finish. The chicken broth finished a strong second.

Though there was a clear winner and loser in the straight broth tasting, the varied results in other applications lead us to believe that the differences between the broths are subtle. If you are using canned vegetable broth in a recipe with lots of other strong flavors, it probably doesn't matter which broth you use. If the flavors of the broth are going to be more up front, as they are in a simple brothy soup or risotto, you should probably use Swanson. And if you are sensitive to salt, you may want to check the sodium level before you buy. As for our jambalaya recipe, you could use vegetable broth instead of chicken broth—it won't make a huge difference.

## GETTING IT RIGHT:
### Properly Cut Vegetables

Using the pulse button on the food processor yields finely chopped vegetables in seconds. Don't overprocess or puree the vegetables—they should remain in distinct pieces.

# Rating Vegetable Broths

EIGHTEEN MEMBERS OF THE *COOK'S ILLUSTRATED* STAFF TASTED ALL THE BROTHS WARMED BUT OTHERWISE STRAIGHT from the package. We also tested our favorite and least favorite broths in a hearty vegetable soup and an asparagus risotto. The broths are listed in order of preference based on their scores in the plain broth tasting. Note that when the broths were used in soup or risotto, some (but not all) of these differences faded away. All brands are sold in supermarkets nationwide.

**RECOMMENDED**
## Swanson Vegetable Broth
**$.99 for 14.5 ounces**

970mg sodium per cup

This top-rated broth had the most flavor, though some tasters found it too salty.

**RECOMMENDED WITH RESERVATIONS**
## Better than Bouillon Vegetable Base
**$4.99 for 8 ounces (enough to make 38 cups of broth)**

560mg sodium per cup

Most tasters liked this thick liquid base, deeming it "good, nicely flavored, and salty"; some tasters nonetheless found it "sour" and "wheaty."

**RECOMMENDED WITH RESERVATIONS**
## Herb-Ox Granulated Vegetable Bouillon Cubes
**$2.39 for 3.33 ounces (enough to make 25 cups of broth)**

980mg sodium per cup

With the highest level of sodium, this powdered base earned one taster's comment: "Tastes like a veggie-flavored salt lick."

**RECOMMENDED WITH RESERVATIONS**
## Morga Instant Vegetable Broth
**$7.99 for 5 ounces (enough to make 35 cups of broth)**

520mg sodium per cup

The prettiest of the bunch, with flakes of parsley floating in a pale gold broth, this powdered base produced broth that was "pale and nondescript," though some found it "quite vegetabley."

**RECOMMENDED WITH RESERVATIONS**
## Health Valley Vegetable Broth
**$2.39 for 32 ounces**

360mg sodium per cup

While some tasters found the flavor "cardboardy," others praised the "natural," "oniony" taste.

**RECOMMENDED WITH RESERVATIONS**
## College Inn Garden Vegetable Broth
**$1.19 for 13.75 ounces**

780mg sodium per cup

"Pretty good," wrote one taster about this supermarket standby, but others found it "too sour" and "very bland."

**RECOMMENDED WITH RESERVATIONS**
## Pacific Foods Organic Vegetable Broth
**$2.99 for 32 ounces**

530mg sodium per cup

Though it had "some depth and richness," many tasters found it "too strong and manufactured tasting."

**RECOMMENDED WITH RESERVATIONS**
## Hain Vegetable Broth
**$2.15 for 14.5 ounces**

480mg sodium per cup

Several tasters detected a "thick, nutmeg flavor," with a scent like "allspice and clove." Other tasters found this broth to be "very tomatoey," with "almost no flavor at all."

**RECOMMENDED WITH RESERVATIONS**
## Kitchen Basics Vegetable Stock
**$2.39 for 32 ounces**

330mg sodium per cup

This last-place broth, deemed "supersweet," with an earthy vegetal flavor, had the lowest sodium content of all the brands.

# BANANAS FOSTER

**WHAT WE WANTED**: A quick, reliable dessert with tender yet not mushy bananas and a flavorful yet not boozy sauce.

Bananas Foster is a classic, simple dessert that hails from New Orleans. The dish is often made tableside at restaurants (or at home, for guests) in a chafing dish. Bananas are cooked in a caramel-type sauce of melted butter and brown sugar, then flambéed with rum, brandy, banana liqueur, or a combination of liquors. The luscious mixture is then spooned over scoops of vanilla ice cream.

Although bananas Foster is quick and simple, with very few ingredients, it can go wrong. Sometimes the bananas are overcooked and mushy. The sauce can be too thin, overly sweet, or taste too strongly of alcohol.

To begin our testing, we first settled on the amounts of dark brown sugar and butter. Sauces made with high ratios of butter to sugar were thin, greasy, and not sweet enough, while too little butter made a sauce that was sugary and sticky. Four tablespoons of butter to ½ cup of brown sugar created a slightly thickened, buttery (but not greasy) sauce.

We pulled brandy, rum, and banana liqueur from the test kitchen liquor cabinet to determine which would be best for this dish. We chose to use dark rum; its full-bodied flavor was a perfect foil for the sweetness of the bananas and brown sugar.

The recipes we had uncovered called for anywhere from 1 tablespoon to a whopping 2 cups of spirits. We started with 1 tablespoon of dark rum and worked our way up to 4 tablespoons, which was just enough to impart a definite rum flavor but not so much as to turn the dessert into an after-dinner drink. We decided to add 1 tablespoon of the rum to the sauce and use the rest to flambé the bananas.

**WHAT WE LEARNED**: Use the proper ratio of brown sugar to butter so the sauce will be nice and thick but not too sweet. Rum is the best liquor for this dish, and a little cinnamon and lemon zest add complexity to the sauce.

## BANANAS FOSTER  Serves 4

While the bananas cook, scoop the ice cream into individual bowls so they are ready to go once the sauce has been flambéed. Before flambéing, make sure to roll up long shirt sleeves, tie back long hair, turn off the exhaust fan (otherwise the fan may pull the flames up), and turn off any lit burners (this is critical if you have a gas stove).

- 4 tablespoons unsalted butter
- ½ cup packed (3½ ounces) dark brown sugar
- 1 cinnamon stick
- 1 strip lemon zest, 2 inches long by about ½ inch wide
- 4 tablespoons dark rum
- 2 large, firm, ripe bananas, peeled and halved lengthwise and then crosswise
- 1 pint vanilla ice cream, divided among four bowls

**1.** Place the butter, sugar, cinnamon stick, lemon zest, and 1 tablespoon rum in a heavy-bottomed 12-inch skillet. Turn the heat to medium-high and cook, stirring constantly, until the sugar dissolves and the mixture is thick, about 2 minutes.

**2.** Reduce the heat to medium and add the bananas to the pan, spooning some sauce over each piece. Cook until the bananas are glossy and golden on the bottom, about 1½ minutes. Turn the bananas and continue cooking until very soft but not mushy or falling apart, about 1½ more minutes.

> **FOOD FACT: Bananas**
> Americans consume an average of 28 pounds of bananas every year. With three medium bananas weighing about a pound, the average American eats about 84 bananas every year.

**3.** Remove the skillet from the heat. Add the remaining 3 tablespoons rum and wait until the rum has warmed slightly, about 5 seconds. Wave a lit match over the pan until the rum ignites, shaking the pan to distribute the flame over the entire pan. When the flames subside (this will take 15 to 30 seconds), divide the bananas and sauce (discarding the cinnamon stick and lemon zest) among the four bowls of ice cream and serve.

## EQUIPMENT CORNER: Ice Cream Scoops

WE'VE ALL STRUGGLED WITH AN INTRACTABLE PINT OF rock-hard ice cream. That's where a good ice cream scoop comes in handy; it can release even hard-frozen ice cream from bondage. We gathered 10 readily available scoops and dipped our way through 20 pints of vanilla to find the best one. We tested three basic types of scoop: classic, mechanical-release (or spring-loaded), and spade-shaped. Prices ranged from $3.99 to $22.

Classic ice cream scoops sport a thick handle and curved bowl. They can be used by lefties and righties with equal comfort. There are a few variations on the theme; among the classic scoops we purchased, one had a pointed "beak" scoop, another offered a "comfort grip" rubber handle, and another contained a self-defrosting liquid. Testers were unanimous in assigning first place—in both its own category and overall—to the Zeroll Classic Ice Cream Scoop ($22). Its thick handle was comfortable for large and small hands, and its nonstick coating and self-defrosting liquid (which responds to heat from the user's hand) contributed to perfect release, leaving only traces of melted cream inside the scoop. The defrosting fluid and the elegantly curved bowl allowed the scoop to take purchase immediately, curling a perfect scoop with minimal effort. Only one caveat: Don't run this scoop through the dishwasher, as it will lose its magical defrosting properties.

Coming in second among the other classic scoops tested was the Oxo Beak Scoop ($11.99). The beak point dug into ice cream with ease, and the ice cream curled up nicely. Our only minor quibble was the short handle, which forced testers with larger hands to choke up close to the head. If price is a concern, you might consider this model.

Mechanical-release scoops come in various sizes and operate with a spring-loaded, squeezable handle (or thumb trigger) that connects to a curved steel lever inside the scoop. When the handle or lever is released, the ice cream pops out in a perfectly round ball. Although we frequently use a mechanical-release scoop to measure out even portions of cookie dough and muffin batter, we found these scoops to be less than ideal when it came to ice cream. They are designed for right-handed users only, and their thin, straight-edged handles were distinctly uncomfortable when considerable pressure was applied. Of the four models we tested, none was worthy of recommendation.

Spades, with their flat, paddle-type heads, are useful when you need to scoop a lot of ice cream quickly, say, for an ice cream cake or sandwiches, but they are too big to fit into pint containers. If you make frozen desserts frequently or need to work your way through multiple gallon-size containers of ice cream, a spade might be for you. Our preferred model, made by the same manufacturer as our winning scoop, is the Zeroll Nonstick Ice Cream Spade ($19.60).

**BEST ICE CREAM SCOOPS**
The Zeroll Classic Ice Cream Scoop (left) was the favorite model tested. If you need to scoop a lot of ice cream for an ice cream cake, you might consider the Zeroll Nonstick Ice Cream Spade (right), but this tool is too big to fit into pint containers.

Chris quizzes Bridget about the names of Italian pasta shapes and their literal translations. This one seems pretty easy—shells anyone?

# FREEDOM FROM
## red sauce

CHAPTER 6

### IN THIS CHAPTER

**THE RECIPES**

Pasta with Sautéed Mushrooms
and Thyme
Pasta with Mushrooms, Peas, and
Camembert
Pasta with Mushrooms, Pancetta,
and Sage

Orecchiette with Broccoli Rabe
and Sausage

**EQUIPMENT CORNER**

Herb Choppers

**SCIENCE DESK**

Why Are Shiitake Stems So
Tough?

**TASTING LAB**

Boutique Extra-Virgin Olive Oil

Tired of the same old marinara sauce? Tomatoes and pasta are a classic (and delicious) pairing, but sometimes you want a change. Vegetable sauces, like the two included in this chapter, one with mushrooms and one with broccoli rabe, are appealing options—at least in theory.

We've had plenty of mushroom pasta dishes that seem like little more than noodles and cream of mushroom soup. We were confident that we could create something special if we started with good, fresh (not canned) mushrooms.

Pasta with broccoli rabe is common in southern Italy. When made in this country, it's often too oily or the broccoli rabe is too wilted and mushy. We wanted to investigate this classic (and very simple) recipe and figure out how to make it right.

# PASTA WITH MUSHROOMS

**WHAT WE WANTED:** We wanted a woodsy, creamy sauce that would enhance the pasta and be ready to serve as quickly as possible.

Transforming an ordinary box of pasta and a package of mushrooms into something special is weeknight cooking at its best: quick, simple, and delicious. But that doesn't mean that it's easy. Mushrooms easily turn out slippery, pale, and watery, not unlike those packed in a tin can. When this dish is done right, however, the mushrooms are woodsy, distinctive, and full-flavored. We'd need to figure out how to cook them properly and then choose a sauce that would marry them best with pasta.

We soon discovered that there is no definitive recipe for this dish; cookbook and Internet research turned up limitless options. We chose four recipes representing the most common mushroom sauce preparations. Pasta with mushrooms simmered in tomato sauce was unanimously dismissed; the delicate mushrooms took a back seat to the tomatoes, and we all wanted a stronger mushroom presence. A sauce made with rehydrated dried mushrooms had intense mushroom flavor, but tasters wanted something fresher and lighter in color (the dried mushrooms had stained the pasta an unappealing dark brown). An Alfredo-like recipe of mushrooms cloaked in a dense cream sauce showed promise—the milky sauce nicely offset the earthy mushrooms. The problem was that it was too heavy and rich, curbing tasters' appetites after just a few forkfuls. A simple topping of sautéed mushrooms, garlic, and herbs made an intoxicating sauce but left the pasta itself dry and bland. If we could find a way to combine the intense flavor of these sautéed mushrooms with a lightened version of the cream sauce, we'd be in business.

Clearly, our next step was to choose the mushrooms. Not willing to shell out $18 per pound on exotic mushrooms, we limited ourselves to cultivated mushrooms that could be purchased for modest prices at the supermarket. The list included white button mushrooms, portobellos, cremini, and shiitakes. A quick taste test confirmed the obvious: White button mushrooms have the least flavor of the group. We also found that portobellos are tasty, but they darken sauces unless the gills are removed, a tedious process. We settled on a combination of cremini and shiitakes; tasters enjoyed the rich and meaty nature of cremini, while shiitakes have a hearty flavor and a pleasant chewy texture.

From experience, we knew the basics of mushroom cookery: They leach liquid a few minutes after exposure to high heat and then, after the moisture evaporates, they begin to brown. We cranked the heat on the stove and threw in a chunk of butter, followed by very thinly sliced mushrooms. The mushrooms quickly absorbed all of the butter and burned slightly. We started anew, adding a good drizzle of olive oil to reduce the risk of burning, but keeping some butter for flavor and slicing the mushrooms thicker. This time they cooked the way we expected them to, ending up lightly browned.

We turned to other variables to refine our technique. Salt draws moisture out of vegetables, and we suspected it might do the same with mushrooms. In a side-by-side test, mushrooms salted at the onset of sautéing released more liquid than an unsalted batch, which was a bonus. The more juices that were released, the more deeply the mushrooms browned (dry food always browns more readily than moist). Because shiitakes contain more moisture than cremini, we gave them a two-minute head start in the pan. (Note that it is possible to overcook mushrooms; we learned to keep them in the skillet just until they are browned; any longer and they become tough and rubbery.) A traditional skillet is our usual choice for sautéing, but we wondered if a nonstick pan was better for delicate mushrooms. A head-to-head test proved that the traditional skillet was best because the resulting fond (the browned bits on the bottom of the pan)

We knew from the first recipes we tested that we wanted a light creamy sauce. We removed the mushrooms from the skillet and made a quick pan sauce by deglazing the pan with chicken broth and then tested a few additions. Sour cream caused the sauce to separate, and it was too tangy. A swirl of heavy cream, however, did the trick, creating a smooth, mild sauce. However, with ½ cup chicken broth and ½ cup cream, the pasta turned dry within minutes of saucing. We added more chicken broth in ¼ cup increments and ended up using quite a bit more than we had expected; 1¼ cups creates a saucy, but not soupy consistency. An acidic element (alcohol, citrus, or vinegar) is often the key ingredient in a recipe—it sharpens and refines competing flavors. We tried small amounts of white wine, vermouth, Marsala, sherry, Madeira, balsamic vinegar, and lemon juice, the latter being the test kitchen favorite.

Chunky sauces pair well with stubby, molded pasta shapes that have crevices in which the sauce can nestle. We found the best choices to be an unusual, frilly, flower-shaped pasta called campanelle and the readily available farfalle (bow ties). Rather than reducing the sauce and tossing it with the pasta, we simmered al dente pasta in the sauce for a couple of minutes. This way, the pasta and sauce became fully integrated, with the pasta absorbing a good amount of flavor. The sauce also thickens slightly during this step as the pasta leaches starch. As with many pasta dishes, this one is improved by a handful of grated Parmesan cheese, a speck of black pepper, and chopped fresh parsley.

contribute flavor to the sauce. (Nonstick skillets produce little fond.) When we added dried porcinis, the resulting sauce was richer, but rehydrating dried mushrooms complicated this otherwise simple recipe and the fresh shiitakes and cremini on their own were just fine.

Garlic and thyme have a natural affinity with mushrooms, so we added generous amounts of both, saving other herbs for variations. Adding the thyme after the mushrooms were fully cooked preserved its pungency. We also experimented with a variety of choices from the onion family and settled on mild shallots, which didn't compete with the mushrooms.

WHAT WE LEARNED: **Use a combination of shiitake and cremini mushrooms for optimum flavor and texture. Cook the mushrooms in a skillet (not in the sauce) to improve their flavor. Create the pasta sauce by adding chicken broth and cream to the browned bits left in the skillet after the mushrooms have been removed. Use a pasta shape that cradles the mushrooms.**

## PASTA WITH SAUTÉED MUSHROOMS AND THYME

**Serves 4 as a main course or 6 to 8 as side dish**

Vegetable broth can be substituted for the chicken broth to make this dish vegetarian. If you add the pasta to the boiling water at the same time the cremini go into the skillet, the pasta and sauce will finish at the same time.

|       | Salt |
|-------|------|
| 1     | pound campanelle or farfalle pasta |
| 2     | tablespoons unsalted butter |
| 2     | tablespoons extra-virgin olive oil |
| 3–4   | large shallots, chopped fine (about 1 cup) |
| 3     | medium cloves garlic, minced or pressed through garlic press (about 1 tablespoon) |
| 10    | ounces shiitake mushrooms, stems discarded, caps wiped clean and sliced ¼ inch thick |
| 10    | ounces cremini mushrooms, wiped clean and sliced ¼ inch thick |
| 1     | tablespoon plus 1 teaspoon minced fresh thyme leaves |
| 1¼    | cups low-sodium chicken broth |
| ½     | cup heavy cream |
| 1     | tablespoon juice from 1 lemon |

Ground black pepper
| 2 | ounces finely grated Parmesan (1 cup) |
| 2 | tablespoons minced fresh parsley leaves |

**1.** Bring 4 quarts water to a rolling boil, covered, in a stockpot; add 1 tablespoon salt and the pasta, stir to separate, and cook until just shy of al dente. Drain and return the pasta to the stockpot.

**2.** Meanwhile, heat the butter and oil over medium heat in a 12-inch skillet until foaming. Add the shallots and cook, stirring occasionally, until softened and translucent, about 4 minutes. Add the garlic and cook until fragrant, about 30 seconds. Increase the heat to medium-high; add the shiitakes and cook, stirring occasionally, for 2 minutes. Add the cremini and ½ teaspoon salt; cook, stirring occasionally, until the moisture released by the mushrooms has evaporated and the mushrooms are golden brown, about 8 minutes. Stir in the thyme and cook 30 seconds. Transfer the mushrooms to a bowl and set aside. Add the chicken broth to the skillet and bring to a boil, scraping up the browned bits on the bottom of the pan; off heat, stir in the cream, lemon juice, and salt and pepper to taste.

---

### GETTING IT RIGHT: Mushroom Cooking 101

1. Raw mushrooms initially soak up all the fat in a pan. Don't give in to temptation and add more oil and butter.

2. After several minutes, the mushrooms begin to release a significant amount of liquid, which will evaporate with continued cooking.

3. The liquid has evaporated and the mushrooms turn golden brown. They are done. If the mushrooms continue to cook, they become dry and rubbery.

**3.** Add the mushrooms, chicken broth/cream mixture, cheese, and parsley to the pasta in the stockpot. Toss over medium-low heat until the cheese melts and the pasta absorbs most of the liquid, about 2 minutes; serve immediately.

VARIATIONS

**PASTA WITH MUSHROOMS, PEAS, AND CAMEMBERT**

Follow the recipe for Pasta with Sautéed Mushrooms and Thyme, omitting the thyme and adding 1 cup frozen peas, thawed, to the skillet along with the chicken broth; substitute 6 ounces Camembert cut into ½-inch cubes (do not remove the rind) for the Parmesan, and 2 tablespoons finely chopped chives for the parsley.

**PASTA WITH MUSHROOMS, PANCETTA, AND SAGE**

Cook 4 ounces pancetta, cut into ¼-inch cubes, in 2 tablespoons olive oil, stirring occasionally, until lightly browned and crisp, about 6 minutes. Using a slotted spoon, transfer the pancetta to a paper towel–lined plate. Follow the recipe for Pasta with Sautéed Mushrooms and Thyme, substituting the fat in the skillet for the butter and olive oil and an equal amount minced fresh sage leaves for the thyme; add the pancetta to the pasta along with the sautéed mushrooms.

## SCIENCE:
### Why Are Shiitake Stems So Tough?

FORGET TO REMOVE THE STEMS FROM SHIITAKES BEFORE cooking, and you'll spend a good part of the dinner hour picking inedible, chewy bits from your plate. Seasoned cooks know to either discard the stems or save them for stock, but most learned this lesson the hard way. Why are shiitake stems so tough while white button and other cultivated mushrooms have tender, edible stems?

Many of the experts we contacted suggest that a sturdy stem with a tightly packed cellular structure evolved over

---

**FOOD FACT: Mushrooms**

Of the more than 5,000 known varieties of mushroom, about 100 are poisonous. Every year, about 9,000 cases of mushroom poisoning are reported to the American Association of Poison Control Centers.

---

time to support the shiitake's wide cap, which can range from the size of a quarter to 5 inches in diameter. Two experts—Judy Rogers, mycologist and executive secretary of the North American Mycological Association, and David Ellis, associate professor of mycology at the University of Adelaide in Australia—concur that the way shiitakes are grown also contributes to the sturdy composition of their stems.

Shiitakes are cultivated on either natural hardwood logs or on man-made sawdust logs. Mushrooms grown this way are called wood-decomposing fungi, a family of mushrooms in which tough, woody stems are characteristic. For these mushrooms, woody stems are a necessity; a tender, flimsy stem would not be able to establish growth in the tough environment of a log. (This hardiness amounts to more long-lived mushrooms, too; shiitakes exist in nature for several weeks without rotting and are slower to rot in the refrigerator than white mushrooms.)

Common white button mushrooms, on the other hand, are raised in composted and sterilized manure. These materials decompose quickly by nature, and the mushrooms grown in them are significantly more delicate with respect to texture and longevity; all but the very ends of their stems are perfectly edible.

## EQUIPMENT CORNER: Herb Choppers

IS THERE AN EASIER WAY TO ACHIEVE FINELY MINCED PILES of parsley, basil, and mint than rocking a chef's knife back and forth a hundred times? We tested several kinds of herb choppers and mincers to find out.

The first gadgets tested were herb mills, a stainless

steel mill by KüchenProfi and a plastic mill by Zyliss. Each has a hopper in which you put the herbs and a series of small blades that chop them when you turn a hand crank. For all of the herb choppers tested we used basil, parsley, rosemary, and garlic. The seemingly solid KüchenProfi gagged on the herbs, and they had to be pinched and pried out of the hopper. The Zyliss didn't choke, but it could not mince either. Shreds of leafy herb and shards of garlic would be more like it.

Next in line were herb rollers, which depend on a row of wheel-like blades that are pushed back and forth over the item to be minced by means of a handle (as in the Oxo we tested) or some sort of protective casing (as in the International Cutlery). Rollers are comfortable, easy to use, and fast—so fast that they crushed and bruised the parsley and basil leaves into a slimy green mush in about 30 seconds. The rosemary and garlic didn't fare much better, being reduced to odd-shaped bits and pieces, and the garlic tended to stick to the blades.

The most newfangled entry in our lineup was the Rev'n Chef by Chef'n, a round plastic case with a ripcord inside that, when pulled and released, turned a blade that tore up everything we gave it into large, rough, unevenly sized pieces. And more pulls of the ripcord didn't help much. A beat-up clove of garlic looked much the same after 75 pulls as it did after 25.

The only worthwhile alternative to a chef's knife was the mezzaluna, a cutting tool named for its half-moon shape that has been in use for hundreds of years. We tried three styles: one with a single blade and a single handle meant to be used in a wooden bowl, one with a single blade and two handles, and one with two blades and two handles. The first of these minced well but was a bit awkward to use as well as labor-intensive. The latter pair, each with a handle on either end, let you get a rocking motion going that cut through herbs—especially tough, woody rosemary—cleanly and quickly. The double-bladed mezzaluna was faster (usually 30 to 60 seconds faster than the single blade when producing ¼ cup of minced herbs), but it was tough on the basil, bruising it badly. Neither mezzaluna could mince garlic as perfectly as a garlic press.

What do we recommend? If your knife skills aren't quite what you'd like them to be, try a single-bladed, two-handled mezzaluna. It's not only effective, it's fun. And purchase one with a 7-inch blade rather than a 6-inch blade. The 7-inch really rocks.

# Rating Herb Choppers

WE TESTED EIGHT HERB CHOPPERS BY MINCING BASIL, PARSLEY, ROSEMARY, AND GARLIC WITH EACH DEVICE. The choppers are listed in order of preference based on their performance in these tests as well as their ease of use and design. See www.americastestkitchen.com for up-to-date prices and mail-order sources for the top-rated product.

**RECOMMENDED**
### Henckels 7-Inch Single-Blade Mezzaluna

**$17.99**

With a handle at either end, this tool rocked through piles of herbs—especially tough, woody rosemary—cleanly and quickly.

**RECOMMENDED WITH RESERVATIONS**
### Schaaf Double-Blade Mezzaluna

**$55.00**

With two blades, this mezzaluna works especially fast, but it was tough on the basil, bruising it badly.

**RECOMMENDED WITH RESERVATIONS**
### KüchenProfi Single-Blade Mezzaluna (with Wooden Bowl)

**$31.95**

With just a single handle that sits on top of the blade, this tool is designed for use inside a wooden bowl. Although it produces nicely minced herbs, testers found it awkward to use.

**NOT RECOMMENDED**
### Zyliss Herb Mill

**$12.95**

Although better than the KüchenProfi mill, this plastic mill shredded herbs rather than mincing them.

**NOT RECOMMENDED**
### KüchenProfi Herb Mill

**$14.99**

This seemingly solid stainless steel tool gagged on every herb.

**NOT RECOMMENDED**
### Oxo Rolling Herb Mincer

**$6.50**

The parsley and basil were badly bruised. The garlic was oddly chopped and stuck to the blade.

**NOT RECOMMENDED**
### International Cutlery Rolling Mincer/Vegetable Cutter

**$12.50**

Turned delicate herbs into a slimy green mush in seconds but could not mince them.

**NOT RECOMMENDED**
### Chef'n Rev'n Chef Herb Processor

**$19.74**

The ripcord design is intriguing, but the results—roughly torn leaves—weren't very impressive. A beat-up garlic clove looked much the same after 75 pulls as it did after 25.

# PASTA WITH BROCCOLI RABE AND SAUSAGE

**WHAT WE WANTED:** A quick sauce that yields properly cooked broccoli rabe in a moist and flavorful (but not oily) pasta dish.

Southern Italy is renowned for its pasta dishes, and one of these is the combination of broccoli rabe (also known as *rapini, cime de rape, rape, raab,* and *brocoletti*) and orecchiette, which loosely translates as "little ears." With the addition of sausage, this pasta dish from Puglia, located in the heel of Italy's boot, quickly makes a satisfying meal.

A search of Italian cookbooks turned up a number of recipes for orecchiette with broccoli rabe. After several tests, we identified some common problems with these recipes. The first was that they used three pans to cook a dish with just a handful of ingredients. The second was that the sauces were bland. The third was that the pasta was dry. We wanted to rectify these problems and streamline the cooking process without sacrificing flavor.

The first issue we tackled was the cooking procedure. Most recipes call for blanching the broccoli rabe in one pot, sautéing the sausage in another pan, and, finally, cooking the pasta in a third pot. Thinking we could eliminate the pot in which the rabe was blanched, we tried several cooking methods.

Our first thought was to add the rabe directly to the pot with the pasta. While this worked, we found it hard to judge the proper time to put the rabe in the pot; it was difficult to cook through both ingredients without overcooking either. We next tried cooking the rabe in the pan in which we cooked the sausage. Sautéing the rabe in the hot pan along with the sausage did not work; some of the rabe was fully cooked while other pieces were undercooked. It was obvious that the rabe required moist-heat cooking, such as steaming, rather than dry-heat cooking (sautéing). So we tried adding a small amount of liquid to the hot pan after we browned the sausage. Because the pan was quite hot, it created a fair amount of steam. By covering the pan, we captured this steam to cook the rabe. This method of pan-steaming turned out to be the solution. We eliminated the extra pot and still had consistently cooked pasta and rabe.

Now that we had mastered a cooking method for the rabe, we focused on the problems of bland flavor and dry pasta. The blanching of the rabe in previous tests resulted in loss of flavor, and our new cooking method seemed to alleviate this problem, but not fully. We therefore decided to steam the rabe in chicken broth rather than water. This did the trick. As the broth reduced, it added richness and depth to the dish. In addition, it moistened the pasta without making it oily or heavy.

Tasters preferred spicy Italian sausage to the sweet version, and most wanted even more heat (remember, the pasta is bland), so we added some hot red pepper flakes. A hefty dose of garlic (we ended up adding six cloves) was also a must. A dusting of grated Parmesan finished off the dish nicely.

**WHAT WE LEARNED:** Brown the sausage, add the broccoli rabe and chicken broth, and then cover the pan to steam the rabe with the other sauce ingredients. Besides eliminating the need for a separate pot to blanch the rabe, this cooking method won't wash away the pleasantly bitter flavor of this Italian vegetable.

---

**FOOD FACT:** Pasta Consumption

The average American eats about 20 pounds of pasta every year. Italians consume three times as much. Italian authorities have recorded more than 500 different pasta shapes, from common shapes such as spaghetti and linguine to the exotic, such as gemelli (the name means "twins" and refers to the two identical strands of pasta that are twisted together to form this shape) and orecchiette (which means "little ears" and refers to their curved bowl shape, which resembles the human ear).

## ORECCHIETTE WITH BROCCOLI RABE AND SAUSAGE Serves 4

If you prefer to use broccoli instead of broccoli rabe in this recipe, use 2 pounds broccoli cut into 1-inch florets and increase the cooking time by several minutes. If you prefer a less spicy dish, use sweet Italian sausage.

     Salt
1    pound orecchiette
8    ounces hot Italian sausage, casings removed
6    medium cloves garlic, minced or pressed through a garlic press (2 tablespoons)
½    teaspoon hot red pepper flakes
1    bunch broccoli rabe (about 1 pound), trimmed and cut into 1½-inch lengths (see the illustrations below)
½    cup low-sodium chicken broth
1    tablespoon extra-virgin olive oil
½    cup (1 ounce) grated Parmesan cheese

**1.** Bring 4 quarts water to a rolling boil in a large pot. Add 1 tablespoon salt and the pasta, stir to separate, and cook until al dente. Drain and return the pasta to the pot.

**2.** While the pasta is cooking, cook the sausage until browned in a large nonstick skillet over medium-high heat, breaking it into ½-inch pieces with a wooden spoon, about 3 minutes. Stir in the garlic, red pepper flakes, and ½ teaspoon salt. Cook, stirring constantly, until the garlic is fragrant and slightly toasted, about 1½ minutes. Add the broccoli rabe and chicken broth, cover, and cook until the broccoli rabe turns bright green, 2 minutes. Uncover and cook, stirring frequently, until most of the broth has evaporated and the broccoli rabe is tender, 2 to 3 minutes.

**3.** Add the sausage-rabe mixture, oil, and cheese to the pot with the pasta and toss to combine. Serve immediately.

## TASTING LAB:
## Boutique Extra-Virgin Olive Oil

ONE OF THE ENDURING MYTHS ABOUT PURCHASING food products, especially gourmet foods, is that price and

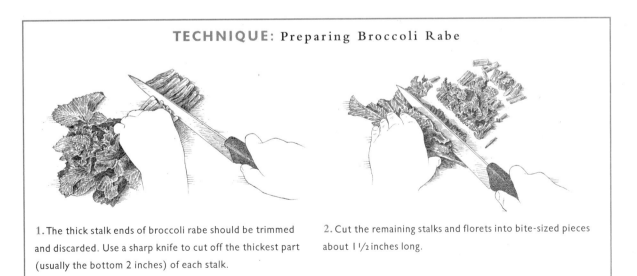

TECHNIQUE: Preparing Broccoli Rabe

1. The thick stalk ends of broccoli rabe should be trimmed and discarded. Use a sharp knife to cut off the thickest part (usually the bottom 2 inches) of each stalk.

2. Cut the remaining stalks and florets into bite-sized pieces about 1½ inches long.

packaging indicate something about the quality of the product. Sometimes this is true. A boutique brand of chocolate such as Scharffen Berger is indeed much better than Baker's, at least in the opinion of our tasters. But this is by no means any sort of universal rule. In fact, price and packaging often have virtually nothing to do with quality. Take the case of premium extra-virgin olive oils.

Many food experts make a big deal about pricey olive oils. To find out if these boutique oils (all made in relatively small quantities) are worth those big bucks, we purchased eight different bottles of expensive extra-virgin olive oils, with prices ranging from $27 to $80 per liter. We also threw in Da Vinci extra-virgin olive oil, winner of a previous tasting of supermarket oils and priced at just $8.50 per liter.

The cheap supermarket oil, Da Vinci, took fourth place, and the two least expensive boutique oils (Antica Azienda Raineri,

$32 per liter, and Columela-Hojiblanca, $27 per liter) took first and second place. One of the most expensive oils, Salvatore Mirisola ($80 per liter) came in next to last. How can this be?

All of the oils were, in fact, pretty good. To earn the designation "extra-virgin," an olive oil must meet a number of criteria and be free from defects. Technically, all of the oils we tasted were fine. They were, however, very different. Some were grassy and mild, others sharp and peppery. In large measure, personal taste will determine favorites. Our panel did object to flavor traits in several oils, especially those that were especially aggressive, but these oils might be delicious when drizzled over grilled vegetables or a spicy soup. In the end, you have to taste for yourself and find an oil that you like. Of course, choosing an inexpensive supermarket oil (such as Da Vinci) is a good option and will save you the bother and expense of holding your own tasting.

# Rating Boutique Extra-Virgin Olive Oils

ELEVEN TASTERS SAMPLED NINE BRANDS OF OLIVE OIL STRAIGHT FROM CUPS. THE LINEUP INCLUDED EIGHT EXPENSIVE oils sold in gourmet shops and Italian markets as well as our favorite supermarket olive oil, Da Vinci. The olive oils are listed in order of preference based on scores from the tasting. See www.americastestkitchen.com for up-to-date prices and mail-order sources for top-rated products.

### RECOMMENDED
**Antica Azienda Raineri Extra-Virgin Olive Oil**

**$31.99 for 1 liter**

This top-rated oil, which hails from northern Italy, won points for its "smooth, easy flavor" and "fruity finish."

### RECOMMENDED
**Columela-Hojiblanca Extra-Virgin Olive Oil**

**$13.49 for 500 ml ($26.98 per liter)**

This "very dark green" oil was praised for its "strong olive taste" and "fruity aroma." Some, however, found it "rubbery" and "very mild." This Spanish oil was the cheapest boutique oil that we tested and offers a good value.

### RECOMMENDED
**Olio Verde Extra-Virgin Olive Oil**

**$21.99 for 500 ml ($43.98 per liter)**

"Smells like freshly cut grass," wrote one taster. Most approved of the "grassy" flavor, though some found it "metallic" and "sour."

### RECOMMENDED
**Da Vinci Extra-Virgin Olive Oil**

**$8.49 for 1 liter**

The least expensive of the bunch, this supermarket staple won points for its "light, natural olive flavor" and "fruity, mild aroma," although several tasters found it "bland." You certainly can't go wrong for the price.

### RECOMMENDED WITH RESERVATIONS
**Frantoio Galantino Extra-Virgin Olive Oil**

**$40.00 for 500 ml ($80.00 per liter)**

With its "light taste" and "very faint olive aroma," most tasters found this oil "uninteresting" and "unremarkable."

### RECOMMENDED WITH RESERVATIONS
**Piccolo Molino-Dolce Verde Extra-Virgin Olive Oil**

**$24.99 for 500 ml ($49.98 per liter)**

Though many tasters found this oil "full-bodied" and "grassy," several described it as "bitter," with a "slightly medicinal aroma."

### RECOMMENDED WITH RESERVATIONS
**Exentia Extra-Virgin Olive Oil**

**$32.99 for 500 ml ($65.98 per liter)**

Tasters found this oil "medicinal tasting," with a "pine-forest scent" and a "hit of pepper at the back of the throat."

### RECOMMENDED WITH RESERVATIONS
**Salvatore Mirisola Extra-Virgin Olive Oil**

**$40.00 for 500 ml ($80.00 per liter)**

Detractors of this oil likened the flavor to "paint thinner" and "motor oil." Kinder tasters simply found it "flat" and "not very fruity."

### RECOMMENDED WITH RESERVATIONS
**Rendola Extra-Virgin Olive Oil**

**$34.99 for 750 ml ($46.55 per liter)**

"Like furniture polish," wrote one taster of this "mineral-ly," "woody," and "one-dimensional" oil.

Chris drains pasta before it's al dente—it will finish cooking in the oven with the four cheeses.

# QUICK pasta

## CHAPTER 7

IN THIS CHAPTER

**THE RECIPES**

Weeknight Bolognese Sauce

Creamy Baked Four-Cheese
  Pasta
Baked Four-Cheese Pasta with
  Tomatoes and Basil
Baked Four-Cheese Pasta with
  Prosciutto and Peas

**SCIENCE DESK**

Why Does Milk Make Meat
  Tender?

**TASTING LAB**

Tomato Paste

Everyone knows pasta is quick. That's one of the reasons Americans (and Italians) love it. Some pasta dishes, however, take a considerable amount of time to prepare. We wanted to take two such recipes—bolognese, a slow-simmering tomato and meat sauce, and baked four-cheese pasta—and figure out how to make them less than an all-day—or even all-afternoon—affair.

True bolognese simmers lazily for half a day on the stove. The real deal is rich and delicious. Many short-cut recipes are nothing more than browned ground beef and tomatoes. These recipes may be quick, but they have none of the finesse or complexity of the original.

Baked four-cheese pasta often yields overcooked pasta in a stringy, curdled sauce. Given all the work involved (grating and shredding all those cheeses, making the sauce, cooking the pasta, and then baking the casserole for half an hour or more), this dish should be better.

# BOLOGNESE SAUCE

**WHAT WE WANTED:** A lush, decadent, unctuous meat sauce ready in less than an hour rather than the usual three hours.

Bolognese gets its big flavor from the braising of ground meat and softened vegetables in slowly reducing liquids—most often milk and wine—and then, finally, tomatoes. The process is often given as much as three hours, but the result is a bold, meaty pasta sauce with sweet resonance and ultra-tender meat.

Just try to short-cut the process and you'll be left with bits of rubbery meat floating in a subpar tomato sauce. We wanted to make bolognese weeknight-friendly. If perfect, it would be everything that we expected from the long-cooked sauce, but we wanted this sauce on table in less than an hour.

There is not exactly a wealth of "quick" bolognese recipes. We found only two, one of them no more than ground beef and jarred tomato sauce. We decided to take the test kitchen's favorite bolognese sauce, which uses the traditional slow-cooking technique, and try to pare the cooking time. Armed with a pitifully small amount of knowledge, we went into the test kitchen, started the clock, and began to cook.

The original test kitchen recipe calls for equal parts ground beef, pork, and veal, and, unfortunately, we found all three to be necessary. We were, however, able to avoid buying several packages of meat by purchasing the trusty supermarket "meatloaf mix" made from equal parts of each. To boost the flavor of our quick-cooked sauce, we tested additions such as pancetta, prosciutto, and even porcini mushrooms. Prosciutto was out owing to its salty flavor and big price tag, but pancetta was a perfect fit—a little went a long way. Porcini mushrooms had such an amazingly beefy impact on the sauce that we just couldn't refuse them.

Vegetables were next under the microscope. Our favorite three-hour recipe called for celery, carrots, and onion, but we found celery could go by the wayside. Garlic found a home, but tasters thought herbs were distracting. Either butter or olive oil can be used to sauté the vegetables, but we chose butter for its richer flavor.

Tomatoes add sweetness to the sauce, and their juice is used to braise the meat. We tried all kinds—crushed, diced, sauce—and in the end liked the juicier whole canned tomatoes best because they come packed in so much juice. To provide some deeper, slow-cooked tomato flavor, we added some tomato paste.

Now hold on a minute! Our goal was to shorten this recipe, not to complicate it with an epic ingredient list. We could already count at least 10 minutes of prep time. The solution? We whipped out a food processor and used it to chop just about everything: carrots, onions, mushrooms, tomatoes, even the pancetta. Only the garlic was spared from the food processor (it never chopped up completely), but a garlic press made quick work of that step, too. Now what had been taking 10 minutes was being accomplished in less than two.

In a true bolognese, liquids are reduced slowly one at a time to tenderize the meat and develop the characteristic sweetness of the sauce. Because we didn't have all day, we had to find a quicker method. To sweeten the sauce, we added a pinch of sugar. But it wasn't until we started thinking outside the box and tried sweeter white wines like Riesling and Gewürztraminer in place of the traditional dry Sauvignon Blanc that our sauce achieved the proper sweetness. We even tried a white Zinfandel—the "other" white wine—often snubbed for its grapey-sweet flavor. Guess what? It worked beautifully.

Now all we had to do was get around that slow simmer. Sure, cooking everything at a raging boil was an obvious option, but the meat (which was still tough) became downright springy when boiled. Our trick for minimizing cooking time was to reduce the wine on the side in a separate skillet; 1¼ cups went down to 2 tablespoons in 20 minutes.

Now meaty, sweet, and fast, this 45-minute sauce had everything going for it—well, almost. The meat still presented itself in the form of little rubber pellets, and no sauce, however good, could mask that.

A hint of an answer came when we thought about the milk. In Italian cooking, milk and meat are often braised together, producing very tender results. What if we soaked the ground meat in milk before cooking? We tried it. After sautéing the vegetables, we added the milk-soaked meat to the hot pan and watched as the meat disintegrated into grainy, mushy bits. OK, this was not the perfect solution, but at least the meat wasn't tough.

Next we added the meat directly to the pan along with the milk (no soaking). Same as before, the meat fell apart into bits, but this time, no mush. Sure that we were on the right track, the next time we added the meat to the pan we quickly broke it into large pieces with a wooden spoon (letting it spend no more than a minute in the pan alone) and then added the milk. We stirred the two together to break up the meat and—success! This meat was incredibly tender. Actually, it made sense. As any fan of steak tartare will tell you, raw ground meat is already tender. Because we weren't browning the meat, it never obtained that tough crust that takes hours upon hours to return to its tender state.

So we had done it. Making no sacrifices in flavor, texture, or our pride, we had made a sauce that was rich and meaty, sweet and bold, luxuriously tender, and on the table in 45 minutes.

---

WHAT WE LEARNED: Beef up the flavor of the ground meats with pancetta and dried porcini mushrooms. Use the food processor to prepare the ingredients. Don't brown the meat and cook it through in milk. Use a sweet white wine and sugar to achieve the flavor traditionally imparted by prolonged simmering.

## WEEKNIGHT BOLOGNESE SAUCE Serves 4 to 6

Sweet white wines such as Gewürztraminer, Riesling, and even white Zinfandel work especially well in this sauce. To obtain the best texture, be careful not to break up the meat too much when cooking it with the milk in step 4. With additional cooking and stirring, it will continue to break up. Just about any pasta shape complements this meaty sauce, but spaghetti and linguine are the test kitchen favorites. If using pancetta that has been sliced thin rather than cut into 1-inch chunks, reduce the processing time in step 3 from 30 seconds to about 5 seconds.

| | |
|---|---|
| ½ | ounce dried porcini mushrooms |
| 1¼ | cups sweet white wine (see note) |
| ½ | small carrot, peeled and chopped into rough ½-inch pieces (about ½ cup) |
| ½ | small onion, chopped into rough ½-inch pieces (about ¼ cup) |
| 3 | ounces pancetta, cut into 1-inch pieces |
| 1 | can (28 ounces) whole tomatoes with juice |
| 1½ | tablespoons unsalted butter |
| 1 | small clove garlic, minced or pressed through a garlic press (about ½ teaspoon) |
| 1 | teaspoon sugar |
| 1¼ | pounds meatloaf mix (or equal amounts 80 percent lean ground beef, ground veal, and ground pork) |
| 1½ | cups whole milk |
| 2 | tablespoons tomato paste |
| | Salt |
| ⅛ | teaspoon ground black pepper |
| 1 | pound pasta |
| | Grated Parmesan cheese, for serving |

1. Cover the porcini mushrooms with ½ cup water in a small microwave-safe bowl; cover the bowl with plastic

Transfer the vegetables to a small bowl. Process the softened porcini until well ground, about 15 seconds, scraping down the bowl if necessary. Transfer the porcini to the bowl with carrot and onion. Process the pancetta until the pieces are no larger than ¼ inch, 30 to 35 seconds, scraping down the bowl if necessary; transfer to a small bowl. Pulse the tomatoes with juice until chopped fine, six to eight 1-second pulses.

**4.** Heat the butter in a 12-inch skillet over medium-high heat; when the foaming subsides, add the pancetta and cook, stirring frequently, until well browned, about 2 minutes. Add the carrot, onion, and porcini; cook, stirring frequently, until the vegetables are softened but not browned, about 4 minutes. Add the garlic and sugar; cook until fragrant, about 30 seconds. Add the ground meats, breaking the meat into 1-inch pieces with a wooden spoon, about 1 minute. Add the milk and stir to break the meat into ½-inch bits; bring to a simmer, reduce the heat to medium, and continue to simmer, stirring to break up the meat into small pieces, until most of the liquid has evaporated and the meat begins to sizzle, 18 to 20 minutes. Stir in the tomato paste and cook until combined, about 1 minute. Add the tomatoes, reserved porcini soaking liquid, ¼ teaspoon salt, and pepper; bring to a simmer over medium-high heat, then reduce the heat to medium and simmer until the liquid is reduced and the sauce is thickened but still moist, 12 to 15 minutes. Stir in the reduced wine and simmer to blend the flavors, about 5 minutes.

wrap, cut a few steam vents with a paring knife, and microwave on high power for 30 seconds. Let stand until the mushrooms have softened, about 5 minutes. Using a fork, lift the porcini from the liquid and transfer to a second small bowl; pour the soaking liquid through a paper towel–lined mesh strainer. Set the porcini and the strained liquid aside.

**2.** Bring the wine to simmer in a 10-inch nonstick skillet over medium heat; reduce the heat to low and simmer until the wine is reduced to 2 tablespoons, about 20 minutes. Set the reduced wine aside.

**3.** Meanwhile, pulse the carrot in a food processor until broken down into rough ¼-inch pieces, about ten 1-second pulses. Add the onion; pulse until the vegetables are broken down into ⅛-inch pieces, about ten 1-second pulses.

**5.** Meanwhile, bring 4 quarts water to a rolling boil, covered, in a stockpot. Add 1 tablespoon salt and the pasta, stir to separate, and cook until al dente. Drain, reserving ¼ cup pasta cooking water, and return the pasta to the stockpot. Add 2 cups sauce and 2 tablespoons pasta water to the pasta; toss well, adding the remaining pasta water, if necessary, to help distribute the sauce. Divide the pasta among individual bowls and top each portion with about ¼ cup remaining sauce. Serve immediately, passing the Parmesan separately.

## SCIENCE DESK:
### Why Does Milk Make Meat Tender?

BROWNING ADDS FLAVOR, BUT IT ALSO CAUSES THE PROTEIN molecules in ground meat to denature (unwind). As the proteins unwind, they link up to create a tighter network and squeeze out some of the water in the meat. Long simmering allows some of that liquid to be reabsorbed. But if you skip the browning and cook the meat in milk (or any other liquid) at the outset, you limit the temperature of the meat to about 212 degrees (browning occurs in dry heat and at higher temperatures). As a result, meat cooked in milk does not dry out and toughen but remains tender. This means you can simmer the sauce just until the liquid has reduced to the right consistency rather than waiting for the meat to soften.

## TASTING LAB: Tomato Paste

A CELEBRATED INGREDIENT IN ITS POST–WWII HEYDAY, when the long-cooked tomato sauce was king, tomato paste has fallen by the wayside as discerning cooks have favored fresher, more brightly flavored tomato sauces. These days, our use of tomato paste comes with a more conservative hand. We reserve it for occasions when a deep tomato flavor is warranted, such as in a chili or our slow-simmering bolognese sauce.

Given this limited use, we wondered if it mattered which brand we used. To find out, we went to local supermarkets to gather seven brands for a tasting: six American brands in small cans and an Italian import in a toothpaste-like tube. We asked tasters to try the tomato paste as is—no cooking, no sauce.

Every brand did well in providing a big tomato punch, but the Amore brand, imported from Italy, was the unanimous winner owing to its "intense" and "fresh" flavor. Amore is the only tomato paste tested that contains fat, which could account for its bigger flavor. The Amore brand

also scored points because of its tube packaging. Just squeeze out what you need and store the rest in the refrigerator. No fuss, no waste.

How did the flavor of this tomato paste hold up in cooking? We tasted it, along with Hunt's, the brand that came in last, in our bolognese recipe, to see if we could detect a difference. We did indeed pick out (and downgrade) the distinct dried herb flavor of the Hunt's paste. On the other hand, we liked the sauce made with the Amore tomato paste for its deep, round tomato flavor.

### GETTING IT RIGHT: The Pan Matters

When the sauce is simmered in a Dutch oven, it doesn't reduce quickly enough, and the consistency is watery (left). When the sauce is simmered in a 12-inch skillet, the texture is thicker, and the sauce reduces more quickly (right).

COOKED IN DUTCH OVEN    COOKED IN SKILLET

### GETTING IT RIGHT: Pancetta

Just like bacon, pancetta comes from the belly of the pig, but it has a very different flavor. American bacon is cured with salt, sugar, and spices and then smoked. Pancetta is not smoked, and the cure does not contain sugar—just salt, pepper, and, usually, cloves. As a result, pancetta has a richer, meatier flavor than bacon. Pancetta is rolled tightly, packed in casing, and then sliced thin or thick as desired.

# Rating Tomato Pastes

ELEVEN MEMBERS OF THE *COOK'S ILLUSTRATED* STAFF TASTED SEVEN TOMATO PASTES STRAIGHT FROM THE CAN OR TUBE. Tasters were asked to evaluate each sample for intensity of tomato flavor, freshness, sweetness, and saltiness. The tomato pastes are listed in order of preference based on tasters' scores. All brands are sold in supermarkets nationwide.

### HIGHLY RECOMMENDED
### Amore Italian Tomato Paste
**$2.49 for 4.5 ounces**

Tasters described this paste-in-a-tube as "intense" and "fresh." The only sample tasted that contains fat. No-fuss, no-waste packaging is appealing.

### RECOMMENDED
### Redpack California Tomato Paste
**$.60 for 6 ounces**

This familiar brand finished a distant second. Panelists commented on its "sweet," "bold" flavor, but it was not as fresh tasting as the winner.

### RECOMMENDED
### Cento Tomato Paste
**$.50 for 6 ounces**

"Good tomato flavor" was the general consensus about this brand, which showed fairly well.

### RECOMMENDED WITH RESERVATIONS
### Rienzi Tomato Paste
**$.75 for 6 ounces**

This Italian brand elicited mixed reviews. Some tasters praised its "fruity" flavor, but quite a few thought it was "unbalanced" and "too strong."

### RECOMMENDED WITH RESERVATIONS
### Muir Glen Organic Tomato Paste
**$.99 for 6 ounces**

Tasters were not impressed with this brand, which has scored well in our tastings of other tomato products. "OK" and "dull" were typical comments.

### NOT RECOMMENDED
### Contadina Tomato Paste
**$.50 for 6 ounces**

This brand was deemed "bland" and "lifeless," and it tied for last place in the scoring. Tasters had no positive comments about this sample.

### NOT RECOMMENDED
### Hunt's Tomato Paste
**$.99 for 6 ounces**

Tasters demonstrated a real aversion to the "fishy," "herbal" flavors in this paste. Many tasters picked up strong hits of dried herbs.

# BAKED FOUR-CHEESE AND PASTA CASSEROLE

**WHAT WE WANTED:** We set out to make a creamy casserole with great flavor, properly cooked pasta, and a crisp bread-crumb topping—all in record time.

Pasta ai quattro formaggi, the classic Italian pasta dish with four cheeses and heavy cream, is a great idea in theory. In reality, however, it often turns into an inedible mess: tasteless, stringy, heavy, and greasy. We wanted to discover what made this dish great in the first place, delivering a pasta dinner that was silky smooth and rich but not heavy—a grown-up, sophisticated version of macaroni and cheese with Italian flavors.

The cheese was first up for consideration, in terms of both flavor and texture. We were committed to Italian cheeses, but this barely diminished our choices; research turned up varying combinations and amounts (1 cup to 6½ cups cheese per 1 pound pasta) of Asiago, Fontina, Taleggio, Pecorino Romano, mascarpone, mozzarella, Gorgonzola, Parmesan, and ricotta. Initial testing reduced the scope quickly: Mascarpone and ricotta added neither flavor nor texture, and Asiago was bland. Pasta tossed with mozzarella was gooey and greasy, whereas Taleggio was not only difficult to obtain but also made the pasta too rich and gluey. After testing numerous combinations of the remaining cheeses, tasters favored a 2½-cup combination of Italian Fontina (which is creamier and better-tasting than versions of this cheese made elsewhere), Gorgonzola, Pecorino Romano, and Parmesan.

The techniques of heating the cheeses and cream together and of adding the cheeses separately to the hot pasta both produced nasty messes. Each attempt caused the cheeses to curdle, separate, and/or turn greasy. Some recipes solved this problem by beginning with a *besciamella* (known in French as a *béchamel*). This basic white sauce starts by cooking butter and flour and then adding milk or cream. The cheeses can then be added to the white sauce, which, because

of the flour, will not separate. As we soon found out, the white sauce kept the sauce from breaking, but it also had an unintended side effect: The flavor of the cheeses was diminished. The solution was to radically reduce the amount of flour and butter to two teaspoons each instead of the usual three to four tablespoons each. Now the sauce was silky and smooth and allowed the flavor of the cheeses to stand out.

After making this recipe a half-dozen more times, we were bothered by the notion of heating the cheeses ahead of time with the béchamel. We wanted to cook the cheeses as little as possible for the best flavor, so we put the shredded/crumbled/grated cheeses in a large bowl and added the hot pasta and hot béchamel. A quick toss melted the cheeses without cooking them. We had now both simplified the recipe and produced a cleaner tasting, more flavorful dish.

We found that the sauce worked best with tubular pasta shapes (penne was ideal), which could be coated inside and out. Many recipes suggest cooking the pasta fully and then baking it for 30 minutes. This approach not only consumes extra time but is a recipe for mushiness. To keep the pasta from overcooking, we found it necessary to drain the pasta several minutes before it was al dente and then minimize the baking time. Just seven minutes in a 500-degree oven (the pasta heats more quickly in a shallow baking dish) is enough to turn the pasta and sauce into a casserole.

Many recipes add a bread crumb topping that browns and crisps in the oven. We tried this casserole with and without the crumb topping, and tasters unanimously voted for the topping. It contrasts nicely with the creamy pasta and helps balance the richness of the sauce.

**WHAT WE LEARNED:** To preserve the fresh flavor of the cheeses, don't cook them along with the sauce and use just a tiny bit of roux (cooked butter and flour) to stabilize the sauce. Undercook the pasta and then bake the casserole in a very hot oven for just seven minutes to prevent mushiness.

## CREAMY BAKED FOUR-CHEESE PASTA

Serves 4 to 6 as main course, 6 to 8 as side dish

To streamline the process, prepare the bread-crumb topping and shred, crumble, and grate the cheeses while you wait for the pasta water to come to a boil. This dish can be on the table in about half an hour.

### bread-crumb topping

| | |
|---|---|
| 3–4 | slices white sandwich bread with crusts, torn into quarters |
| ¼ | cup (½ ounce) grated Parmesan cheese |
| ¼ | teaspoon salt |
| ⅛ | teaspoon ground black pepper |

### pasta and cheese

| | |
|---|---|
| 4 | ounces Italian Fontina cheese, shredded (about 1 cup) |
| 3 | ounces Gorgonzola cheese, crumbled (about ¾ cup) |
| ½ | cup (1 ounce) grated Pecorino Romano cheese |
| ¼ | cup (½ ounce) grated Parmesan cheese |
| 1 | pound penne |
| | Salt |
| 2 | teaspoons unsalted butter |
| 2 | teaspoons all-purpose flour |
| 1½ | cups heavy cream |
| ¼ | teaspoon ground black pepper |

**1.** FOR THE TOPPING: Pulse the bread in a food processor until the mixture resembles coarse crumbs, about ten 1-second pulses (you should have about 1½ cups). Transfer to a small bowl; stir in the Parmesan, salt, and pepper. Set the mixture aside.

**2.** FOR THE PASTA: Adjust an oven rack to the middle position and heat the oven to 500 degrees.

**3.** Bring 4 quarts water to a rolling boil in a stockpot. Combine the cheeses in a large bowl; set aside. Add the pasta and 1 tablespoon salt to the boiling water; stir to separate the pasta. While the pasta is cooking, melt the butter in a small saucepan over medium-low heat; whisk the flour into the butter until no lumps remain, about 30 seconds. Gradually whisk in the cream, increase the heat to medium, and bring to a boil, stirring occasionally; reduce the heat to medium-low and simmer 1 minute to ensure that the flour cooks. Stir in ¼ teaspoon salt and pepper; cover the cream mixture to keep hot and set aside.

**4.** When the pasta is almost al dente (when bitten into, the pasta should be opaque and slightly underdone at the very center), drain about 5 seconds, leaving the pasta slightly wet. Add the pasta to the bowl with the cheeses; immediately pour the cream mixture over, then cover the bowl with foil or a large plate and let stand 3 minutes. Uncover the bowl and stir with a rubber spatula, scraping the bottom of the bowl, until the cheeses are melted and the mixture is thoroughly combined.

**5.** Transfer the pasta to 13 by 9-inch baking dish, then sprinkle evenly with the reserved bread crumbs, pressing down lightly. Bake until the topping is golden brown, about 7 minutes. Serve immediately.

### VARIATIONS

### BAKED FOUR-CHEESE PASTA WITH TOMATOES AND BASIL

Follow the recipe for Creamy Baked Four-Cheese Pasta, adding one 14½-ounce can diced tomatoes, drained, to the pasta along with the cream mixture and stirring in ¼ cup coarsely chopped fresh basil leaves just before transferring the pasta to the baking dish.

### BAKED FOUR-CHEESE PASTA WITH PROSCIUTTO AND PEAS

Follow the recipe for Creamy Baked Four-Cheese Pasta, omitting the salt from the cream mixture and adding 4 ounces prosciutto, chopped, and 1 cup frozen peas to the pasta along with the cream mixture.

Classic Gazpacho **page 16**

Chicken Provençal **page 152**

Tomato and Mozzarella Tart **page 22**

Chicken and Shrimp Jambalaya **page 55**

Wilted Spinach Salad with Warm Bacon Dressing **page 11**

Pan-Roasted Chicken Breast with Sage-Vermouth Sauce **page 133**

Beef Chili with Kidney Beans **page 32**

Pad Thai **page 194**

Charcoal-Grilled Filet Mignon **page 158** with Lemon, Garlic, and Parsley Butter **page 159**

Stir-Fried Pork, Green Beans, and Red Bell Pepper with Gingery Oyster Sauce **page 186**

92

Charcoal-Grilled Steak Tips **page 172**

Maple-Glazed Pork Roast **page 114**

Wild Rice Pilaf with Pecans and Dried Cranberries **page 117**

Chicken with 40 Cloves of Garlic **page 144**

Stir-Fried Beef and Broccoli with Oyster Sauce **page 182**

Pot Roast with Root Vegetables **page 102**

# POT roast

CHAPTER 8

IN THIS CHAPTER

**THE RECIPES**

Simple Pot Roast
Pot Roast with Root Vegetables
Pot Roast with Mushrooms,
    Tomatoes, and Red Wine

Quick Green Bean "Casserole"
Garlic-Lemon Green Beans with
    Toasted Bread Crumbs
Green Beans with Orange
    Essence and Toasted Maple
    Pecans

**EQUIPMENT CORNER**

Vegetable Choppers

**SCIENCE DESK**

How Does Braising Work?
What's So Special about
    Collagen?

Pot roast can be the ultimate comfort food or a huge waste of time. When it comes out right, pot roast is tender, succulent, and richly flavored. When it turns out wrong, the meat is dry, gray, tough, and full of fat and sinew.

Good pot roast begins at the market. Some cuts will never make good pot roast. But there's more to pot roast than careful shopping. We've found that technique matters just as much as the cut. We bought a dozen kinds of roasts and tested as many cooking methods to develop our foolproof recipe for pot roast. Green beans are a natural accompaniment to pot roast, and we've developed an unusual technique to cook and sauce them in just one skillet.

# POT ROAST

**WHAT WE WANTED**: Tender, moist, flavorful meat floating in a savory liquid that becomes a sauce.

A good pot roast by definition entails the transformation of a tough (read cheap), nearly unpalatable cut of meat into a tender, rich, flavorful main course by means of a slow, moist cooking process called braising. It should not be sliceable; rather, the tension of a stern gaze should be enough to break it apart. Nor should it be pink or rosy in the middle—save that for prime rib or steak.

The meat for pot roast should be well marbled with fat and connective tissue to provide the dish with flavor and moisture. Recipes typically call for roasts from the sirloin (or rump), round (leg), or chuck (shoulder). When all was said and done, we cooked a dozen cuts of meat to find the right one.

The sirloin roasts tested—the bottom rump roast and top sirloin—were the leanest of the cuts and needed longer cooking to be broken down to a palatable texture. The round cuts—top round, bottom round, and eye of round—had more fat running through them than the sirloin cuts, but the meat was chewy. The chuck cuts—shoulder roast, boneless chuck roast, cross rib, chuck mock tender, seven-bone roast, top-blade roast, and chuck-eye roast—cooked up the most tender, although we gave preference to three of these cuts (see "Getting It Right: Chuck Roasts" on page 104). The high proportion of fat and connective tissue in these chuck cuts gave the meat much-needed moisture and superior flavor.

Tough meat, such as brisket, can benefit from the low, dry heat of oven roasting, and it can be boiled. With pot roast, however, the introduction of moisture by means of a braising liquid is thought to be integral to the breakdown of the tough muscle fibers. (We also tried dry-roasting and boiling pot roast just to make sure. See page 103 to find out why braising was the winner.) It was time to find out what kind of liquid and how much was needed to best cook the roast and supply a good sauce.

Before we began the testing, we needed to deal with the aesthetics of the dish. Because pot roast is traditionally cooked with liquid at a low temperature, the exterior of the meat will not brown sufficiently unless it is first sautéed in a Dutch oven on the stovetop. High heat and a little oil were all that were needed to caramelize the exterior of the beef and boost both the flavor and appearance of the dish.

Using water as the braising medium, we started with a modest ¼ cup, as suggested in a few recipes. This produced a roast that was unacceptably fibrous, even after hours of cooking. After increasing the amount of liquid incrementally, we found that the moistest meat was produced when we added liquid halfway up the sides of the roast (depending on the cut, this amount could be between 2 and 4 cups). The greater amount of liquid also accelerated the cooking process, shaving nearly one hour off the cooking time needed for a roast cooked in just ¼ cup of liquid.

Next we tested different liquids, hoping to add flavor to the roast and sauce. Along with our old standby, water, we tested red wine, low-sodium canned chicken broth, and low-sodium canned beef broth. Red wine had the most startling effect on the meat, penetrating it with a potent flavor that most tasters agreed was "good, but not traditional pot roast." However, tasters did like the flavor of a little red wine added to the sauce after the pot roast was removed from the pan. Each of the broths on their own failed to win tasters over completely—the chicken broth was rich but gave the dish a characteristic poultry flavor, while the beef broth tasted sour when added solo. In the end, we found that an equal amount of each did the job, with the beef broth boosting the depth of flavor and the chicken broth tempering any sourness. Because different amounts of liquid would have to be added to the pot depending on the size and shape of each individual roast, we chose to be consistent in the amount of chicken and beef broth used—1 cup each—

and to vary the amount of water to bring the liquid level halfway up the roast.

Trying to boost the flavor of the sauce even more, we added carrot, celery, onion, and garlic to the pot as the meat braised. Unfortunately, the addition of raw vegetables made the pot roast taste more like a vegetable stew. We then tried sautéing them until golden brown and found that the caramelized flavor of the vegetables added another layer of flavor to the sauce. Tomato paste, an ingredient found in several recipes, was not a welcome addition. Tasters appreciated the sweetness it added but not the "tinny" flavor. A little sugar (2 teaspoons) added to the vegetables as they cooked gave the sauce the sweetness tasters were looking for.

Some recipes thicken the sauce with a mixture of equal parts butter and flour (beurre manié); others use a slurry of cornstarch mixed with a little braising liquid. Both techniques made the sauce more gravy-like than we preferred, and we didn't care for the dilution of flavor. We chose to remove the roast from the pot, then reduce the liquid over high heat until the flavors were well concentrated and the texture more substantial.

As for the best cooking method for pot roast, there are two schools of thought: on the stove or in the oven. After a few rounds of stovetop cooking, we felt that it was too difficult to maintain a steady, low temperature, so we began pot-roasting in the oven, starting out at 250 degrees. This method required no supervision, just a turn of the meat every 30 to 40 minutes to ensure even cooking. We then tested higher temperatures to reduce the cooking time. Heat levels above 350 degrees boiled the meat to a stringy, dry texture because the exterior of the roast overcooked before the interior was cooked and tender. The magic temperature turned out to be 300 degrees—enough heat to keep the meat at a low simmer while high enough to shave a few more minutes off the cooking time.

As said above, pot roast is well-done meat—meat cooked to an internal temperature above 165 degrees. Up to this point, we were bringing the meat to an internal temperature of 200 to 210 degrees, the point at which the fat and connective tissue begin to melt. In a 300-degree oven, the roast came up to that temperature in a neat 2½ hours, certainly by no means a quick meal but still a relatively short time in which to cook a pot roast. But we still had not achieved our goal of fall-apart tenderness. We went back and reviewed our prior testing to see what we might have missed.

Once in a great while in the test kitchen we happen upon a true "Eureka!" moment, when a chance test result leads to a breakthrough cooking technique. Some days before, we had forgotten to remove one of the roasts from the oven, allowing it to cook one hour longer than intended. Racing to the kitchen with our instant-read thermometer, we found the internal temperature of the roast was still 210 degrees, but the meat had a substantially different appearance and texture. The roast was so tender that it was starting to separate along its muscle lines. A fork poked into the meat met with no resistance and nearly disappeared into the flesh. We took the roast out of the pot and "sliced" into it. Nearly all the fat and connective tissue had dissolved into the meat, giving each bite a soft, silky texture and rich, succulent flavor. We "overcooked" several more roasts. Each roast had the same great texture. The conclusion? Not only do you have to cook pot roast until it reaches 210 degrees internally, but the meat has to remain at that temperature for a full hour. In other words, cook the pot roast until it's done—and then keep on cooking!

WHAT WE LEARNED: Start with a cut from the chuck and brown the meat to build flavor and enhance its appearance. Use chicken and beef broths as the braising medium and cook the pot roast until the internal temperature reaches 210 degrees, and then cook it another hour. It's hard to overcook pot roast but easy to undercook it.

## SIMPLE POT ROAST  Serves 6 to 8

Our favorite cut for pot roast is a chuck-eye roast. Most markets sell this roast with twine tied around the center (see the photo on page 104); if necessary, do this yourself. Seven-bone and top-blade roasts are also good choices for this recipe. Remember to add only enough water to come halfway up the sides of these thinner roasts, and begin checking for doneness after 2 hours. If using a top-blade roast, tie it before cooking (see the illustrations on page 105) to keep it from falling apart. Mashed or boiled potatoes are a good accompaniment to pot roast.

| | |
|---|---|
| 1 | boneless chuck-eye roast (about 3½ pounds) |
| | Salt and ground black pepper |
| 2 | tablespoons vegetable oil |
| 1 | medium onion, chopped medium |
| 1 | small carrot, chopped medium |
| 1 | small rib celery, chopped medium |
| 2 | medium cloves garlic, minced |
| 2 | teaspoons sugar |
| 1 | cup low-sodium chicken broth |
| 1 | cup low-sodium beef broth |
| 1 | sprig fresh thyme |
| 1–1½ | cups water |
| ¼ | cup dry red wine |

**1.** Adjust an oven rack to the middle position and heat the oven to 300 degrees. Thoroughly pat the roast dry with paper towels; sprinkle generously with salt and pepper.

**2.** Heat the oil in a large heavy-bottomed Dutch oven over medium-high heat until shimmering but not smoking. Brown the roast thoroughly on all sides, reducing the heat if the fat begins to smoke, 8 to 10 minutes. Transfer the roast to a large plate; set aside. Reduce the heat to medium; add the onion, carrot, and celery to the pot and cook, stirring occasionally, until beginning to brown, 6 to 8 minutes. Add the garlic and sugar; cook until fragrant, about 30 seconds. Add the chicken and beef broths and thyme, scraping the bottom of the pan with a wooden spoon to loosen the browned bits. Return the roast and any accumulated juices to the pot; add enough water to come halfway up the sides of the roast. Place a large piece of foil over the pot and cover tightly with a lid; bring the liquid to a simmer over medium heat, then transfer the pot to the oven. Cook, turning the roast every 30 minutes, until fully tender and a meat fork or sharp knife easily slips in and out of the meat, 3½ to 4 hours.

**3.** Transfer the roast to a carving board; tent with foil to keep warm. Allow the liquid in the pot to settle about 5 minutes, then use a wide spoon to skim the fat off the surface; discard the thyme sprig. Boil over high heat until reduced to about 1½ cups, about 8 minutes. Add the red wine and reduce again to 1½ cups, about 2 minutes. Season to taste with salt and pepper.

**4.** Using a chef's or carving knife, cut the meat into ½-inch-thick slices, or pull apart into large pieces; transfer the meat to a warmed serving platter and pour about ½ cup sauce over the meat. Serve, passing the remaining sauce separately.

### VARIATIONS
### POT ROAST WITH ROOT VEGETABLES

In this variation, carrots, potatoes, and parsnips are added near the end of cooking to make a complete meal.

**1.** Follow the recipe for Simple Pot Roast. In step 2, when the roast is almost tender (a sharp knife should meet little resistance), transfer the roast to a cutting board. Pour the braising liquid through a mesh strainer and discard the solids. Return the liquid to the empty pot and let it settle for 5 minutes; use a wide spoon to skim the fat off the surface. Return the roast to the liquid and add 1½ pounds (about 8 medium) carrots, sliced ½ inch thick (about 3 cups), 1½ pounds small red potatoes, halved if larger than 1½ inches in diameter (about 5 cups), and 1 pound (about

5 large) parsnips, sliced ½ inch thick (about 3 cups), submerging them in the liquid. Continue to cook until the vegetables are almost tender, 20 to 30 minutes.

**2.** Transfer the roast to a carving board; tent with foil to keep warm. Add the wine and salt and pepper to taste; boil over high heat until the vegetables are fully tender, 5 to 10 minutes. Using a slotted spoon, transfer the vegetables to a warmed serving bowl or platter; using a chef's or carving knife, cut the meat into ½-inch-thick slices or pull apart into large pieces; transfer to the bowl or platter with the vegetables and pour about ½ cup sauce over. Serve, passing the remaining sauce separately.

### POT ROAST WITH MUSHROOMS, TOMATOES, AND RED WINE

This recipe is based on stracotto, an Italian pot roast with tomatoes and red wine.

**1.** Follow the recipe for Simple Pot Roast, adding 10 ounces white button mushrooms, cleaned and quartered, to the Dutch oven along with the onion, carrot, and celery in step 2. Decrease the chicken and beef broths to ½ cup each and add ½ cup dry red wine and 1 can (14½ ounces) diced tomatoes, with juice, along with the broths.

**2.** After skimming fat off the liquid in step 3, add 1 sprig fresh rosemary; omit the red wine. Boil the liquid over high heat until reduced to 1½ cups; discard the rosemary and thyme sprigs. Season to taste with salt and pepper.

**3.** Using a chef's or carving knife, cut the meat into ½-inch-thick slices or pull apart into large pieces; transfer the meat to a warmed serving platter or bowl, pour the sauce and vegetables over the meat, and serve.

## SCIENCE DESK:
### How Does Braising Work?

BRAISING—SEARING MEAT, PARTIALLY SUBMERGING IT IN liquid in a sealed pot, and then cooking it until fork-tender—is a classic technique used with tough cuts of meat. A variety of cooks have put forward theories about why and how braising works (as opposed to roasting or boiling). We set out to devise a series of experiments that would explain the mystery of braising.

Before kitchen testing began, we researched the meat itself to better understand how it cooks. Meat (muscle) is made up of two major components: muscle fibers, the long thin strands visible as the "grain" of meat, and connective

**GETTING IT RIGHT:** Roasting versus Braising

A distinctive pattern of fat and connective tissue runs through the meat of a chuck roast (left). When cooked in dry heat, or roasted (middle), the fat and sinew do not break down sufficiently, even after many hours in the oven. Cooking the meat in moist heat, or braising (right), promotes a more complete breakdown of the fat and connective tissue, yielding very tender meat.

tissue, the membranous, translucent film that covers the bundles of muscle fiber and gives them structure and support. Muscle fiber is tender because of its high water content (up to 78 percent). Once meat is heated beyond about 120 degrees, the long strands of muscle fiber contract and coil, expelling moisture in much the same way that it's wrung out of a towel. In contrast, connective tissue is tough because it is composed primarily of collagen, a sturdy protein that is in everything from the cow's muscle tendons to its hooves. When collagen is cooked at temperatures exceeding 140 degrees, it starts to break down to gelatin, the protein responsible for the tender, rich meat and thick sauces of braised dishes.

In essence, then, meat both dries out as it cooks (meat fibers lose moisture) and becomes softer (the collagen melts). That is why (depending on the cut) meat is best either when cooked rare or pot-roasted—cooked to the point at which the collagen dissolves completely. Anything in between is dry and tough, the worst of both worlds.

This brings us to why braising is an effective cooking technique for tough cuts of meat. To determine the relative advantages of roasting, braising, and boiling, we constructed a simple test. One roast was cooked in a 250-degree oven, one was braised, and one was simmered in enough liquid to cover it. The results were startling. The dry-cooked roast never reached an internal temperature of more than 175 degrees, even after four hours, and the meat was tough and dry (see "Roasting versus Braising" on page 103). To our great surprise, both the braised and boiled roasts cooked in about the same amount of time, and the results were almost identical. Cutting the roasts in half revealed little difference—both exhibited nearly full melting of the thick bands of connective tissue. As far as the taste and texture of the meat, tasters were hard pressed to find any substantial differences between the two. Both roasts yielded meat that was exceedingly tender, moist, and infused with rich gelatin.

The conclusion? Dry heat (roasting) is ineffective because the meat never gets hot enough to fully melt the collagen. It does not appear that steam heat (braising) enjoys

## GETTING IT RIGHT: Chuck Roasts

The seven-bone pot roast (left) is a well-marbled cut with an incredibly beefy flavor. It gets its name from the bone found in the roast, which is shaped like the number seven. Because it is only 2 inches thick, less liquid and less time are needed to braise this roast. Do not buy a seven-bone pot roast that weighs more than 3 1/2 pounds, as it will not fit into a Dutch oven. This roast is also sometimes referred to as a seven-bone steak.

The top-blade pot roast (middle) is also well-marbled with fat and connective tissue, which make this roast very juicy and flavorful. Even after thorough braising, this roast retains a distinctive strip of connective tissue, which is not unpleasant to eat. This roast may also be sold as a blade roast.

The chuck-eye roast (right) is the fattiest of the three roasts and the most commonly available. Its high proportion of fat gives pot roast great flavor and tenderness. Because of its thicker size, this roast takes the longest to cook.

**SEVEN-BONE POT ROAST**

**TOP-BLADE POT ROAST**

**CHUCK-EYE ROAST**

any special ability to soften meat over boiling. Braising has one advantage over simmering or boiling, however—half a pot of liquid reduces to a sauce much faster than a full pot.

## SCIENCE DESK:
### What's So Special about Collagen?

COLLAGEN IS THE PREDOMINANT PROTEIN IN CONNECTIVE tissue and is quite tough to chew. It is found in abundance in tough cuts of meat. Braising is a slow cooking technique that is applied to tough cuts of meat. The meat is covered halfway with cooking liquid and heated, covered, at a low temperature. By the time the meat reaches 150 degrees the muscle tissue has tightened fully and has expelled a great deal of its moisture into the braising liquid. If the meat is pulled from the pot at this temperature it will be dry and tough, but the braising liquid will be rich and flavorful.

Upon further heating, the collagen in the muscle will break down progressively into soft gelatin. The tightened muscle tissue strands can then separate a little, and moisture from the cooking liquid will accumulate between the fibers. Now, though the finished product still is tough muscle tissue, it is more succulent owing to the conversion of collagen to soft gelatin and to the resultant opening of gaps between the tough strands of muscle.

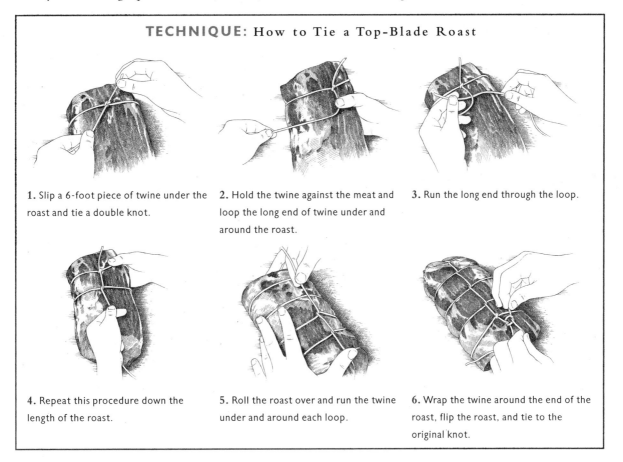

**TECHNIQUE: How to Tie a Top-Blade Roast**

**1.** Slip a 6-foot piece of twine under the roast and tie a double knot.

**2.** Hold the twine against the meat and loop the long end of twine under and around the roast.

**3.** Run the long end through the loop.

**4.** Repeat this procedure down the length of the roast.

**5.** Roll the roast over and run the twine under and around each loop.

**6.** Wrap the twine around the end of the roast, flip the roast, and tie to the original knot.

## EQUIPMENT CORNER:
### Vegetable Choppers

EVERY NIGHT OWL HAS SEEN THE MIDNIGHT INFOMERCIALS advertising do-it-all food preparation devices that will "make superfresh salads, pizza, coleslaw, tacos, and more in seconds!" Real people give testimonials in which they claim these gadgets quickly and effortlessly chop, mince, slice, dice, julienne, and shred.

Such gadgets would probably not tempt cooks with a sharp knife and passable skill in its use. But there are countless cooks with dull knives or limited time, interest, or facility who might well part with their hard-earned cash for the lure of easily and speedily dispatching all manner of foodstuffs. Wondering how well they'd be served by these devices, we gathered eight models—several of them courtesy of the toll-free number on the television screen—and repaired to the test kitchen to chop, mince, slice, and shred everything from garlic and parsley to cheese and potatoes.

The models tested showcased a variety of designs. Of the five units intended to chop and mince, three—the Zyliss, Gemco, and Dalla Piazza—use a chamber to contain the food and a pump-operated, rotating, zigzag-shaped blade that descends over the food to chop it. The first few pumps chop the food roughly; continued pumping minces it. The New & Improved Quick Chopper operates like a hand-cranked food processor, with a blade spinning in a workbowl. The last of the five chopper models, the Kitchen Magic, combines a nonadjustable slicing blade mounted in the handle with a series of circular blades, which you roll back and forth over the slices you've made to chop them.

The remaining three models slice and shred. The Culinary 2000 Rocket Chef, like the Quick Chopper, is a hand-cranked manual food processor that includes slicing and shredding blades. The Presto Salad Shooter pushes food through a feed tube onto a rotating, cone-shaped slicing or shredding blade, and the Veg-o-Matic makes the cook push food through blades using a plunger and two hands.

In the course of running 11 separate tests on each unit, it didn't take long to reach the conclusion that this bunch of kitchen gadgets is unimpressive. The shortcomings include uneven processing, whether chopping, shredding, or slicing; poor design in terms of rinsing, cleaning, and even safety; and lackluster manufacturing quality.

First, the cutting quality. Not one machine did a decent job on parsley, and several choked when we tried to chop nuts. In general, we found it best to process small amounts of food at one time because ½ cup of nuts or even a small onion brought several units to a halt.

Cleaning or rinsing these units between runs through the dishwasher (so they could be used on different foods being prepared for the same meal) was no walk in the park. Most designs included numerous hard-to-reach nooks and crannies and multiple pieces. Only the Zyliss opened up to reveal the entire blade, which made it easy to clean.

Because our test cooks are not the target consumer for these products—we have both a sharp knives and enough skill to use them comfortably—we expanded the testing to include four less experienced cooks who work in the production and accounting departments at *Cook's Illustrated* magazine. We asked each individual to finely chop an onion and to mince a knob of ginger, using both a freshly honed 8-inch chef's knife and the winning chopper.

It goes almost without saying that average onion-chopping times with the machine were much faster than those with the knife—one minute, 19 seconds, versus four minutes, 45 seconds, respectively. But, like our test cooks, three of the four novice testers were not pleased with the quality (fineness and evenness) of the chop. To be fair, the tester who took the longest to get through the onion and ginger with a knife was very enthusiastic about the chopper.

All in all, we would rather see money spent on a decent chef's knife (which can be had for about $30) and an adult education course in knife skills than on any of these machines. That said, if you are really averse to using a knife and think that one of these machines might help you out, the Zyliss is the one to go for.

# Rating Vegetable Choppers

WE RATED EIGHT FOOD CHOPPER/SLICER/SHREDDER DEVICES AND EVALUATED THEM IN 11 TESTS: CHOPPING GARLIC, ginger, parsley, chocolate, almonds, dried apricots, and onion, and slicing or shredding cheddar cheese, carrots, tomatoes, and potatoes. We've divided the devices into two categories based on their intended uses. The devices are listed in order of preference in each category based on their performance in these tests as well as ease of use and ease of cleaning. See www.americastestkitchen.com for up-to-date prices and mail-order sources for top-rated products.

## FOOD CHOPPERS

**BEST CHOPPER**
### Zyliss Comfort Food Chopper **$19.99**
Clever design and best performance by a wide margin make this a handy kitchen tool if you hate to use a knife. Parsley was the only test it failed.

**RECOMMENDED WITH RESERVATIONS**
### Gemco—The Chopper **$4.99**
Simple, cheap, and a bit flimsy, but it might be worth keeping around if you chop a lot of chocolate. Good with dried fruit, but lousy on ginger, garlic, nuts, and parsley.

**RECOMMENDED WITH RESERVATIONS**
### Dalla Piazza Brushed Stainless Steel Food Chopper **$22.00**
Performance was acceptable in some cases (nuts and chocolate), mediocre in most.

**NOT RECOMMENDED**
### New & Improved Quick Chopper **$14.95**
Performance in key tests ranged from subpar to terrible.

**NOT RECOMMENDED**
### Kitchen Magic Chopper **$17.25**
Two words characterize this unit best: "dangerous" and "useless."

## FOOD SLICERS/SHREDDERS

**NOT RECOMMENDED**
### Presto 2972 Pro Salad Shooter/Shredder **$49.92**
Shredding is its strong suit; slicing performance is fickle.

**NOT RECOMMENDED**
### K-Tel Veg-o-Matic Food Cutter **$22.35**
Flimsy, unstable, and a disgracefully poor performer.

**NOT RECOMMENDED**
### Culinary 2000 New Rocket Chef & Supreme Ice Cream **$28.99**
The phrase "piece of junk" could have been coined for this unit.

# GREEN BEANS

**WHAT WE WANTED:** To skip the traditional, multipot method and cook the beans and sauce together in a skillet.

For eleventh-hour cooks (like us), the conventional rigmarole for cooking green beans—boiling, shocking in ice water, drying, and, finally, reheating in a separately made sauce—simply takes too long and dirties too many dishes. We wanted a streamlined technique that would yield tender beans and a flavorful sauce.

The plan was to steam the beans in a covered skillet with a little water, remove the lid part way through to evaporate the water, then build a quick pan sauce around the beans as they finished cooking. The beans, however, steamed in only eight minutes, leaving little time to make a decent sauce after the water had evaporated. Switching the cooking order, we then tried making the sauce first. Building good flavor and texture by sautéing aromatics (such as garlic and onion) and a little flour, we then stirred in broth and some fresh herbs. Adding the beans right to the sauce, we covered the skillet and cooked them until almost tender (omitting the water altogether), then removed the lid to thicken the sauce. Not only did these beans turn out more flavorful, but by removing the lid near the end of cooking, we were able to closely monitor the doneness of the beans.

When made in a nonstick skillet, these beans are easy to gussy up with some toasted bread crumbs or glazed nuts. The toppings are made first, then the pan is simply wiped clean with paper towels and returned to the stove. Putting this one-pan technique to the ultimate test, we also re-create a green bean "casserole," complete with a mushroom cream sauce and fried shallots.

**WHAT WE LEARNED:** Build a sauce in the skillet with aromatics, broth, and a little flour; add the beans, cover, and steam until almost done; then uncover during the final phase of cooking to thicken the sauce.

## QUICK GREEN BEAN "CASSEROLE" Serves 8

| | |
|---|---|
| 3 | large shallots, sliced thin (about 1 cup) |
| | Salt and ground black pepper |
| 3 | tablespoons all-purpose flour |
| 5 | tablespoons vegetable oil |
| 10 | ounces cremini mushrooms, stems discarded, caps wiped clean and sliced ¼-inch thick |
| 2 | tablespoons unsalted butter |
| 1 | medium onion, minced (about 1 cup) |
| 2 | medium cloves garlic, minced |
| 1½ | pounds green beans, stem ends trimmed |
| 3 | sprigs fresh thyme |
| 2 | bay leaves |
| ¾ | cup heavy cream |
| ¾ | cup low-sodium chicken broth |

**1.** Toss the shallots with ¼ teaspoon salt, ⅛ teaspoon pepper, and 2 tablespoons flour in a bowl. Heat 3 tablespoons oil in a 12-inch nonstick skillet over medium-high heat until smoking; add the shallots and cook, stirring frequently, until golden and crisp, about 5 minutes. Transfer the shallots with the oil to a baking sheet lined with paper towels.

**2.** Wipe out the skillet and return to medium-high heat. Add the remaining 2 tablespoons oil, mushrooms, and ¼ teaspoon salt; cook, stirring occasionally, until the mushrooms are well browned, about 8 minutes. Transfer to a plate and set aside.

**3.** Wipe out the skillet. Heat the butter in the skillet over medium heat; when the foaming subsides, add the onion, and cook, stirring occasionally, until the edges begin to brown, about 2 minutes. Stir in the garlic and remaining 1 tablespoon flour; toss in the green beans, thyme, and bay. Add the cream and chicken broth, increase the heat to medium-high, cover, and cook until the beans are partly tender but still crisp at the center, about 4 minutes. Add the mushrooms, and continue to cook, uncovered, until the green beans are tender, about 4 minutes. Off heat, discard the bay and thyme; adjust the seasonings with salt and pepper. Transfer to a serving dish, sprinkle evenly with the shallots, and serve.

## GARLIC-LEMON GREEN BEANS WITH TOASTED BREAD CRUMBS Serves 8

- 3 tablespoons unsalted butter
- 2 slices high-quality sandwich bread, ground fine in a food processor
  Salt and ground black pepper
- 2 tablespoons grated Parmesan cheese
- 6 medium cloves garlic, minced
- 2 teaspoons all-purpose flour
- 1/8 teaspoon red pepper flakes
- 1 teaspoon minced fresh thyme leaves
- 1 1/2 pounds green beans, stem ends trimmed
- 1 cup low-sodium chicken broth
- 1 tablespoon juice from 1 lemon

**1.** Heat 1 tablespoon butter in a 12-inch nonstick skillet over medium-high heat; when melted, add the bread crumbs and cook, stirring frequently, until golden brown, 3 to 5 minutes. Transfer to a medium bowl, stir in 1/4 teaspoon salt, 1/8 teaspoon pepper, and the Parmesan; set aside.

**2.** Wipe out the skillet. Add the remaining 2 tablespoons butter, garlic, and 1/4 teaspoon salt; cook over medium heat, stirring constantly, until the garlic is golden, 3 to 5 minutes. Stir in the flour, pepper flakes, and thyme, then toss in the green beans. Add the broth and increase the heat to medium-high; cover and cook until the beans are partly tender but still crisp at the center, about 4 minutes. Uncover and cook, stirring occasionally, until the beans are tender, about 4 minutes. Stir in the lemon juice; adjust the seasonings with salt and pepper. Transfer to a serving dish, sprinkle with bread crumbs, and serve.

## GREEN BEANS WITH ORANGE ESSENCE AND TOASTED MAPLE PECANS Serves 8

- 3/4 cup pecans (about 1 3/4 ounces), chopped coarse
- 3 tablespoons unsalted butter
- 2 tablespoons maple syrup
  Salt
- 2 medium shallots, minced (about 1/2 cup)
- 1/2 teaspoon grated zest plus 1/3 cup juice from 1 large orange
  Pinch cayenne
- 2 teaspoons all-purpose flour
- 1 1/2 pounds green beans, stem ends trimmed
- 2/3 cup low-sodium chicken broth
- 1 teaspoon minced fresh sage leaves
  Ground black pepper

**1.** Toast the pecans in a 12-inch nonstick skillet over medium-high heat, stirring occasionally, until golden brown and fragrant, about 3 minutes. Off heat, stir in 1 tablespoon butter, maple syrup, and 1/8 teaspoon salt. Return the skillet to medium heat and cook, stirring constantly, until the nuts are dry and glossy, about 45 seconds; transfer to a large plate and set aside.

**2.** Wipe out the skillet. Heat the remaining 2 tablespoons butter in the skillet over medium heat; when the foaming subsides, add the shallots, orange zest, and cayenne and cook, stirring occasionally, until the shallots are softened, about 2 minutes. Stir in the flour until combined, then toss in the green beans. Add the chicken broth and orange juice; increase the heat to medium-high, cover, and cook until the beans are partly tender but still crisp at the center, about 4 minutes. Uncover and cook, stirring occasionally, until the beans are tender and the sauce has thickened slightly, about 4 minutes. Off heat, adjust the seasonings with salt and pepper. Transfer to a serving dish, sprinkle evenly with the pecans, and serve.

Maple-glazed pork loin is browned on the stovetop and then finished—still in its skillet—in the oven.

# MAPLE-GLAZED
## pork roast

CHAPTER 9

IN THIS CHAPTER

**THE RECIPES**

Maple-Glazed Pork Roast
Maple-Glazed Pork Roast with
    Rosemary
Maple-Glazed Pork Roast with
    Orange Essence
Maple-Glazed Pork Roast with
    Star Anise
Maple-Glazed Pork Roast with
    Smoked Paprika

Wild Rice Pilaf with Pecans and
    Dried Cranberries

**EQUIPMENT CORNER**

Food Storage Containers

**SCIENCE DESK**

Why Brown and Glaze a Roast?

The marketing of the "other white meat" would be amusing if today's pork weren't so lean and flavorless. Pork producers have worked so hard to remove fat from their pigs that most pork roasts have little character. Glazing a pork roast with maple syrup is an attractive way to boost flavor, but all too often the meat becomes too sweet and candyish. We wanted to perfect this simple recipe, figuring out how to apply the glaze as well as how to cook this lean roast without having the meat dry out.

Wild rice is as all-American as maple syrup. Too bad, then, that most wild rice dishes are better fed to farm animals than human beings. Most wild rice is mushy and starchy or tough and crunchy. And forget about those horrible boxed mixes. We wanted to develop a simple pilaf that would showcase the unusual flavor and texture of this indigenous ingredient.

# MAPLE-GLAZED PORK ROAST

**WHAT WE WANTED:** Tender, juicy pork with a rich, clingy glaze that packs a lot of pure maple flavor—all in less than an hour.

From pancakes to pineapple, New Englanders will slather maple syrup on just about anything. Among the multitude of dishes done right by a dash of maple, classic New England maple-glazed pork roast is one of our favorites. Sweet maple, with its delicate flavor notes of smoke, caramel, and vanilla, makes an ideal foil for pork, which has a faint sweetness of its own. The result of this marriage is a glistening maple-glazed pork roast, which, when sliced, combines the juices from tender, well-seasoned pork with a rich maple glaze to create complex flavor in every bite.

When we tested five different recipes, however, we found that this dish often falls short of its savory-sweet promise. Of course, many of the roasts turned out dry (a constant concern when cooking today's lean pork), but we were surprised to discover that the glazes presented even bigger problems. Most of them were too thin to coat the pork properly, some were so sweet that they required a hotline to the dentist's office, and none of them had a pronounced maple flavor.

Good maple-glazed roast pork starts out as good plain roast pork. We wanted a boneless cut, of which there are four popular choices: the blade roast, which is cut from the animal's shoulder; the blade-end loin roast, cut from the loin near the shoulder blade; the center loin roast, cut from the center of the loin; and the sirloin roast, cut from the posterior of the loin. Tasters preferred the blade-end loin roast for its flavor and juiciness, which it receives in part from a deposit of fat that separates the two muscle sections at one end of the roast.

As is the custom in our test kitchen, we tried brining the meat (soaking it in a saltwater solution to season and boost juiciness), and brining did, indeed, yield tender, juicy, well-seasoned pork. On the other hand, the unbrined pork was almost as good (as long as we took care not to overcook it), and it was nice to dispense with the 2½-hour brining time. Tasters also noted that the minor improvements realized by brining were lost to the assertively sweet glaze, so brining was out. We also ran a series of tests using "enhanced" pork, a common supermarket product that has been injected with a solution of water, salt, and sodium phosphate to season the meat and add moisture. Tasters were put off by the flood of liquid these roasts released when they were sliced, as well as by the overly wet, spongy texture of the meat.

In cooking more than a dozen roasts up to this point, we had learned that the real key to juicy pork is simple. Don't overcook it. In the old days, when pork had more fat and the trichinosis parasite was a more persistent threat, pork was routinely cooked to an internal temperature of 160 degrees. Today, pork is considerably leaner, and the possibility of contamination with trichinosis has been reduced to almost nil. This means that pork can be safely served at 145 to 150 degrees (measured in the center of the roast). If, however, you take the roast out of the oven once it reaches this temperature, it will be overcooked. The reason is simple: The temperature of the roast continues to rise, by as much as 15 degrees. The thing to do is to remove the roast when it hits a mere 135 degrees and then let it rest on the cutting board before slicing.

Innumerable tests in the kitchen have proven that roasts with a deep brown, caramelized crust look and taste better than those without. Trying to brown the meat using high oven heat at the beginning or end of roasting produced marginal results, so we decided to sear it on the stovetop. Because the meat was tied into a neat bundle, it fit well in a skillet, which made for great browning and gave us lots of control over the process. From the hot skillet, the loin went onto a rack in a roasting pan placed in a 325-degree oven, which proved to be the temperature of choice for even cooking.

Now it was time to get serious about developing maple flavor. The recipes we had researched touted dozens of glaze concoctions and methods for marrying them to the pork. Most of the flavoring ingredients added to the maple syrup either diluted it (so that it was too thin to use as a glaze) or were simply unwelcome. This list included soy sauce, vinegar, lemon juice, cranberry juice, cider, and bourbon for liquid ingredients and herbs, spices, jams, jellies, brown sugar, maple sugar, mustards, and chiles for flavor boosters. (We reserved the best of these flavorings for recipe variations.) Everyone agreed, however, that small amounts of complementary spices added subtle dimension to the maple, thus cinnamon, ground cloves, and cayenne all found their way into the glaze recipe. Still, we wanted more maple flavor and a glaze that would really stick to the meat. We even tried brining one loin in maple syrup and wrapping another with maple-flavored bacon. The former added no discernible maple flavor, while the latter tasted mildly artificial. We finally hit upon a simple solution to enhance flavor when we reduced the maple syrup in a saucepan. But we were frustrated when it dripped down off the roast onto the bottom of the roasting pan and burned.

Then we had an idea. Remember the hot pan we had left from searing the roast? How about putting it to additional use? We decided to use it to flash-reduce the maple syrup. We removed the loin from the pan after searing, poured off excess fat, added the syrup, and let it heat for 30 seconds. This allowed us to use the drippings that had formed in the pan when the meat seared and also eliminated the extra pan we had been using to reduce the syrup. Next we decided to lose the roasting pan (as well as the basting brush, which we invariably trashed with the sticky glaze) in favor of using the same skillet. Instead of pouring the glaze mixture over the pork in the roasting pan, where it would run to the edges and scorch, we returned the seared loin to the skillet with the syrup, twirled the pork around in the glaze a couple of times with tongs, and then popped the whole thing into the oven, with the skillet serving as the roasting pan.

The smaller surface area of the skillet prevented the glaze from spreading out and burning. This pan also made it easier to coat the pork thoroughly because it was sitting right in the glaze, like a belle in her bath. The roast emerged from the oven with a thick, uniform, glistening coating of glaze and an impressive, concentrated maple flavor. We had managed to turn this into a one-pan dish by searing, reducing the glaze, and roasting all in the same skillet. And there was yet another bonus. Starting with a hot skillet shaved a little time off the whole process. This skillet-roasted, burnished beauty was now out of the oven in 45 minutes or less.

---

**WHAT WE LEARNED:** Use a blade-end pork loin. Brown the meat in a large skillet, remove it to reduce the syrup and the spices, then return the meat to the pan and pop the whole thing—pan and all—into the oven.

## MAPLE-GLAZED PORK ROAST Serves 4 to 6

A nonstick ovenproof skillet will be much easier to clean than a traditional one. Whichever you use, remember that the handle will be blistering hot when you take it out of the oven, so be sure to use a pot holder or oven mitt. Note that you should not trim the pork of its thin layer of fat. The flavor of grade B maple syrup (sometimes called "cooking maple") is stronger and richer than grade A, but grade A syrup will work well, too. This dish is unapologetically sweet, so we recommend side dishes that take well to the sweetness. Garlicky sautéed greens, braised cabbage, and soft polenta are good choices.

   ⅓   cup maple syrup, preferably grade B
   ⅛   teaspoon ground cinnamon
        Pinch ground cloves
        Pinch cayenne pepper
   1   boneless blade-end pork loin roast (about 2½ pounds), tied at even intervals along length with 5 pieces butcher's twine (see the photo on page 115)
   ¾   teaspoon salt
   ½   teaspoon ground black pepper
   2   teaspoons vegetable oil

**1.** Adjust an oven rack to the middle position; heat the oven to 325 degrees. Stir the maple syrup, cinnamon, cloves, and cayenne together in a measuring cup or small bowl; set aside. Pat the roast dry with paper towels, then sprinkle evenly with the salt and pepper.

**2.** Heat the oil in a heavy-bottomed ovenproof 10-inch nonstick skillet over medium-high heat until just beginning to smoke, about 3 minutes. Place the roast fat-side down in the skillet and cook until well browned, about 3 minutes. Using tongs, rotate the roast one-quarter turn and cook until well browned, about 2½ minutes; repeat until the roast is well browned on all sides. Transfer the roast to a large plate. Reduce the heat to medium and pour off the fat from the skillet; add the maple syrup mixture and cook until fragrant, about 30 seconds (the syrup will bubble immediately). Turn off the heat and return the roast to the skillet; using tongs, roll the roast to coat with glaze on all sides.

**3.** Place the skillet in the oven and roast until the center of the roast registers about 135 degrees on an instant-read thermometer, 35 to 45 minutes, using tongs to roll and spin the roast to coat with glaze twice during roasting time. Transfer the roast to a carving board; set the skillet aside to cool slightly to thicken the glaze, about 5 minutes. Pour the glaze over the roast and let rest 15 minutes longer (the center of the loin should register about 150 degrees on an instant-read thermometer). Snip the twine off the roast, cut into ¼-inch slices, and serve immediately.

---

**FOOD FACT:** Pancake Syrup

Many pancake syrups sold in supermarkets do not contain a drop of maple syrup. In fact, they are nothing more than corn syrup with artificial colors and flavors.

---

### MAPLE-GLAZED PORK ROAST WITH ROSEMARY

Follow the recipe for Maple-Glazed Pork Roast, substituting 2 teaspoons minced fresh rosemary for the cinnamon, cloves, and cayenne.

### MAPLE-GLAZED PORK ROAST WITH ORANGE ESSENCE

Follow the recipe for Maple-Glazed Pork Roast, adding 1 tablespoon grated orange zest to the maple syrup along with the spices.

### MAPLE-GLAZED PORK ROAST WITH STAR ANISE

Follow the recipe for Maple-Glazed Pork Roast, adding 4 star anise pods to the maple syrup along with the spices.

### MAPLE-GLAZED PORK ROAST WITH SMOKED PAPRIKA

Follow recipe for Maple-Glazed Pork Roast, adding 2 teaspoons smoked hot paprika to maple syrup along with spices.

## SCIENCE DESK:
### Why Brown and Glaze a Roast?

IT MIGHT SEEM A LITTLE RIDICULOUS TO GO TO THE TROUBLE of browning a pork roast when all of that beautiful color ends up being covered in a thick maple glaze. But pork requires extra attention to flavor development because the meat alone is plain. Our pork roast develops great flavor from two different reactions, both involving sugar.

The first reaction happens when we brown the meat and is called the Maillard reaction. Heat from the pan denatures proteins on the surface of the meat, and these proteins recombine with the natural sugars present in the meat to cause browning. This combination of protein with sugar has hundreds of possible chemical outcomes, leading to exceptional flavor depth.

The second reaction happens when the sugar in the maple glaze reaches a temperature of about 310 degrees, which generates hundreds of new compounds by means of caramelization. No wonder caramel is so much more interesting than sugar.

## GETTING IT RIGHT:
### The Importance of Tying

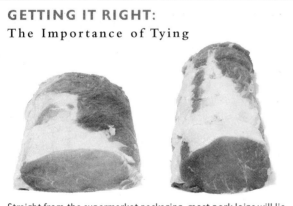

Straight from the supermarket packaging, most pork loins will lie flat in the pan and cook unevenly (left). Tying the roast not only yields more attractive slices but ensures that the roast will have the same thickness from end to end so that it cooks evenly (right).

## GETTING IT RIGHT:
### Don't Buy Enhanced Pork

Many markets sell enhanced pork, which has been injected with a water/salt/sodium phosphate solution meant to season the meat and improve juiciness. During testing, we found that an enhanced roast exuded nearly one and a half times as much juice as a regular roast when carved. We recommend buying regular pork.

JUICES LOST FROM ENHANCED PORK    JUICES LOST FROM REGULAR ROAST

# WILD RICE

WHAT WE WANTED: Too often, this American grain resembles mulch and has a taste to match. We wanted to figure out how to tame the flavor and turn out properly cooked rice every time.

Like a couture evening gown, wild rice is slinky black, demurely elegant, and exorbitantly pricey. But like the dress, the rice's inky sheath is no guarantee of what lies underneath. More often than not, that sleek ebony coating masks a chewy interior tasting of little but the marsh from whence the rice came. The question before us was how to make wild rice taste as good as it looks.

Properly cooked wild rice is a study in contrasts: chewy yet tender and cottony—like popcorn. Ideally, the cooked grains remain discreet, doubling to quadrupling in size from their uncooked state. Undercooked rice is tough and, quite literally, hard to chew. At the other end of the spectrum, overcooked wild rice is gluey.

To find the best cooking method, we first tried steaming and boiling, but both methods produced poorly cooked wild rice. Research revealed the best approach to be slow simmering, although the timing varied from batch to batch. The key is to stop the cooking process at just the right moment; otherwise the texture goes quickly from

tough to gluey. The solution? Once the rice had simmered for 35 minutes, we checked it for doneness every couple of minutes.

Finding good flavor was another story. Plain water made for distinctly bad-tasting rice, and the addition of wine only accentuated the off flavor. Beef broth was overwhelming, but chicken broth was a revelation. Mild yet rich, the chicken broth tempered the rice's muddy flavor to a pleasant earthiness and affirmed its subdued nuttiness. Bay leaves and thyme added finesse and complexity.

Although it was now perfectly cooked, tasters found the wild rice alone to be overwhelming. Perhaps it could be better appreciated if complemented by a mellower grain, such as brown or white rice. Brown rice offered too little contrast, so we quickly settled on white. Cooking both rices in the same pot (adding the white rice midway through the simmer) caused the texture of the white rice to suffer, so an additional pot was called for. To make the most of this second saucepan, we decided to add flavoring ingredients in the style of a pilaf, a simple technique that guarantees flavorful, fluffy rice. Aromatics are first softened in oil or butter, and then the rice is lightly toasted in the pan, after which the liquid is added (in a smaller amount than for conventional cooking) and the rice steamed until tender. The winning pilaf ingredients turned out to be onions, carrots, dried cranberries, and toasted pecans.

WHAT WE LEARNED: Simmer wild rice in plenty of chicken broth and check the pot often as it nears completion to make sure the grains do not overcook. Mellow the intense flavor of wild rice with some white rice pilaf.

---

## FOOD FACT: Wild Rice

While wild rice (*Zizania aquatica*) and traditional cultivated rice (*Oryza sativa*) are both members of the grass family, wild rice is not considered a cereal grass (as are wheat, corn, oats, barley, rye, and traditional cultivated rice). Truly "wild" wild rice is native to the northern Great Lakes, where it is still harvested. But most so-called wild rice is now cultivated on farms in California. Cultivated wild rice grown in man-made paddies costs between $3 and $5 per pound, while hand-harvested rice from lakes and streams in Minnesota and Canada costs about $9 per pound.

---

## WILD RICE PILAF WITH PECANS AND DRIED CRANBERRIES Serves 6 to 8

Wild rice goes quickly from tough to pasty, so begin testing the rice at the 35-minute mark and drain the rice as soon as it is tender.

1¾ cups low-sodium chicken broth

2 bay leaves

8 sprigs thyme, divided into 2 bundles, each tied together with kitchen twine

1 cup wild rice, rinsed well in a strainer and picked over

1½ cups long-grain white rice

3 tablespoons unsalted butter

1 medium onion, chopped fine (about 1¼ cups)

1 large carrot, chopped fine (about 1 cup)

Salt

¾ cup sweetened or unsweetened dried cranberries

¾ cup pecans, toasted in small dry skillet over medium heat until fragrant and lightly browned, about 6 minutes, then chopped coarse

1½ tablespoons minced fresh parsley leaves

Ground black pepper

**1.** Bring the chicken broth, ¼ cup water, bay leaves, and 1 bundle thyme to a boil in a medium saucepan over medium-high heat. Add the wild rice, cover, and reduce the heat to low; simmer until the rice is plump and tender and has absorbed most of the liquid, 35 to 45 minutes. Drain the rice in a mesh strainer to remove excess liquid. Return the rice to the now-empty saucepan; cover to keep warm and set aside.

**2.** While the wild rice is cooking, place the white rice in a medium bowl and cover with 2 of inches water; gently swish the grains to release excess starch. Carefully pour off the water, leaving the rice in the bowl. Repeat about 5 times, until the water runs almost clear. Drain the rice in a mesh strainer.

**3.** Heat the butter in a medium saucepan over medium-high heat until foam subsides, about 2 minutes. Add the onion, carrot, and 1 teaspoon salt; cook, stirring frequently, until softened but not browned, about 4 minutes. Add the rinsed white rice and stir to coat the grains with the butter; cook, stirring frequently, until the grains begin to turn translucent, about 3 minutes. Meanwhile, bring 2¼ cups water to a boil in a small saucepan or a microwave. Add the boiling water and the second thyme bundle to the rice; return to a boil, then reduce the heat to low, sprinkle the cranberries evenly over the rice, and cover. Simmer until all of the liquid is absorbed, 16 to 18 minutes. Off the heat, fluff the rice with a fork.

**4.** Combine the wild rice, white rice mixture, toasted pecans, and parsley in a large bowl; toss with a rubber spatula until ingredients are evenly mixed. Adjust the seasonings with salt and pepper to taste; serve immediately.

---

### GETTING IT RIGHT: The Texture Matters

Undercooked wild rice is tough and hard to chew. At the other end of the spectrum, overcooked wild rice bursts, revealing the pasty starch concealed beneath the glossy coat. Perfectly cooked wild rice is chewy but tender, the individual grains plumped but intact.

UNDERCOOKED       PERFECTLY       OVERCOOKED
                  COOKED

## EQUIPMENT CORNER:
### Food Storage Containers

CIRCA 1950, LEFTOVERS WENT INTO TUPPERWARE. . .
period. Today, some 50 years later, you can store leftovers in
any number of containers made from plastic, glass, or metal
and including features such as vacuum sealing, stain resistance,
locking lids, and special venting. We wanted to find out if any
of the newer models offered a higher level of protection for
your food, more useful features, or significantly better design.

"Food storage containers?" grimaced one test kitchen
skeptic, "Just how do you rate those?" After much discus-
sion, we came up with several reliable, if slightly unconven-
tional, methods to test the seal between the container and
its lid. The "sink test" was first. We filled each container with
2 pounds of pie weights topped with a layer of sugar and,
with the lid in place, submerged the whole thing in water.
Then we fished out the container, dried it, and inspected the
sugar inside. To further assess the seal, we devised the "shake
test." We filled each container with soup, fixed the lid in
place, and shook vigorously. If we ended up wearing soup,
the seal wasn't tight enough.

Preventing the transfer of food odors is also largely up
to the seal between container and lid. After all, you don't
want your last few bites of chocolate mousse to smell like the
anchovies next to it in the fridge, do you? To gauge odor protection, we conducted "stink tests" by loading slices of white
sandwich bread into each container, positioning the lids, and
storing them in the fridge with a huge, uncovered bowl of
diced raw onions. Over the course of five days, we sniffed the
bread daily to see if we could detect any "eau de allium."

We chose chili to test stain resistance, refrigerating it in
the containers for three days, microwaving it to serving temperature (about three minutes), and then immediately running the containers through the dishwasher. Last, to mimic
the ravages of time, we ran the containers through 100
cycles in the dishwasher, and then repeated every test.

Our lineup of 12 containers included Tupperware, two

Rubbermaid models (Seal'n Saver and Stain Shield), several
competing plastic containers, two inexpensive disposable containers, two vacuum-sealing models, and models made from
both ovensafe glass and metal. The Genius VakSet container,
with its pump-operated vacuum seal, performed impressively
in the sink, shake, and stink tests. Several other containers with
tight-fitting lids, particularly the Tupperware, both
Rubbermaid models, and the Tramontina stainless steel, held
their own against the vice grip of the Genius.

The "stink tests" produced no clear pattern among the
odor control champs, including the Genius, GladWare,
Tupperware, Tramontina, Betty Crocker, and Rubbermaid
Seal'n Saver, which just edged out the Rubbermaid Stain
Shield. The Pyrex glass container was a loser in both the
stink and sink tests.

The results of the staining tests, on the other hand, did
reveal a pattern. The winners were made of the hardest materials. The glass Pyrex and stainless steel Tramontina containers
proved stain resistant, though the same cannot be said of the latter's plastic lid. Among the plastic containers, those made from
hard, clear polycarbonate (the same stuff used for lightweight
eyeglass lenses and compact disks), including the Tupperware,
Rubbermaid Stain Shield, Genius, and Snapware, resisted stains
best in our tests. The remaining plastic containers were made
of polypropylene, a somewhat softer polymer that seems more
susceptible to staining, as we observed in our tests.

To our surprise, several containers matched or surpassed
the performance of the reigning king, Tupperware. Strictly
speaking, the vacuum-sealed Genius VakSet edged out the
Tupperware by one point in the performance tests. Yet despite
stellar performance, we'd still hesitate to buy it because of its
design. We fear that some cooks will lose the pump and the
containers will become useless. Also, no one in our test kitchen
could figure out how to release the vacuum seal without first
reading the instruction manual. Throwing leftovers in the
fridge shouldn't be any hassle at all. That's why our nod goes
to the Tupperware, followed closely by the two Rubbermaid
models. Their performance was excellent, and you don't have
to think twice to use them.

# Rating Food Storage Containers

WE TESTED 12 FOOD STORAGE CONTAINERS, ASSESSING THE QUALITY OF THE SEAL BETWEEN THE CONTAINER AND LID, the resistance of the sealed container to food odors, and the resistance of the container to staining. Containers are listed in order of preference based on results from these tests, tests performed after the containers went through the dishwasher 100 times, and design features. See www.americastestkitchen.com for up-to-date prices and mail-order sources for top-rated products.

**RECOMMENDED**
### Tupperware Rock 'N Serve Medium Deep Container
**$12.99**
Well designed (handles, flat lid, vent for microwaving) with performance to match.

**RECOMMENDED**
### Rubbermaid Stain Shield Square Container
**$4.99**
Lives up to the marketing claims of stain resistance. Odor-control performance was not perfect, though.

**RECOMMENDED**
### Genius VakSet: Four Vacuum Storage Containers with Pump
**$57.99/set of four**
Its impressive performance comes with some hassle factor, and the containers are rendered useless if you lose the pump.

**RECOMMENDED**
### Rubbermaid Seal'n Saver
**$4.99**
Staining was the only problem we encountered in this sturdy container with an excellent seal.

**RECOMMENDED WITH RESERVATIONS**
### Betty Crocker Servables Container
**$3.99**
A decent container that didn't stand up well to the submersion and staining tests.

**RECOMMENDED WITH RESERVATIONS**
### GladWare Containers/Deep Dish Size
**$2.89/package of three**
Despite some staining and minor leaking, a good overall performer, which surprised us given its flimsy feel. A good value.

**RECOMMENDED WITH RESERVATIONS**
### Ziploc Brand Containers/Large Rectangle
**$2.99/package of two**
Only odor protection was truly subpar. We're not crazy for the flimsy feel, but you can't argue with the performance.

**RECOMMENDED WITH RESERVATIONS**
### Sterilite Ultra Seal
**$3.29**
Less leakage, less staining, and better odor protection after 100 dishwasher cycles.

**RECOMMENDED WITH RESERVATIONS**
### Snapware Snap N' Serve Stainproof Six-Piece Storage Container Set
**$19.97**
Cracked during the 100 dishwasher cycles, which impaired the seal. We're concerned about durability.

**NOT RECOMMENDED**
### Tramontina Stainless Steel Gourmet Collection Storage Containers
**$29.75**
Despite good performance, testers found it so difficult to affix the lid to the container securely that we would avoid this model.

**NOT RECOMMENDED**
### Pyrex Storage Plus/Rectangle Dish
**$5.99**
Stain resistant for sure, but also heavy, hard to handle when hot, and seals poorly.

**NOT RECOMMENDED**
### SK Enterprises Vacuum Seal Storage Containers
**$19.94/set of three**
Midway through the testing, the vacuum mechanism broke and never worked again.

Becky and Susan check to make sure that all the food and equipment are on the set.

# TRUCK STOP favorites

## CHAPTER 10

IN THIS CHAPTER

**THE RECIPES**
Chicken-Fried Steak

Coconut Cream Pie

**EQUIPMENT CORNER**
Meat Pounders

**TASTING LAB**
Graham Cracker Crusts

Truckers often know where to find the best home cooking. After long days on the road, most would rather tuck into real food, prepared from scratch, than the prefab food offered by roadside chains. And what could be better than chicken-fried steak with cream gravy and real coconut cream pie?

Chicken-fried steak can go wrong in many places. If you use the wrong cut of meat, the steak will be tough. If you don't bread and fry the steak properly, the coating can be pale, soggy, or greasy. And, if you don't take care with the gravy, it will be no better than the canned version.

Coconut cream pie almost always looks good. More often than not, it tempts with mile-high looks but then disappoints with lackluster flavor (some versions taste nothing like coconut) or gummy texture. And let's not even think about that soggy crust. The test kitchen wanted to perfect these roadside classics.

# CHICKEN-FRIED STEAK

**WHAT WE WANTED:** Thin cutlets of beef that have been breaded and fried until crisp and golden brown. The creamy gravy that accompanies the steaks would be well seasoned and not too thick.

Although this truck-stop favorite often gets a bad rap, chicken-fried steak can be delicious when cooked just right. When cooked wrong, however, the dry, rubbery steaks snap back with each bite and are coated in a damp, pale breading and topped with a bland, pasty white sauce.

The first question we encountered on the road to good chicken-fried steak was what type of steak to use. By design, chicken-fried steak is a technique used with only the cheapest of cuts. No one would use strip steaks or filet mignon in this recipe, but steaks from the round, chuck, and sirloin are all contenders. We tested cube, Swiss, top-round, bottom-round, eye-round, chuck, and top sirloin steaks and came up with one winner. The cube steak was our favorite. This steak is lean yet tender; most of the other cuts tested were either fatty or difficult to chew.

Cube steak is usually cut from the round and tenderized (cubed) by the butcher, who uses a special machine to give the steak its unique, bumpy texture. We found that this lean, tender steak required little trimming and was easy to pound out to a thin cutlet, about 1/3 inch thick. Regular top, bottom-, and eye-round steaks, on the other hand, were thick and tough, requiring lots of muscle to pound out and chew. Swiss and chuck steaks, which come from the shoulder, were slightly less tough but still chewy and resilient. Top sirloin tasted great and had a nice texture, but the meat was laced with wide strips of gristle. Trimming the gristle reduced this steak to small, awkwardly sized pieces, making for unusual portions and cooking times.

What really makes chicken-fried steak great is the coating and subsequent frying. But what kind of coating is best?

To find out, we tested straight flour against various contenders, including cornflakes, Melba toast, cornmeal, matzo crumbs, ground saltines, and panko (Japanese bread crumbs). Straight flour was light and clung well to the steak but was simply too delicate for the toothsome meat and cream gravy. Cornflakes and Melba toast both burned and became tough, while the grittiness of cornmeal was simply out of place. Matzo, saltines, and panko all tasted great but quickly grew soggy under the rich, cream gravy.

We figured our single-breading technique might to be blame and decided to try double (or bound) breading. With single breading, meat is dipped into egg and then into flour, while double breading starts off with an initial dip in flour, then into egg, and again into flour (or into a coating such as those we tried with the steak). In side-by-side tests, we were surprised to discover that single breading was actually messier than double. When initially dipped in flour, the meat became dry and talcum-smooth, allowing the egg to cling evenly to the surface. The double breading also produced a more substantial base coat that didn't become overly thick or tough. Seasoned flour and a double-breading technique yielded a much improved crust.

Although this double breading was far superior to any other breading so far, we were still left wanting a heartier and crunchier crust. We wondered if we could bolster the egg wash with some buttermilk, baking soda, and baking powder, something that we knew worked well with fried chicken. Sure enough, these ingredients turned the egg wash into a thick, foamy concoction. This created a wet yet airy layer that stuck to and hydrated both layers of flour. This wet-looking, skin-like coating fried up to an impressive dark mahogany color and had a resilient texture that didn't weaken under the gravy. Because the coating is such a big part of the dish, we found it necessary to season it heavily with salt, black pepper, and cayenne.

After frying a few batches of these steaks, we found the

flavor of peanut oil preferable to that of vegetable oil or even shortening. Because the steaks are thin, they fry evenly in just 1 inch of oil. To keep splattering to a minimum, we used a deep Dutch oven. We also noted that the steaks fried to a dark, beautiful brown without tasting too greasy when the oil was heated initially to 375 degrees. Although the thick breading offers substantial protection from the hot oil, the steaks usually cook through completely within the time it takes for the crust to brown, about 2½ minutes per side.

Equally important to the crust is the cream gravy made from the fried drippings. Not wanting to waste any time while the fried steaks were kept warm in the oven, we found it easy to strain the small amount of hot oil used to fry the steaks right away. Adding the strained bits of deep-fried crumbs back to the Dutch oven, we were ready to make gravy. Most recipes simmer the drippings with some milk and thicken it with flour. To avoid making a floury-tasting sauce, we decided to cook the flour in the fat (that is, to

make a roux) and then add the milk, along with a splash of chicken stock. We found this technique quick and easy, and it also produced an authentic-tasting sauce.

We tested recipes using cream, half-and-half, and evaporated milk, but tasters preferred the fresh, clean flavor and lighter texture of whole milk. Onions and cayenne are traditional seasonings for the gravy, but tasters also liked small additions of thyme and garlic (neither of which is authentic). Topped with the light, well-seasoned gravy, this chicken-fried steak is the best any trucker has ever tasted.

---

WHAT WE LEARNED: **Start with cube steaks pounded to an even thickness. Double-bread the steaks, dredging them in heavily seasoned flour, dipping in a thick buttermilk and egg mixture aerated with baking power and baking soda, and then returning to the seasoned flour for a second coat. Build flavor in the cream sauce by using the fried bits that fall off the steaks as they cook and by making a roux.**

## CHICKEN-FRIED STEAK Serves 6

Getting the initial oil temperature to 375 degrees is key to the success of this recipe. An instant-read thermometer with a high upper range is perfect for checking the temperature; a clip-on candy/deep-fry thermometer is also fine. If your Dutch oven measures 11 inches across (as ours does), you will need to fry the steaks in two batches.

### steak

| | |
|---|---|
| 3 | cups unbleached all-purpose flour |
| | Salt and ground black pepper |
| ⅛ | teaspoon cayenne |
| 1 | large egg |
| 1 | teaspoon baking powder |
| ½ | teaspoon baking soda |
| 1 | cup buttermilk |
| 6 | cube steaks, about 5 ounces each, pounded to ⅓-inch thickness |
| 4–5 | cups peanut oil |

### cream gravy

| | |
|---|---|
| 1 | medium onion, minced |
| ⅛ | teaspoon dried thyme |
| 2 | medium cloves garlic, minced or pressed through a garlic press |
| 3 | tablespoons unbleached all-purpose flour |
| ½ | cup low-sodium chicken broth |
| 2 | cups whole milk |
| ¾ | teaspoon salt |
| ¼ | teaspoon ground black pepper |
| | Pinch cayenne |

**1.** FOR THE STEAKS: Measure the flour, 5 teaspoons salt, 1 teaspoon black pepper, and cayenne into a large shallow dish. In a second large shallow dish, beat the egg, baking powder, and baking soda; stir in the buttermilk (the mixture will bubble and foam).

**2.** Set a wire rack over a rimmed baking sheet. Pat the steaks dry with paper towels and sprinkle each side with salt and pepper to taste. Drop the steaks into the flour and shake the pan to coat. Shake excess flour from each steak, then, using tongs, dip the steaks into the egg mixture, turning to coat well and allowing the excess to drip off. Coat the steaks with flour again, shake off the excess, and place them on the wire rack.

**3.** Adjust an oven rack to the middle position, set a second wire rack over a second rimmed baking sheet, and place the sheet on the oven rack; heat the oven to 200 degrees. Line a large plate with a double layer of paper towels. Meanwhile, heat 1 inch of oil in a large (11-inch diameter) Dutch oven over medium-high heat to 375 degrees. Place three steaks in the oil and fry, turning once, until deep golden brown on each side, about 5 minutes (oil temperature will drop to around 335 degrees). Transfer the steaks to the paper towel–lined plate to drain, then transfer them to the wire rack in the oven. Bring the oil back to 375 degrees and repeat the cooking and draining process (use fresh paper towels) with the three remaining steaks.

**4.** FOR THE GRAVY: Carefully pour the hot oil through a fine-mesh strainer into a clean pot. Return the browned bits from the strainer along with 2 tablespoons of frying oil back to the Dutch oven. Turn the heat to medium, add the onion and thyme, and cook until the onion has softened and is beginning to brown, 4 to 5 minutes. Add the garlic and cook until aromatic, about 30 seconds. Add the flour to the pan and stir until well combined and starting to dissolve, about 1 minute. Whisk in the broth, scraping any browned bits off the bottom of the pan. Whisk in the milk, salt, pepper, and cayenne; bring to a simmer over medium-high heat. Cook until thickened (gravy should have a loose consistency—it will thicken as it cools), about 5 minutes.

**5.** Transfer the chicken-fried steaks to individual plates. Spoon a generous amount of gravy over each steak. Serve immediately, placing any remaining gravy in a small bowl.

## EQUIPMENT CORNER: Meat Pounders

IN BOXING, WEIGHT MATTERS SO MUCH THAT IT SETS THE contenders apart; it just wouldn't be fair to put a heavyweight in the ring with a lightweight. In our test of five "official" meat pounders plus a couple of ringers (a rubber mallet and a small skillet), we learned that weight matters in this arena, too, but the advantage doesn't necessarily go to the big guys.

The challenge was to flatten halved boneless chicken breasts into ¼-inch-thick paillards and to pound 1½-inch-thick slices of pork tenderloin into ½-inch cutlets. What counted was efficiency (as judged by the number of strokes it took to get the job done), quality (we wanted even, perfectly smooth cutlets and paillards, without marred or torn surfaces), and comfort and ease of use. Here are the results, by category.

Lightweights: More featherweight than lightweight and very cheap at $2.99, the 5-ounce wood hammer was the least efficient tool we tried, needing an average of about 90 strokes to produce one paillard and close to 40 for a pork cutlet. It was easy enough to use (we flattened the meat with its flat rectangular sides; the teeth on the square sides of the head are for tenderizing), but the sharp edges on the corners of the head tore into the meat a bit. This was not the performance we were looking for.

Also in this category was an 11-ounce rubber and metal pounder from Oxo, available for $9.95. It was more effective than the wood pounder—needing about 60 strokes for a paillard and 35 for a cutlet—but it also tore the meat, if very slightly.

Middleweight: The one entrant in this category was a standout. It may look a little odd, with its offset handle, but the 1-pound, 10-ounce Norpro meat pounder, which costs just $14.99, produced flawlessly smooth paillards (about 35 strokes) and cutlets (about 20) with a modicum of effort. Its moderate weight and offset handle make it very easy to control.

Heavyweights: The performance of two stainless steel tools from Mouli—the disk pounder and the square pounder—suffered from their excesses. The disk, which was not cheap at $44.95, weighed in at 3 pounds, 3 ounces. It produced very nice paillards and cutlets in relatively few strokes (35 and 20, respectively), but it felt so heavy compared with the Norpro, which was also much cheaper. *Cheap* is not a word that applies to Mouli's 2-pound, 4-ounce square pounder, which costs $99.95. It did a very good job and required very few strokes (about 25 for the paillards and only 12 for the cutlets), but even if we could use it as a snow shovel as well as a meat pounder, we'd have a hard time justifying that price. Its large size (12 inches tall with a 4-inch-square head) also made it a little hard to handle, with the corners of the head sometimes missing the meat and hitting the countertop.

Ringers: If you're not in the mood to bring yet another tool into your kitchen, we found that you can make do with a rubber mallet (20 strokes for paillards, 13 for cutlets) or a sturdy 8-inch skillet (25 strokes for paillards, 15 for pork). The skillet may not be as elegant or ergonomic as the Norpro (our top choice among models tested), but it will suffice for any home cook who rarely takes to pounding meat.

**BEST MEAT POUNDERS**
The Norpro Offset Pounder (left) was the clear favorite in our tests. Its offset handle and moderate weight make it both effective and easy to control. If you don't want to buy a meat pounder, we found that a small skillet (right) works pretty well if not terribly elegantly.

# COCONUT CREAM PIE

**WHAT WE WANTED:** A dreamily soft, delicately perfumed, luscious filling nestled in a crisp crust.

Coconut cream pie evokes happy thoughts—a fluffy cloud of a dessert, a sweet finish to a satisfying home-cooked meal. But imagining the taste of a perfect coconut cream pie can be a much different experience from eating a piece that's right in front of you. We discovered this first-hand when we whipped up a few recipes. These coconut cream pies did not have the smooth and satiny fillings and crisp crusts we had hoped for. Instead, they were disappointingly heavy, leaden, pasty, noxiously sweet, bland vanilla puddings in soggy pie shells. Hardly what we had in mind.

First, we went to work on the crust. Though a plain pastry crust is typical of a coconut cream pie, we were not the least bit wowed. The crust was fully prebaked and started out perfectly crisp, but when the filling went in, it quickly became soggy. For cream pies, we have in the past advocated rolling out a basic pie pastry in graham cracker crumbs. This speckled crust stayed crispy longer than the plain pie pastry, but we still had misgivings, mostly about its texture. It was a crust made entirely of graham crackers—a somewhat unorthodox but not completely odd option—that was the crowd-pleaser. Its crisp, sandy texture, sturdy construction, and substantial presence was the perfect contrast to the creamy smooth filling. Its sweet, toasty flavor also complemented the mild flavor of the filling.

It occurred to us, though, that the flavor of the graham cracker crust could be heightened and made to better fit its role by adding some coconut to it. In our next attempts, we toasted some shredded coconut until it was golden brown, then processed it along with the graham crackers so that it could be broken down into the finest bits. The coconut was a welcomed addition; though it offered only a little flavor, ¼ cup of it dispersed throughout the cracker crumbs gave

the crust that characteristic fibrous, nubby coconut crunch.

Coconuts are exotic tropical nuts (seeds, actually). They hail from lands of balmy breezes, palm trees, and ocean air, but recipes for coconut cream pie fillings are often boring and domesticated. They consist of no more than eggs, sugar, cornstarch or flour, and cream or milk. In a nutshell, they are vanilla cream pies garnished with a spray of toasted shredded coconut. We wanted to breathe some life into this downtrodden pie by pumping the filling full of true coconut flavor.

As with other cream pies, the filling for coconut cream pie is made on the stovetop in the same manner as a home-cooked pudding. In developing a filling, the first thing we needed to do was find the right kind of cream or "milk" to use. We made versions with half-and-half, whole milk, and coconut milk. As we expected, the first two made for boring, bland puddings. The coconut milk filling had a delicate coconut flavor and aroma, but it was far too rich to be palatable. We pulled back on the coconut milk and tried a filling made with one 14-ounce can of coconut milk cut with a cup of whole milk. Much better, but still we felt we needed to work in more coconut flavor.

We stirred some toasted shredded coconut into the filling, but the long stringy shreds suspended in the otherwise smooth filling were unappealing. Next, we took the advice of a recipe that suggested steeping unsweetened shredded coconut (which comes shredded in fine flecks and is available in natural foods and Asian grocery stores) in the milk to extract some of its flavor; the coconut was then strained out and pressed to remove any liquid that it was withholding. Though this technique didn't yield the results expected—the steeped mixture didn't have much more flavor and was a nuisance to boot—we did make the fortuitous discovery that the unsweetened shredded coconut itself had good, pure coconut flavor. We captured this delicate coconut flavor by leaving the tiny bits in the filling. The coconut also

#416 Coconut Cream Pie

As for eggs, some recipes called for whole eggs, some for just yolks, and a few for both. The number called for ranged from two to six. Our preference was for five yolks. This number made a filling with a smooth, lush, supple texture and a full, deep flavor. By comparison, fillings made with whole eggs—even with whole eggs plus yolks—had a leaner, gummier texture and a hollow flavor. In addition, their color wasn't as appealing as that of the all-yolk filling.

We were now very close to a final recipe. The last adjustments were to add some salt and vanilla to heighten and round out the flavors. Some butter whisked into the hot filling just before pouring it into its shell was the final touch that smoothed out any rough edges and made the coconut cream superbly creamy, rich, and silky—yet not so unctuous as to make one slice—topped with a puff of whipped cream—a challenge to eat.

Operationally, our coconut cream pie came together seamlessly. First, we made and prebaked the crust. While it sat cooling, we made the filling. As soon as the filling was done, we poured it—hot—into the cooled shell, covered the surface flush with plastic wrap (so that it didn't form a "skin"), and shuttled it into the refrigerator. Three or so hours later, when the pie was chilled and firm and ready to serve, we whipped up the cream with a bit of sugar and some vanilla (and some dark rum for those who cared for it), piled the cream on top, and gave it a sprinkle of toasted coconut. Finally, a truly memorable coconut cream pie that lived up to our notions of what it should be.

WHAT WE LEARNED: A graham cracker crust flavored with shredded coconut may not be traditional, but it is crisp, sweet, and, to our way of thinking, just what this pie needs. For the best flavor, use coconut milk and unsweetened shredded coconut in the filling. For the best texture, use cornstarch (not flour) and egg yolks (rather than whole eggs) to thicken the filling.

offered up its gritty coconut crunch. One-half cup of coconut in the filling was good; any more and it overran the smoothness of the filling.

Next we tasted one filling thickened with cornstarch and another with flour. The cornstarch, as we expected, made a filling with a lighter, more natural feel; the flour made a heavy and starchy goo. One-quarter cup of cornstarch was just the right amount to allow the filling to set up into a firm texture. When chilled, the pie sliced neatly and cleanly. The filling had just enough resistance to keep it from slipping and sliding onto the plate.

## COCONUT CREAM PIE Serves 8 to 10

When toasting the coconut, keep a close eye on it because it burns quite easily.

### coconut–graham cracker crust

|   |   |
|---|---|
| 5 | tablespoons unsweetened shredded coconut |
| 10 | graham crackers (5 ounces, or 1 package), broken into rough pieces |
| 2 | tablespoons sugar |
| 5 | tablespoons unsalted butter, melted |

### coconut cream filling

|   |   |
|---|---|
| 1 | can (14 ounces) coconut milk, well stirred |
| 1 | cup whole milk |
| ½ | cup (1¼ ounces) unsweetened shredded coconut |
| ⅔ | cup (4¾ ounces) sugar |
| ¼ | teaspoon salt |
| 5 | large egg yolks |
| ¼ | cup (1 ounce) cornstarch |
| 1½ | teaspoons vanilla extract |
| 2 | tablespoons unsalted butter, cut into 4 pieces |

### whipped cream topping

|   |   |
|---|---|
| 1½ | cups heavy cream, chilled |
| 1½ | tablespoons sugar |
| 1½ | teaspoons dark rum, optional |
| ½ | teaspoon vanilla extract |

**1.** FOR THE CRUST: Adjust an oven rack to the middle position and heat the oven to 325 degrees. Spread the 5 tablespoons coconut in a 9-inch Pyrex glass pie plate and toast in the oven until golden brown, about 9 minutes, stirring 2 or 3 times. When cool enough to handle, reserve 1 tablespoon for garnishing the finished pie.

**2.** Pulse the graham crackers and the remaining 4 tablespoons toasted coconut in a food processor until the crackers are broken down into coarse crumbs, about ten 1-second pulses. Process the mixture until evenly fine crumbs form, about 12 seconds. Transfer the crumbs to a medium bowl and stir in the sugar to combine; add the melted butter and toss with a fork until the crumbs are evenly moistened. Wipe out the now-empty pie plate and empty the crumb mixture into it. Using the bottom of a ramekin or measuring cup, press the crumbs evenly into the bottom and up the sides. Bake the crust until deep golden brown and fragrant,

**TECHNIQUE:**
**Whipping Cream to Soft and Stiff Peaks**

**SOFT PEAKS**
Cream whipped to soft peaks droops slightly from the ends of the beaters or whisk.

**STIFF PEAKS**
Cream whipped to stiff peaks clings tightly to the ends of the beaters or whisk and holds its shape.

about 22 minutes. Cool the crust on a wire rack while making the filling.

**3.** FOR THE FILLING: Bring the coconut milk, milk, shredded coconut, ⅓ cup sugar, and salt to a simmer in a medium saucepan over medium-high heat, stirring occasionally with a wooden spoon to dissolve the sugar. When the mixture reaches a simmer, whisk the egg yolks in a medium bowl to break them up, then whisk in the remaining ⅓ cup sugar and cornstarch until well-combined and no lumps remain. Gradually whisk the simmering liquid into the yolk mixture to temper it, then return the mixture to the saucepan, scraping the bowl with a rubber spatula. Bring the mixture to a simmer over medium heat, whisking constantly, until 3 or 4 bubbles burst on the surface and the mixture is thickened, about 30 seconds. Off heat, whisk in the vanilla and butter. Pour the filling into the cooled crust, press a sheet of plastic wrap directly on the surface of the filling, and refrigerate until the filling is cold and firm, at least 3 hours.

**4.** FOR THE TOPPING: Just before serving, whip the cream, sugar, rum, and vanilla in a chilled bowl with chilled beaters on low speed until small bubbles form, about 30 seconds. Increase the speed to medium and continue beating until beaters leave a trail, about 30 seconds longer. Increase the speed to high and beat until the cream is nearly doubled in volume and forms soft peaks, 30 to 60 seconds longer.

**5.** TO SERVE: Spread or pipe the whipped cream over the chilled pie filling. Sprinkle the reserved 1 tablespoon toasted coconut over the cream. Cut the pie into wedges and serve.

## TASTING LAB: Graham Cracker Crusts

SAVING TIME IS ALWAYS A GOOD IDEA—JUST AS LONG AS you're not sacrificing quality. With this in mind, we thought we'd see if store-bought graham cracker pie crusts were worth their weight in pie tins. All you have to do is fill, chill, then serve. We sampled three such crusts (Nabisco Honey Maid Graham Pie Crust, Keebler Graham Cracker Ready Crust, and our local supermarket brand) and unanimously rejected all of them. Tasters described them as pale in color, with a "chalky," "sandy" texture, and "bland," "artificial" flavor. This could be attributed to the fact that all are made with vegetable shortening (already present in the graham cracker itself, but in much less quantity).

After this test, it was obvious to us that adding real butter to ground graham crackers was the best way to get a good-flavored crust and was well worth the few extra minutes. But are all graham crackers the same?

After experimenting with the three leading brands, we discovered subtle but distinct differences between them and found that these differences carried over into crumb crusts made with each kind of cracker. Our favorite was Nabisco Original Graham Crackers. Tasters liked the hardy molasses flavor in these crackers. The two other brands tested (Nabisco Honey Maid and Keebler Graham Crackers) both use honey and yielded crusts that were on the sweet side. We did find that packaged graham cracker crumbs are an acceptable substitute to making your own (they don't have the off flavors we found in premade crusts), but we could not find them made with Nabisco Original's.

**BEST GRAHAM CRACKERS**

Nabisco Original Graham Crackers have a hardy molasses flavor and make the best-tasting pie crust. Other graham crackers can be used, but don't bother with store-bought crusts—they are made with shortening rather than butter and taste terrible.

Once the chicken breasts have been roasted, it takes just five minutes to make a sauce in the empty skillet.

# CHICKEN
## in a skillet

CHAPTER 11

IN THIS CHAPTER

**THE RECIPES**

Pan-Roasted Chicken Breasts
   with Sage-Vermouth Sauce
Pan-Roasted Chicken Breasts
   with Garlic-Sherry Sauce
Pan-Roasted Chicken Breasts
   with Sweet-Tart Red Wine
   Sauce
Pan-Roasted Chicken Breasts
   with Onion and Ale Sauce

Almond-Crusted Chicken
   Cutlets with Wilted
   Spinach—Orange Salad
Macadamia Nut—Crusted
   Chicken Breasts with Wilted
   Spinach—Pineapple Salad

**EQUIPMENT CORNER**

Traditional Skillets

**SCIENCE DESK**

When Is the Pan Hot Enough?

A skillet can turn out hundreds of chicken dinners. For most Americans, chicken breasts are the holy grail of weeknight cooking. (We think thighs are more flavorful, but that's another story.) We like to cook split breasts (with the bones and skin still attached) as well as boneless, skinless cutlets. Adding a quick pan sauce enhances the split breasts, and a coating turns cutlets into something special.

Although these chicken dinners are quick to prepare, they can go terribly wrong. Part of the problem is the chicken itself—the breast meat has very little fat and will become dry and chalky if overcooked. The other major source of trouble is improper cooking methods. If you try to brown skin-on chicken breasts in a nonstick skillet, they won't produce the lovely browned bits that later must flavor the sauce. Likewise, if you use bad technique, it's easy to turn out breaded chicken cutlets that are greasy, soggy, and/or poorly browned.

Because Americans eat so much chicken, we decided to tackle these issues with some creativity. The inspired recipes that follow are foolproof and intriguing—a combination that is sure to please, night after night after night.

# PAN-ROASTED CHICKEN BREASTS

WHAT WE WANTED: **Crisp skin, moist meat, and a quick pan sauce.**

Bone-in, skin-on chicken breasts look primitive compared with their boneless, skinless, trimmed, and filleted brethren, and the best way to cook them is primitive as well—over a live fire on a hot grill. But during the colder months of the year, cooking them becomes a challenge. Oven-roasting fails to impress us because the delicate white meat cooks faster than the skin can crisp. This cut of chicken is also difficult to sauté or cook through on the stovetop because it has great girth on one end and is thin and tapered on the other. If overcooked, it becomes dry and takes on the texture of overchewed bubble gum. And last, this piece of chicken has a mild—some might say bland— flavor that could certainly use a boost.

Our immediate thought was to try pan-roasting, a restaurant technique in which food is browned in a skillet on the stovetop and then placed, skillet and all, in a hot oven to finish cooking. We often employ this technique to cook a whole cut-up chicken and wondered if pan-roasting could be adapted to breasts only, where the meat is thicker and more prone to drying out than in the legs and thighs. The goal was to produce moist, tender, and crisp-skinned, bone-in chicken breasts.

The first problem we encountered was the packaging and quality of chicken breasts in the supermarket. Curiously, bone-in, skin-on split chicken breasts are often sold three to a package. (This makes no sense from either an anatomical or culinary perspective.) More problematic are the facts that split chicken breasts are often covered only by shreds of skin and that large portions of the meat near the breastbone are often missing. An additional reason not to buy split chicken breasts is that the pieces within one package can differ greatly in size (we found 9-ounce and 13-ounce pieces in one pack). Obviously, smaller pieces cook more quickly, so when cooking pieces of divergent sizes, we were forced to closely monitor them and pull the smaller breasts out earlier. Not ideal. Consequently, we found we prefer to purchase whole chicken breasts and split them ourselves so that we'd have more control over their size, quantity, and condition.

With these matters resolved, we tried brining the chicken—soaking it in a saltwater solution—before cooking it. It was no surprise that this chicken was superior—more moist and better seasoned than unbrined chicken. Brining also mitigated the dryness and blandness typical of chicken breasts. The sugar that the test kitchen typically likes in brines was omitted because it caused scorching in the skillet. We also found it necessary to rinse the brined chicken before cooking; otherwise the skin was unpalatably salty.

When it came to browning, we heated a mere teaspoon of vegetable oil in the skillet until it was smoking and then browned both sides of the chicken before transferring the skillet to the oven. We tried oven temperatures from 375 degrees up to 500. Five hundred caused profuse smoking and sometimes singed drippings. Temperatures on the lower end meant protracted cooking times. At 450, however, the skin was handsomely brown and crackling crisp.

The bonus of pan-roasting is that the skillet is left with caramelized drippings, or fond. To let the fond go to waste would be criminal; it is ideal for making a rich, flavorful pan sauce to accompany the chicken. Shallots, wine, chicken broth, herbs, and butter, or a variation on this combination, created pan sauces that added flavor interest and made these crisp-skinned, pan-roasted chicken breasts as good as, if not better than, their grilled incarnations.

WHAT WE LEARNED: **Buy whole breasts and split them yourself to control their size, brine the breasts for maximum moistness, and then sear on the stovetop before letting them cook through in a 450-degree oven.**

## PAN-ROASTED CHICKEN BREASTS WITH SAGE-VERMOUTH SAUCE Serves 4

We prefer to split whole chicken breasts ourselves because store-bought split chicken breasts are often sloppily butchered. However, if you prefer to purchase split chicken breasts, try to choose 10- to 12-ounce pieces with skin intact. If split breasts are of different sizes, check the smaller ones a few minutes early to see if they are cooking more quickly, and remove them from the skillet if they are done ahead.

### chicken

- 1 cup kosher salt (or ½ cup table salt)
- 2 whole bone-in, skin-on chicken breasts, about 1½ pounds each, split in half along breast bone and trimmed of rib sections
  Ground black pepper
- 1 teaspoon vegetable oil

### sage-vermouth sauce

- 1 large shallot, minced (about 4 tablespoons)
- ¾ cup low-sodium chicken broth
- ½ cup dry vermouth
- 4 medium fresh sage leaves, each leaf torn in half
- 3 tablespoons unsalted butter, cut into 3 pieces
  Salt and ground black pepper

**1.** FOR THE CHICKEN: Dissolve the salt in 2 quarts cold water in a large container or bowl; submerge the chicken in the brine and refrigerate until fully seasoned, about 30 minutes. Rinse the chicken pieces under running water and pat dry with paper towels. Season the chicken with pepper.

**2.** Adjust an oven rack to the lowest position and heat the oven to 450 degrees.

**3.** Heat the oil in a heavy-bottomed 12-inch ovenproof skillet over medium-high heat until beginning to smoke; swirl the skillet to coat with the oil. Brown the chicken skin-side down until deep golden, about 5 minutes; turn the chicken and brown until golden on the second side, about 3 minutes longer. Turn the chicken skin-side down and place the skillet in the oven. Roast until the juices run clear when the chicken is cut with a paring knife, or the thickest part of the breast registers 160 degrees on an instant-read thermometer, 15 to 18 minutes. Transfer the chicken to a platter, and let it rest while making the sauce. (If you're not making the sauce, let the chicken rest 5 minutes before serving.)

**4.** FOR THE SAUCE: Using a potholder to protect your hands from the hot skillet handle, pour off most of the fat from the skillet; add the shallot, then set the skillet over medium-high heat and cook, stirring frequently, until the shallot is softened, about 1½ minutes. Add the chicken broth, vermouth, and sage; increase the heat to high and simmer rapidly, scraping the skillet bottom with a wooden spoon to loosen the browned bits, until slightly thickened and reduced to about ¾ cup, about 5 minutes. Pour the accumulated chicken juices into the skillet, reduce the heat to medium, and whisk in the butter 1 piece at a time; season to taste with salt and pepper and discard the sage. Spoon the sauce around the chicken breasts and serve immediately.

### VARIATIONS

### PAN-ROASTED CHICKEN BREASTS WITH GARLIC-SHERRY SAUCE

Peel 7 medium cloves garlic and cut crosswise into very thin slices (you should have about 3 tablespoons). Follow the recipe for Pan-Roasted Chicken Breasts with Sage-Vermouth Sauce, substituting the sliced garlic for the shallots and cooking the garlic until light brown, about 1½ minutes; also, substitute dry sherry for the vermouth and 2 sprigs fresh thyme for the sage. Add ½ teaspoon lemon juice along with the salt and pepper.

### PAN-ROASTED CHICKEN BREASTS WITH SWEET-TART RED WINE SAUCE

This sauce is a variation on the Italian sweet-sour flavor combination called *agrodolce*.

Follow the recipe for Pan-Roasted Chicken Breasts with Sage-Vermouth Sauce, substituting ¼ cup each red wine and red wine vinegar for the vermouth and 1 bay leaf for the sage leaves. Add 1 tablespoon sugar and ¼ teaspoon ground black pepper to the skillet with chicken broth.

### PAN-ROASTED CHICKEN BREASTS WITH ONION AND ALE SAUCE

Brown ale gives this sauce a nutty, toasty, bittersweet flavor. Newcastle Brown Ale and Samuel Smith Nut Brown Ale are good choices.

Follow the recipe for Pan-Roasted Chicken Breasts with Sage-Vermouth Sauce, substituting ½ medium onion, sliced very thin, for the shallot; cook the onion until softened, about 3 minutes. Also, substitute brown ale for the vermouth and 1 sprig fresh thyme for the sage. Add 1 bay leaf and 1 teaspoon brown sugar along with the chicken broth. Add ½ teaspoon cider vinegar along with the salt and pepper.

## SCIENCE DESK:
### When Is the Pan Hot Enough?

COOKS COMMONLY USE A DROP OF WATER TO HELP decide if the pan is warm enough to begin searing; when the drop begins to dance around the pan, the meat is added. But how often have you added the meat to the pan only to discover that it won't brown? Simple math tells us why. We all know that water boils at 212 degrees; what we may not know is that meat begins to brown well at above 310 degrees—that's a difference of about 100 degrees between the boiling point and the browning point.

Oil begins to break down when exposed to high heat and will release an acrid smoke. Olive oil smokes at about 375 degrees, peanut oil at about 440 degrees. If a drop of oil placed in the bottom of your pan is beginning to smoke, the temperature of the pan is plenty hot enough for good browning. We generally add food to the pan just as oil begins to smoke.

## EQUIPMENT CORNER:
### Traditional Skillets

HAVE YOU SHOPPED FOR A SKILLET RECENTLY? THE choices in material, weight, brand, and price—from $10 to $140—are dizzying. Preliminary tests on a lightweight discount store special selling for $10 confirmed our suspicions that cheap was not the way to go. But how much do you need to spend on this vital piece of kitchen equipment? To find out what more money buys, we zeroed in on a group of eight pans from well-known manufacturers, ranging in price from $60 to more than twice that, and sautéed our way to some pretty surprising conclusions.

All of the pans tested had flared sides, a design that makes it easier to flip foods in the pan (accomplished by jerking the pan sharply on the burner). Oddly, this design feature has created some confusion when it comes to nomenclature. Different manufacturers have different names for their flare-sided pans, including sauté pan, skillet, frypan, chef's pan, and omelet pan. In the test kitchen, we refer to flare-sided pans as skillets and to pans with straight sides (and often lids as well) as sauté pans. All of the pans tested also fall into a category we refer to as traditional—that is, none of the pans were nonstick. Most had uncoated stainless steel cooking surfaces, which we prize for promoting a *fond* (the brown, sticky bits that cling to the interior of the pan when food is sautéed and that help flavor sauces). We also included a Le Creuset model made from enameled cast iron.

The pans tested measured 12 inches in diameter (across the top) or as close to that as we could get from each manufacturer. We like this large size in a skillet because it can accommodate a big steak or all of the pieces cut from a typical 3½-pound chicken. Because the pan walls slope inward, the cooking surface of each pan is considerably smaller than 12 inches. In fact, we found that a loss of even ¼ inch of cooking space could determine whether all of the chicken pieces fit without touching and therefore how well they would brown. (If a pan is too crowded, the food tends to steam rather than brown.) For instance, the All-Clad, with its 9¼-inch cooking surface, accommodated the chicken pieces without incident, whereas the 9-inch cooking surface of the Viking caused the pieces to touch.

Skillet construction also varies, and our group included the three most popular styles: clad, disk bottom, and cast. The All-Clad, Viking, Calphalon, Cuisinart, and KitchenAid units are clad, which means that the whole pan body, from the bottom up through the walls, is made from layers of the same metal that have been bonded under intense pressure and heat. These layers often form a sandwich. The "filling" is made of aluminum, which has the fourth highest thermal conductivity of all metals, behind silver, copper, and gold, and each slice of "bread" is made of stainless steel, which is attractive, durable, and nonreactive with acidic foods but is also a lousy heat conductor on its own.

In the disk-bottom construction style, only the pan bottom is layered and the walls are thus thinner than the bottom. In our group, the Farberware has an aluminum sandwich base and the Emerilware has disks of both aluminum and copper in its base.

Casting is the third construction style, represented here by Le Creuset, in which molten iron is molded to form the pan, body and handle alike. Cast iron pans are known to be heavy, to heat up slowly, and to retain their heat well. The French Le Creuset pans are also enameled, which makes them nonreactive inside and out.

Did we uncover any significant differences in performance based on these three construction styles? Although some manufacturers tout the benefits of cladding, our kitchen testing did not support this. The two skillets with disk bottoms, the Farberware and the Emerilware, did heat up a little faster than the rest of the field, but it was easy to accommodate this difference by adjusting the stovetop burner.

To get a more precise answer to our question, we set up an experiment. Around the perimeter of pans of each construction type (and in the lightweight $10 pan mentioned earlier), we placed rings of solder with a melting point of 361 degrees and heated them from dead center. Over the course of several trials, we averaged the time it took the pans to reach 361 degrees all around (that is, the time it took all of the solder beads to melt). The difference between the clad and disk-bottomed pans was less than 15 percent (they all reached 361 degrees in four to five minutes), with the disk-bottomed pans heating up a little faster than the clad pans. This difference was of little significance.

We checked our observations with an industry expert, who, after expressing the desire to remain anonymous, admitted to reaching the same conclusion about skillets after trying many different models over the years. Because you cook on the bottom of a skillet (not the sides), cladding is not that important. It may be more important in saucepans and Dutch ovens, in which it's common practice to cook liquids, which are of course in contact with the sides of the pan.

The weight of the pans turned out to be more important than construction, especially in our solder tests. The lightweight (1 pound, 1 ounce) aluminum budget pan was the quickest to reach 361 degrees, at an average of 2.8 minutes, while the heavy 6.5-pound Le Creuset was the slowest, at an average of 10.1 minutes. The lightweight pan performed poorly in kitchen tests, while Le Creuset did well. Still, cast iron does have its disadvantages. The heavy Le Creuset pan is difficult to lift on and off the burner and to handle while cleaning. If your strength is limited, these factors can mean a lot. In addition, the pan's iron handle gets just as hot as the rest of the pan, so it's necessary to use a potholder both during and just after use.

We concluded that a range of 3 to 4 pounds is ideal in a 12-inch skillet. The medium-weight pans (especially those from All-Clad, Viking, and Calphalon) brown foods beautifully, and most testers handled them comfortably. These pans have enough heft for heat retention and structural integrity but not so much that they are difficult to lift or manipulate.

Which skillet should you buy? For its combination of excellent performance, optimum weight and balance, and overall ease of use, the All-Clad was our favorite. But the Calphalon and Farberware nearly matched the All-Clad and did so for less than half the price, making these pans best buys.

# Rating Traditional Skillets

WE TESTED EIGHT TRADITIONAL SKILLETS WITH A 12-INCH DIAMETER (OR AS CLOSE TO IT AS WE COULD FIND IN THAT manufacturer's line) in six applications (cooking crêpes, searing steaks, simmering a pan sauce, browning stew meat, pan-roasting chicken, and sautéing onions). The skillets are listed in order of preference based on their performance in these tests as well as design factors. See www.americastestkitchen.com for up-to-date prices and mail-order sources for top-rated products.

---

### HIGHLY RECOMMENDED
**All-Clad Stainless 12-Inch Fry Pan $125.00**

From crêpes to steak to chicken, this pan browned foods perfectly. Sometimes, however, more fond stuck to the pan than was left on the food. Spacious and easy to handle. A star performer.

---

### HIGHLY RECOMMENDED
**Viking 7-Ply 11-Inch Frying Pan $140.00**

Eight pieces of chicken were a trifle crowded, but that was the only misstep in an otherwise excellent performance. Good news for the most expensive pan in the group.

---

### BEST BUY
**Calphalon Tri-Ply Stainless 12-Inch Omelette Pan $63.95**

Really shines when it heats up for heavy searing and browning. Onions and crêpes, both cooked at moderate heat, were a tad pale but still acceptable. Easy to lift and maneuver. A fine pan at an attractive price.

---

### BEST BUY
**Farberware Millennium 18/10 Stainless Steel 12-Inch Covered Skillet $69.99**

Easy to manipulate and wide open in terms of space, but this pan sautés a bit too quickly, which can lead to very dark fond when browning meat. Watch it carefully and adjust the heat if necessary.

---

### RECOMMENDED WITH RESERVATIONS
**Emerilware Stainless 12-Inch Frypan $59.99**

Does well in higher-heat applications, such as searing steak and browning chicken, but sauté speed is fast, so keep an eye on the heat. Runs a little hot and is a bit heavy to lift, but by no means a bad pan.

---

### RECOMMENDED WITH RESERVATIONS
**Cuisinart MultiClad Stainless 12.5-Inch Skillet $99.99**

A respectable performer with ample space for large batches, but required some attention to control the sauté speed. Plenty of space and a helper handle, but you have to watch the heat and take care with the handle, which ran hot in some tests.

---

### RECOMMENDED WITH RESERVATIONS
**KitchenAid Hi-Density Hard Anodized 12-Inch Skillet $119.00**

Despite reliable performance, this pan was downgraded because the chicken was a bit crowded, the handle heated up, and the pan felt bulky and poorly balanced in the hands of some testers.

---

### RECOMMENDED WITH RESERVATIONS
**Le Creuset 12-Inch Iron Handle Skillet $85.50**

Spacious and terrific at searing meat but also heavy, unwieldy, and hot-handled. Requires extra preheating time, and the pan's dark surface can make it difficult to judge fond development. Retains heat like a pro, but have a potholder handy and be prepared for some heavy lifting.

# NUT-CRUSTED CHICKEN CUTLETS

**WHAT WE WANTED:** To create a new kind of breaded chicken cutlet, with nuts taking the place of bread crumbs. We also wanted to add a salad to make the dish a complete meal.

Sautéed chicken cutlets are basic fare in most every cook's repertoire. In many homes, they appear on the dinner table at least once a week. Although fast to prepare, sautéed cutlets can become a bit boring. By replacing bread crumbs with nuts, a simple breaded chicken cutlet can be quickly transformed. Yet, for the transformation to be a success, we had to make a few adjustments to our technique.

Using boneless skinless chicken breasts, we began by adapting our standard breading technique: dredge the chicken in flour, dip it in an egg wash, then coat with bread crumbs. We first tried replacing the bread crumbs with sliced almonds, but the thin almond slices refused to stick to the chicken. We had more success when the almonds were processed into fine crumbs in the food processor, but even then the crust tasted dense, oily, and sodden after it was cooked. In an effort to lighten the crust, we mixed the nuts with some bread crumbs. Testing various ratios of nuts to bread crumbs, we landed on a ratio of 2 parts freshly ground nuts to 1 part crumbs. We also found that the light, crispy Japanese-style bread crumbs called panko worked especially well.

Because the nut/bread crumb mixture was so dense, we wondered if the initial step of flouring the chicken was necessary. In cooking two nut-crusted pieces of chicken, one floured and one flourless, side by side, we found the differences to be minor; in the spirit of streamlining, we decided to omit the flouring step. It is sufficient just to dip the cutlets (already trimmed of excess fat and any tough tendons) in beaten egg and then in the nut-bread crumb mixture.

Cooking the chicken turned out to be fairly straightforward. The keys were to use a skillet large enough to comfortably cook four pieces of chicken and to use plenty of oil. Much like regular breaded chicken, the cutlets need to be pan-fried in a fair amount of oil rather than sautéed in a wisp of oil. We found that four cutlets are best cooked in six tablespoons of vegetable oil in a 12-inch skillet. When pan-frying almost anything, we have found that a nonstick skillet is best because there's no chance that any food or coating will cling to the pan surface. In addition, cleaning a nonstick surface is much easier; pan-frying can really make a mess in a conventional skillet.

As for flavor, we were surprised to find that the nut crust tasted relatively mild. To spruce it up, we tried flavoring the egg wash by introducing ingredients such as Dijon mustard and/or citrus zest; this was both easy and effective.

Noticing how well the nut-crusted chicken tasted with fruit, it was a short jump to pair the chicken with a wilted spinach salad with fruit-based dressings. Holding the chicken warm in a 200-degree oven, we simply wiped the oil out of the pan and returned it to the stovetop to make a warm dressing, which served to lightly wilt baby spinach without it turning wet or slimy. Cooked from start to finish in merely 45 minutes, this exotic-tasting meal is far from your average chicken and salad supper.

**WHAT WE LEARNED:** Ground almonds paired with panko create a rich-tasting crust for chicken that is light and crisp. Pan-fry the chicken for the best results. To make a quick side dish, heat some fruit and dressing in the empty pan and use it to wilt spinach salad.

---

**FOOD FACT:** Panko

Japanese bread crumbs, called panko, have a coarser texture than ordinary breadcrumbs, and they make for a much lighter and crunchier casserole topping and coating for deep-fried foods like tempura. We also like to use panko as a coating for breaded chicken cutlets.

## ALMOND-CRUSTED CHICKEN CUTLETS WITH WILTED SPINACH–ORANGE SALAD

Serves 4

It should take about 10 seconds to process the almonds into fine crumbs—don't overprocess or the nuts will become oily. If you like, serve with couscous.

2   large eggs
1   teaspoon Dijon mustard
1¼  teaspoons grated zest from 1 orange, zested
    orange cut into 4 wedges
    Salt and ground black pepper
1   cup sliced almonds, processed into fine crumbs
    in the food processor
½   cup panko (Japanese-style bread crumbs)
4   boneless, skinless chicken cutlets (5 to 6 ounces
    each), trimmed (see the illustrations on page
    139) and dried thoroughly with paper towels
½   cup vegetable oil
5   ounces baby spinach (about 6 cups)
2   medium oranges, peel and pith removed (see
    the illustrations at right), and then quartered
    through the ends and sliced crosswise into
    ¼-inch-thick pieces
1   small shallot, minced (about 2 tablespoons)

**1.** Lightly beat the eggs, mustard, 1 teaspoon orange zest, ½ teaspoon salt, and ¼ teaspoon pepper together in a shallow dish. Mix the almonds and panko in a separate shallow dish. Working with one piece of chicken at a time, dip the chicken into the egg mixture using tongs, turning to coat well and allowing excess to drip off. Drop the chicken into the nut mixture and press the nuts into the chicken with your fingers. Transfer the breaded chicken to a wire rack set over a baking sheet and repeat with the remaining chicken. Adjust an oven rack to the middle position and heat the oven to 200 degrees.

**2.** Heat 6 tablespoons oil in a heavy-bottomed, 12-inch nonstick skillet over medium-high heat until just smoking.

Place the chicken in the skillet gently and cook until golden brown and crisp on the first side, about 2½ minutes. Using tongs, flip the chicken; reduce the heat to medium and continue to cook until the meat feels firm when pressed gently, the second side is deep golden brown and crisp, and the chicken is no longer pink in the center, about 2 minutes longer. Transfer the chicken to a paper towel–lined plate and place the plate in the oven. Discard the oil in the skillet and, using tongs and paper towels, wipe the skillet clean.

### TECHNIQUE:
#### Removing the Peel and Pith from Oranges

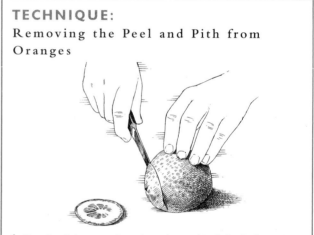

1. Start by slicing a small section, about ½ inch thick, from the top and bottom ends of the orange.

2. Use a very sharp paring knife to slice off the rind, including all of the bitter white pith. Slide the knife edges from the top to the bottom of the orange, following the outline of the fruit as closely as possible to minimize waste.

**3.** Place the spinach in a large bowl. Heat 1 tablespoon oil in the cleaned skillet over high heat until just smoking. Add the orange slices and cook until lightly browned around the edges, 1½ to 2 minutes. Remove the pan from the heat and add remaining 1 tablespoon oil, shallot, remaining ¼ teaspoon zest, ¼ teaspoon salt, and ⅛ teaspoon pepper and allow residual heat to soften the shallot, 30 seconds. Pour the warm dressing with the oranges over the spinach and toss gently to wilt. Remove the chicken from the oven and serve it immediately with the salad and orange wedges.

VARIATION

## MACADAMIA NUT–CRUSTED CHICKEN BREASTS WITH WILTED SPINACH–PINEAPPLE SALAD

Buy peeled and cored pineapple at the supermarket to save time. Round out the meal with white rice.

Follow the recipe for Almond-Crusted Chicken Breasts with Wilted Spinach-Orange Salad, omitting the mustard. Substitute lime zest and lime wedges for the orange zest and orange wedges and macadamia nuts for the almonds. Substitute 2 cups fresh pineapple cut into ¾-inch dice for the orange slices in step 3, sautéing the pineapple for 2 minutes.

---

**TECHNIQUE:**
Trimming Chicken Cutlets

1. Place each cutlet tenderloin-side down and smooth the top with your fingers. Any fat will slide to the periphery, where it can be trimmed with a knife.

2. To remove the tough, white tendon, turn the cutlet tenderloin-side up and peel back the thick half of the tenderloin so it lies top-down on the work surface. Use the point of a paring knife to cut around the top of the tendon to expose it, then scrape the tendon free with a knife.

---

**TECHNIQUE:** Freezing Small Portions

1. Place two portions of food (such as two chicken cutlets) in different locations inside a large zipper-lock freezer bag. Flatten the bag, forcing the air out in the process, so that the portions do not touch.

2. Fold the bag over in the center and freeze. The bag divides the two portions so they will freeze separately. Best of all, you have the option of using one or both frozen portions.

The back kitchen is filled with food being prepared for use on the set.

# CHICKEN
**CHAPTER 12**

*in a pot*

**IN THIS CHAPTER**

**THE RECIPES**
Chicken with 40 Cloves of
Garlic

Chicken Provençal
Chicken Provençal with Saffron,
Orange, and Basil

**EQUIPMENT CORNER**
Kitchen Shears

**TASTING LAB**
Garlic
Dry Vermouth

Herbert Hoover may have promised Americans a chicken in every pot, but no one said that chicken couldn't be French. In fact, French country cooking has a way with chicken in a pot, whether it's the famous chicken with 40 cloves of garlic or the lesser-known chicken Provençal with tomatoes and olives. When made correctly, these dishes take chicken to new heights.

But these dishes can also go astray. The 40 cloves of garlic may be raw tasting and harsh, or the sauce may be thin and vapid. Chicken Provençal can be greasy or overwhelmed by a thick, sweet tomato sauce. The goal for the test kitchen was simple: Rework these French classics so that all Americans would welcome such chickens into their pots.

# CHICKEN WITH 40 CLOVES OF GARLIC

WHAT WE WANTED: Well-browned, crisp-skinned chicken paired with sweet, nutty garlic and a savory sauce.

Poulet à quarante gousses d'ail, or chicken with 40 cloves of garlic, is a classic Provençal dish that entered into the American culinary consciousness several decades ago, when our interest in French gastronomy was sparked. But since its introduction, chicken with 40 cloves of garlic has failed to make it onto many dinner tables or into many cooks' repertoires . . . and not without reason.

Recipes for chicken with 40 cloves of garlic involve a whole or cut-up chicken. Sometimes the chicken is browned, sometimes not. It is put into a pot along with raw garlic cloves (most often unpeeled), some liquid (usually wine and/or chicken broth), sometimes onions and other aromatic vegetables and herbs, and then the lot is cooked, covered, for an hour or more. The garlic becomes soft and spreadable, but its flavor is spiritless, not like that of sweet, sticky roasted garlic. With such prolonged cooking, the chicken becomes tender, but the breast meat takes on a dry chalky quality, and the flavor of the chicken in general is vapid, as if it had been washed out into the liquid. In addition, as cannot be helped in moist heat cookery, the chicken skin is soggy, flabby, and wholly unappealing, even if the chicken had first been browned.

A diagnostic test of several recipes found all tasters in agreement. We all sought richer, more concentrated flavors like those imparted by roasting, not braising. We wanted the chicken browned, full-flavored, and crisp-skinned, the garlic browned, sweet, and nutty. And we wanted a savory sauce to unite the elements.

Our first decision was to use a cut-up chicken rather than a whole bird because it cooks faster and more evenly. We brined the chicken, browned it in a large skillet, tossed in the unpeeled garlic cloves from three medium heads (42

cloves, so pretty true to the name), and slipped the skillet into a hot oven. About 12 minutes later, the chicken was fully cooked; we removed the chicken pieces, leaving the garlic in the skillet, and made a pan sauce with the drippings, wine, chicken broth, and butter. The gravest offense of this attempt came from the garlic: The cloves were far from done. Although they were browned, they were neither creamy nor spreadable, and they had a raw, fiery flavor. The second problem was that the chicken, though flavorful and crisp-skinned, seemed divorced from the other elements. Third, the sauce lacked depth and tasted of neither the chicken nor the garlic. Despite its demerits, this technique showed enough promise that we were compelled to pursue it.

We grappled with the garlic first. We knew that to soften and gain color the cloves would have to roast in dry heat, but they would require considerably more time to roast than was built into the pan-roasting technique. Hence, they would need to be at least partially roasted by the time they joined the chicken. Some tests later, we arrived at roasting the garlic cloves, tossed with a little olive oil, salt, and pepper, in a small baking dish for 40 minutes in a 400-degree oven. For the first 30 minutes, they cooked under foil to speed things along. For the final 10 minutes, they went uncovered to finish browning. At this point, the garlic cloves were soft, sweet, and mellow but could still withstand some additional cooking with the chicken and sauce. Because the garlic could be roasted while the chicken was being brined and browned, this step did not add time to the recipe.

We then focused on refining the cooking technique. In a braise, the chicken cooks half-submerged in simmering liquid, and an exchange of flavors thereby occurs to the benefit of both the chicken and the liquid that becomes the sauce. This made us think to modify the pan-roasting technique. After we browned the chicken, we poured off the rendered fat, added chicken broth and dry vermouth (we came to use vermouth because it is herbaceous, slightly

sweet, and more flavorful than most white wines of the same price), added the roasted garlic cloves, returned the chicken skin-side up, and then put the skillet into the 400-degree oven from which the garlic had emerged. Things were slightly improved with this pan-roasting/braising technique. The sauce had better flavor, although it was still mousy, especially in texture, and the chicken seemed to be more a part of the dish. The skin, however, had turned soggy from the moisture.

To counter the effects of the moisture, we tried increasing the oven temperature to 450 degrees. This produced acceptably crisp skin. The ultimate solution, however, was a quick blast of broiler heat, which crisped the skin very nicely in less than five minutes. Because cooks with drawer-type gas broilers might find this step inconvenient, if not impossible, we made it optional. We were nonetheless pleased with the results of this hybrid pan-roasting/braising technique.

Now a different issue came into play. The brined chicken, cooked in the liquid that eventually becomes the sauce, seemed to exude juices that resulted in an overseasoned sauce, even for those tasters who love salt. We pulled back on the salt in the brine until we were using only ¼ cup of table salt per 2 quarts of water. Unsure that this small amount was of any benefit to the dish as a whole, we compared it with a batch made with unbrined chicken. Even this weak brine improved the flavor and juiciness of the cooked chicken.

Finally, we worked on the flavor of the sauce. Inspired by those recipes that included onions, we roasted some shallots—milder in flavor than onions—with the garlic cloves to see if they would affect the flavor of the sauce. Indeed they did. The sauce tasted fuller and rounder. Some tasters even found the roasted shallots to be good eating. Herbs—thyme, rosemary, and bay—all had pleasing effects on the flavor of the sauce, offering depth and complexity.

We had seen in another recipe the recommendation of mashing a few of the garlic cloves and adding them back to the sauce. Using a mesh sieve and rubber spatula, we made a paste of a dozen or so peeled garlic cloves and whisked it into the sauce (peeling the cloves and then mashing them on a cutting board with the back of a fork is another effective method). What an extraordinarily good idea. The garlic paste endowed the sauce with the velvety texture of a well-made gravy, and the sauce was now richly flavored with garlic as well as chicken and wine. Last, a couple tablespoons of butter to enrich the sauce met with applause. *Enfin, un nouveau poulet à quarante gousses d'ail est arrivé.*

---

**WHAT WE LEARNED :** To give this dish the complete overhaul it needs, brown a cut-up chicken in a skillet, build a sauce in the pan with roasted garlic and shallots, and then roast the chicken (now back in the pan) in the oven. Then give the chicken a final run under the broiler to ensure crisp skin. Finally, puree some of the garlic to thicken and flavor the sauce.

## CHICKEN WITH 40 CLOVES OF GARLIC

**Serves 3 to 4**

Try not to purchase heads of garlic that contain enormous cloves; if unavoidable, increase the foil-covered baking time to 40 to 45 minutes so that the largest cloves soften fully. A large Dutch oven can be used in place of a skillet, if you prefer. Broiling the chicken for a few minutes at the end of cooking crisps the skin, but this step is optional. Serve the dish with slices of crusty baguette; you can dip them into the sauce or spread them with the roasted garlic cloves.

    Salt
1   chicken (3½ to 4 pounds), cut into 8 pieces (4 breast pieces, 2 thighs, 2 drumsticks) and trimmed of excess fat
    Ground black pepper
3   medium heads garlic (about 8 ounces), outer papery skins removed, cloves separated and unpeeled
2   medium shallots, peeled and quartered pole to pole
1   tablespoon olive oil
2   sprigs fresh thyme
1   sprig fresh rosemary
1   bay leaf
¾   cup dry vermouth or dry white wine
¾   cup low-sodium chicken broth
2   tablespoons unsalted butter

**1.** Adjust an oven rack to the middle position and heat the oven to 400 degrees. Dissolve ¼ cup salt in 2 quarts cold tap water in a large container; submerge the chicken pieces in the brine and refrigerate until fully seasoned, about 30 minutes. Rinse the chicken pieces under running water and thoroughly pat dry with paper towels. Season both sides of the chicken pieces with pepper.

**2.** Meanwhile, toss the garlic and shallots with 2 teaspoons olive oil and salt and pepper to taste in a 9-inch pie plate; cover tightly with foil and roast until softened and beginning to brown, about 30 minutes, shaking the pan once to toss the contents after 15 minutes (the foil can be left on during tossing). Uncover, stir, and continue to roast, uncovered, until browned and fully tender, 10 minutes longer, stirring once or twice. Remove from the oven and increase the oven temperature to 450 degrees.

---

### GETTING IT RIGHT: Developing the Flavor of the Garlic

Remove the outer papery skins from three heads of garlic and separate but do not peel the individual cloves (far left). Lightly oil the cloves and roast them in a pie plate covered with foil; remove the foil (second from left) and continue to roast until the cloves are fully tender. Add the roasted cloves to the braising liquid in the skillet (center), return the chicken to the pan, and place the skillet in the oven. When the chicken is done, use a rubber spatula to push a dozen garlic cloves through a mesh sieve to remove the skins and obtain a smooth paste (second from right). Whisk the garlic paste into the sauce just before serving (right).

**3.** Using kitchen twine, tie together the thyme, rosemary, and bay; set aside. Heat remaining 1 teaspoon oil in a 12-inch heavy-bottomed ovenproof skillet over medium-high heat until beginning to smoke; swirl to coat the pan with oil. Brown the chicken pieces skin-side down until deep

## TECHNIQUE: Cutting Up a Chicken

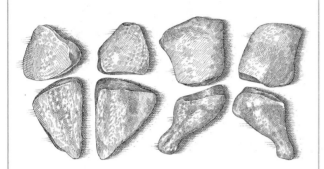

For chicken with 40 cloves of garlic, cut a whole chicken into two drumsticks, two thighs, and four breast pieces. Discard the wings and back or save them for making stock.

## TECHNIQUE: An Extra-Large Trivet

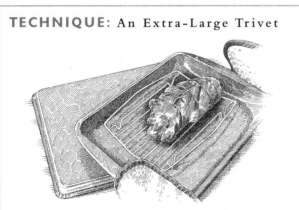

There never seem to be enough spots in the kitchen to place a hot pan or pot. To solve this problem, we place an overturned rimmed baking sheet on the counter and use it as a trivet on which to rest a hot roasting pan, Dutch oven, or skillet.

golden, about 5 minutes; using tongs, turn the chicken pieces and brown until golden on second side, about 4 minutes longer. Transfer the chicken to a large plate and discard the fat; off heat, add the vermouth, chicken broth, and herbs, scraping the bottom of the skillet with a wooden spoon to loosen browned bits. Set the skillet over medium heat, add the garlic/shallot mixture, then return the chicken, skin-side up, to the pan, nestling the pieces on top of and between the garlic cloves.

**4.** Place the skillet in the oven and roast until an instant-read thermometer inserted into the thickest part of the breast registers about 160 degrees, 10 to 12 minutes. If desired, increase the heat to broil and broil to crisp the skin, 3 to 5 minutes. Using potholders or oven mitts, remove the skillet from oven and transfer the chicken to a serving dish. Remove 10 to 12 garlic cloves to a mesh sieve and reserve; using a slotted spoon, scatter the remaining garlic cloves and shallots around the chicken and discard the herbs. With a rubber spatula, push the reserved garlic cloves through a sieve and into a bowl; discard the skins. Add the garlic paste to the skillet. Bring the liquid to a simmer over medium-high heat, whisking occasionally to incorporate the garlic; adjust the seasoning with salt and pepper to taste. Whisk in the butter; pour the sauce into a sauceboat, and serve.

## EQUIPMENT CORNER: Kitchen Shears

A PAIR OF KITCHEN SHEARS IS NOT AN ESSENTIAL KITCHEN implement. But when you need to butterfly or trim chicken, there is no better tool. To test their versatility, we also used kitchen shears to cut lengths of kitchen twine, trim pie dough, and cut out parchment paper rounds. We found two pairs to recommend.

Wüsthof Kitchen Shears ($27.99) made easy, smooth cuts even through small chicken bones and completed all tasks flawlessly. The size and proportion of the shears felt ideal—the blades could open wide for large jobs and to

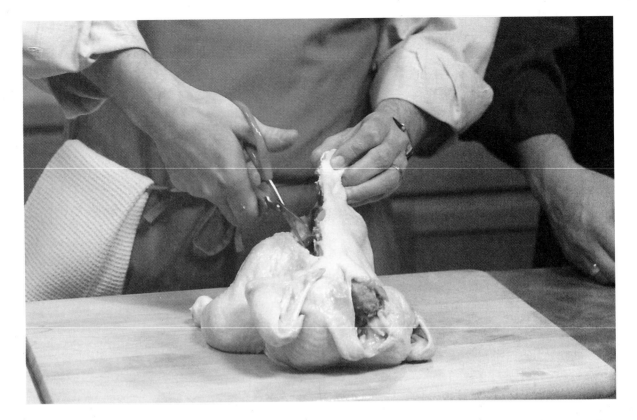

achieve more forceful cutting, but the shears were also suited to smaller, more detailed tasks such as snipping pieces of twine. These shears boasted heft, solid construction, and textured handles that were comfortable, even when wet and greasy. They were also suitable and comfortable for left-handed users.

Messermeister Take Apart Kitchen Shears ($16.99) were also great performers, though the blades didn't have quite the spread of those on the Wüsthof. These shears, too, made clean, easy cuts and accomplished all tasks without hesitation. The Messermeister shears came apart for cleaning, which we found to be neither a benefit nor a disadvantage. The soft, rubber-like handles proved extremely comfortable but were clearly designed for right-handed users.

Three pairs of shears fall into the category of "recommended with reservations." The first pair is Henckels Twin M Kitchen Shears ($39.99). These shears were of nice size and proportion and made smooth, clean, easy cuts. They were also handsome—in fact, too much so. The design of the handle seemed to sacrifice comfort for style. More effort was

needed to butterfly a chicken with the Chicago Cutlery Walnut Signature Kitchen Scissors ($9.95). When making cuts requiring some force, the handles were hard and unforgiving. Joyce Chen Scissors ($18.00) cut through chicken bones with ease but slipped when cutting through skin, and their relatively diminutive size sometimes made the cutting motion feel more like a snipping motion. Given their size and feather weight, these scissors were suitable to more detailed tasks, such as cutting parchment paper rounds.

The two pairs of shears that we cannot recommend are F. Dick Come-Apart Kitchen Scissors ($31.60) and Oxo Good Grips Kitchen Scissors ($11.95). The F. Dick pair failed miserably at butterflying a chicken. The handles were actually painful to use and slippery when greasy and wet. Their ponderous weight was also a disadvantage, particularly for smaller, finer cutting. The Oxo Kitchen Scissors struggled to get through the chicken and were the only pair that had trouble snipping kitchen twine. The spring-loaded design made the scissors feel rather uncontrollable and difficult to use with precision.

# Rating Kitchen Shears

WE TESTED SEVEN PAIRS OF KITCHEN SHEARS IN A VARIETY OF KITCHEN TASKS—EVERYTHING FROM BUTCHERING A chicken to trimming pie dough. The shears are listed in order of preference based on their performance in these tests as well as on design and ease of use. See www.americastestkitchen.com for up-to-date prices and mail-order sources for top-rated products.

**RECOMMENDED**
## Wüsthof Kitchen Shears
**$27.99**
These shears made smooth, easy cuts through bones and performed all tasks flawlessly. Suitable and comfortable for both lefties and righties.

**RECOMMENDED**
## Messermeister Take Apart Kitchen Shears
**$16.99**
These shears cut cleanly in all tests. Righties found the soft rubber-like handles comfortable, but lefties were less enthusiastic. An excellent value.

**RECOMMENDED WITH RESERVATIONS**
## Henckels Twin M Kitchen Shears
**$39.99**
Excellent performance but uncomfortable handles bothered most testers. Sharp edges between the two handles gave pause to some users.

**RECOMMENDED WITH RESERVATIONS**
## Chicago Cutlery Walnut Signature Kitchen Scissors
**$9.95**
Butterflying a chicken required some force, and the handles were hard and unforgiving.

**RECOMMENDED WITH RESERVATIONS**
## Joyce Chen Scissors
**$18.00**
These small scissors are better suited to snipping chives than cutting up a chicken.

**NOT RECOMMENDED**
## F. Dick Come-Apart Kitchen Scissors
**$31.60**
Handles are painful to use and slippery when greasy or wet. Heavier than the rest of the pack and less comfortable to use.

**NOT RECOMMENDED**
## Oxo Kitchen Scissors
**$11.95**
These spring-loaded scissors struggled to snip kitchen twine; forget about cutting through bone.

## TASTING LAB: Garlic

GARLIC FALLS INTO TWO PRIMARY CATEGORIES: HARDNECK and softneck. The garlic that most of us cook with is softneck, so called because its neck is soft and braidable. Softneck garlic contains a circle of plump cloves shrouding a second circle of smaller cloves, all enveloped by many papery layers. Because softneck garlic is heat tolerant and produces and stores well, it has become the favored commercial garlic. Supermarket garlics are almost invariably softneck.

Hardneck, which is the original cultivated garlic variety, is distinguished by its stiff center staff, around which large uniform cloves hang. Hardneck garlic has a relatively sparse parchment wrapper that makes it easier to peel (and damage) than softneck. It is considered superior in flavor—more complex and intense than softneck. Its thinly wrapped cloves lose moisture quickly, however, and do not winter over, as do the cloves of the robust softneck.

We tasted eight garlic varieties, softneck and hardneck, raw and cooked, and found a wide range of flavors. We enjoyed several softneck and hardneck varieties, but our favorites were Porcelain Zemo and Rocambole Carpathian, both of which are hardnecks.

**HARDNECK GARLIC**     **SOFTNECK GARLIC**

Hardneck garlic has a stiff center staff around which its large, uniformly sized cloves hang. Softneck garlic, the kind found most commonly in supermarkets, has cloves of varying sizes (larger on the outside, smaller near the center) and no central staff.

## TASTING LAB: Dry Vermouth

THOUGH IT'S OFTEN USED IN COOKING, AND EVEN MORE often in martinis, dry vermouth is a potable that is paid very little attention. Imagine our surprise, then, when we did a little research and turned up nearly a dozen different brands. We pared them down to eight and tasted the vermouths straight (chilled) and in simple pan sauces for chicken (containing only shallots, chicken broth, and butter in addition to the vermouth).

First, a quick description of what dry vermouth is. Its base is a white wine, presumably not of particularly high quality, as evidenced by the relatively low prices of most vermouths. The wine is fortified with neutral grapes spirits that hike the alcohol level up a few percentage points to 16 to 18 percent, and it is "aromatized," or infused with "botanicals," such as herbs, spices, and fruits. In this country, dry vermouth, also called extra-dry vermouth, is imported from France and Italy (Italian vermouths being most common here) or is made domestically in California.

Two vermouths found their way into the top three in both tastings: Gallo Extra Dry and Noilly Prat Original French Dry. Gallo is the fruitier of the two and made the favorite pan sauce, which tasters called balanced, complex, smooth, and round. Noilly Prat is more woodsy and herbaceous and made a pan sauce that tasted fresh and balanced.

# Rating Dry Vermouths

WE GATHERED EIGHT DRY VERMOUTHS MADE IN CALIFORNIA, FRANCE, AND ITALY, AND NINE TASTERS SAMPLED THEM straight (chilled) and in a simple pan sauce for chicken made with just chicken broth, shallots, butter, and vermouth. Panelists were asked to rate each vermouth and describe its aroma and flavor. The vermouths are listed below in order of preference based on their combined scores from the two tastings.

**RECOMMENDED**
### Gallo Extra Dry Vermouth (California)
**$5.00 for 750 ml**
Simple but floral and fruity, with hints of melons and apples.

**RECOMMENDED**
### Noilly Prat Original French Dry Vermouth (France)
**$6.79 for 750 ml**
Honeyed, herbaceous, and woodsy, with faint anise notes and a subtle bitterness.

**NOT RECOMMENDED**
### Boissiere Vermouth (Italy)
**$6.99 for I liter**
Floral aroma and flavors, and a sherry-like finish. The pan sauce tasted sweet and stale.

**NOT RECOMMENDED**
### Martini & Rossi Extra Dry Vermouth (Italy)
**$6.79 for 750 ml**
Medicinal and harsh tasted straight. The vermouth made a sweet-sour pan sauce.

**NOT RECOMMENDED**
### Cinzano Extra Dry Vermouth (Italy)
**$6.79 for 750 ml**
Sweet, woodsy, and tannic. The pan sauce was dull and unremarkable.

**NOT RECOMMENDED**
### Stock Extra Dry Vermouth (Italy)
**$6.79 for I liter**
Fruity nose, very dry, and slightly tart. Acidic and vinegary in a pan sauce.

**NOT RECOMMENDED**
### Tribuno Extra Dry Vermouth (California)
**$4.99 for I liter**
Harsh, bitter, and alcoholic tasted straight. Harsh and acidic in a pan sauce.

**NOT RECOMMENDED**
### Vya Extra Dry Vermouth (California)
**$19.99 for 750 ml**
Smoky, earthy, and spicy. Sour, woodsy, and a bit unbalanced in a pan sauce.

# CHICKEN PROVENÇAL

**WHAT WE WANTED:** A chicken dish that was meltingly tender, moist, and flavorful, napped in an aromatic, garlicky tomato sauce that we could mop up with a good loaf of crusty bread.

Chicken Provençal may represent the best of French peasant cooking—chicken pieces on the bone simmered in a liquid flavored with tomatoes, garlic, herbs, and olives—but it is not well known here in the United States. We soon discovered why. The handful of recipes we tested produced rubbery, dry chicken, dull and muddy flavors, and a sauce that was too thick or too thin, too sweet or too greasy.

Most recipes we reviewed began with browning a cut-up whole chicken, removing the parts from the pot, sautéing some aromatic vegetables, deglazing the pot with white wine or dry vermouth, adding stock, tomatoes, olives, and herbs, and then simmering the chicken in the liquid until it was cooked. When we used a whole cut-up chicken, we encountered several problems. First, the breast pieces always dried out and lacked flavor after cooking. Second, the skin, although crisp after browning, turned soggy and unappealing after braising. Finally, the wings contained mostly inedible skin and very little meat. We tried again, using only dark meat, which, with its extra fat and connective tissue, was better suited to braising. The meat turned out tender, moist, and flavorful—far more appealing than either the breasts or the wings. We had used whole legs for this first test with dark

meat, but because tasters preferred the meatier thighs to the drumsticks, we decided to make the dish with thighs only.

Next we addressed the skin. Its flabby texture after cooking made it virtually inedible. When we began with skinless thighs, however, they stuck to the pan, the outer layer of meat becoming tough and dry with browning. The skin, it turns out, acts as a necessary cushion between the meat and the pan, so we left it on for browning and then discarded it. We also wondered if the amount of browning mattered. A side-by-side taste test—one batch made with lightly browned thighs, the other with deeply browned thighs—revealed that more browning renders more fat and results in more chicken flavor.

We assumed that olive oil was essential to this dish (it is ostensibly from Provence, after all), but most recipes (which use about three tablespoons) were too greasy. We browned a batch of thighs in a meager 1 tablespoon of oil and found that the skin quickly rendered a couple of additional tablespoons of fat. But even with this reduced amount of fat, tasters found the final dish to be greasy. Pouring off all but 1 tablespoon of fat after browning the chicken eliminated the greasiness, but now the flavor of the sauce was lacking. We were throwing flavor out with the rendered fat. We tried another test using just 1 teaspoon of oil. Sure enough, using less olive oil at the beginning allowed for a stronger chicken flavor in the final dish because we were discarding less chicken fat. We had one more test in mind—drizzling 2 teaspoons of extra-virgin olive oil over the finished dish just before serving. Tasters approved of the additional fruity olive flavor.

Our final tests with the chicken focused on the cooking method. Almost by definition, chicken Provençal is braised (browned and then cooked in a tightly covered pot in a small amount of liquid over low heat for a lengthy period of time). Stovetop braising proved unreliable. The cooking time varied, and, despite the fact that we set the

---

## FOOD FACT: Chicken Provençal

The term Provençal refers to the dishes prepared in the style of Provence, a region in southeastern France. Garlic, tomatoes, and olive oil are the trademarks of Provençal cooking. Onions, olives, mushrooms, anchovies, and eggplant also play a prominent part in many of these dishes.

---

flame at the same heat level every time, the heat transfer was not uniform. Braising in a 300-degree oven was much more reliable, producing a predictably even, consistent level of heat. Next we tested the optimal braising time. Technically, thighs are considered done when they reach an internal temperature of 170 degrees, or after 30 minutes of braising. Unfortunately, 30 minutes of braising produced thighs that were not as meltingly tender as desired, and the chicken did not have enough flavor. What if we were to cook them longer? Would they dry out?

To our great surprise, after trying longer and longer cooking times, we ended up keeping the dish in the oven for a whopping 1½ hours. At this point, the meat simply falls off the bone; it is exceedingly tender and flavorful, and the thighs did not seem overcooked. Additional tests, however, revealed that slightly less time—1¼ hours, wherein the meat reaches an internal temperature of 210 degrees—was perfect, as the meat then stays on the bone. Why this long cooking time? The long stay in the oven breaks down the connective tissue in the thighs, much as it does in a pot roast, yielding more tender meat. (White meat contains little connective tissue, so there's no benefit to cooking it longer.) In addition, thighs have plenty of fat that keeps them moist as they braise away.

Many recipes call for browning onions after the chicken is browned and taken out of the pot. Tasters approved of some onion, but not a lot, commenting that a modest amount of its pungent flavor was enough to balance the sweetness of the tomatoes. Garlic is most often added next and sautéed briefly to bring forth its flavor. Preliminary tests showed that both dry white wine and dry vermouth work well for deglazing the pan, but the wine turned out to be the favorite among tasters. The vermouth seemed to exaggerate the acidity of the tomatoes.

Crushed and pureed canned tomatoes each produced a thick, sweet, overbearing sauce reminiscent of a bad Italian restaurant. Canned diced tomatoes, though more promising, presented the opposite problem: Even when drained they contain a fair amount of liquid, and the resulting sauce was too thin. We added a few tablespoons of tomato paste to the diced tomatoes and the texture improved dramatically—now the sauce coated the chicken without overwhelming it. Chicken broth rounded out the flavors.

Whole niçoise olives appeared in just about every recipe, but tasters complained about the pits. Niçoise are so small that pitting by hand with a knife is unreasonable. We tried kalamatas, gaetas, and oil-cured olives, but none of them sufficed. The flavors of their brine or oil were too strong and inappropriate. While discussing this predicament with colleagues, a solution surfaced that involved a mallet and clean kitchen towels (see the illustration on page 152). Olives are best stirred in at the end of cooking, just before serving.

As for seasonings, the combination of dried herbs referred to as herbes de Provence (lavender, marjoram, basil, fennel seed, rosemary, sage, summer savory, and thyme) seemed like a shoe-in. But tasters said that when used alone, these dried herbs were too strong, giving the sauce a flavor that bordered on medicinal. Fresh thyme, oregano, and parsley with a bay leaf were preferred, and a teaspoon of the dried blend became an optional item. A pinch of cayenne balanced the sweet tomatoes.

Inspired by one of the better initial recipes tested, we tried adding a teaspoon of minced anchovies before deglazing. Although tasters could not identify the ingredient, everyone agreed the sauce tasted richer and fuller. The final item on our list was lemon zest, a common and, as it turned out, welcome addition. We found that the zest is best added at two points: first to the braising liquid while it is being reduced (just before serving) and second to the finished dish itself, sprinkled on top along with the parsley.

WHAT WE LEARNED: Use chicken thighs for the best flavor and texture. Brown the thighs in a sheer film of oil and then spoon off excess fat to keep the sauce from becoming greasy. Braise the chicken until it is meltingly tender—about one and one-quarter hours, which is far longer than most recipes suggest.

## CHICKEN PROVENÇAL Serves 4

This dish is often served with rice or slices of crusty bread, but soft polenta is also a good accompaniment. Niçoise olives are the preferred olives here; the flavor of kalamatas and other types of brined or oil-cured olives is too potent.

| | |
|---|---|
| 8 | bone-in, skin-on chicken thighs (about 3 pounds), trimmed of excess skin and fat |
| | Salt |
| 1 | tablespoon extra-virgin olive oil |
| 1 | small onion, chopped fine (about ⅔ cup) |
| 6 | medium cloves garlic, minced or pressed through a garlic press (about 2 tablespoons) |
| 1 | anchovy fillet, minced (about 1 teaspoon) |
| ⅛ | teaspoon cayenne |
| 1 | cup dry white wine |
| 1 | cup low-sodium chicken broth |
| 1 | can (14.5 ounces) diced tomatoes, drained |
| 2½ | tablespoons tomato paste |
| 1½ | tablespoons chopped fresh thyme leaves |
| 1 | teaspoon chopped fresh oregano leaves |
| 1 | bay leaf |
| 1 | teaspoon herbes de Provence (optional) |
| 1½ | teaspoons grated zest from 1 lemon |
| ½ | cup niçoise olives, pitted (see the illustration at right) |
| 1 | tablespoon chopped fresh parsley leaves |

**1.** Adjust an oven rack to the lower-middle position; heat the oven to 300 degrees. Sprinkle both sides of the chicken thighs with salt to taste. Heat 1 teaspoon oil in a large Dutch oven over medium-high heat until shimmering but not smoking. Add 4 chicken thighs, skin-side down, and cook without moving them until the skin is crisp and well browned, about 5 minutes. Using tongs, turn the chicken pieces and brown on the second side, about 5 minutes longer; transfer to a large plate. Add the remaining 4 chicken thighs to the pot and repeat, then transfer them to a plate and set aside. Discard all but 1 tablespoon of fat from the pot.

**2.** Add the onion to the fat in the Dutch oven and cook, stirring occasionally, over medium heat until softened and browned, about 4 minutes. Add the garlic, anchovy, and cayenne; cook, stirring constantly, until fragrant, about 1 minute. Add the wine and scrape up browned bits from the pan bottom with a wooden spoon. Stir in the chicken broth, tomatoes, tomato paste, thyme, oregano, bay, and herbes de Provence (if using). Remove and discard the skin from the chicken thighs, then submerge the chicken pieces in the liquid and add the accumulated chicken juices to the pot. Increase the heat to high, bring to a simmer, cover, then set the pot in the oven; cook until the chicken offers no resistance when poked with the tip of a paring knife but is still clinging to the bones, about 1¼ hours.

**3.** Using a slotted spoon, transfer the chicken to a serving platter and tent with foil. Discard the bay leaf. Set the Dutch oven over high heat, stir in 1 teaspoon lemon zest, bring to

**TECHNIQUE:** Pitting Niçoise Olives

Removing the pits from tiny niçoise olives by hand is not an easy job. We found the following method to be the most expedient. Cover a cutting board with a clean kitchen towel and spread the olives on top, about 1 inch apart from each other. Place a second clean towel over the olives. Using a mallet, pound all of the olives firmly for 10 to 15 seconds, being careful not to split the pits. Remove the top towel, and, using your fingers, press the pit out of each olive.

a boil, and cook, stirring occasionally, until slightly thick-ened and reduced to 2 cups, about 5 minutes. Stir in the olives and cook until heated through, about 1 minute. Meanwhile, mix the remaining ½ teaspoon zest with the parsley. Spoon the sauce over the chicken, drizzle the chicken with the remaining 2 teaspoons olive oil, sprinkle with the parsley mixture, and serve.

## CHICKEN PROVENÇAL WITH SAFFRON, ORANGE, AND BASIL

Follow the recipe for Chicken Provençal, adding ⅛ tea-spoon saffron threads along with the wine and substituting orange zest for the lemon zest and 2 tablespoons fresh chopped basil for the parsley.

Erin carries hot coals to the outdoor "test kitchen."

# STEAK
## CHAPTER 13
# & potatoes

**IN THIS CHAPTER**

**THE RECIPES**

Charcoal-Grilled Strip or Rib
   Steaks
Gas-Grilled Strip or Rib Steaks
Charcoal-Grilled Filets Mignons
Gas-Grilled Filets Mignons
Roasted Red Pepper and
   Smoked Paprika Butter
Lemon, Garlic, and Parsley
   Butter

Mashed Potatoes with Blue
   Cheese and Port-Caramelized
   Onions
Mashed Potatoes with Scallions
   and Horseradish
Mashed Potatoes with Smoked
   Cheddar and Grainy Mustard
Mashed Potatoes with Smoked
   Paprika and Toasted Garlic

**EQUIPMENT CORNER**

Large Saucepans

**SCIENCE DESK**

Why Do Juicy Meats Seem
   Tender?

**TASTING LAB**

Mail-Order Steaks

It's hard to beat steak and mashed potatoes for both simplicity and flavor. When you've purchased a good steak and cooked it properly, it needs little more than salt and pepper, and, of course, a side of spuds. Unfortunately, many of the inexpensive steaks labeled "great for grilling" at supermarkets turn out tough and dry and have little flavor.

We think premium steaks—the strip, rib-eye, and filet—are worth the extra money, but you certainly don't want to spend big bucks and then use the wrong grilling technique. We know many home cooks have trouble timing steaks on the grill—it can be a struggle to achieve a browned, crisp crust and a perfectly cooked center at the same time. We knew the test kitchen could fire up the grill and solve this problem.

When the steak is special, we think the potatoes should be, too. But all too often, mashed potatoes are gluey or runny. We wanted potatoes with perfect texture and big flavor—something unusual to accompany a great steak and a good bottle of wine.

# GRILLED STEAKS

**WHAT WE WANTED:** A sure-fire technique for grilling the three most popular premium steaks—strip, rib-eye, and filet.

Grilled steaks have many attractive qualities: rich, beefy flavor; a thick, caramelized crust; and almost no prep or cleanup for the cook. But sometimes a small bonfire fueled by steak fat can leave expensive steaks charred and tasting of resinous smoke. And sometimes the coals burn down so low that the steaks end up with those pale, wimpy grill marks and just about no flavor at all. In those cases, you try leaving the steaks on the grill long enough to develop flavor, but they just overcook.

We went to work, promising ourselves we'd figure out how to use the grill to get the results we were after: meat seared evenly on both sides so that the juices are concentrated into a powerfully flavored, dark brown, brittle coating of crust; the juicy inside cooked a little past rare; and the outside strip of rich, soft fat crisped and browned slightly on the edges.

We decided to focus on the steaks from the short loin and rib sections of the animal that we think are the best the cow has to offer—the strip and filet mignon (both from the short loin) and the rib-eye (from the rib section). We figured these steaks were bound to take to pretty much the same cooking technique because they were all cut from the same general part of the cow.

Early on in our testing, we determined that we needed a very hot fire to get the crust we wanted without overcooking the steak. We could get that kind of heat by building the charcoal up to within 2 or 2½ inches of the grilling grate. But with this arrangement, we ran into problems with the fat dripping down onto the charcoal and flaming. We had already decided that a thick steak—at least 1½ inches thick, to be precise—was optimal because at that thickness we got a tasty contrast between the charcoal flavoring on

the outside of the steak and the beefy flavor on the inside. The problem was that we couldn't cook a thick steak over consistently high heat without burning it.

After considerable experimentation, we resolved this dilemma: We had to build a fire with two levels of heat. Once we realized that we needed a fire with a lot of coals on one side and far fewer coals on the other, we could sear the steak properly at the beginning of cooking, then pull it onto the cooler half of the grill to finish cooking at a lower temperature. And we could use the dual heat levels to cook thin steaks as well as thick ones properly. The system also provided insurance against bonfires—if a steak flared up, we simply moved it off the high heat.

We found we could be sure we had the right levels of heat on both sides of the fire by holding a hand about five inches over the cooking grate. When the hot side of the grill was hot enough for searing, we could hold a hand over the grill for only about two seconds. For the cooler side of the grill, we could count four to five seconds. (This is how we adapted our recipes for a gas grill, using burners set to high and medium.)

Common cooking wisdom suggests that bringing meat to room temperature before grilling will cause it to cook

---

**FOOD FACT: Steak Names**

Steaks have curious names, and many of these names have interesting histories. Legend has its that England's King Henry VIII was so impressed with meat from the sirloin that he dubbed it "Sir Loin." (The more likely source for this word is the French *surlonge*, which translates as "over the loin.") The châteaubriand, the premium portion of the filet mignon, takes its name from the French statesman François Châteaubriand. The term *porterhouse* comes from the early 1800s, when travelers stopped to dine on steak and ale at coach stops, which were also known as porter houses.

more evenly and that letting it rest for five minutes after taking it off the grill will both preserve the juices and provide a more even color. We tested the first of these theories by simultaneously grilling two similar steaks, one straight from the refrigerator and a second that stood at room temperature for one hour. We noticed no difference in the cooked steaks except that the room temperature steak cooked a couple of minutes faster than the other. The second test was more conclusive. Letting a cooked steak rest for five minutes does indeed help the meat retain more juices when sliced and promotes a more even color throughout the meat.

We tried lightly oiling steaks before grilling to see if they browned better that way and tried brushing them with butter halfway through grilling to see if the flavor improved. Although the oiled steaks browned a tiny bit better, the difference wasn't significant enough to merit the added ingredient. (The filets mignons were an exception; oiling them improved browning in these leaner steaks.) As for the butter, we couldn't taste any difference.

We did find proper seasoning with salt and pepper before grilling to be essential. Seasonings added after cooking sit on the surface and don't penetrate as well as salt and pepper added before cooking. Be liberal with the salt and pepper. A fair amount falls off during the cooking process. Finally, consider using coarse sea salt or kosher salt. In our tests, tasters consistently preferred steaks sprinkled with coarse salt before grilling compared with those sprinkled with table salt. The larger crystals are easier to pick up and sprinkle evenly over the meat.

---

**WHAT WE LEARNED:** Cook these premium steaks over a two-level fire, searing them first over a high stack of coals and then moving them to a cooler part of the grill to cook through. Oil lean filets mignons to encourage browning, but otherwise don't fuss with these steaks before cooking them—salt and pepper are all that they need.

## CHARCOAL-GRILLED STRIP OR RIB STEAKS Serves 4

Strip and rib steaks, on or off the bone, are our first choice for individual steaks. A steak that's between 1 1/4 to 1 1/2 inches thick gives you a solid meat flavor as well as a little taste of the grill; cut any thicker and the steak becomes too thick for one person to eat. If your guests are more likely to eat only an 8-ounce steak, grill two 1-pounders, slice them, and serve each person a half steak. The most accurate way to judge doneness is to stick an instant-read thermometer through the side of the steak deep into the meat, so that most of the shaft is embedded in the steak (see the illustration on page 159).

4   strip or rib steaks, with or without the bone,
    1 1/4 to 1 1/2 inches thick (12 to 16 ounces each),
    patted dry
    Salt and ground black pepper

**1.** Light a large chimney starter filled with hardwood charcoal (about 6 quarts) and allow to burn until all the charcoal is covered with a layer of fine gray ash. Build a two-level fire by stacking most of the coals on one side of the grill for a medium-hot fire and arranging the remaining coals in a single layer on the other side of the grill for a medium-low fire. Set the cooking rack in place, cover the grill with the lid, and let the rack heat up, about 5 minutes. Use a wire brush to scrape clean the cooking rack.

**2.** Meanwhile, sprinkle both sides of the steaks with salt and pepper to taste. Grill the steaks, uncovered, over the hotter part of the fire until well browned on one side, 2 to 3 minutes. Turn the steaks; grill until well browned on the other side, 2 to 3 minutes. (If the steaks start to flame, pull them to the cooler part of the grill and/or extinguish the flames with a squirt bottle.)

**3.** Once the steaks are well browned on both sides, slide them to the cooler part of grill. Continue grilling, uncovered, to the desired doneness, 5 to 6 minutes more for rare (120 degrees on an instant-read thermometer), 6 to 7 minutes for medium-rare on the rare side (125 degrees), 7 to 8 minutes for medium-rare on the medium side (130 degrees), or 8 to 9 minutes for medium (135 to 140 degrees).

**4.** Remove the steaks from the grill and let rest for 5 minutes. Serve immediately.

VARIATION

### GAS-GRILLED STRIP OR RIB STEAKS

Depending on the heat output of your gas grill, you may need to cook the steaks over the cooler part of the grill for an extra minute or two.

Turn on all burners to high, close the lid, and heat the grill until very hot, about 15 minutes. Scrape the grill grate clean with a grill brush. Leave one burner on high and turn the other burner(s) to medium. Follow the recipe for Charcoal-Grilled Strip or Rib Steaks from step 2.

### CHARCOAL-GRILLED FILETS MIGNONS

Serves 4

Filet mignon steaks are cut from the tenderloin, which is, as the name indicates, an extremely tender portion of meat. Though tender, the steaks are not extremely rich. To prevent the steaks from drying out on the grill and to encourage browning, we found it helpful to lightly rub each steak with a little oil before grilling. We suggest that you drizzle the grilled steaks with olive oil and serve them with lemon wedges, or serve the steaks with one of the flavored butters on page 159.

    4   center-cut filets mignons, about 1½ to 2 inches thick (7 to 8 ounces each), patted dry
    4   teaspoons olive oil
        Salt and ground black pepper

**1.** Light a large chimney starter filled with hardwood charcoal (about 6 quarts) and allow to burn until all the charcoal is covered with a layer of fine gray ash. Build a two-level fire by stacking most of the coals on one side of the grill for a medium-hot fire. Arrange the remaining coals in a single layer on the other side of the grill for a medium-low fire. Set the cooking rack in place, cover the grill with the lid, and let the rack heat up, about 5 minutes. Use a wire brush to scrape clean the cooking rack.

**2.** Meanwhile, lightly rub the steaks with the oil and sprinkle both sides of the steaks with salt and pepper to taste. Grill the steaks, uncovered, over the hotter part of the fire until well browned on one side, 2 to 3 minutes. Turn the steaks; grill until well browned on the other side, 2 to 3 minutes.

**3.** Once steaks are well browned on both sides, slide them to the cooler part of the grill. Continue grilling, uncovered,

---

## GETTING IT RIGHT:
### The Eight Primal Cuts of Beef

If you want to buy beef, it helps to understand the anatomy of a cow. Butchers divide the meat into eight primal cuts. Steaks generally come from six places on the cow—not from the brisket or plate. We find that best steaks come from the rib and short loin sections.

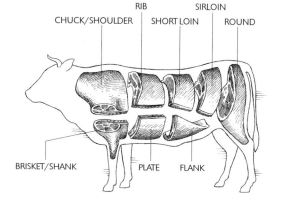

to the desired doneness, 6 minutes more for rare (120 degrees on an instant-read thermometer), 7 minutes for medium-rare on the rare side (125 degrees), 8 minutes for medium-rare on the medium side (130 degrees), or 9 to 10 minutes for medium (135 to 140 degrees).

**4.** Remove the steaks from the grill and let rest for 5 minutes. Serve immediately.

VARIATION
### GAS-GRILLED FILETS MIGNONS

Depending on the heat output of your gas grill, you may need to cook the steaks over the cooler part of the grill for an extra minute or two.

Turn on all burners to high, close the lid, and heat the grill until very hot, about 15 minutes. Scrape the grill grate clean with a grill brush. Leave one burner on high and turn the other burner(s) to medium. Follow the recipe for Charcoal-Grilled Filets Mignons from step 2.

### ROASTED RED PEPPER AND SMOKED PAPRIKA BUTTER

Makes 4 tablespoons, enough for 4 steaks
Serve this butter with filets mignons.

    4    tablespoons unsalted butter, softened
    2    tablespoons very finely minced jarred roasted red bell peppers (about 1 ounce)
    1    tablespoon minced fresh thyme leaves
    ¾    teaspoon smoked paprika
    ½    teaspoon salt
        Ground black pepper

Using a fork, beat all of the ingredients, including pepper to taste, together in a small bowl until combined. Just before serving the steaks, spoon about 1 tablespoon butter onto each and serve.

### LEMON, GARLIC, AND PARSLEY BUTTER

Makes 4 tablespoons, enough for 4 steaks
This is a variation on maître d'hôtel butter, a classic French accompaniment to meat, fish, and vegetables. It works well with filets.

    4    tablespoons unsalted butter, softened
    ½    teaspoon grated lemon zest
    1    tablespoon minced fresh parsley leaves
    1    medium clove garlic, minced to a puree or pressed through a garlic press (about 1 teaspoon)
    ½    teaspoon salt
        Ground black pepper

Using a fork, beat all of the ingredients, including pepper to taste, together in a small bowl until combined. Just before serving the steaks, spoon about 1 tablespoon butter onto each and serve.

## TECHNIQUE:
### Judging When Steaks Are Done

Hold the steak with a pair of tongs and push the tip of the thermometer through the edge of the steak until most of the shaft is embedded in the meat and not touching any bone. Pull the steak off the grill when it registers 120 degrees for rare; 125 to 130 degrees for medium-rare; and 135 to 140 degrees for medium. Note that the internal temperature will rise another 5 degrees or so as the steak rests.

## SCIENCE DESK:
### Why Do Juicy Meats Seem Tender?

THE SENSATION OF TENDERNESS IN MEAT HAS A LOT TO do with the condition of the muscle fiber. Loss of water invariably leads to toughness (just think about beef jerky). Meats such as turkey or ham are often "enhanced" by the injection of water. When these meats are cooked, they seem more tender than when untreated because they retain more moisture.

Why does extra water make us think "tender"? One reason could be that as meat cooks the muscle cells contract and water is expelled. What was once a moist, thick cut of meat is now more thin and sinewy. The net effect is that you need to (specifically, your jaw needs to) expend more effort to bite through the same number of cells over a shorter distance. Juiciness, or water content, also affects the structure of the cells. A normal, healthy cell has suppleness primarily because of the presence of water; the contents can readjust their position because water serves as a lubricant. When water is eliminated through cooking, the cell becomes more rigid.

Thus, loss of water may contribute to the sensation of toughness in two ways. First, cells become smaller and denser, and, second, they become less supple. It is not surprising that "tender" and "juicy" have become inseparable partners in the cook's mind.

## TASTING LAB: Mail-Order Steaks

TO CONNOISSEURS, STEAKS ARE THE STARS OF THE BEEF world, and strip steaks are the divas. Long and lean, with a heartier chew and a lot more flavor, strip steaks put their more popular brethren, filets mignons, to shame. Beef is a tricky business, however, and too often you can find your steak more dud than stud. To guarantee quality, more and more people are looking beyond the confines of their local supermarket butcher case and buying their steaks through mail-order sources. These outlets promise all-star beef with a price tag to match. But do the mail-order steaks really outshine the ones you can get around the corner?

We gathered seven widely available mail-order strip steaks and two from local supermarkets (Coleman Natural—hormone- and antibiotic-free—from our local Whole Foods market and choice steak from the regular market). Our candidates included Niman Ranch, a high-end, all-natural, restaurant favorite; Peter Luger, a New York steakhouse that many consider to be the best in the country; Omaha, probably the most well-known mail-order steak company, with two steaks in the running (their "private reserve" as well as their standard); Allen Brothers, a Chicago-based company that supplies many of this country's steakhouses; and Lobel's, a New York butcher shop. In

# Rating Mail-Order Steaks

TWENTY-THREE MEMBERS OF THE *COOK'S ILLUSTRATED* STAFF TASTED SEVEN MAIL-ORDER STEAKS ALONG WITH TWO supermarket samples. All samples were boneless strip steaks, pan-seared in a thin film of vegetable oil and then sliced for the tasting. (The steaks were not seasoned with salt or pepper.) The steaks are listed in order of preferences based on their scores in this tasting. Prices do not include shipping, which can add another $15 to $30 to the overall cost. See www.americastestkitchen.com for up-to-date prices and mail-order sources for top-rated products.

---

**HIGHLY RECOMMENDED**
Lobel's Wagyu (Kobe-Style) Boneless Strip Steak (from Oakleigh Ranch, Australia) **$68.00 per pound**
"Incredibly tender" and "awesome." The clear favorite, but incredibly expensive.

---

**HIGHLY RECOMMENDED**
Niman Ranch New York Steak **$22.00 per pound**
Tasters thought this steak, which is a favorite with chefs, had "good flavor" and was "very tender."

---

**HIGHLY RECOMMENDED**
Coleman Natural Boneless Strip Steak **$14.00 per pound**
This all-natural supermarket option was praised by tasters for its "great flavor" and "rich, meaty" quality.

---

**HIGHLY RECOMMENDED**
Peter Luger Strip Steak **$29.00 per pound**
This steak from the famed Brooklyn steakhouse was "extremely tender" and "mild."

---

**RECOMMENDED**
Lobel's Boneless Strip Steak **$34.00 per pound**
The steak from this famous New York butcher was "juicy" and "chewy."

---

**RECOMMENDED**
Allen Brothers Dry-Aged Boneless Sirloin Strip Steak **$35.00 per pound**
"Very tender" but "kind of bland" was the consensus on this steak.

---

**RECOMMENDED**
Stop & Shop Choice Boneless Strip Steak **$10.00 per pound**
"Very juicy" but "not much flavor" was how most tasters judged this supermarket steak.

---

**NOT RECOMMENDED**
Omaha Boneless Strip Steak **$25.00 per pound**
This basic steak from the famed mail-order company was judged "beefy but generic" and "too thin."

---

**NOT RECOMMENDED**
Omaha Private Reserve Boneless Strip Steak **$45.00 per pound**
This premium offering from Omaha was "a little chewy" and "tough and stringy."

addition to Lobel's boneless strip steak we included Lobel's Wagyu, or Kobe-style, steak from Oakleigh Ranch in Australia. Kobe beef comes from Wagyu cattle raised to certain specifications in Kobe, Japan. Considered the foie gras of beef, the meat is extremely well-marbled, tender, and rich. Wagyu is the more generic name for the same type of beef, but not from Japan. Although few of us could afford the hefty $68/pound price tag for Wagyu beef, we wanted to see if it was really worth that much.

Well, it was. After pan-searing three dozen steaks (four of each type for perhaps the largest tasting turnout in the test kitchen), we found that money can buy you happiness, if happiness for you is the best steak you ever ate.

"Wow," wrote one happy taster of our first-place Wagyu steak. "This is unlike any strip that I've had." Others deemed the Wagyu steak "tender like a filet" and "very rich and meaty." But the overwhelming richness—which one taster likened to "foie gras–infused beef"—was not everyone's cup of tea. A minority of tasters agreed with the one who wrote, "This doesn't taste like beef at all."

Three steaks shared the spot for second place: Niman Ranch ($22 per pound), praised for its "good flavor" and "nice texture"; Coleman Natural, deemed "very robust"; and Peter Luger, described as having "strong beef flavor" and "great juiciness."

Unfortunately, the brand most people turn to when ordering steak through the mail took the last two spots in our tasting. The Omaha strip steak had "off flavors" and was "grainy tasting," while the Omaha Private Reserve (at almost twice the price) finished last, with tasters finding it "a little chewy" and "very dry."

The good news is that you don't have to spend a small fortune (or pay for shipping) to get a great steak. Coleman Natural steak, available at all-natural supermarkets, tied for second place and was a comparative bargain at $14 per pound (just $4 more than the low-ranked Stop & Shop beef). If you want to sample true steak greatness, however, we recommend splurging on the Wagyu beef...at least once.

# MASHED POTATOES

**WHAT WE WANTED:** Mashed potatoes packed with enough flavor to stand as an equal partner with a great grilled steak.

When it comes to mashed potatoes, most cooks (including those here in the test kitchen) worry so much about getting the texture right that they forget about flavor. Butter and half-and-half make for mashed potatoes that are rich tasting but not terribly exciting. Giving flavor second-tier status is fine if the potatoes are going to be smothered with gravy, but with just a bit of help they can stand proudly on their own.

Based on work done in the test kitchen a few years ago, we knew how to make potatoes with great texture. The formula is simple: Use russets for the fluffiest texture (other varieties turn out soggy, heavy mashed potatoes), boil them whole and in their skins to keep them from soaking up water, add melted butter to coat the starch molecules, and finish with half-and-half. A ricer or food mill delivers the smoothest (and best) texture, but a potato masher can be used if you don't mind lumps. With our method for cooking and mashing the potatoes decided, our goal was to jazz up the flavor.

We tried multiple flavor combinations and found that adding too many ingredients served only to muddy the flavor of the potatoes. Tasters preferred simple pairings of contrasting but complementary flavors. Sweet caramelized onions balance the tang and sharpness of blue cheese. The richness of smoked cheddar is cut with the vinegary bite of grainy mustard. Scallions add a fresh, light onion flavor to potatoes spiked with spicy horseradish. The warmth of toasted garlic softens the smoky edge of Spanish paprika.

**WHAT WE LEARNED:** A few well-chosen ingredients can elevate mashed potatoes to star status.

## MASHED POTATOES WITH BLUE CHEESE AND PORT-CARAMELIZED ONIONS Serves 4

We especially like this dish with Roquefort cheese.

onions

| | |
|---|---|
| 1½ | teaspoons unsalted butter |
| 1½ | teaspoons vegetable oil |
| ¼ | teaspoon salt |
| ½ | teaspoon light brown sugar |
| 1 | pound yellow onions, sliced ¼ inch thick |
| ⅓ | cup port, preferably ruby port |

potatoes

| | |
|---|---|
| ¾ | cup half-and-half |
| 1 | teaspoon chopped fresh thyme leaves |
| 2 | pounds russet potatoes, unpeeled and scrubbed |
| 6 | tablespoons unsalted butter, melted |
| 1¼ | teaspoons salt |
| ½ | teaspoon ground black pepper |
| 4 | ounces blue cheese, crumbled |

**1.** FOR THE ONIONS: Heat the butter and oil in an 8-inch nonstick skillet over high heat; when the foam subsides, stir in the salt and sugar. Add the onions and stir to coat; cook, stirring occasionally, until the onions begin to soften and release some moisture, about 5 minutes. Reduce the heat to medium; cook, stirring frequently, until the onions are deeply browned and sticky, about 35 minutes longer (if the onions are sizzling or scorching, reduce the heat; if the onions are not browning after 15 minutes, increase the heat). Stir in the port; continue to cook until the port reduces to a glaze, 4 to 6 minutes. Set the onions aside.

**2.** FOR THE POTATOES: While the onions are cooking, bring the half-and-half and thyme to boil in a small saucepan; cover to keep warm.

**3.** Place the potatoes in a large saucepan with water to cover by 1 inch. Bring to a boil over high heat, reduce the heat to medium, and simmer until the potatoes are just tender (a paring knife can be slipped into and out of the potato with very little resistance), 20 to 30 minutes. Drain.

**4.** Set a food mill or ricer over the now-empty but still-warm saucepan. Spear the potato with a dinner fork, then peel back the skin with a paring knife; repeat with the remaining potatoes. Working in batches, cut the peeled potatoes into rough chunks and drop them into the hopper of a food mill or ricer. Process or rice the potatoes into the saucepan, or mash the potatoes with a potato masher directly in the saucepan.

**5.** Stir the butter into the potatoes until just incorporated. Sprinkle the salt and pepper over the potatoes. Add the warm half-and-half and blue cheese; stir until just combined. Serve immediately, topping individual servings with a portion of the onions.

## MASHED POTATOES WITH SCALLIONS AND HORSERADISH Serves 4

Prepared horseradish gives the potatoes a vinegary kick, while fresh horseradish adds a sweeter, more mellow horseradish flavor without pungency.

    2  pounds russet potatoes, unpeeled and scrubbed
    8  tablespoons (1 stick) unsalted butter, melted
 1½  teaspoons salt
   ½  teaspoon ground black pepper
    2  tablespoons prepared hot horseradish
   ¼  cup grated fresh horseradish
    3  medium scallions, green parts only, minced
       (about ½ cup)
    1  cup half-and-half, warm

**1.** Place the potatoes in a large saucepan with water to cover by 1 inch. Bring to a boil over high heat, reduce the heat to medium, and simmer until the potatoes are just tender (a paring knife can be slipped into and out of the potato with very little resistance), 20 to 30 minutes. Drain.

**2.** Set a food mill or ricer over the now-empty but still-warm saucepan. Spear the potato with a dinner fork, then peel back the skin with a paring knife; repeat with the remaining potatoes. Working in batches, cut the peeled potatoes into rough chunks and drop into the hopper of a food mill or ricer. Process or rice the potatoes into the saucepan or mash the potatoes with a potato masher directly in the saucepan.

**3.** Stir the butter into the potatoes until just incorporated. Sprinkle the salt and pepper over the potatoes. Whisk the horseradish and scallions into the warm half-and-half; add the mixture to the potatoes and stir until just combined. Serve immediately.

## MASHED POTATOES WITH SMOKED CHEDDAR AND GRAINY MUSTARD Serves 4

Because of the cheese, this recipe uses a bit less salt. Coarse Dijon mustard is ideal in this recipe.

    2  pounds russet potatoes, unpeeled and scrubbed
    8  tablespoons (1 stick) unsalted butter, melted
 1¼  teaspoons salt
   ½  teaspoon ground black pepper
    1  cup half-and-half, warm
    2  tablespoons grainy mustard
    3  ounces smoked cheddar cheese, grated (1 cup)

**1.** Follow the recipe for Mashed Potatoes with Scallions and Horseradish through step 2.

**2.** Stir the butter into the potatoes until just incorporated. Sprinkle the salt and pepper over the potatoes; add the warm half-and-half, mustard, and cheese and stir until just combined. Serve immediately.

## MASHED POTATOES WITH SMOKED PAPRIKA AND TOASTED GARLIC Serves 4

Smoked paprika is a Spanish specialty. It gives these mashed potatoes a flavor that is deep, earthy, and complex, with a mild smokiness. Sweet paprika can be substituted, but the flavor won't be quite the same.

|   |   |
|---|---|
| 2 | pounds russet potatoes, unpeeled and scrubbed |
| 1 | teaspoon sweet or bittersweet smoked paprika |
| 8 | tablespoons (1 stick) unsalted butter |
| 3 | medium-large cloves garlic, minced or pressed through a garlic press (about 1 generous tablespoon) |
| 1½ | teaspoons salt |
| ½ | teaspoon ground black pepper |
| 1 | cup half-and-half, warm |

**1.** Follow the recipe for Mashed Potatoes with Scallions and Horseradish through step 2.

**2.** While the potatoes are cooking, toast the paprika in a small dry skillet over medium heat, stirring frequently, until fragrant, about 2 minutes. (Do not let the paprika burn, or it will taste bitter.) Transfer to a small bowl; set aside. Heat the butter in a small saucepan over medium-low heat; when melted, add the garlic and reduce the heat to low. Cook, stirring frequently, until the garlic begins to brown, 12 to 14 minutes; remove the saucepan from the heat immediately and set aside for 5 minutes (the garlic will continue to brown). Pour the butter mixture through a mesh strainer; reserve the butter and set the toasted garlic aside.

**3.** With a wooden spoon, stir the reserved butter into the mashed potatoes until just incorporated. Sprinkle the potatoes with salt, pepper, and toasted paprika; add the warm half- and-half and stir until just combined. Serve immediately, sprinkling individual servings with a portion of the reserved toasted garlic.

## EQUIPMENT CORNER:
### Large Saucepans

WHEN COOKING MOST VEGETABLES, WE REACH FOR A three- to four-quart saucepan. Which begs an obvious question: Does the brand of pan matter? With prices for these large saucepans ranging from $24.99 for a Revere stainless-steel model with thin copper cladding at the base up to $140 for an All-Clad pan with a complete aluminum core and stainless-steel interior and exterior cladding, a lot of money is riding on the answer. To let us offer guidance, we tested eight models, all between three and four quarts in size, from well-known cookware manufacturers.

The tests we performed were based on common cooking tasks and designed to highlight specific characteristics of the pans' performance. Sautéing minced onions illustrated the pace at which the pan heats up and sautés. Cooking white rice provided a good indication of the pan's ability to heat evenly as well as how tightly the lid sealed. Making pastry cream let us know how user-friendly the pan was—was it shaped such that a whisk reached into the corners without trouble, was it comfortable to pick up, and could we pour liquid from it neatly? These traits can make a real difference when you use a pan day in and day out.

Of the tests we performed, sautéing onions was the most telling. In our view, onions should soften reliably and evenly (and with minimal attention and stirring) when sautéed over medium heat. In this regard, the All-Clad, Calphalon, KitchenAid, and Sitram pans all delivered. The Chantal and Cuisinart pans sautéed slightly faster, necessitating a little more attention from the cook, but still well within acceptable bounds. Only the Revere and Farberware Millennium sautéed so fast that we considered them problematic.

Incidentally, the Revere and Farberware pans that sautéed onions too fast for us were the lightest pans of the bunch, weighing only 1 pound 10 ounces and 2 pounds 6 ounces, respectively. This indicates that they were made from thinner metal, which is one reason they heat quickly.

On the flip side of the weight issue, however, we found that too heavy a pan, such as the 4-pound Calphalon, could be uncomfortable to lift when full. The ideal was about 3½ pounds; pans near this weight, including the All-Clad, KitchenAid, Chantal, Sitram, and Cuisinart, balanced good heft with easy maneuverability.

While none of the pans failed the rice test outright, there were performance differences. In the Sitram, Revere, and Farberware pans, the rice stuck and dried out at the bottom, if only a little bit. Although this did not greatly affect the texture, the flavor, or the cleanup, we'd still choose a pan for which this was not an issue.

Every pan in the group turned out perfect pastry cream. During this test, we did observe one design element that made it easy to pour liquid from the pan neatly, without dribbles and spills. A rolled lip that flares slightly at the top of the pan helped control the pour. Only two pans in the group did not have a rolled lip: the All-Clad and the Calphalon.

So which pan do you want to buy? That depends largely on two things: your budget and your attention span. Based on our tests, we'd advise against really inexpensive pans—those that cost less than $50. For between $50 and $100, you can get a competent pan such as the Chantal, Sitram, or Cuisinart. The only caveat is that you may have to watch them carefully; they offer less room for error than our favorite pans, made by All-Clad, Calphalon, and KitchenAid.

# Rating Large Saucepans

WE TESTED EIGHT LARGE SAUCEPANS, EACH WITH A CAPACITY OF THREE TO FOUR QUARTS, IN THREE APPLICATIONS: sautéing onions, steaming rice, and preparing pastry cream. The pans are listed in order of preference based on their performance in these tests as well as on design factors. See www.americastestkitchen.com for up-to-date prices and mail-order sources for top-rated products.

**RECOMMENDED**
### All-Clad Stainless Steel 3 Quart Saucepan
**$139.99**
Performed beautifully, but why not include a rolled lip for neat pouring? A long, indented handle helps the cook maintain a secure grip when lifting this pan.

**RECOMMENDED**
### Calphalon Commercial Hard-Anodized 3½ Quart Saucepan
**$110.99**
The bruiser of the group—are we cooking or weight-training here? Performed well but has minor design shortcomings, including a lip that is not rolled.

**RECOMMENDED**
### KitchenAid Stainless Steel 3 Quart Saucepan
**$119.00**
The rolled lip makes for neat pouring, but the handle is too short for some testers. Otherwise, a solid performer.

**RECOMMENDED WITH RESERVATIONS**
### Chantal 3 Quart Saucepan #35-200S
**$89.99**
Sautés at a faster than usual clip, so it requires a bit of extra attention. Nothing unacceptable, however.

**RECOMMENDED WITH RESERVATIONS**
### Sitram Professional Induction 3.17 Quart Saucepan
**$56.90**
Especially light lid allowed steam to escape, so rice began to stick to the pan bottom. Otherwise, a decent pan.

**RECOMMENDED WITH RESERVATIONS**
### Cuisinart Everyday Stainless 3¾ Quart, Model 919-20
**$79.99**
Watch the sauté speed, which is a little faster than we like. Otherwise, a very serviceable saucepan.

**NOT RECOMMENDED**
### Revere Stainless Steel Copper Clad Bottom 3 Quart Saucepan
**$24.99**
This featherweight heats up and sautés exceptionally fast, so it can be difficult to control. Lid allowed significant steam to escape so rice browned and stuck a bit.

**NOT RECOMMENDED**
### Farberware Millennium 3 Quart Saucepan
**$44.99**
The handle was hot at the base and the performance far from ideal; this pan turned out dry rice and over-browned onions.

Geof keeps Chris on his toes as the crew lights our outdoor grilling location.

# STEAK tips

IN THIS CHAPTER

## THE RECIPES

Charcoal-Grilled Steak Tips
Gas-Grilled Steak Tips
Southwestern Marinade
Garlic, Ginger, and Soy Marinade

Steak Fries

## EQUIPMENT CORNER

Grill Brushes

## SCIENCE DESK

How to Infuse Meat with
    Moisture and Flavor

## TASTING LAB

Steak Tips

Steak tips and steak fries sound like bad menu offerings from your local low-rent steakhouse. The meat is tough and weirdly seasoned, and the thick fries are pale and soggy. No doubt the restaurant has used the cheapest scraps of meat for the steak tips (you really don't want to think about that), and the fries probably came frozen from their food purveyor.

But there is something appealing about taking a relatively inexpensive cut of meat and making it special. And there's no reason why steak fries have to be greasy and bland. If you started out with decent quality meat and fresh potatoes, could you make this humble fare special? The test kitchen felt confident that we could rescue these dishes from the clutches of the fast food empire and turn them into something you would actually welcome into your home.

# STEAK TIPS

**WHAT WE WANTED:** A way to turn this inexpensive cut into something worth grilling.

Steak tips have never been on our list of favorite meats. It's not that we're premium steak snobs, but we were skeptical about a cut of meat that has long been the darling of all-you-can-eat restaurant chains, where quantity takes precedence over quality. There is also some confusion about what constitutes a steak tip. Some steak tips are sautéed and served with a sauce (these are often called pub-style steak tips), some are marinated and grilled (known as tailgate tips). We were drawn to grilling and so began by testing five such recipes.

The recipes differed in the ingredients used to marinate the meat and in the marinating time. The simplest recipe marinated the tips in a bottled Italian-style salad dressing for 24 hours. The most complex marinated the meat for three days in a mixture that included aromatics and herbs. Despite such variations in time and ingredients, none of these grilled tips was very good. Some were mushy, but most were tough and dry. At this point, steak tips still seemed like a cheap cut of meat, with promising beefy flavor but poor texture.

Thinking that the problem might be the cut of meat, we went to the supermarket only to discover a confusing array of meats—cubes, strips, and steaks—labeled "steak tips." Still more confusing, these cubes, strips, and steaks could be cut from a half-dozen different parts of the cow.

After grilling more than 50 pounds of tips, it became clear that the only cut worth grilling is one referred to by butchers as flap meat. (For more information, see "Buying Steak Tips," page 172.) When we grilled whole flap meat steaks and then sliced them on the bias before serving, tasters were impressed. Although the meat was still a bit chewy, choosing the right cut was a start.

We now turned to marinades. Given the long-held belief that acidic marinades tenderize tough meat, we created four recipes using four popular acids: yogurt, wine, vinegar, and fruit juice. To determine the best timing, we let the meat sit in each marinade for four hours and for 24 hours. Curious about marinades' other claim to fame—flavoring—we added aromatics, spices, and herbs.

The yogurt marinade was the least favorite, producing dry meat that was chewy and tough. Tasters also panned the wine-based marinade. The meat was tough and dry, the flavors harsh and bland. Some tasters liked the complex flavor of the vinegar marinade, but everyone found the tips to be "overly chewy." The marinade prepared with pineapple juice was the favorite. Both the four-hour and 24-hour versions yielded juicy, tender, flavorful meat.

Why did pineapple juice make the best marinade? Our first thought was proteases, enzymes that help to break down proteins. Proteases are found in pineapple, papaya, and other fruits. One of them, *papain*, from papayas, is the active component of meat tenderizers such as Adolph's. The juice we had been using was pasteurized, however, and the heat of pasteurization is thought to disable such enzymes. To see if proteases were in fact at work, we devised three tests in which we made three more marinades: one with pasteurized pineapple juice from the supermarket; a second with pasteurized pineapple juice heated to the boiling point and then cooled; and a third with fresh pineapple pureed in a food processor.

The result? The fresh juice was a much more aggressive "tenderizer," so much so that it turned the meat mushy on the inside and slimy on the outside. We had learned three things: proteases do break down meat, but they don't make it any better (tasters universally disapproved of these tenderized tips); pasteurization does kill this enzyme (the fresh juice was much more powerful than the supermarket variety); and proteases were not responsible for the strong showing made by the original pineapple marinade. Why, then, did tasters prefer the pineapple marinade to those made with yogurt, wine, and vinegar?

After rereading the ingredient list in our pineapple marinade, we devised a new theory. The pineapple marinade included soy sauce, an ingredient that is packed with salt and that was not used in any of the other marinades. Was the soy sauce tenderizing the meat by acting like a brine of salt and water? In the past, the test kitchen has demonstrated the beneficial effects of brining on lean poultry and pork.

To answer these questions, we ran another series of tests, trying various oil-based marinades made with salt or soy sauce (in earlier tests, we had determined that oil helped to keep the meat moist and promoted searing). To use salt in a marinade, we first had to dissolve it. Because salt doesn't dissolve in oil, we used water, but the liquid prevented the meat from browning properly. That said, brining did make these steak tips tender and juicy.

We concluded that soy sauce, not pineapple juice, was the secret ingredient in tasters' favorite marinade. The salt in soy sauce improved the texture of the meat, and the soy sauce also promoted browning. We experimented with brining times and found that an hour was optimal. It allowed the thicker parts of the meat to become tender while preventing the thinner sections from becoming too salty.

We then went to work on flavor variations, adding garlic, ginger, orange zest, hot pepper, brown sugar, and scallions for an Asian marinade and making a Southwest-inspired marinade that included garlic, chili powder, cumin, cayenne, brown sugar, and tomato paste. We found that a squeeze of fresh citrus served with the steak provided a bright acidic counterpoint.

Because this relatively thin cut of meat cooks quickly, high heat is necessary to achieve a perfect crust. The uneven thickness of many of the steak tips presented a problem, though. The exterior would scorch by the time the thick portions were cooked, and the thin parts would be overcooked. A two-level fire, with more coals on one side of the grill to create hotter and cooler areas, solved the problem. We started cooking the tips over high heat to sear them and then moved them to the cooler area to finish cooking.

We prefer steaks grilled rare, so we were surprised to find that when cooked rare the meat was rubbery, whereas longer cooking gave it a tender chew—without drying out the meat. Even when cooked until well done, these tips were exceptionally juicy. We had the brine to thank again: The salty soy marinade helped the meat hold onto its moisture.

Conventional wisdom prompted one more test. We grilled two more batches of tips and sliced one immediately after it came off the grill and the other five minutes later. Sure enough, the rested tips were both more juicy and more tender. Finally, a recipe for steak tips as pleasing to the palate as they are to the pocketbook.

WHAT WE LEARNED: Buy flap meat sirloin tips, marinate the meat for at least an hour in a soy-based marinade, grill over a two-level fire, let the meat rest for five minutes, then slice thinly against the grain for meat that is tender and flavorful.

**CHARCOAL-GRILLED STEAK TIPS** Serves 4 to 6

A two-level fire allows you to brown the steak over the hot side of the grill, then move it to the cooler side if it is not yet cooked through. If your steak is thin, however, you may not need to use the cooler side of the grill. The times in the recipe below are for relatively even, 1-inch-thick steak tips. When grilling, bear in mind that even those tasters who usually prefer rare beef preferred steak tips cooked medium-rare to medium because the texture is firmer and not quite so chewy. Serve lime wedges with the Southwestern-marinated tips and orange wedges with the tips marinated in garlic, ginger, and soy sauce.

1   recipe marinade (recipes follow)
2   pounds flap meat sirloin steak tips, trimmed of excess fat
    Lime or orange wedges for serving

**1.** Combine the marinade and meat in a gallon-size zipper-lock bag; press out as much air as possible and seal the bag. Refrigerate for 1 hour, flipping the bag after 30 minutes to ensure that the meat marinates evenly.

**2.** About halfway through the marinating time, light a large chimney starter filled with hardwood charcoal (about 6 quarts) and allow to burn until all the charcoal is covered with a layer of fine gray ash. Build a two-level fire by stacking most of the coals on one side of the grill for a medium-hot fire. Arrange the remaining coals in a single layer on the other side of the grill for a medium-low fire. Set the cooking rack in place, cover the grill with the lid, and let the rack heat up, about 5 minutes. Use a wire brush to scrape clean the cooking rack.

**3.** Remove the steak tips from the marinade and pat dry with paper towels. Grill, uncovered, until well seared and dark brown on the first side, about 4 minutes. Using tongs, flip the steak tips and grill until the second side is well seared and the thickest part of the meat is slightly less done than

desired, 4 to 5 minutes for medium-rare (about 130 degrees on instant-read thermometer), 6 to 8 minutes for medium (about 135 degrees); if the exterior of the meat is browned but the steak is not yet cooked through, move the steak tips to the cooler side of the grill and continue to grill to the desired doneness.

**4.** Transfer the steak tips to a cutting board; tent the tips loosely with foil and let rest for 5 minutes. Slice the steak tips very thinly on the bias; serve immediately with the lime or orange wedges.

VARIATION

**GAS-GRILLED STEAK TIPS**

Follow the recipe for Charcoal-Grilled Steak Tips through step 1. When about 15 minutes of marinating time remains, turn all of the burners on the gas grill to high, close the lid, and heat the grill until hot, about 15 minutes. Continue with the recipe from step 3, grilling the steak tips covered.

---

### GETTING IT RIGHT: Buying Steak Tips

Steak tips can be cut from a half-dozen muscles and are sold in three basic forms: cubes, strips, and steaks. To make sure that you are buying the most flavorful cut (called flap meat sirloin tips by butchers and pictured at right), buy whole steaks.

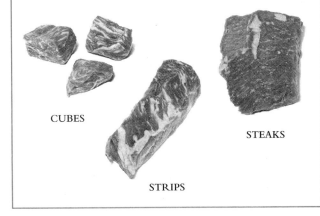

CUBES

STRIPS

STEAKS

## SOUTHWESTERN MARINADE

**Makes enough for 2 pounds of steak tips**

⅓  cup soy sauce

⅓  cup vegetable oil

3  medium cloves garlic, minced or pressed through a garlic press (about 1 tablespoon)

1  tablespoon dark brown sugar

1  tablespoon tomato paste

1  tablespoon chili powder

2  teaspoons ground cumin

¼  teaspoon cayenne

Combine all of the ingredients in a small bowl.

## GARLIC, GINGER, AND SOY MARINADE

**Makes enough for 2 pounds of steak tips**

⅓  cup soy sauce

3  tablespoons vegetable oil

3  tablespoons toasted sesame oil

3  medium cloves garlic, minced or pressed through a garlic press (about 1 tablespoon)

1  piece (1 inch) fresh ginger, minced (about 1 tablespoon)

2  tablespoons dark brown sugar

2  teaspoons grated zest from 1 orange

½  teaspoon red pepper flakes

1  medium scallion, sliced thin

Combine all of the ingredients in a small bowl.

## TASTING LAB: Steak Tips

STEAK TIPS CAN COME FROM TWO AREAS OF THE COW. One kind comes from tender, expensive cuts in the middle of the cow, such as the tenderloin. These tips are a superior cut but not what we consider to be a true steak tip, which should be a more pedestrian cut that is magically transformed into a desirable dish through marinating and cooking. If the steak tips at your market cost $8 to $10 per pound, the meat likely comes from the tenderloin.

True steak tips come from various muscles in the sirloin and round and cost about $5 per pound. After tasting 50 pounds of cheap steak tips, tasters had a clear favorite: a single muscle that butchers call flap meat and that is typically labeled "sirloin tips." A whole piece of flap meat weighs about 2½ pounds. One piece can range in thickness from ½ inch to 1½ inches and may be sold as cubes, strips, or small steaks. It has a rich, deep beefy flavor and a distinctive longitudinal grain.

We found that it's best to buy flap meat in steak form rather than cubes or strips, which are often cut from nearby muscles in the hip and butt that are neither as tasty nor as tender. Because meat labeling is so haphazard, you must visually identify this cut; buying it in steak form makes this easy.

## SCIENCE DESK: How to Infuse Meat with Moisture and Flavor

IN BRINING, TWO NATURAL PHENOMENA COMBINE TO yield great-tasting meat: osmosis and diffusion. Osmosis controls the movement of water. In brining, the net flow of water is into the meat, producing moister meat after cooking. Diffusion is the movement of molecules from an area of higher concentration to one of lower concentration. In brining, salt penetrates the meat through diffusion. It serves a cook well to remember diffusion when placing food in a liquid. Soaking, simmering, and marinating all present the cook with a golden opportunity to infuse any flavor—not just that of salt—into food simply by adding it to the liquid. The net result is always more flavor. A little patience is required, though, because diffusion can be quite slow. Our steak tips, for example, need a full hour for complete flavor development.

## EQUIPMENT CORNER: Grill Brushes

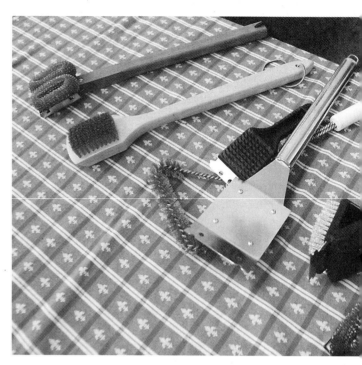

ANYONE WHO HAS GRILLED A RACK OF STICKY BARBECUED ribs has had to deal with the task of removing the sugary, burned-on mess that gets left behind. The ideal time to do this is soon after your food comes off the grill, but, if you're like most of us, you close the lid, walk away, and save the mess for the next time grill duty calls. We set out to find a grill brush that could make the tedious task of cleaning a gunked-up grill grate more efficient. And we did not want to exert superhuman strength to get the job done.

To test the brushes, we concocted a "paint"—a mixture of honey, molasses, mustard, and barbecue sauce—that we could burn onto our grates. We coated the grates four times, baking them for one hour in the test kitchen ovens between coats. The result was a charred mess that would be sure to challenge even the hardiest of brushes. The grates were put back on the grills, which were then heated so we could test the brushes under real-life conditions.

The seven brushes we tested were chosen based on the construction and design of the handle and the scrubbing head. The handle of the stainless steel model was decidedly the heaviest and looked to be the most durable, but it absorbed heat at an alarming rate. Plastic performed adequately if you didn't spend too much time in one place on the grill (melting occurred) and if the handle was long enough. One plastic-handled brush, the Grill Pro, with a skimpy 5-inch handle, didn't even make it through the first test. The handle was so short that we couldn't get the brush to the far side of the grill without getting burned. A combination plastic/aluminum brush handle was so flexible it caused burnt knuckles when pressed with any strength. The material of choice for grill brush handles is clearly wood, which is relatively comfortable and durable.

In terms of the scrubbing heads, six of the seven brushes tested had brass bristles. Among these six, those with stiffer bristles fared better than their softer counterparts, but none of them worked all that well. The bristles on most bent after a few strokes and trapped large quantities of gunk, thereby decreasing their efficiency.

In the end, only one brush was able to successfully clean our molten mess down to the grill grate in a reasonable number of strokes. The unusual but incredibly effective Grill Wizard has no brass bristles to bend, break, or clog with unwanted grease and grime. Instead, this brush comes equipped with two large woven mesh stainless steel "scrubbie" pads. The pads are able to conform to any grill grate's spacing, size, and material, including porcelain. Best of all, the pads are detachable, washable, and replaceable. The 14-inch handle, made of poplar, is smooth, with rounded edges (unlike its square-cut competitors), with a hook for easy storage.

The one downside to this brush was the two-page instruction sheet that came affixed to the underside of the scrubbie head (yes, a grill brush with instructions). Had we not seen a corner of the instructions sticking out, we would have used the brush and burned the instructions. Not only do the instructions need better placement, but operating a grill brush should not be made to seem as difficult as programming a DVD player. Still, though the instructions were confusing, the process of replacing the scrubbies was fairly easy.

# Rating Grill Brushes

WE TESTED SEVEN GRILL BRUSHES ON GRILL GRATES WE HAD DIRTIED WITH A BAKED-ON MIXTURE OF HONEY, molasses, mustard, and barbecue sauce. The brushes were rated on effectiveness, design, and ease of use and are listed in order of preference. See www.americastestkitchen.com for up-to-date prices and mail-order sources for top-rated products.

### HIGHLY RECOMMENDED
#### Grill Wizard China Grill Brush $19.99
The most-odd looking of the bunch, with no bristles; instead, stainless steel "scrubbie" pads are held in place by stainless bars. The hardwood handle is very comfortable and smooth. The Grill Wizard cleaned the grate completely in 40 strokes. The scrubbies were very dirty after the test, but they can be removed and washed (or replaced for $2.50). After being cleaned, the scrubbies were in great shape.

### RECOMMENDED WITH RESERVATIONS
#### Weber 18-Inch Grill Brush $6.99
This classic brush with brass bristles and a hardwood handle cleaned fairly well, but the bristles showed wear and tear in our tests.

### NOT RECOMMENDED
#### Brushtech Wide-Faced, Industrial Quality Grill Brush $12.99
The bristles on this wide brush were the stiffest of the lot, but they wore down to the metal in just 70 strokes. The plastic handle was too flexible and the unusual design did not win any fans among our testers.

### NOT RECOMMENDED
#### Grill Pro Two-Sided Grill Brush $10.00
The bristles looked bad after 50 strokes. The scrubber on the other side did not work at all; it just burned. The scraper did not work because of the location of both scrubber and bristles.

### NOT RECOMMENDED
#### Original Char Buster Grill Brush $7.95
This brush did not clean at all. The short brass bristles collapsed during testing, and we ended up scraping the grill with the brush head. The 12-inch plastic handle was fairly comfortable though.

### NOT RECOMMENDED
#### Mr. BBQ Premium Grill Brush $9.99
Even after 150 strokes, this brush could not clean the grill. The soft bristles collapsed almost immediately after we started using this brush. The metal handle absorbed too much heat and became impossible to hold.

### NOT RECOMMENDED
#### Grill Pro Grill Brush $3.83
The 5-inch plastic handle is so short that we could not complete the test without risking serious burns on our hands. Yes, this brush is cheap, but its design makes absolutely no sense to us.

# STEAK FRIES

**WHAT WE WANTED:** Much like good french fries, good steak fries should be crisp on the outside and tender on the inside. They should never be oily, dry, mealy, or soggy.

Steak fries are the rustic, country cousin to french fries. With their skin left on and their shape determined largely by the shape of the potato, these wedge-shaped fries are easier to prepare and less wasteful than the typical french fry, where much effort is expended to obtain a ruler-perfect consistency of shape. They are much easier for the home cook to prepare.

As with regular french fries, we found that starchy russets fried up beautifully. Their dense, starchy texture cooked to a consistently tender interior while the thick skin fried up good and crisp. Russets we bought in 5-pound bags, however, came in various sizes and were difficult to cut into uniformly sized wedges. We found that the russets sold loose, in bins, are more consistent in size and are easier to cut into same-size wedges for more consistent cooking times. After cooking up fries of various thicknesses, we found that we preferred wedges with an outside edge measuring ¾ inch wide; this works out to one large potato cut into 12 wedges. Any thicker or thinner, and the ratio of tender interior to crisp exterior was thrown off.

Many recipes for deep-fried potatoes suggest refrigerating the raw wedges before frying them, and we found this step to be crucial. Cooling the potatoes down before plunging them in the hot oil allows them to cook more slowly and evenly. By soaking the wedges in a refrigerated bowl of ice water for at least 30 minutes, we were able to ensure that the inner pulp was fully cooked before the outside turned overly brown.

Like most who've fried potatoes before us, we found that simply dunking the chilled, raw fries in hot oil and cooking them until they are done will not produce a good fry. By the time the inside of the fry is cooked and the outside is well browned, the fry itself is wooden and overcooked. We first par-fried them at a relatively low temperature to help them cook through without much browning. We then gave them a brief repose to cool off before refrying them quickly in oil at a higher temperature until nicely browned. In combination with the ice water bath, this technique worked like a dream. The thick wedges of potato were evenly cooked, with tender middles and crisp, browned exteriors.

What is the right fat for making perfect steak fries? To find out, we experimented with lard, vegetable shortening, canola oil, corn oil, and peanut oil. Lard and shortening make great fries, but we figured that many cooks won't want to use these products. We moved on to canola oil, the ballyhooed oil of the '90s, but we were unhappy with the results: bland, almost watery fries. Corn oil was the most forgiving oil in the test kitchen. It rebounded well from temperature fluctuations and held up very well in subsequent frying, and the fries tasted marvelous. A potato fried in peanut oil is light, and the flavor is rich but not dense. The earthy flavor of the potato is there, as with corn oil, but is not overbearing. It is our top choice.

**WHAT WE LEARNED:** Cut russet potatoes into ¾-inch wedges, soak them in ice water for at least 30 minutes, and then fry the potatoes twice (the first time to cook through the centers and the next time to brown and crisp the exteriors) in peanut oil.

---

**FOOD FACT: Potatoes**

Potatoes are America's favorite vegetable, easily outpacing tomatoes, which are in second place. Each man, woman, and child in this country consumes about 135 pounds of potatoes every year. What's our favorite way to eat potatoes? French fries are king. In fact, 13 percent of Americans eat French fries every day.

---

**STEAK FRIES** Serves 4

See the illustrations below for tips on cutting potatoes into wedges. The potatoes must be soaked in cold water, fried once, cooled, and then fried a second time—so start this recipe at least one hour before dinner.

4    large russet potatoes (about 10 ounces each),
     scrubbed and cut lengthwise into ¾-inch-thick
     wedges (about 12 wedges per potato)
2    quarts peanut oil
     Salt and ground black pepper

**1.** Place the cut fries in a large bowl, cover with cold water by at least 1 inch, and then cover with ice cubes. Refrigerate at least 30 minutes or up to 3 days.

**2.** In a 5-quart pot or Dutch oven fitted with a clip-on candy thermometer, or in a large electric fryer, heat the oil over medium-low heat to 325 degrees. (The oil will bubble up when you add fries, so be sure you have at least 3 inches of room at the top of the pot.)

**3.** Pour off the ice and water, quickly the wrap potatoes in a clean kitchen towel, and thoroughly pat them dry. Increase the heat to medium-high and add the fries, one handful at a time, to the hot oil. Fry, stirring with a Chinese skimmer or large-holed slotted spoon, until the potatoes are limp and soft and have turned from white to gold, about 10 minutes. (The oil temperature will drop 50 to 60 degrees during this frying.) Use a skimmer or slotted spoon to transfer the fries to a triple thickness of paper towels to drain; let rest at least 10 minutes. (The fries can stand at room temperature up to 2 hours or be wrapped in paper towels, sealed in a zipper-lock bag, and frozen up to 1 month.)

**4.** When ready to serve the fries, reheat the oil to 350 degrees. Using the paper towels as a funnel, pour the potatoes into the hot oil. Discard the paper towels and line a wire rack with another triple thickness of paper towels. Fry the potatoes, stirring fairly constantly, until medium brown and puffed, 8 to 10 minutes. Transfer to the paper towel–lined rack to drain. Season to taste with salt and pepper. Serve immediately.

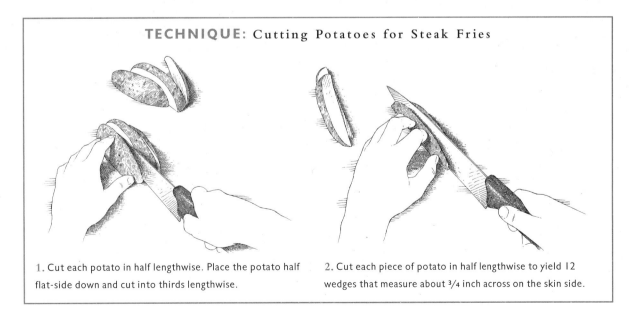

**TECHNIQUE:** Cutting Potatoes for Steak Fries

1. Cut each potato in half lengthwise. Place the potato half flat-side down and cut into thirds lengthwise.

2. Cut each piece of potato in half lengthwise to yield 12 wedges that measure about ¾ inch across on the skin side.

Ingredients are assembled for the pork and eggplant stir-fry.

# STIR-FRY 101

CHAPTER 15

**IN THIS CHAPTER**

**THE RECIPES**

Stir-Fried Beef and Broccoli with
    Oyster Sauce

Stir-Fried Pork, Eggplant, and
    Onions with Garlic and Black
    Pepper
Stir-Fried Pork, Green Beans,
    and Red Bell Pepper with
    Gingery Oyster Sauce
Spicy Stir-Fried Pork, Asparagus,
    and Onions with Lemon
    Grass

**EQUIPMENT CORNER**

Electric Woks

**TASTING LAB**

Broccoli Relations
Oyster Sauce

Ordering Chinese take-out is like playing Russian roulette. Once in a great while, those little white cartons deliver tasty morsels of stir-fried meat and vegetables in a lightly thickened, potent, and savory sauce, with the flavors of garlic and ginger clean and invigorating. Unfortunately, the reality is usually something quite different. The meat is tough, the vegetables are overcooked, and the sauce is thick and gloppy. The garlic and ginger taste scorched and the sauce is bland, greasy, or overly sweet.

We think the best stir-fries are made at home, where it's easier to pay attention to detail and the food can be served immediately. Over the years, the test kitchen has developed some foolproof guidelines that guarantee great stir-fries.

# STIR-FRIED BEEF AND BROCCOLI

**WHAT WE WANTED:** Tender beef and jade green, crisp-tender broccoli coated (not smothered) in a deeply flavored, silky sauce.

Order beef and broccoli in most restaurants and you are served a pile of chewy, gray "beef" surrounded by a forest of giant, overcooked army-issue broccoli. Worst of all is the thick-as-pudding brown sauce (more suitable for meatloaf than stir-fry), which, aside from being flavored with burnt garlic, is otherwise tasteless.

We turned to several recipes in cookbooks for help. Although most produced that gloppy, tasteless mass of beef and broccoli that we were trying to avoid, a couple of recipes showed promise. In these recipes, we found that each component of the dish—the beef, the broccoli, and even the sauce—was distinct and cooked to the best of its ability. Grateful for this glimmer of hope, we grabbed a 12-inch, nonstick skillet (our pan of choice when it comes to stir-frying because its flat surface perfectly matches the surface of the American stovetop) and started cooking.

Although flank steak—a chewy cut from the underbelly beneath the loin—is most often called for, in this stir-fry, we also tested a few other boneless cuts. Tender and expensive filet mignon (from the tenderloin) was mushy and dull flavored in this application. Strip steak (from the loin) was good, but not as good as the flank. A blade steak (cut from the shoulder blade area of the chuck) was similar to the tenderloin—too soft and too mild tasting. Flank steak clearly offered the biggest beefy taste. Slicing the steak thinly across the grain made it tender, but when we used a less than razor-sharp knife (like the knives found in most home kitchens), the steak tugged on the blade. We threw the steak in the freezer for 20 minutes to stiffen it up enough to make slicing easier.

Having recently discovered that using soy sauce in a marinade aids in tenderizing meat (see Chapter 14, "Steak Tips"), we tested one batch of unmarinated flank steak against batches marinated in soy sauce for two hours, one hour, and ten minutes. The results were dramatic. Two hours was overkill; the steak became gummy and spongy. One hour was perfect. The steak was tender and full of great soy flavor. Just a few minutes of marinating, however, made a big difference, which is good news if you don't have the full hour to marinate the steak.

But marinating introduced a new problem. The soaked beef expunged its liquid well before the meat had time to brown. We found that the best way to counter this was to limit the time the beef spent in the pan. The skillet had to be incredibly hot so that the meat would begin to brown in seconds. Also, many recipes simply throw all of the beef at once into the pan. The result was beef that steamed in its own juices and never browned (ergo the gray mass). We found it best to cook the beef in two batches and give it plenty of room to sear. Finally, getting rid of some of the marinade by way of draining the soaked beef before cooking helped immensely.

Cooking the broccoli evenly was the next test, and our first decision here was to get rid of those gargantuan pieces of broccoli we found in both the restaurant and recipe versions of this dish. Fork-friendly 1-inch pieces of broccoli floret seemed right, and by trimming the tough exterior from the broccoli stems and slicing them into thin ⅛-inch slices, we were able to cook the stems right along with the florets.

Most recipes cook the broccoli either by straightforward stir-frying or by steaming or blanching. While the former technique produced unevenly cooked broccoli, steaming or blanching made for tender broccoli every time. Unfortunately, this technique required an additional pan. In an effort to avoid this, we modified our use of the pan we'd already been using. After cooking the beef and removing it from the skillet, we stir-fried the broccoli for a few seconds, added water to the pan, and covered it tightly in hopes of

steaming the broccoli. This greatly simplified the recipe and produced superior broccoli—steamed to perfect tenderness and a brilliant emerald hue.

As for other vegetables, tasters wanted to keep this dish true to its name, save for the addition of red bell pepper, which added sweetness and vivid color. After removing the broccoli, we tossed the peppers into the hot pan and cooked them briefly to retain their crispness.

Garlic was a must, but we had to figure out the best way to add it to the mix. Added to the marinade, the garlic scorched in the skillet as it cooked with the beef. Added with the broccoli, it tasted raw. In the end we added minced garlic (along with some well-received ginger) to the skillet when the red peppers were nearly finished cooking.

Oyster-flavored sauce is the typical base for the sauce in this dish. Indeed, in some restaurants, it is referred to as "beef and broccoli in oyster sauce." We found no need to depart from the tradition of oyster sauce, as its deep, earthy notes provided the right flavor base and its thick consistency (think ketchup) added great body to the sauce. Soy sauce was next up for consideration, but we found it unnecessary; there was already enough in both the oyster sauce and the beef marinade. Rice vinegar and sherry are common additions, but only the latter was approved for its warm flavor.

Chicken stock was also welcomed to balance the flavors. Just a little toasted sesame oil and light brown sugar and the sauce took a sweet and nutty turn for the better.

Finally, satisfied with the flavor of the sauce, we added it to the pan along with the browned beef and steamed broccoli. We tossed the mixture together, but the sauce pooled on the bottom of the skillet. Clearly, the sauce wasn't thick enough, so we reluctantly returned to an often used but frequently troublesome ingredient: cornstarch. While many recipes (including some used in our early failed tests) called for a tablespoon or more of this thickener, we started more modestly. With a tentative hand, we stirred in the cornstarch until we had used only 1 teaspoon.

And now we had it: a sensuous sauce that barely clung to the deeply browned, tender beef and perfectly cooked jade green broccoli. The kitchen was studded with the heady aroma of garlic, and we knew that Chinatown had come home.

**WHAT WE LEARNED:** Use thinly sliced flank steak for the best texture and flavor, marinate it in soy sauce to improve on that texture and flavor, stir-fry the meat in batches to make sure it browns, and then coat with an oyster sauce mixture that is lightly thickened with cornstarch.

## STIR-FRIED BEEF AND BROCCOLI WITH OYSTER SAUCE Serves 4

To make slicing the flank steak easier, freeze it for about 20 minutes before slicing. Steamed white rice is the perfect accompaniment for this stir-fry.

  1    pound flank steak, sliced according to the illustrations at right
  3    tablespoons soy sauce
  1    tablespoon dry sherry
  2    tablespoons low-sodium chicken broth
  5    tablespoons oyster sauce
  1    tablespoon light brown sugar
  1    teaspoon Asian sesame oil
  1    teaspoon cornstarch
  6    medium cloves garlic, minced or pressed through a garlic press (about 2 tablespoons)
  1    piece (1 inch) ginger, minced (about 1 tablespoon)
  3    tablespoons peanut or vegetable oil
  1¼   pounds broccoli, florets cut into bite-sized pieces, stems trimmed, peeled, and cut on the diagonal into ⅛-inch-thick slices
  ⅓    cup water
  1    small red bell pepper, cored, seeded, and diced
  3    medium scallions, sliced ½ inch thick on the diagonal

**1.** Combine the beef and soy sauce in a medium bowl; cover with plastic wrap and refrigerate at least 10 minutes or up to 1 hour, stirring once. Meanwhile, whisk the sherry, chicken broth, oyster sauce, sugar, sesame oil, and cornstarch in a measuring cup. Combine the garlic, ginger, and 1½ teaspoons peanut oil in a small bowl.

**2.** Drain the beef and discard the liquid. Heat 1½ teaspoons peanut oil in a 12-inch nonstick skillet over high heat until smoking. Add half of the beef to the skillet and break up clumps; cook without stirring, 1 minute, then stir and cook

until the beef is browned about the edges, about 30 seconds. Transfer the beef to a medium bowl. Add 1½ teaspoons peanut oil to the skillet, heat until just smoking, and repeat with the remaining beef.

**3.** Add 1 tablespoon peanut oil to the now-empty skillet; heat until just smoking. Add the broccoli and cook 30 seconds; add the water, cover the pan, and lower the heat to medium. Steam the broccoli until tender-crisp, about 2 minutes; transfer to a paper towel–lined plate. Add the remaining 1½ teaspoons peanut oil to the skillet; increase the heat to high and heat until just smoking. Add the bell

---

**TECHNIQUE:**
**Slicing Flank Steak for Stir-Fries**

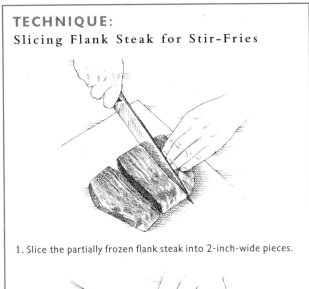

1. Slice the partially frozen flank steak into 2-inch-wide pieces.

2. Cut each piece of flank steak against the grain into very thin slices.

pepper and cook, stirring frequently, until spotty brown, about 1½ minutes. Clear the center of the skillet; add the garlic and ginger to the clearing and cook, mashing the mixture with a spoon, until fragrant, about 15 to 20 seconds, then stir the mixture into the peppers. Return the beef and broccoli to the skillet and toss to combine. Whisk the sauce to recombine, then add to the skillet; cook, stirring constantly, until the sauce is thickened and evenly distributed, about 30 seconds. Transfer to a serving platter, sprinkle with the scallions, and serve.

---

## TECHNIQUE: Stir-Frying 101

Whether you are making beef and broccoli, kung pao shrimp, or chicken with ginger, there are six key steps you should follow to turn out a perfect stir-fry. Use very little oil, preferably peanut, at each step listed below—no more than 1 tablespoon and less when possible.

**1.** Preparing the ingredients in advance is key. While the meat, seafood, or chicken is marinating, whisk the sauce ingredients together in a measuring cup and add a small amount of oil to the garlic and ginger.

**2.** Heat the oil in a 12-inch nonstick skillet until smoking. Drain the meat, seafood, or chicken and add half to the pan. Cook until well browned. Remove to a large bowl and repeat with more oil and the remaining meat, seafood, or chicken.

**3.** Stir-fry long-cooking vegetables—such as broccoli, asparagus, or green beans—in oil in the empty pan, add a little water, cover, and then steam. Once the vegetables are crisp-tender, transfer them to a bowl.

**4.** Stir-fry short-cooking vegetables—such as peppers or onions—for a minute or two in oil in the empty pan.

**5.** When the vegetables are slightly browned, add the garlic and ginger to the center of the pan. Cook until fragrant (15 to 20 seconds), and then stir the aromatics into vegetables.

**6.** Add the meat and long-cooking vegetables back to the skillet. Whisk the sauce to recombine, then pour it into the skillet and toss with the meat and vegetables. Once everything is hot (30 to 60 seconds), serve immediately.

## TASTING LAB: Broccoli Relations

BESIDES SUPERMARKET STANDARD BROCCOLI, WE TESTED some other "broccoli" options in our beef and broccoli recipe and found that all worked well.

Chinese broccoli, sometimes referred to as Chinese kale or *gai lan*, is the broccoli called for in many authentic recipes. Made of mostly thick stems and leaves, it has a mildly bitter flavor that tastes of bell pepper. Trim the yellowed or bruised leaves and bottom 1 inch of the stem from 1 pound of Chinese broccoli, then cut into 2-inch-long pieces. Chinese broccoli can be cooked exactly like regular broccoli in the recipe.

Broccoli rabe, also known as *rapini*, is actually a type of turnip green. Also made mostly of leaves and stems, broccoli rabe has a much stronger flavor. Cut off the bottom 2 inches of the stems from 1 pound of broccoli rabe, then cut into 2-inch-long pieces. Cook according to the recipe instructions, increasing the steaming time to 3 minutes.

Baby broccoli, also sold under the trademarked names Broccolini or Asperation, looks like a mix of broccoli and asparagus, but it's actually a cross between broccoli and Chinese broccoli. Very mild in flavor, the stalks are tender and do not need to be peeled. Remove any leaves from 1 pound of baby broccoli, then cut into 2-inch-long pieces. Baby broccoli may be cooked exactly according to recipe.

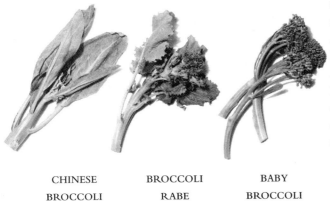

CHINESE
BROCCOLI

BROCCOLI
RABE

BABY
BROCCOLI

## TASTING LAB: Oyster Sauce

OYSTER SAUCE, WHICH IS ACTUALLY CALLED OYSTER-FLAVORED sauce, is a rich, concentrated mixture of oyster extracts, soy sauce, brine, and assorted seasonings. This brown sauce is thick, salty, and strong tasting. It is used sparingly to enhance the flavor of many dishes, including those—like some of the stir-fries in this chapter—without any seafood.

A trip to our local grocery store and Asian market turned up five different brands of bottled oyster sauce. Lee Kum Kee dominated the shelves with three varieties: Choy Sun, Panda Brand, and Premium Brand. Coin Tree and Sa Cheng rounded out the list. Although oyster sauce is too strong to be used as a condiment, we thought it important to take note of the raw, unadulterated flavor of each bottle before using it in a recipe. Each brand of the potent sauce received the same standard comments: "salty," "biting," and "fishy." However, when we mixed the bottled oyster sauces with other ingredients—sherry, soy sauce, sesame oil, sugar, and freshly ground black pepper—and then made simple stir-fries, our tasters were able to detect a wider range of flavors.

The most authentic of the group was undoubtedly Lee Kum Kee's Premium Brand Oyster Flavored Sauce with Dried Scallop. Admittedly intense and somewhat fishy, it was the only sauce with true depth of flavor; its saltiness was balanced by sweet caramel undertones, and the oyster flavor was strong. However, this sauce is not for the faint of heart, as one taster proclaimed, "My American taste buds can't take it." According to Jason Wong, president of AsiaFoods.com, Lee Kum Kee's Premium sauce is the favorite among the Asian-American population and the "only one" used in restaurants. It is also the most expensive sauce we tested ($5.79 for an 18-ounce bottle). All of this notwithstanding, the other favorite among tasters was Sa Cheng Oyster Flavored Sauce ($1.59 for a 15-ounce bottle), preferred because it was mild and "gravylike." The other three bottled sauces we tried didn't seem to add much to our stir-fries. As one taster put it, they "may just as well have been soy sauce."

# PORK AND VEGETABLE STIR-FRIES

**WHAT WE WANTED:** Stir-fries with tender, flavorful pork and perfectly cooked vegetables. They would taste authentic but would not have epic ingredient lists.

From a pork and vegetable stir-fry—homemade or ordered out—we usually expect nothing more than tough, tasteless pork and barely cooked vegetables in a thick, slithery sauce. We set out to make pork and vegetable stir-fries that were both tasty and tender without being labor-intensive.

Pork shoulder is often called for in authentic pork stir-fry recipes, but because pieces weighing less than several pounds can be difficult to find, we excluded pork shoulder as a possibility. Instead, we tried stir-frying the more sensible options: boneless loin chops and tenderloin, both cut into strips small enough to eat with a piece or two of vegetable. The loin chops cooked into dry, tight, tough pieces not unlike shoe leather. The tenderloin was the uncontested winner. Tender and yielding, it had the textural quality of a filet mignon.

The next task was to determine whether marinating the pork was worth the trouble. We tossed one plain batch of tenderloin strips unceremoniously into the skillet and a second batch with some soy and sherry to marinate a few minutes before cooking. The marinade, which boosted flavor quickly and easily, was the clear winner. But it also dealt us a setback when the pork failed to brown properly, even in the hottest skillet. The reason? Pork tenderloin is almost always sold in shrink-wrapped packages and therefore contains a lot of moisture (and we were adding more). We discovered that the answer was to cook the pork in batches over high heat. This way, the moisture that the pork released evaporated rapidly, and, after it did, the pork was free to take on color. Each batch needed to cook for only 2 minutes—quite a flash in the pan.

With the pork out of the skillet and set aside in a bowl, we worked on the vegetables and flavorings. Because different vegetables cook at different rates, batch cooking was necessary (batch cooking also prevents overcrowding, so that the vegetables, too, can brown their way to good flavor). We added various mixes of aromatics (such as garlic and ginger) using our standard stir-fry method (add at the end of cooking to a clearing in the center of the skillet, where they can cook long enough to develop their flavors but not long enough to burn).

We were not after an abundance of sauce, just enough light-bodied liquid to cling to the pork and vegetables and provide succulence. If we added enough soy sauce or fish sauce to provide the bulk of the sauce, saltiness or fishy pungency prevailed. If we added water, the flavor was hollow. Chicken broth was the solution. It provided a liquid element that gave the sauce backbone and did not dilute flavor. We also found that a small addition of acid—lime juice or rice vinegar—did a lot to brighten flavors. Finally, just a teaspoon of cornstarch allowed the sauce to lightly cloak the meat and vegetables instead of pooling at the bottom of the plate.

**WHAT WE LEARNED:** Use pork tenderloin for the best texture, marinate the meat to improve its flavor, stir-fry it in batches to promote browning, and cloak everything in potently flavored sauce that has been lightly thickened with cornstarch.

---

## FOOD FACT: Rice

Americans don't eat much rice, at least compared with rest of the world. Our per capita consumption of rice is about 20 pounds per year. In many Asian countries, annual per capita consumption runs about 300 pounds, and, in the United Arab Emirates, that figure is an astonishing 450 pounds. The French, who eat about 10 pounds of rice per person every year, are one of the few peoples to eat less rice than Americans do.

## STIR-FRIED PORK, EGGPLANT, AND ONIONS WITH GARLIC AND BLACK PEPPER

**Serves 4 as a main dish with rice**

This classic Thai stir-fry is not for those with timid palates.

| | |
|---|---|
| 12 | ounces pork tenderloin, prepared according to the illustrations on page 188 |
| 1 | teaspoon plus 2½ tablespoons fish sauce |
| 1 | teaspoon plus 2½ tablespoons soy sauce |
| 2 | tablespoons low-sodium chicken broth |
| 2 | teaspoons juice from 1 lime |
| 2½ | tablespoons light brown sugar |
| 1 | teaspoon cornstarch |
| 12 | cloves garlic, minced or pressed through a garlic press (about 3½ tablespoons) |
| 2 | teaspoons ground black pepper |
| 3½ | tablespoons peanut or vegetable oil |
| 1 | pound eggplant, cut into ¾-inch cubes |
| 1 | large onion, cut into ¼- to ⅜-inch wedges |
| ½ | cup fresh cilantro leaves, chopped coarse |

**1.** Combine pork, 1 teaspoon fish sauce, and 1 teaspoon soy sauce in a small bowl. Whisk remaining 2½ tablespoons each fish sauce and soy sauce, chicken broth, lime juice, sugar, and cornstarch in a measuring cup. Combine the garlic, pepper, and 1 tablespoon oil in a small bowl.

**2.** Heat 1½ teaspoons oil in a 12-inch nonstick skillet over high heat until smoking; add half of the pork to the skillet and cook, stirring occasionally and breaking up clumps, until well-browned, about 2 minutes. Transfer the pork to a medium bowl. Repeat with an additional 1½ teaspoons oil and the remaining pork. Add 1 tablespoon oil to the now-empty skillet; add the eggplant and cook, stirring every 30 seconds, until browned and no longer spongy, about 5 minutes; transfer to the bowl with the pork. Add the remaining 1½ teaspoons oil to the skillet; add the onion and cook, stirring occasionally, until beginning to brown and soften, about 2 minutes. Clear the center of the skillet, add the garlic/pepper mixture to the clearing; cook, mashing the mixture with a spoon, until fragrant and beginning to brown, about 1½ minutes, then stir the mixture into the onions. Add the pork and eggplant; toss to combine. Whisk the sauce to recombine, then add to the skillet; cook, stirring constantly, until the sauce is thickened and evenly distributed, about 30 seconds. Transfer to a serving platter; sprinkle with the cilantro and serve.

## STIR-FRIED PORK, GREEN BEANS, AND RED BELL PEPPER WITH GINGERY OYSTER SAUCE

**Serves 4 as a main dish with rice**

See page 184 for more information on oyster sauce.

| | |
|---|---|
| 12 | ounces pork tenderloin, prepared according to the illustrations on page 188 |
| 2 | teaspoons soy sauce |
| 2 | teaspoons plus 1 tablespoon dry sherry |
| ⅓ | cup low-sodium chicken broth |
| 2½ | tablespoons oyster sauce |
| 2 | teaspoons toasted sesame oil |
| 1 | teaspoon rice vinegar |
| ¼ | teaspoon ground white pepper |
| 1 | teaspoon cornstarch |
| 2 | cloves garlic, minced or pressed through a garlic press (about 2 teaspoons) |
| 1 | piece (about 2 inches) fresh ginger, grated (about 2 tablespoons) |
| 3 | tablespoons peanut or vegetable oil |
| 12 | ounces green beans, cut on the diagonal into 2-inch lengths |
| ¼ | cup water |
| 1 | large red bell pepper, cut into ¾-inch squares |
| 3 | medium scallions, sliced thin on the diagonal |

**1.** Combine the pork, soy sauce, and 2 teaspoons sherry in a small bowl. Whisk the remaining 1 tablespoon sherry, chicken broth, oyster sauce, sesame oil, rice vinegar, white pepper, and cornstarch in a measuring cup. Combine the garlic, ginger, and 1½ teaspoons peanut oil in a small bowl.

**2.** Heat 1½ teaspoons peanut oil in a 12-inch nonstick skillet over high heat until smoking; add half of the pork to the skillet and cook, stirring occasionally and breaking up clumps, until well-browned, about 2 minutes. Transfer the pork to a medium bowl. Repeat with an additional 1½ teaspoons peanut oil and the remaining pork. Add 1 tablespoon peanut oil to the now-empty skillet; add the green beans and cook, stirring occasionally, until spotty brown, about 2 minutes. Add the water, cover the pan, and lower the heat to medium. Steam until the beans are tender-crisp, 2 to 3 minutes; transfer beans to the bowl with the pork. Add the remaining 1½ teaspoons oil to the skillet; add the bell pepper and cook, stirring frequently, until spotty brown, about 2 minutes. Clear the center of the skillet, then add the garlic/ginger mixture to the clearing; cook, mashing the mixture with a spoon, until fragrant, about 45 seconds, then stir the mixture into the peppers. Add the pork and green beans; toss to combine. Whisk the sauce to recombine, then add to the skillet; cook, stirring constantly, until the sauce is thickened and evenly distributed, about 30 seconds. Transfer to a serving platter; sprinkle with the scallions and serve.

## SPICY STIR-FRIED PORK, ASPARAGUS, AND ONIONS WITH LEMON GRASS

**Serves 4 as a main dish with rice**

To use lemon grass, peel off the tough outer leaves to reveal a creamy white interior, then trim off the bottom inch of the stalk. Of what remains, the bottom 4 or 5 inches can be minced.

| | |
|---|---|
| 12 | ounces pork tenderloin, prepared according to the illustrations on page 188 |
| 1 | teaspoon plus 2 tablespoons fish sauce |
| 1 | teaspoon soy sauce |
| ⅓ | cup low-sodium chicken broth |
| 2 | teaspoons juice from 1 lime |
| 1 | tablespoon light brown sugar |
| 1 | teaspoon cornstarch |
| 2 | medium cloves garlic, minced or pressed through a garlic press (about 2 teaspoons) |
| ¼ | cup minced lemon grass from 2 stalks (see note) |
| ¾ | teaspoon red pepper flakes |
| 3½ | tablespoons peanut or vegetable oil |
| 1 | pound asparagus, cut on the diagonal into 2-inch pieces |
| ¼ | cup water |
| 1 | large onion, cut into ¼- to ⅜-inch wedges |
| ¼ | cup chopped fresh basil leaves |

**1.** Combine the pork, 1 teaspoon fish sauce, and soy sauce in a small bowl. Whisk the remaining 2 tablespoons fish sauce, chicken broth, lime juice, sugar, and cornstarch in a measuring cup. Combine the garlic, lemon grass, red pepper flakes, and 1 tablespoon oil in a small bowl.

**2.** Heat 1½ teaspoons oil in a 12-inch nonstick skillet over high heat until smoking; add half of the pork to the skillet and cook, stirring occasionally and breaking up clumps, until well browned, about 2 minutes. Transfer the pork to a medium bowl. Repeat with an additional 1½ teaspoons oil and remaining pork. Add 1 tablespoon oil to the now-empty skillet; add the asparagus and cook, stirring every 30 seconds, until lightly browned, about 2 minutes. Add the water, cover the pan, and lower the heat to medium. Steam the asparagus until tender-crisp, about 2 minutes; transfer the asparagus to the bowl with the pork. Add the remaining 1½ teaspoons oil to the skillet; add the onion and cook, stirring occasionally, until beginning to brown and soften, about 2 minutes. Clear the center of the skillet, add the garlic/lemon grass mixture to the clearing; cook, mashing the mixture with a spoon, until fragrant, about 1 minute, then stir the mixture into the onion. Add the pork and asparagus; toss to combine. Stir the sauce to recombine, then add to the skillet; cook, stirring constantly, until the sauce is thickened and evenly distributed, about 30 seconds. Transfer to a serving platter; sprinkle with the basil and serve.

## EQUIPMENT CORNER: Electric Woks

WE'VE SAID IT PLAINLY SEVERAL TIMES: WE DON'T LIKE woks. The relatively small base of a wok means only modest burner contact, which translates to less than maximal heat. Quite simply, the design of a wok is not meant for cooking on a Western stovetop, where a large open skillet is much more successful at achieving optimum sizzle and sear.

We wondered, however, if electric woks offered advantages over stovetop woks. We collected six of them, ranging in price from $30 to $100, then stir-fried and deep-fried in each, looking for differences in heating ability and design. To our surprise, one wok—and a modestly priced one at that—excelled in all areas and another did quite well.

The runaway winner was the Maxim Nonstick Electric Wok with Dome Cover ($60). It stir-fried on par with a skillet, and it managed the oil for deep-frying like a pro. The temperature dial was accurate and easy to read. The size of this wok is generous (14 inches in diameter, 6½-quart capacity), and the long-handled design makes it possible to simultaneously empty and scrape ingredients out of the wok when cooking in batches.

The runner-up was the Toastmaster High Performance Electric Wok ($30). This wok had the heat output of the winner, but it was not nearly as commodious (12¾ inches in diameter, with a 4½-quart capacity). With use, its temperature dial became hot to the touch, and the wok's two short handles made it impossible to scrape out food while turning the wok to empty it.

The remaining four woks tested weren't worth the space they occupied on the countertop. Problems included flimsy construction, odd design, and hot spots. Moreover, none of these woks had good heat output—in fact, three couldn't get the oil for deep-frying above 350 degrees, though their thermostats were set for 375 and indicated that the temperature had been reached. In comparison, our favorite woks maintained temperatures of 365 to 375 degrees, ideal for deep-frying.

Should you purchase an electric wok? If you're a frequent fryer or you like to use a bamboo steamer (which requires a wok of some sort, electric or not), our winning model, the Maxim, might be a worthwhile investment. However, if stir-frying is your limit, stick with a large, heavy, totally utilitarian nonstick skillet.

---

## TECHNIQUE:
### Slicing Pork Tenderloin for Stir-Fries

**1.** Pork tenderloin is easier to slice when partially frozen. Freeze the tenderloin until firm but not frozen solid, 45 minutes to 1 hour. Cut the tenderloin crosswise into ¼-inch slices.

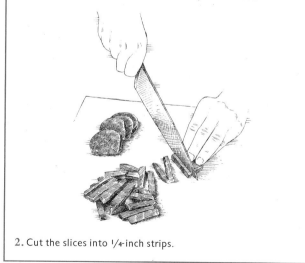

**2.** Cut the slices into ¼-inch strips.

# Rating Electric Woks

WE TESTED SIX ELECTRIC WOKS BY STIR-FRYING AND DEEP-FRYING IN EACH ONE. WE PREHEATED EACH WOK AND THEN prepared a batch of our stir-fried pork with eggplant. We also heated peanut oil in each wok, with the temperature dial set to 375 degrees, and then deep-fried chicken wings. The woks are listed in order of preferences based on their performance in these tests as well as their heating ability and design. See www.americastestkitchen.com for up-to-date prices and mail-order sources for top-rated products.

**RECOMMENDED**

### Maxim Nonstick Electric Wok with Dome Cover

**$60.00**

This large wok stir-fries like a skillet and is perfect for deep-frying. We particularly like the long handle (which makes it easy to pick up) and the no-fuss cleanup. The temperature dial was accurate and easy to read.

**RECOMMENDED WITH RESERVATIONS**

### Toastmaster High Performance Electric Wok

**$30.00**

This wok heats up quite well but is considerably smaller than our top choice. The two short handles are not ideal, but the nonstick interior made cleanup a snap. Also, the temperature dial became hot to the touch as the wok heated up.

**NOT RECOMMENDED**

### Rival Stainless Steel Electric Wok

**$90.00**

Food stuck horribly to the stainless steel surface of this flawed wok, which did not get hot enough to deep-fry properly.

**NOT RECOMMENDED**

### West Bend Electric Wok

**$48.00**

This wok heated very unevenly and erratically, and it was difficult to brown foods evenly. Better at deep-frying than stir-frying.

**NOT RECOMMENDED**

### Martin Yan Professional Wok

**$90.00**

This pricey wok had little sizzle, and food browned only moderately. After 15 minutes of heating, oil only reached 312 degrees, much too low for proper deep-frying.

**NOT RECOMMENDED**

### Circulon Hard Anodized Electric Wok

**$100.00**

This expensive wok was slow to heat and cooled down quickly when food was added. Small surface grooves ensnared small bits of food. Could not achieve high enough temperature to deep-fry.

Bean sprouts, stored and stacked,
are ready for use in our pad Thai recipe.

# ASIAN noodles

## CHAPTER 16

IN THIS CHAPTER

**THE RECIPES**
Pad Thai

Sesame Noodles with Shredded
  Chicken
Sesame Noodles with Sweet
  Peppers and Cucumbers

**EQUIPMENT CORNER**
Flat-Bottom Woks

**SCIENCE DESK**
Why Do Some Peanut Butters
  Separate?

**TASTING LAB**
Tamarind Options
Peanut Butter

We no longer think of noodles as just Italian. Asian noodles are everywhere, from slippery udon noodles in Japanese soups to delicate cellophane noodles in Vietnamese salads. Pad thai and cold sesame noodles are two of our favorite Asian noodle recipes, but both have fallen victim to their popularity. We've been served more bad Americanized versions of these dishes than we care to admit. More often than not, the noodles are much too starchy (Asian noodles cannot be handled as if they were Italian pasta) and the sauces are sweet or greasy.

We decided to take matters in our own hands in the test kitchen. We figured that authentic ingredients would be part of the answer, and we were willing to make special shopping expeditions to Asian markets to find the pantry staples we needed. We also wanted to better understand the fundamental cooking techniques associated with the noodles.

# PAD THAI

**WHAT WE WANTED:** A fresh, vibrant version of this Thai classic, not the greasy, soggy, candy-sweet dish served in so many restaurants.

Pad thai is a remedy for a dead, jaded palate. Hot, sweet, and pungent Thai flavors tangled in an un-Western jumble of textures awaken all of the senses that have grown weary of the usual grub. We have downed numerous platefuls of pad thai, many from an excellent Thai restaurant only a few blocks away from our test kitchen. What we noticed was that from one order to the next, pad thai prepared in the same reliable restaurant kitchen was inconsistent. If it was perfect, it was a symphony of flavors and textures. It balanced sweet, sour, and spicy, and the tender, glutinous rice noodles ensnared curls of shrimp, crisp strands of bean sprouts, soft curds of fried egg, and sturdy bits of tofu. Sometimes, however, it tasted weak and flat, as if seasoned too timidly. At its worst, pad thai suffers from indiscriminate amounts of sugar, from slick, greasy noodles, or from sticky, lifeless strands that glom onto one another to form a chaotic skein.

We have become so enamored of pad thai and so tired of disappointment that we have attempted it several times in the test kitchen with only moderate success, and that we attribute to luck. The recipes were unclear, the ingredient lists daunting, and we stumbled through the steps only to produce dry, undercooked noodles and unbalanced flavors. Happily, though, our pad thai was loaded with plump, sweet shrimp (not the paltry four or five per typical restaurant order), and the flavors tasted clean and fresh. Our goal was to build on these positives and produce a consistently superlative pad thai.

Rice sticks, the type of noodles used in pad thai, are often only partially cooked, particularly when used in stir-fries. We found three different methods of preparing them: soaking in room-temperature water, soaking in hot tap water, and boiling. We began with boiling and quickly realized that this was bad advice. Drained and waiting in the colander, the noodles glued themselves together. When we managed to stir-fry them, they wound up soggy and overdone. Noodles soaked in room-temperature water remained fairly stiff. After lengthy stir-frying, they eventually became tender, but longer cooking made this pad thai drier and stickier. Finally, we tried soaking the rice sticks in hot tap water for about 20 minutes. They "softened," turning limp and pliant, but were not fully tender. Drained, they were loose and separate, and they cooked through easily with stir-frying. The result? Noodles that were at once pleasantly tender and resilient.

Sweet, salty, sour, and spicy are the flavor characteristics of pad thai, and none should dominate; they should coexist in harmony. Although the cooking time is short, the ingredient list isn't, and many components will appear foreign to some. Fish sauce supplies a salty-sweet pungency, sugar gives sweetness, the heat comes from ground chiles, vinegar provides acidity, and tamarind rounds out the dish with its fruity, earthy, sweet-tart molasses-tinged flavor. Garlic and sometimes shallots contribute their heady, robust flavors. Some recipes call for ketchup (sounds dubious but probably worth trying) and some for soy sauce.

With these ingredients in hand, we set off to find out which ones were key to success and how much of each to use to achieve balanced flavor. For 8 ounces of rice sticks, 3 tablespoons of fish sauce and the same amount of sugar were ideal. Three-quarters of a teaspoon of cayenne (many recipes call for Thai chiles, but for the sake of simplicity, we opted not to use them) brought a low, even heat—not a searing burn—and 1 tablespoon of rice vinegar (preferred in pad thai for its mild acidity and relatively complex fermented-grain flavor) greatly vivified the flavors.

Tasters liked the garlic at 1 tablespoon minced. Shallots had a surprising impact on flavor. Just one medium shallot (about 3 tablespoons minced) produced such a round, full

sweetness and depth of flavor that we just couldn't say no. To coax the right character out of these two aromatics, we found that cooking them to the point of browning was critical; they tasted mellow, sweet, and mildly toasty.

Tamarind was the most enigmatic ingredient on our list. Tamarind is a fruit that grows as a round brown pod about 5 inches long and is often sold as a paste (a hard, flat brick) or as a sticky concentrate. (For more information, see page 195.) Although we eschew hard-to-find ingredients in the test kitchen, we came to the conclusion that tamarind is central—if not essential—to the unique flavor of pad thai. Testing showed that tamarind paste has a fresher, brighter, fruitier flavor than concentrate, which tasted dull by comparison. For those who cannot obtain either tamarind paste or concentrate, we worked out a formula of equal parts lime juice and water as a stand-in. This mixture produces a less interesting and less authentic dish, but we polished off several such platefuls with no qualms.

We tried a little ketchup, but its vinegary tomato flavor was out of place. As for soy sauce, even just a mere tablespoon was a big bully—its assertive flavor didn't play nicely with the others.

The other ingredients in pad thai are sautéed shrimp, scrambled eggs, chopped peanuts, bean sprouts, and scallions.

For more textural intrigue and to achieve authentic pad thai flavor, dried shrimp and Thai salted preserved radish are worthy embellishments (both sold in Asian grocery stores). Dried shrimp are sweet, salty, and intensely shrimpy, and they add tiny bursts of incredible flavor. We used 2 tablespoons of the smallest dried shrimp we could find and chopped them up finer still, because tasters asked that their firm, chewy texture be mitigated. Thai salted preserved radish is brownish-yellow in color, dry, and a bit wrinkled, and it is sold in long sections (think daikon radish) folded into a flimsy plastic package. Two tablespoons of chopped salted radish added piquant, savory bits with a good crunch.

Oddly, after consuming dozens of servings of pad thai, we did not feel glutted. We were addicted. These days, if we order it in a restaurant, we prepare ourselves for disappointment. We've come to think that pad thai is not unlike chocolate chip cookies: It's always best homemade.

WHAT WE LEARNED: Soak the rice noodles in hot water before stir-frying them. Tamarind paste is the key flavor in the sauce, although lime juice and water make an adequate substitute. Fish sauce, sugar, and rice vinegar are the other key components in the sauce, and browned garlic and shallot add tremendous flavor.

## PAD THAI Serves 4 as a main dish

A wok might be the implement of choice in restaurants and the old country, but a large 12-inch skillet (nonstick makes cleanup easy) is more practical for home cooks. Although pad thai cooks very quickly, the ingredient list is long, and everything must be prepared and within easy reach at the stovetop when you begin cooking. For maximum efficiency, use the time during which the tamarind and noodles soak to prepare the other ingredients. Tofu is a good and common addition to pad thai. If you like, add 4 ounces of extra-firm tofu or pressed tofu (available in Asian markets) cut into 1/4-inch cubes (about 1 cup) to the noodles along with the bean sprouts.

2 tablespoons tamarind paste or substitute (see "Tasting Lab: Tamarind Options" on page 195)
3/4 cup boiling water
3 tablespoons fish sauce
1 tablespoon rice vinegar
3 tablespoons sugar
3/4 teaspoon cayenne pepper
4 tablespoons peanut or vegetable oil
8 ounces dried rice stick noodles, about 1/8 inch wide (the width of linguine)
2 large eggs
1/4 teaspoon salt
12 ounces medium (31/35 count) shrimp, peeled and deveined, if desired
3 cloves garlic, minced or pressed through a garlic press (about 1 tablespoon)
1 medium shallot, minced (about 3 tablespoons)
2 tablespoons dried shrimp, chopped fine (optional)
2 tablespoons chopped Thai salted preserved radish (optional)
6 tablespoons chopped roasted unsalted peanuts
3 cups (6 ounces) bean sprouts
5 medium scallions, green parts only, sliced thin on a sharp diagonal
1/4 cup loosely packed cilantro leaves (optional)
Lime wedges

### GETTING IT RIGHT: Soaking the Noodles

**STIFF NOODLES**
Soaking the rice sticks in room-temperature water yields hard noodles that take too long to stir-fry.

**STICKY NOODLES**
Fully cooking the rice sticks in boiling water results in soft, sticky, gummy, overdone noodles.

**PERFECT NOODLES**
Soaking the rice sticks in hot water yields softened noodles. When stir-fried, they are tender but resilient.

**1.** Rehydrate the tamarind paste in boiling water (see the instructions in "Tasting Lab: Tamarind Options" at right). Stir the fish sauce, rice vinegar, sugar, cayenne, and 2 tablespoons oil into the tamarind liquid and set aside.

**2.** Cover the rice sticks with hot tap water in a large bowl; soak until softened, pliable, and limp but not fully tender, about 20 minutes. Drain the noodles and set aside. Beat the eggs and ⅛ teaspoon of the salt in a small bowl; set aside.

**3.** Heat 1 tablespoon oil in a 12-inch skillet (preferably nonstick) over high heat until just beginning to smoke. Add the shrimp and sprinkle with the remaining ⅛ teaspoon salt; cook, tossing occasionally, until the shrimp are opaque and browned about the edges, about 3 minutes. Transfer the shrimp to a plate and set aside.

**4.** Off heat, add the remaining tablespoon oil to the skillet and swirl to coat; add the garlic and shallot, set the skillet over medium heat, and cook, stirring constantly, until light golden brown, about 1½ minutes; add the eggs to the skillet and stir vigorously with a wooden spoon until scrambled and barely moist, about 20 seconds. Add the noodles and the dried shrimp and salted radish (if using) to the eggs; toss with 2 wooden spoons to combine. Pour the fish sauce mixture over the noodles, increase the heat to high, and cook, tossing constantly, until the noodles are evenly coated. Scatter ¼ cup peanuts, bean sprouts, all but ¼ cup scallions, and cooked shrimp over the noodles; continue to cook, tossing constantly, until the noodles are tender, about 2½ minutes (if not yet tender add 2 tablespoons water to the skillet and continue to cook until tender).

**5.** Transfer the noodles to a serving platter, sprinkle with the remaining scallions, 2 tablespoons peanuts, and cilantro; serve immediately, passing lime wedges separately.

## TASTING LAB: Tamarind Options

SWEET-TART, BROWNISH-RED TAMARIND IS A NECESSARY ingredient for a pad thai that looks and tastes authentic. It's commonly sold in paste (also called pulp) and in concentrate form. But don't fret if neither is available—you can still make a very good pad thai using lime juice and water. Here are your three options.

Tamarind Paste or Pulp: Tamarind paste, or pulp, is firm, sticky, and filled with seeds and fibers. We favored this product because it had the freshest, brightest flavor. To use it in the pad thai recipe, soak 2 tablespoons in ¾ cup boiling water for about 10 minutes, then push it through a mesh strainer to remove the seeds and fibers and extract as much pulp as possible.

Tamarind Concentrate: Tamarind concentrate looks more like a scary pomade than a foodstuff. It's black, thick, shiny, and gooey. Its flavor approximates that of tamarind paste, but it tastes less fruity and more "cooked," and it colors the pad thai a shade too dark. To use in the pad thai recipe, mix 1 tablespoon with ⅔ cup hot water.

Lime Juice and Water Substitute: If tamarind is out of the question, combine ⅓ cup lime juice and ⅓ cup water and use it in its place; use light brown sugar instead of granulated to give the noodles some color and a faint molasses flavor. Because it will already contain a good hit of lime, do not serve this version with lime wedges.

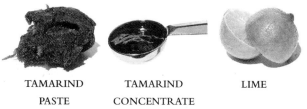

TAMARIND    TAMARIND    LIME
PASTE    CONCENTRATE

# EQUIPMENT CORNER:
## Flat-Bottom Woks

WE DON'T LIKE STOVETOP WOKS—AT LEAST NOT conventional rounded models. The traditional wok is designed to sit in an open cooking pit with flames licking the sides of the vessel. Of course, on a flat American stovetop, a round wok wobbles and has little direct contact with the heat source. For these reasons, we prefer a 12-inch nonstick skillet for stir-frying. When we decided to revisit the wok issue yet again, this time with flat-bottom woks, we thought we'd wait to pass judgment. We needn't have bothered. We can now safely say that we don't like stovetop woks, period.

There are dozens of flat-bottom woks on the market, which are also sold as stir-fry pans. To narrow the field, we set a few guidelines. First was size. We chose woks that had a diameter of at least 12 inches when measured across the top. Second was interior material. We like to use a nonstick pan in stir-fries, so we limited our field to nonstick woks only. We found eight popular brands of nonstick flat-bottom woks and brought them into the kitchen for a marathon stir-fry session, making batch after batch of beef and broccoli. The woks ranged in price from $16.99 to $139.99. Did price correlate to quality? Not at all.

The best performer, the 14-inch Joyce Chen Original Stir Fry Pan ($43.95), held a roomy 6½ quarts and measured 6½ inches across the bottom (the widest bottom area we could find). The wok was balanced, sturdy, and easy to use, though it was a bit heavy for one petite tester. The best part about this wok was that it got hot and stayed hot, taking a respectable three minutes to get the oil smoking initially and a quick 49 seconds to get it smoking for the second batch of beef. That heat is key to developing a brown crust on the beef, which this wok achieved to some degree, though not quite as nicely as our trusty 12-inch skillet. A 12-inch skillet has twice as much surface in direct contact with the heating source as the Joyce Chen wok. This larger area

allows for the meat to be spread in an even layer, ensuring even browning.

Our second-place finisher, the Anolon Classic Stir Fry Pan ($39.99), had the same size bottom as the Joyce Chen but was significantly smaller overall, with a 12-inch diameter at the top and a 5-quart capacity. Beef and broccoli browned somewhat, but the wok's tipsy and unstable design made us nervous. This thin wok didn't hold heat well; it took almost twice as long as the Joyce Chen wok to get the oil hot for the second batch of beef.

The woks that fared worst in our tests were the Scanpan Ergonomic Stir Fry Pan ($139.99) and the Circulon Steel Stir Fry Pan ($39.99). Neither browned the beef or the broccoli at all. The large-capacity Scanpan was sturdy and easy to work with, but its relatively small bottom (5¾-inches) made browning difficult; instead of lying in an even layer across the bottom, the pieces of meat stacked up into a pile, oozing juice and steaming rather than searing. Despite the heft of this wok, it didn't hold heat at all; at 2 minutes, 15 seconds, it took the longest to get hot again after searing the first batch of beef.

One tester described last-place finisher Circulon as a "mixing bowl with a handle." The Circulon pan's tippy design made it difficult to work with, and its 5½-inch flat bottom never gave the beef a chance.

Though the Joyce Chen Stir Fry Pan fared the best in our testing, we'd still reach first for a 12-inch nonstick skillet when stir-frying. If you were using a bamboo steamer, for which you need a wok, or cooking a large batch of fried rice, the Joyce Chen might come in handy. But if you're sticking to stir-fry, stick to your skillet. Its large, flat bottom is better suited for flat Western stovetops.

# Rating Flat–Bottom Woks

WE TESTED EIGHT WOKS WITH FLAT BOTTOMS, PREPARING A BEEF AND BROCCOLI STIR-FRY IN EACH. THE WOKS ARE listed in order of preference based on their ability to brown foods, the time it took them to heat up, and their design. For up-to-date prices and mail-order sources for the top-rated product see www.americastestkitchen.com.

**RECOMMENDED WITH RESERVATIONS**
## Joyce Chen Original Stir Fry Pan
**$43.95**

Best browning with large capacity. Better than the rest of the pack but not as good as a 12-inch nonstick skillet.

**NOT RECOMMENDED**
## Anolon Classic Stir Fry Pan with Lid
**$39.99**

This small wok did not heat up well, and the tipsy designed was worrisome. "Feels cheap," wrote one tester.

**NOT RECOMMENDED**
## Excalibur (Williams-Sonoma) Nonstick Wok with Lid
**$59.00**

Decent browning, but this pan was slightly awkward to use.

**NOT RECOMMENDED**
## Calphalon Commercial Nonstick Flat Bottom Wok
**$99.99**

Decent browning, but this model was tipsy and unbalanced.

**NOT RECOMMENDED**
## Asian Traditions (Target) Nonstick Stir Fry Pan
**$16.99**

This wok got very hot, very fast, but lost its heat as soon as we put food in it.

**NOT RECOMMENDED**
## Anolon Professional Stir Fry Pan
**$31.99**

Slight browning, but this pan was very wobbly.

**NOT RECOMMENDED**
## Scanpan Ergonomic Stir Fry Pan
**$139.99**

Stable and sturdy, but no browning in this expensive pan.

**NOT RECOMMENDED**
## Circulon Steel Stir Fry Pan
**$39.99**

Small flat bottom means that very little browning can occur. High handle is awkward.

# COLD SESAME NOODLES

**WHAT WE WANTED:** We set out to avoid the sticky noodles, gloppy texture, and lackluster flavor typically found in this Chinese classic.

Much like a Chinese finger trap that lures by appearing to be a toy, sesame noodles are not what they seem. You may think of them as merely a humble bowl of cold noodles, but don't be fooled—just one bite and you're hooked on these Chinese wheat noodles with shreds of tender chicken, all tossed with a fresh sesame sauce. And now you've got a real problem: Once you get the hankering, good versions of the dish are hard to find. The cold noodles have a habit of turning gummy, the chicken often dries out, and the sauce is notorious for turning bland and pasty. We wanted a recipe that could not only quell a serious craving but could do it in less time than it would take to grab a bus to Chinatown.

Though immediately drawn to the softer texture and milder flavor of fresh Chinese wheat noodles, we conceded that dried spaghetti could serve as a second-string substitute. The trouble with both types of noodles, however, was that after being cooked and chilled, they gelled into a rubbery skein. After trying a number of ways to avoid this problem, we found it necessary to rinse the noodles under cold tap water directly after cooking. This not only cooled the hot noodles immediately but washed away much of their sticky starch. To further forestall any clumping, we tossed the rinsed noodles with a little toasted sesame oil; this kept them slack and separated for hours.

Boneless, skinless chicken breasts are quick to cook and easy to shred; the real question is how to cook them. The microwave seemed easy in theory, but we found the rate of cooking difficult to monitor. Many recipes suggested poaching the chicken in water or broth, but this chicken had a washed-out flavor. Roasting caused the outer meat to dry out before the interior was fully cooked. Cooking under the broiler, however, worked perfectly. We found it necessary to position the chicken six inches from the broiler; any closer and the exterior of the cutlets will burn before the middle is cooked through. Once the internal temperature of chicken reaches 160 degrees, the cutlets are done.

To be authentic, the sesame sauce should be made with an Asian sesame paste (not to be confused with Middle Eastern tahini), but most recipes substitute peanut butter because it's easier to find. Somewhat surprisingly, tasters preferred chunky peanut butter over smooth, describing its flavor as fresh and more peanutty. We had been making the sauce in a blender and realized that the chunky bits of peanuts were being freshly ground into the sauce, resulting in the cleaner, stronger flavor. We found the flavors of both fresh garlic and ginger necessary, along with soy sauce, rice vinegar, hot sauce, and brown sugar. We then stumbled on the obvious way to keep the sauce from being too thick or pasty: Thin it out with water.

Although the sauce was good, tasters still complained that there was not enough sesame flavor. We tried adding toasted sesame seeds. Blended into the sauce along with the peanut butter, the sesame seeds added the final kick of authentic sesame flavor we were all hankering for.

**WHAT WE LEARNED:** Use fresh Chinese noodles or dried spaghetti, but rinse and then oil the cooked noodles to keep them from sticking together. Use toasted sesame seeds and chunky peanut butter to build flavor in the sauce, which should be thinned with hot water to achieve the proper consistency.

---

## FOOD FACT: Peanuts

Two American presidents were peanut farmers. Most of us remember Jimmy Carter on his Georgia peanut farm, but Thomas Jefferson also farmed peanuts on his Virginia plantation.

## SESAME NOODLES WITH SHREDDED CHICKEN
**Serves 4 to 6 as a main course**

In our experience, chicken takes longer to cook in a gas broiler than in an electric one, which is why the cooking times in the recipe range widely. Although our preference is for fresh Chinese egg noodles, we found that dried spaghetti works well, too. Because dried pasta swells so much more than fresh pasta during cooking, 12 ounces of dried spaghetti can replace one pound of fresh noodles.

¼ cup sesame seeds

¼ cup chunky peanut butter

2 medium cloves garlic, minced or pressed through a garlic press (about 2 teaspoons)

1 piece (1-inch) fresh ginger, grated or minced (about 1 tablespoon)

5 tablespoons soy sauce

2 tablespoons rice vinegar

1 teaspoon hot sauce (such as Tabasco)

2 tablespoons lightly packed light brown sugar
 Hot water

3 boneless, skinless chicken breast halves (1½ pounds), trimmed of excess fat

1 tablespoon salt

1 pound fresh Chinese egg noodles or 12 ounces dried spaghetti

2 tablespoons Asian sesame oil

4 scallions, sliced thin on the diagonal

1 medium carrot, peeled and grated on large holes of box grater (about ⅔ cup)

**1.** Toast the sesame seeds in a medium skillet over medium heat, stirring frequently, until golden and fragrant, about 10 minutes. Reserve 1 tablespoon sesame seeds in a small bowl. In a blender or food processor, puree the remaining 3 tablespoons sesame seeds, peanut butter, garlic, ginger, soy sauce, vinegar, hot sauce, and sugar until smooth, about 30 seconds. With the machine running, add hot water 1 tablespoon at a time until the sauce has the consistency of heavy cream, about 5 tablespoons; set the mixture aside (it can be left in the blender jar or food processor workbowl).

**2.** Bring 6 quarts water to a boil in a stockpot over high heat. Meanwhile, adjust an oven rack to 6 inches from the broiler element; heat the broiler. Spray the broiler pan top with vegetable cooking spray; place the chicken breasts on top and broil the chicken until lightly browned, 4 to 8 minutes. Using tongs, flip the chicken over and continue to broil until the thickest part is no longer pink when cut into and registers about 160 degrees on an instant-read thermometer, 6 to 8 minutes. Transfer to a cutting board and let rest 5 minutes. Using 2 forks, shred the chicken into bite-sized pieces and set aside. Add the salt and noodles to the boiling water; boil the noodles until tender, about 4 minutes for fresh and 10 minutes for dried. Drain, then rinse with cold running tap water until cool to the touch; drain again. In a large bowl, toss the noodles with the sesame oil until evenly coated. Add the shredded chicken, scallions, carrot, and sauce; toss to combine. Divide among individual bowls, sprinkle each bowl with a portion of reserved sesame seeds, and serve.

## SESAME NOODLES WITH SWEET PEPPERS AND CUCUMBERS

Core, seed, and cut into ¼-inch slices 1 medium red bell pepper; peel, halve lengthwise, seed, and cut crosswise into ⅛-inch slices 1 medium cucumber. Follow the recipe for Sesame Noodles with Shredded Chicken, omitting the chicken, adding the bell pepper and cucumber to the noodles along with the sauce, and sprinkling each bowl with a portion of 1 tablespoon chopped fresh cilantro leaves along with the sesame seeds.

---

## SCIENCE DESK: Why Do Some Peanut Butters Separate?

THE FIRST FEW STEPS IN MAKING ANY TYPE OF PEANUT butter are essentially the same. Raw, shelled peanuts are roasted, cooled by industrial-strength suction fans, skinned, and ground.

After being ground, natural peanut butters are immediately jarred and shipped. When emulsified peanut butters are made, the peanuts must be ground once more, this time with salt, sweeteners, and hydrogenated stabilizers. During this grinding, the stabilizers trap the oil that is extracted from the peanuts in what scientists call a beta-prime polymorph. In layman's terms, this is a lattice-like structure that holds the peanut oil in its weave, suspending it throughout the creamed mass and protecting it from exposure to oxygen, which is the cause of rancidity. This is why hydrogenated peanut butters have a longer shelf life than natural peanut butters.

---

## TASTING LAB: Peanut Butter

PEANUT BUTTER IS A CUPBOARD STAPLE, USED FOR EVERYTHING from sandwiches and cookies to sesame noodles. In the United States alone, peanut butter accounts for more than $630 million in sales annually, which is pretty amazing considering that just 150 years ago the peanut was thought fit only as fodder for pigs. Because we are constantly turning to peanut butter as a flavor booster for cookies, sauces, and sandwiches, we decided to find out which brand is best.

To do so, we first took a look at how all those brands got onto our supermarket shelves. Early peanut butters were (like today's "natural" versions) essentially just nuts ground into a paste. Because of the peanut's high fat content, these butters turned rancid easily and so were basically local products, with most producers supplying only their home city. In the early 1920s, Swift & Company introduced the first emulsified peanut butter, E. K. Pond, to American consumers. Emulsification made not only for a smoother, more spreadable product but also increased peanut butter's shelf

# Rating Peanut Butters

TWENTY MEMBERS OF THE *COOK'S ILLUSTRATED* STAFF TASTED EIGHT PEANUT BUTTERS IN THREE APPLICATIONS—PLAIN, in peanut sauce, and in peanut butter cookies. Tasters evaluated the peanut butters and the sauces for intensity of peanut flavor and texture (mealy, smooth, pasty, gritty, and the like). The cookies were evaluated for peanut flavor, texture, and appearance. The peanut butters are listed in order of preference based on the combined scores from the three tastings. All brands are sold in supermarkets nationwide.

### HIGHLY RECOMMENDED
## Skippy Creamy Peanut Butter
**$2.09 for 18 ounces**

Overall, tasters felt that Skippy had a "good sweet/salty balance" and "tasted just like peanut butter should." Skippy made a tender and crisp cookie and a satisfying peanut sauce.

### RECOMMENDED
## Jif Creamy Peanut Butter
**$1.99 for 18 ounces**

Many tasters described second-place Jif as having the "perfect thickness" and being "sweet, but not obnoxiously so." Its texture was "silky and smooth," and it produced cookies with brown sugar undertones. In the peanut sauce, however, Jif was relatively sweet.

### RECOMMENDED
## Teddie Smooth Old Fashioned Peanut Butter
**$2.39 for 16 ounces**

Teddie Old Fashioned was the only natural peanut butter to rank in the upper echelons of the tasting. In its raw state, one taster complained that she "couldn't even swallow" it. In the cookie and sauce, however, it was described as "peanutty perfection."

### RECOMMENDED
## Reese's Creamy Peanut Butter
**$1.88 for 18 ounces**

Even though Reese's didn't fare too well in the sauce (tasters found it "unbalanced") or the cookies (it was deemed "gritty," with a "loose, shattery crumb"), tasters loved it raw. Most found it sweet and silky smooth, with a delicious flavor.

### RECOMMENDED
## Simply Jif Creamy Peanut Butter
**$2.19 for 17.3 ounces**

With only two-thirds of the sugar and less than half of the sodium per serving of other brands, Simply Jif scored surprisingly well. Many tasters thought it was very peanutty (albeit a little bland). In the sauce, it was called "fairly peanutty," but in the cookie this peanut butter failed to impress.

### RECOMMENDED WITH RESERVATIONS
## Freshly ground peanuts from a natural foods store
**$1.99 for 16 ounces**

Tasters found the cookies made with this product to be "meaty," with "lots of peanut flavor." When tasted raw, it was thought very bland, with the texture of "cardboard." The sauce made with it was found lacking in "character."

### NOT RECOMMENDED
## Peter Pan Creamy Peanut Butter
**$2.19 for 18 ounces**

Peter Pan was criticized for its "artificial" and "unbalanced" flavor. It gave the sauce a bitter, "fake" flavor, while it made a cookie that was sandy, dry, and generally unpleasant.

### NOT RECOMMENDED
## Smucker's Natural Creamy Peanut Butter
**$2.79 for 16 ounces**

Tasters just couldn't get past the texture when it came to eating the peanut butter raw, calling it "gritty," "grainy," and "pasty." In the sauce it was criticized for being too salty, and the cookie made with it was described as "dense," "tough," and very dry.

life. (See the Science Desk on page 200 for an explanation.) As a result, E. K. Pond became the first nationally available brand of peanut butter. In 1928, Swift changed the E. K. Pond label to Peter Pan; in 1932, a disgruntled Swift employee left the company to make his own brand of peanut butter, which he called Skippy; in 1958, Procter & Gamble lined market shelves with its new brand, Jif.

Over the years, the peanut butter scene hasn't changed much. Shoppers can choose natural, or "old-fashioned," peanut butter, or they can opt for a smooth emulsified peanut butter with a long shelf life.

We decided to focus our tasting on the top-selling peanut butters in grocery stores nationwide. This decision led us to include both natural and emulsified peanut butters, but only in their "creamy" form; "crunchy" peanut butter accounts for only 26 percent of peanut butter sales. In addition, our tasting would confine itself to "real" peanut butters as defined by the Food and Drug Administration: those that contain at least 90 percent peanuts. We tasted the peanut butters raw, in a sauce, and in a baked peanut butter cookie. After many long hours of tasting, we concluded that the peanut butter you choose might well depend on how you plan to use it.

When sampling the peanut butters straight from the jar, tasters chose Reese's as their favorite, with Jif only one point behind and Skippy trailing a distant third. When we checked the labels to try to explain this, we found that Reese's and Jif were the only two brands to include molasses. This, it seemed, added a caramel-like facet to their flavor profiles—an attribute tasters valued.

In the peanut sauce tasting, emulsified peanut butter once again stole the show. The rather grainy texture of the natural peanut butters was at odds with what should be the silky mouthfeel of the sauce. But this time Skippy took the lead, getting twice as many votes as the runner-up, Jif. Both the Jif and Reese's sauces were described by tasters as "very sweet" and "rather unbalanced." We concluded that this was the result of combining the already sweet ingredients in the sauce, which included coconut milk, with the molasses in the peanut butter.

It was in the cookie category, though, that we observed the most dramatic differences from brand to brand. The textures of the cookies were quite distinct. The cookies made with the natural peanut butters (Teddie and Smucker's) and those made with freshly ground peanut butter were hearty and thick, just what you would expect of a "natural" cookie. The cookies made with Reese's and Simply Jif (a version of Jif with reduced salt, molasses, and sugar) were sandy and delicate, while those made with regular Jif were of medium build, with soft, chewy centers and crisp edges. We attributed the semipliant character of the cookies made with regular Jif to the presence and amount of molasses, a hygroscopic substance that helps to retain moisture, giving the cookie its chewy quality. But if the Jif cookie was slightly soft, why wasn't the cookie made with Reese's, which also contains a significant amount of molasses? We once again compared the ingredient lists of Jif and Reese's and found our answer: Reese's contains cornstarch and less fat (1 gram). Robert Parker, a professor in the division of nutritional sciences at Cornell University, explained that the cornstarch in the peanut butter bound the water in the dough, leading to a dry cookie.

When it came to flavor, tasters slightly preferred the cookie made with Skippy, which they described as "tender and crisp." But the cookies made with natural peanut butters (one of which earned second and another third place in the cookie tasting) were consistently called more "peanutty" in flavor. The reason, according to University of Maryland lipids expert Elizabeth Boyle-Roden, is that natural peanut butters have not been doctored with hydrogenated oils, starches, sweeteners, or mono- or diglycerides, which can interfere with the peanut flavor in a cookie after it is baked.

Given all this information, what peanut butter should you buy? If you're looking for an all-purpose peanut butter, you can't go wrong with Skippy—and regular Jif comes in a close second. But if you eat your peanut butter on crackers, in sandwiches, or on an apple more often than you cook with it, you might prefer Reese's for its molasses-enhanced, caramel-like sweetness.

To remove chicken alla diavola from the grill without tearing the crisp skin, grasp the ends of the drumsticks with sturdy tongs.

# ITALIAN classics

## CHAPTER 17

IN THIS CHAPTER

**THE RECIPES**
Frico

Charcoal-Grilled Chicken alla
    Diavola
Gas-Grilled Chicken alla Diavola

Strawberries with Balsamic
    Vinegar

**SCIENCE DESK**
How to Pry Flavor Out of Spices

**TASTING LAB**
Balsamic Vinegar

Americans love Italian food—and rightly so. When prepared correctly (and authentically), most Italian dishes are light, simple, and quick. Italian cooks know that simpler is better, especially if you are starting with good ingredients. Luckily, there seem to be an endless number of appealing Italian dishes that make sense for the American home cook.

The recipes in this chapter start with three staple ingredients—cheese, chicken, and strawberries—but use them in interesting ways to create an easy but unusual Italian menu. Of course, the fact that a dish is simple (or Italian) doesn't mean that it will taste good. It's easy to incinerate chicken on the grill, and berries with balsamic vinegar often turn into a harsh, acidic affair. We wanted to explore these classic Italian dishes and get them right.

# FRICO

**WHAT WE WANTED:** Thin, crisp cheese wafers to serve with cocktails.

*F*rico is probably the simplest and most addictive snack you'll ever eat. It is a thin, golden, flavorful cheese crisp. Classically made from a cheese called Montasio, this snack hails from the region of Friuli in northern Italy. It is nothing more than grated cheese sprinkled into a pan, melted, and then browned to form a crisp wafer. When made well, frico is light and airy, with a heavenly and intense cheese flavor. More often than not, however, it turns out chewy, bitter, and overly salty. Wondering what the key to this one-ingredient wonder was, we set out to make the perfect frico.

Although most of the recipes we researched were similar, we did encounter minor differences in technique. Some recipes call for a regular skillet and butter, while others call for olive oil and a well-seasoned cast-iron pan. After making a few rounds in the test kitchen, we found it easiest to use a medium (10-inch) nonstick skillet. The nonstick surface repels any fat released from the melting cheese, which ensures a smooth and effortless release without the use of butter or olive oil.

As we made and ate batches of frico, we picked up a few more tips for success. First, we discovered an easy way to flip the frico midway through cooking to brown the second side. After the first side browned, we simply removed the pan from the heat for several seconds to cool. As the cheese wafer began to cool and set up, it was easy to flip without tearing or stretching. We then quickly returned the pan to the heat and continued to brown the frico on the second side.

Using the right level of heat is also essential. If the pan is too hot, the cheese cooks too fast and turns bitter. But when cooked slowly over low heat, the cheese dries out, becomes crunchy, and turns a beautiful, golden color. We found it necessary to adjust the heat between medium-high and medium between flips.

Last, we tried using a variety of cheeses other than Montasio, which can be difficult to find in the United States. While many of the recipes we found recommended Parmesan, we found aged Asiago to be a more appropriate substitution. When tasted side by side, the frico made with Parmesan was salty and harsh, while the frico made with aged Asiago was smooth and clean. But for the ultimate frico, with a deep, complex flavor that is neither too bitter nor too salty, a good hunk of Montasio is worth tracking down.

**WHAT WE LEARNED:** Montasio cheese makes the best frico and Asiago is a better substitute than Parmesan. Use a 10-inch nonstick skillet set over medium-high heat. To flip the frico, remove the pan from the burner once the first side has browned, cool briefly, flip with a fork and spatula, and return to the burner on medium heat to finish cooking on the second side.

## FRICO Makes 8 large wafers

Serve frico with drinks and a bowl of marinated olives or marinated sun-dried tomatoes.

1   pound Montasio or aged Asiago cheese, finely grated

Sprinkle 2 ounces (about ½ cup) grated cheese over the bottom of a 10-inch nonstick skillet set over medium-high heat. Use a heat-resistant rubber spatula or wooden spoon to tidy the lacy outer edges of the cheese (see the illustration at right). Cook, shaking the pan occasionally to ensure an even distribution of the cheese over the pan bottom, until the edges are lacy and toasted, about 4 minutes. Remove the pan from the heat and allow the cheese to set for about 30 seconds. Using a fork and a heatproof spatula (see the illustration at right), carefully flip the cheese wafer and return the pan to medium heat. Cook until the second side is golden brown, about 2 minutes. Slide the cheese wafer out of the pan and transfer to a plate. Repeat with the remaining cheese. Serve the frico within 1 hour.

## TECHNIQUE: Making Frico

1. After sprinkling the cheese into the skillet, use a heat-resistant spatula or wooden spoon to gently push the scattered shreds of cheese around the edges inward to form a tidy rim.

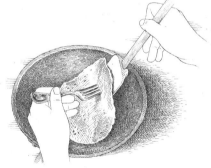

2. Once the first side is browned, remove the pan from the heat and let cool for 30 seconds to allow the frico to firm slightly. Using a fork and a heatproof spatula, carefully flip the cheese wafer and return the pan to medium heat to cook the second side.

# CHICKEN ALLA DIAVOLA

**WHAT WE WANTED:** Chicken that was pleasantly spicy (not searingly hot) and nicely grilled (not charred).

Pounded flat, seasoned with a wicked amount of peppery spice, and pinned beneath a brick over a bed of fiery coals, "devil's chicken" often sounds better than it tastes (or looks). Although its namesake implies plenty of heat, many recipes for chicken alla diavola produce dreary, bland main courses, while others blast the taste buds with raw bits of untamed spice. In addition, this mysterious method of grilling a butterflied chicken under the weight of a brick often left us with a hopelessly charred bird. What we wanted was a reliable grilling technique and a well-rounded diavola flavor that was spicy but not overwhelming. We began by focusing on flavor.

Most chicken alla diavola recipes can be divided into two camps, touting either ground black pepper or red pepper flakes as crucial to both flavor and heat. But no matter what their party alignment in this regard, all recipes develop flavor by marinating the chicken in a traditional mixture of olive oil, lemon juice, garlic, salt, and the party-line pepper, brushing more marinade onto the chicken during the last few minutes of grilling. Not wanting to overlook the benefits of brining (soaking in a saltwater solution), we first tested brined chickens against chickens that had been marinated overnight, brushing both types with marinade as they finished cooking. The marinated-only birds tasted bland and boring compared with the moist, well-seasoned, brined chickens. We now wanted to add some spicy diavola flavor to the brine and tried using both types of pepper, with little luck. (No peppery flavors made their way into the chicken.) By crushing garlic and bay leaves into the brine, however, we were able to make the chicken pleasantly fragrant and reasonably flavorful, albeit not spicy.

Although the marinade was ineffective for marinating, we were still brushing the grilled chicken with it during the last minutes of cooking. We thought that boosting the flavor in the marinade-turned-basting-sauce might be the answer. After many tests, we found that a combination of black and red pepper flakes tasted far better than either on its own. Noting that a quarter cup of oil made plenty of brushing sauce for one chicken, we added teaspoon after teaspoon of both spices to find a good balance of flavor and heat. But instead of getting more flavor with each teaspoon, we merely turned the basting sauce into a crude-textured paste that offered little beyond a burnt tongue and heartburn. The way around this problem was simple enough: We steeped the spices in warm oil and discovered the well-rounded, intense, yet sophisticated flavor we had been looking for (see the Science Desk on page 211 for more information on releasing the flavor of spices). Just 2 teaspoons each of ground black pepper and red pepper flakes did the trick. Tasters liked the additional flavor of garlic. We tried adding lemon to the basting sauce, but this flavor didn't come across. Instead, we served the grilled chicken with fresh wedges of lemon, and this was a huge hit.

Up until now we had been brushing the sauce on the chicken during the last few minutes of grilling. We wondered if brushing it on at the beginning or rubbing it underneath the skin would make a difference. When we brushed the sauce onto the skin before grilling, the garlic and peppers burned. Rubbing it under the skin, however, worked wonders. The rubbed chicken had a fuller, rounder flavor, as the spices were able to seep directly into the meat. We then tried dabbing extra sauce onto the meat after it had been rubbed, grilled, and carved, and hit pay dirt. The fresh kick of garlic and pepper ensured that every bite tasted spicy without going overboard.

To butterfly a chicken, you remove the backbone with poultry shears or a chef's knife, then press the bird flat. Some cooks remove the breastbone, but we found this maneuver to be both tricky and fruitless. It leaves the breast meat

unprotected on the grill and prone to overcooking. Keeping the breastbone intact, we tried pressing the chicken flat with our hands, but this caused the chicken to bow on the grill, resulting in uneven cooking and uneven grill marks. Pounding the chicken flat with a mallet worked well.

So far, we were having little success on the grill. We were consistently burning chickens even though we had yet to weight them down with a brick (a technique that would probably make burning more—not less—likely). To get to the bottom of this problem, we decided to investigate the best method for setting up a charcoal grill.

A charcoal fire can be set up in three basic ways: single level, two level, or modified two level. A single-level fire spreads the coals evenly over the bottom of the grill, a two-level fire spreads a thin layer of coals over the grill and then banks the rest to one side, and a modified two-level fire banks all of the coals to one side of the grill and leaves the other side completely empty. When cooking over a two-level fire (which is often used when grilling meat), you use the hot side of the grill first for searing, then the cooler side to finish the cooking. We placed a foil-wrapped brick on top of the chicken and then tried all three setups to see which worked best. The result? A parade of incinerated chickens. No matter what the type of fire or the heat level, tall menacing flames licked the chickens until they were fully blackened—the devil's chicken, indeed.

Although these last tests were utter failures, they clearly illustrated the problem inherent to grilling chicken alla diavola over a charcoal fire: The oil-based marinade (or, in this case, sauce) seeps out of the chicken (particularly under the weight of the brick) and onto the hot coals, thereby creating unmanageable infernos. Because we were rubbing the sauce underneath the skin, the chicken burned mostly when it was skin-side down. How, then, could we grill the chicken skin-side down without charring it? We tried a modified two-level fire—backward—grilling the chicken skin-side down over the empty side of the grill and flipping it skin-side up over the coals to finish cooking. Although this technique did prevent the skin from burning, it also prevented the skin from receiving any color at all. The empty side of the grill was just too cool. To increase the level of heat without placing any coals directly under the chicken, we tried banking the coals on either side of the grill, leaving the center completely empty. We put the chicken in the center of the cooking grate and then covered the grill to help retain the heat. Finally, we produced a great grilled chicken with a gorgeous brown skin. To render the skin completely crisp, we found it necessary to cook the chicken skin-side down, covered, for the entire 30- to 40-minute grilling time. Developing a technique for the gas grill was no problem. We simply grilled the chicken skin-side down over medium-low heat, covered, until it was done and crisp. There were no flare-ups.

Throughout these tests we faithfully employed the brick, but we had come to find its repeated removal and replacement a real nuisance when checking the chicken. Testing the difference between a bricked chicken and an unbricked chicken with our newfound grilling methods, we suddenly felt like the punch line to an old Italian prank. The brick, it turned out, was little more than a conversation starter.

---

**WHAT WE LEARNED:** Brine the chicken in a mixture of salt, water, garlic, and bay leaves as the first flavor-building step. Rub spicy garlic oil (heated first to intensify the flavors of the garlic as well as the black and hot red pepper) under the skin before grilling the chicken, and then drizzle the bird with more of this oil right before serving. Finally, grill the bird over moderate heat and without bricks, which press oil out of the bird and promote flare-ups.

## CHARCOAL-GRILLED CHICKEN ALLA DIAVOLA Serves 3 to 4

Before building the fire, make sure that the grill is cleaned of residual ash from previous use; if left in the bottom, residual ash catches fat drippings and causes flare-ups that can singe the chicken. For this recipe, we prefer the even, slower heat generated by charcoal briquettes over faster-burning hardwood charcoal.

### chicken and brine

- 2 medium garlic heads
- 3 bay leaves, crumbled
- ½ cup salt
- 1 whole chicken (3 to 3½ pounds), butterflied and pounded according to the illustrations below

### garlic-pepper oil

- 4 medium garlic cloves, minced or pressed through garlic press (about 4 teaspoons)
- 2 teaspoons ground black pepper
- 2 teaspoons red pepper flakes
- ¼ cup olive oil

  Vegetable oil for grill grate
- 1 lemon, cut into wedges, for serving

**1.** TO BRINE THE CHICKEN: Combine the garlic heads, bay leaves, and salt in a gallon-size zipper-lock bag; press out the air and seal the bag. Using a rubber mallet or meat pounder, pound the mixture until the garlic cloves are crushed; transfer the mixture to a large container or stockpot and stir in 2 quarts cold water until the salt is dissolved. Immerse the chicken in the brine and refrigerate until fully seasoned, about 2 hours.

**2.** FOR THE GARLIC-PEPPER OIL: While the chicken is brining, heat the garlic, black pepper, pepper flakes, and oil in a small saucepan over medium heat until the garlic is fragrant and sizzling and the mixture registers about 200 degrees on an instant-read thermometer, about 3 minutes. Remove from the heat and cool to room temperature, about

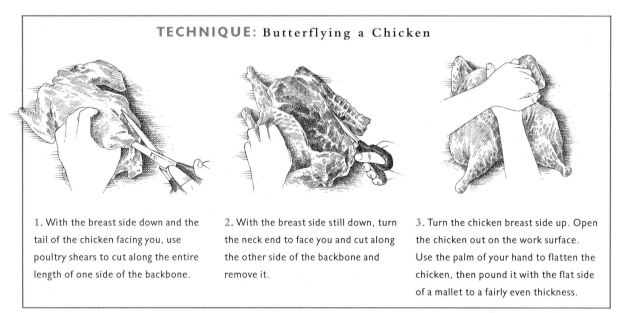

**TECHNIQUE:** Butterflying a Chicken

1. With the breast side down and the tail of the chicken facing you, use poultry shears to cut along the entire length of one side of the backbone.

2. With the breast side still down, turn the neck end to face you and cut along the other side of the backbone and remove it.

3. Turn the chicken breast side up. Open the chicken out on the work surface. Use the palm of your hand to flatten the chicken, then pound it with the flat side of a mallet to a fairly even thickness.

40 minutes. Measure 2 tablespoons garlic-pepper oil into 2 small bowls and set aside.

**3.** TO FLAVOR THE CHICKEN: Remove the chicken from the brine and thoroughly pat dry with paper towels. Slip your fingers underneath the skin of the breast and legs to loosen the membrane and rub 2 tablespoons of the infused oil beneath the skin.

**4.** TO GRILL THE CHICKEN: Light a large chimney starter filled with charcoal briquettes (about 6 quarts) and allow to burn until all the charcoal is covered with a layer of fine gray ash. Empty the coals into the grill and bank half of the coals on either side of the grill, leaving the midsection of the grill free of coals. Set the cooking rack in place, cover the grill with the lid, and let the rack heat up, about 5 minutes. Use a wire brush to scrape clean the cooking rack. Lightly dip a small wad of paper towels in vegetable oil; holding the wad with tongs, wipe the grill rack. Position the chicken skin-side down on the grill rack over area with no coals; cover the grill and fully open the lid vents.

**5.** Cook until an instant-read thermometer inserted into the thickest part of the thigh registers 170 to 175 degrees, 30 to 40 minutes. Transfer the chicken to a cutting board; let rest 10 minutes. Carve the chicken, cutting the bird into 10 pieces (two wings, two drumsticks, two thighs, and four breast quarters), and transfer the pieces to a platter. Drizzle the chicken with the remaining infused oil and serve with the lemon wedges.

**VARIATION**
### GAS-GRILLED CHICKEN ALLA DIAVOLA
To prevent flare-ups that can char the chicken, make sure that the gas grill's fat drainage system is in place. Lava rocks can intensify flare-ups, so be especially vigilant if making this recipe on a grill with these ceramic briquettes. Keep a squirt bottle filled with water near the grill to extinguish any flare-ups.

Follow the recipe for Charcoal-Grilled Chicken alla Diavola through step 3. Turn all burners on a gas grill to high, close the lid, and heat until the grill is very hot, about 15 minutes. Scrape the grill grate clean with a wire brush; lightly dip a small wad of paper towels in vegetable oil and, holding the wad in tongs, wipe the grill grate. Turn all burners to medium-low, position the chicken skin-side down on the center of the grill grate, cover, and continue with the recipe from step 5.

## SCIENCE:
### How to Pry Flavor Out of Spices

AS WE DEVELOPED OUR RECIPE FOR CHICKEN ALLA diavola, we were curious as to why we weren't able to extract much flavor from either the ground black pepper or the red pepper flakes when they were added to the brine or a room-temperature marinade. We were further intrigued when their flavor blossomed, becoming deep and fragrant, after being briefly steeped in warm oil. After some research, we learned that it's simply a matter of solubility.

The essential oils in both black pepper and red pepper flakes are oil-soluble as opposed to water-soluble. This means that they dissolve in oil rather than water. As they dissolve, these flavorful essential oils are released from a solid state into solution form, where they mix and interact, thereby producing a more complex flavor. Like most substances, these essential oils dissolve faster and to a greater extent in a hot solvent (in this case, olive oil) than in a cold solvent. However, if the oil is too hot, the spices can scorch. We prepared five batches of marinade, bringing them to temperatures of 150, 200, 250, 300, and 400 degrees. The differences were dramatic. The 150-degree batch tasted flat and boring, while the marinades brought to 250, 300, and 400 degrees tasted increasingly burnt. When heated to 200 degrees, however, the marinade tasted perfectly spicy and well rounded.

# STRAWBERRIES AND BALSAMIC VINEGAR

**WHAT WE WANTED:** A simple dessert, with vinegar enhancing but not overwhelming the flavor of the berries.

Strawberries with balsamic vinegar may sound like an odd combination or even a bit trendy. But this dessert is neither. At its best, balsamic vinegar is akin to fine port—something to sip in a glass rather than toss in a salad. A few drops of the slightly sweet vinegar enhances the sweetness and fragrant qualities of fresh fruit. As for trendiness, artisan-made balsamic vinegar has been produced in parts of northern Italy for hundreds of years and served over berries for nearly as long.

True balsamic vinegars have brilliantly complex flavors with hints of spice, honey, and caramel. Used primarily as a condiment or liqueur, they are soft, mellow, and not at all acidic. A 3½-ounce bottle of artisan-made balsamic vinegar, otherwise referred to as *tradizionale* or *extra-vecchio tradizionale aceto balsamico*, can fetch up to $300. Of course, most Americans are familiar with industrial balsamic vinegars that cost just a few dollars a bottle. These vinegars are thinner, more acidic, and less complex than the traditional vinegars. Such commercial vinegars are perfectly suited for salads and pan sauces, but would they work in this recipe?

Curious to see how the best supermarket balsamic vinegar would fare, we started with 365 Every Day Value balsamic vinegar, which won our tasting of leading commercial vinegars (see the Tasting Lab on page 213). The result was not totally surprising. The vinegar was somewhat mellow and had a hint of vanilla flavor, but it lacked body and, frankly, tasted like—well—vinegar. As most Americans are not willing to lay down a couple hundred dollars for the real McCoy, we wanted to find some way to use commercial vinegar so that it would approximate the syrupy texture and complex but mellow flavor of aged traditional vinegar.

The obvious solution was to simmer the vinegar to improve its texture and to add sugar and perhaps seasonings

to improve its flavor. Reducing the supermarket vinegar by almost half improved its texture and created a syrupy sauce—a major improvement over the straight vinegar. A tiny bit of sugar tempered its acidity. We also tried reducing the vinegar with vanilla and honey, hoping to create a sauce with more personality. The vanilla was overpowering, and the honey was not noticeably different from the sugar. Finally, we tried a squirt of lemon juice to brighten the flavors; this was well received by tasters.

Now that we had found a viable solution to the vinegar problem, we focused our attention on the strawberries. The strawberries must be sweetened; sugar accentuates the flavors of the berries and balances the balsamic syrup. We found that ¼ cup was ideal for 3 pints of strawberries. Traditionally, strawberries and balsamic vinegar are sweetened with white granulated sugar. We tested different sweeteners, hoping to find a sweetener that might enhance the flavors of the vinegar. Honey produced a funny aftertaste and was distracting. Dark brown sugar was too strong and so also distracting. We tried a coarse natural sugar but found no appreciable difference in flavor over white sugar. Light brown sugar, however, added gentle hints of molasses without being overpowering. Though the difference was subtle, tasters felt that light brown sugar was slightly preferable to granulated white sugar.

After mixing the sliced berries and sugar, we found that it took 10 to 15 minutes for the sugar to dissolve and the berries to release some juice. Don't let the berries macerate for much longer. We found that they will continue to soften and become mushy rather quickly.

**WHAT WE LEARNED:** Simmer an inexpensive vinegar with some sugar to approximate the syrupy texture of aged balsamic vinegar. Toss the berries with light brown sugar—rather than the traditional granulated sugar—for the most complex flavor.

## STRAWBERRIES WITH BALSAMIC VINEGAR

Serves 6

If you don't have light brown sugar on hand, sprinkle the berries with an equal amount of granulated white sugar. Serve the berries and syrup as is or with a scoop of vanilla ice cream or a dollop of lightly sweetened mascarpone cheese.

| | |
|---|---|
| 1/3 | cup balsamic vinegar |
| 2 | teaspoons granulated sugar |
| 1/2 | teaspoon lemon juice |
| 3 | pints strawberries, hulled and cut lengthwise into 1/4-inch-thick slices (small strawberries can be halved or quartered) |
| 1/4 | cup packed light brown sugar |
| | Ground black pepper |

**1.** Bring the vinegar, granulated sugar, and lemon juice to a simmer in a small heavy-bottomed saucepan over medium heat. Simmer until the syrup is reduced by half (to approximately 3 tablespoons), about 3 minutes. Transfer the vinegar syrup to a small bowl and cool completely.

**2.** With a spoon, lightly toss the berries and brown sugar in a large bowl. Let stand until the sugar dissolves and the berries exude some juice, 10 to 15 minutes. Pour the vinegar syrup over the berries, add pepper to taste, and toss to combine. Divide the berries among individual bowls or goblets and serve immediately.

## TASTING LAB: Balsamic Vinegar

YOU CAN BUY A DECENT BOTTLE OF NONVINTAGE French table wine for $8, or you can invest in a bottle of 1975 Château Lafite Rothschild Bordeaux for $300—but no one would ever compare the two. They are two different beasts. The same holds true for balsamic vinegars. There are balsamic vinegars you can buy for $2.50 and those that nudge the $300 mark. The more expensive vinegars bear the title *tradizionale* or *extra-vecchio tradizionale aceto balsamico* (traditional or extra-old traditional). According to Italian law, these traditional vinegars must come from the northern Italian provinces of Modena or Reggio Emilia and be created and aged in the time-honored fashion.

Unfortunately, American consumers cannot really be sure that the industrial-style balsamic vinegar they purchase in their grocery or specialty foods store is a high-quality product. Unlike the makers of trademark-protected products of Italy, including tradizionale balsamico, Parmigiano-Reggiano, and Prosciutto di Parma (all from the Reggio Emilia region), Italian producers of commercial balsamic vinegars failed to unite before market demand for their products ballooned in the United States in the early 1980s. The result has been high consumer demand with little U.S. regulation—the perfect scenario for producers who take advantage of the system by misleading consumers about the integrity of their products.

For hundreds of years, tradizionale balsamico vinegar has been made from Trebbiano grapes grown in the Modena or Reggio Emilia regions of northern Italy. The grapes are crushed and slowly cooked into *must* over an open flame. The must begins mellowing in a large wooden barrel, where it ferments and turns to vinegar. The vinegar is then passed through a series of barrels made from a variety of woods. To be considered worthy of the tradizionale balsamico title, the vinegar must be moved from barrel to barrel for a minimum of 12 years. An extra-vecchio vinegar must be aged for at least 25 years.

Because of its complex flavor and high production cost, tradizionale balsamico is used by those in the know as a condiment rather than an ingredient. The longer the vinegar ages, the thicker and more intensely flavored it becomes, maturing from a thin liquid into a spoon-coating, syrupy one—perfect for topping strawberries or cantaloupe. This is the aristocrat of balsamic vinegars.

The more common varieties—those with a price tag under $30—are categorized as commercial or industrial balsamic vinegars. These vinegars are the kind with which most

Americans are familiar and are often used to complete a vinaigrette or flavor a sauce. The flavor profile of commercial balsamic vinegars ranges widely from mild, woody, and herbaceous to artificial and sour, depending on the producer and the style in which the vinegar was made. Commercial balsamic vinegar may or may not be aged and may or may not contain artificial caramel color or flavor.

We wondered how bad—or good—inexpensive commercial balsamic vinegars would be when compared in a blind tasting. To level the playing field—and ease the burden on our budget—we limited the tasting to balsamic vinegars that cost $15 or less. We included some vinegars from supermarkets (we held a preliminary supermarket balsamic vinegar tasting and included the three most favored by our tasters in the final tasting) and some from mail-order sources and specialty foods stores. We also included samples of the many production styles, including some aged in the traditional fashion, some with added caramel color and flavor, and some made from a blend of aged red wine vinegar and grape must.

We found that a higher price tag did not correlate with a better vinegar. In addition, age seemed to play a less important role than we had expected. There were young vinegars among the winners as well as older vinegars among the losers.

Across the board, tasters found balsamic vinegars containing caramel color or flavor to be "sour" and "uninteresting." The top brands from our tasting contain no artificial colors or flavors whatsoever. Our findings led us to believe that much as *fond* (the browned bits left in a pan after food

has been sautéed) is instrumental in creating a high-quality pan sauce, *must* is paramount to making a full-flavored balsamic vinegar. As the must ages, it becomes thick and sweet, contributing a character almost like sherry or port. Producers who substitute artificial color and flavor for must end up with a shallow product that was routinely derided by our tasters. Some connoisseurs might argue that the only balsamic vinegars worth buying are aged ones, but we found that age didn't make nearly as big a difference as artificial additives did.

Given this information, how can you figure out what type of balsamic vinegar to buy? The easy answer is to check the label. If it discloses that artificial ingredients have been added, don't buy it. Unfortunately, it's not only commonplace but legal for the ingredient label to skirt the issue and completely avoid publishing the contents of the vinegar. This is because Italian law dictates that "Balsamic Vinegar of Modena"—which is how 9 out of 10 vinegars are labeled— is itself an ingredient and product, so no further description of the vinegar's contents is required. Label specifications from the U.S. Food and Drug Administration require only that the producer indicate whether or not the vinegar contains sulfites, a preservative that produces a severe allergic reaction in some people.

"Whatever you want to call a balsamic vinegar, you can call a balsamic vinegar," says John Jack, vice president of sales and marketing for Fiorucci Foods in Virginia. "It's become very much of a commodity-oriented business." Even if a vinegar is labeled "Balsamic Vinegar of Modena," a title that conveys the idea of quality to consumers, it may not have been produced in, or even near, Modena. In fact, several manufacturers bottle their vinegar right here in the United States. Young vinegars can bear the balsamic title, too. As a result of the less-than-stringent regulations, many producers and importers look forward to the passage of a new regulation in Italy that would make it illegal to label a vinegar younger than three years *balsamic.*

For now, check the label. If the vinegar contains artificial color or sweetener, look further.

# Rating Inexpensive Balsamic Vinegars

TWENTY-ONE MEMBERS OF THE *COOK'S ILLUSTRATED* STAFF AND NINE CHEFS RATED EIGHT VINEGARS FOR COLOR, bouquet, flavor, body, and density. The balsamic vinegars were tasted in their natural state, with bread and water provided to cleanse the palate between samples. The vinegars are listed in order of preference. All vinegars are available in supermarkets nationwide.

## HIGHLY RECOMMENDED
### 365 Every Day Value Balsamic Vinegar
**$3.99 for 16.9 ounces**
**MADE IN MODENA**

**Started from must; blend of older (up to five years) and younger balsamic vinegars.**

Tasters described this vinegar as chocolate brown, with a medium thickness. They loved its vanilla, fruit, and caramel-like underpinnings as well as its "balanced acidity."

## HIGHLY RECOMMENDED
### Masserie Di Sant'Eramo Balsamic Vinegar
**$10.95 for 8.5 ounces**
**MADE IN MODENA**

**Started from must; aged a minimum of five years.**

This vinegar was dark reddish-brown in color. Tasters liked its fruit and honey notes as well as its "balanced spice and acidity." One taster called it "demure" and "floral"; another found it "sherry-like."

## HIGHLY RECOMMENDED
### Fiorucci Riserva Balsamic Vinegar
**$8.99 for 8.5 ounces**
**MADE IN MODENA**

**Aged wine vinegar blended with must; aged six years.**

Described as "translucent brown," the Fiorucci vinegar was called "mellow" and "tangy-sweet" in flavor, reminding some tasters of plums and apples.

## RECOMMENDED
### Cavalli Balsamic Seasoning
**$15.00 for 8.5 ounces**
**MADE IN REGGIO EMILIA**

**Started from must; aged three years.**

This was an interesting, "enormously complex" sample, scoring either as a favorite or as a most detested balsamic—which lands it in the middle of the rankings. It had big vanilla and honey attributes, but some tasters couldn't get past the "strange but alluring" cedar/balsam notes.

## RECOMMENDED
### Fini Balsamic Vinegar
**$10.50 for 8.5 ounces**
**MADE IN MODENA**

**Started from must; aged two years.**

**Note: Contains caramel color.**

Tasters called this sample "cloudy" and "muddy," with many objecting to the presence of sediment. It was characterized as having a fermented flavor somewhat reminiscent of soy sauce or raisins.

## RECOMMENDED
### Colavita Balsamic Vinegar
**$8.49 for 16.9 ounces**
**MADE IN MODENA**

**Aged wine vinegar blended with must; aged one year.**

**Note: Contains caramel color and flavor.**

Although this vinegar wasn't considered very complex, tasters were fond of its "fig," "burnt nut," and "tobacco" flavors. It was downgraded for being overly harsh, acidic, and "fleeting."

## NOT RECOMMENDED
### Regina Balsamic Vinegar
**$2.79 for 12 ounces**
**GRAPES FROM MODENA, BOTTLED IN THE UNITED STATES**

**Wine vinegar blended with must; aged two to four years.**

**Note: Contains caramel color and flavor.**

Called a "thin, mousy, unassuming little vinegar," Regina was disliked for its "artificial" qualities.

## NOT RECOMMENDED
### Giuseppe Giusti Balsamic Vinegar
**$11.95 for 8.5 ounces**
**MADE IN MODENA**

**Started from must; aged approximately six years.**

**Note: May contain caramel color and flavor (an industry representative was unable to confirm or deny their presence in this product).**

Tasters called it "salty," "harsh," and "sharp."

Becky readies cassoulet for its final sprinkling with croutons and baking in the oven.

# FRENCH·FOOD
### CHAPTER 18
*in a flash*

## IN THIS CHAPTER

### THE RECIPES
Simplified Cassoulet with Pork
and Kielbasa
Simplified Cassoulet with Lamb
and Andouille Sausage

30-Minute Tarte Tatin
Tarte Tatin with Pears

### TASTING LAB
Diced Canned Tomatoes
Petite Diced Tomatoes

Americans seem to have a love/hate relationship with all things French, including their food. There's no denying that French cuisine is marvelous, but many traditional dishes are best made by an army of sous chefs. Preparing favorite dishes such as cassoulet (a bean and pork stew showered with a crisp bread crumb topping) or tarte Tatin (a caramelized apple tart) calls for a lot of patience and time. By the time you've completed these projects, the day is gone and your kitchen is a mess.

We wondered if we could find ways to simplify these recipes without sacrificing the qualities that make them great. Does a cassoulet really require all of those exotic meats? What about using canned beans rather than dried? Can you make good tarte Tatin with store-bought puff pastry? Do you need to caramelize the apples and bake the pastry in the skillet at the same time?

We decided to roll up our sleeves and rethink these French classics. After much trial and error, the test kitchen developed two novel versions of these dishes that eliminate much of the work but still deliver high-quality results.

# CASSOULET

**WHAT WE WANTED:** Great cassoulet made in a few hours (rather than a few days) that didn't sacrifice the deep, melded flavors that are characteristic of this dish.

Every once in a while, a dish comes around that is so robust, so satisfying to every sense that we deem it comfort food. It warms us from the inside out and assures us that this winter, too, shall pass. Cassoulet is such a dish.

But for most cooks, the reasons to eat cassoulet outnumber the reasons to make it. Cassoulet can take three days to make, and the ingredients can be both hard to find and difficult to prepare.

The cassoulet originated in Languedoc, France, and each area of the region touts its recipe as "the real thing." All versions of the dish contain white beans, but that is where the agreement ends. Some prefer pork loin in their cassoulet, others use a shoulder of lamb, while still others use a combination of both. Mutton, duck, pheasant, garlic sausage, and even fish can be found in the different variations.

But the best known and most often replicated type of cassoulet hails from Toulouse. This cassoulet must start with the preparation of confit. Meat or poultry, most often goose legs (the region of Toulouse also houses the foie gras industry, so goose is plentiful), is placed in a large container, sprinkled heavily with salt, and cured for 24 to 48 hours. This both preserves and tenderizes the meat. After this sojourn in salt, the meat is slowly simmered in its own fat, so that the flavor of the fat penetrates the spaces previously occupied by the juices. The finished confit may be used immediately or stored in an airtight container, covered in its own fat.

But the intricacy of cassoulet doesn't end with the confit. Pork loin and mutton must be slow-roasted for hours to become fully tender, and garlic sausages freshly made. The beans must be presoaked and then simmered with pork rinds to develop flavor. Finally, the entire mixture has to be combined in an earthenware pot, topped with bread crumbs, and placed in a low-temperature oven to simmer slowly for several hours.

The result is nothing short of divine. But while this classic French peasant dish can be replicated at restaurants, it is definitely not a dish for the casual home cook. The time investment alone is impractical, and it can be difficult to achieve a perfect balance of flavors. On more than one occasion we have eaten cassoulets that were overwhelmed by salt or swimming in fat, most often because of the confit and sausages. All the same, we love this dish so much that we decided it would be worth the effort to try to streamline it without compromising its essential nature.

We decided to accept the hardest of the challenges first and conquer the confit. We eliminated the notion of confit made from scratch as far too time-consuming. Assessing our other options, we created three cassoulets. One was prepared with braised duck leg confit (goose leg confit is less widely available) purchased through our butcher. The others we made with no confit at all, starting one version with sautéed and braised duck legs and the other with sautéed and braised chicken thighs, which we wanted to use because they're so easy to find in the supermarket. The results were disheartening, although not surprising. The cassoulet made with the purchased confit was the clear favorite. Those made without it produced dishes more reminiscent of duck and chicken stews.

Unfortunately, ready-made confit is not widely available, so we wanted to develop a recipe that wouldn't rely on it. Somewhat ironically, we arrived at the solution to the problem with some help from the confit itself.

Because confit is salt-cured and then cooked in its own fat, it retains an intense duck flavor when added to the cassoulet, contributing a rich, slightly smoky flavor that was noticeably absent from the dishes prepared with the sautéed duck and chicken. The texture of the dish made with confit was superior as well, the flesh plump with flavor yet tender to the bite; the sautéed and braised duck and chicken became tough and gave up all of their flavor to the broth. Taking an educated guess, we decided to adopt an approach often used in the test kitchen and brine the chicken. Because we had found when making other dishes that brining resulted in poultry that was both more moist and more flavorful, we reasoned that brining the chicken might bring it closer to the tender texture of confit. To approximate the confit's light smokiness, we decided to cook the thighs in bacon fat.

We quick-soaked the chicken thighs for one hour in a concentrated salt and sugar solution, sautéed them quickly in rendered bacon fat, then braised them with the rest of the cassoulet ingredients. What resulted was just what we were hoping for: a suitable substitute for duck confit. The bacon added a smoky flavor, and it enhanced the flavors of the pork and sausage added later. The texture was spot-on for the confit; the chicken thighs were plump and juicy; and the broth became well seasoned because of the brine. With this "mock" confit in hand, we proceeded.

Our next test involved figuring out which meats to use and how to avoid slow roasting. We knew that we wanted to be true to the original recipe and use either fresh pork or lamb. We decided to try stewing the meat in liquid entirely on top of the stove. This method yielded great results in terms of tenderness, but the meat had none of the depth of flavor that occurs with roasting. Searing the meat in some of the rendered bacon fat that we had used with the chicken thighs took care of that problem.

Because we were now stewing the meat, we needed to use cuts that were appropriate for this method. We tried pork loin, the choice in so many cassoulet recipes, but the loin became waterlogged and tasteless during stewing. A suggestion from our butcher led us to try a blade-end roast, which is the part of the loin closest to the shoulder. The blade-end roast, which has more internal fat than the center loin, retained the moisture and flavor. To facilitate

quicker cooking, we cut the roast into 1-inch pieces. We used similar testing with the lamb. Lamb shoulder is the best cut for stewing, but it can be difficult to find in markets. We bought instead thick lamb shoulder chops, which we also cut into 1-inch pieces. Finally, perfectly tender meat without the effort of roasting.

Cassoulets traditionally use white beans. We wanted to make sure that the beans would retain their shape while adding a soft texture to the dish. Canned beans fell apart quickly, so we opted for dried. We tested four varieties, and the winner was the pale green flageolet bean. These small, French, kidney-shaped beans have a creamy, tender texture and delicate flavor that perfectly enhanced the cassoulet. We also cooked the beans on top of the stove along with bacon and the aromatics to let them absorb additional flavor.

The last major decision we had to make concerned the sausage. After ruling out the use of hard-to-find French sausages (and not willing to take the time to make our own), we found that both kielbasa and andouille sausages intensified the smoky flavor that we so desired.

With the major problems out of the way, we were able to concentrate on streamlining the technique used to cook the dish. This proved to be quite simple. With the chicken, meat, and beans now modified for cooking on the stovetop, oven braising became unnecessary. Cooking the dish entirely on the stove at a low simmer, with a quick finish in the oven to brown the bread crumbs, produced perfect results in a short amount of time. At last we had it: a quick cassoulet that was worthy of the name.

---

WHAT WE LEARNED: Use brined chicken thighs cooked in bacon fat to approximate the duck confit traditionally used in this recipe. Stew the meat rather than roast it and use fattier cuts of pork or lamb from the shoulder area. Dried beans are a must (canned beans will turn to mush), and flageolets are our favorites.

## SIMPLIFIED CASSOULET WITH PORK AND KIELBASA Serves 8

This dish can be made without brining the chicken, but we recommend that you do so. To ensure the most time-efficient preparation of the cassoulet, while the chicken is brining and the beans are simmering, prepare the remaining ingredients. Look for dried flageolet beans in specialty food stores. If you can't find a boneless blade-end pork loin roast, a boneless Boston butt makes a fine substitution. Additional salt is not necessary because the brined chicken adds a good deal of it. If you skip the brining step, add salt to taste before serving.

### chicken

- ½ cup salt
- 1 cup sugar
- 10 bone-in skinless chicken thighs (about 3½ pounds), excess fat removed

### beans

- 1 pound dried flageolet or great Northern beans, picked over and rinsed
- 1 medium onion, peeled and left whole
- 1 medium head garlic, outer papery skin removed and top ½ inch sliced off
- 1 teaspoon salt
- ½ teaspoon ground black pepper

- 6 ounces (6 slices) bacon, chopped medium
- 1 pound boneless blade-end pork loin roast, trimmed of excess fat and cut into 1-inch pieces
- 1 small onion, chopped fine
- 2 medium garlic cloves, minced or pressed through garlic press
- 1 can (14.5 ounces) diced tomatoes, drained
- 1 tablespoon tomato paste
- 1 large sprig fresh thyme
- 1 bay leaf
- ¼ teaspoon ground cloves

Ground black pepper
- 3½ cups low-sodium chicken broth
- 1½ cups dry white wine
- ½ pound kielbasa, halved lengthwise and cut into ¼-inch slices

### croutons

- 6 slices good-quality white sandwich bread, cut into ½-inch dice (about 3 cups)
- 3 tablespoons unsalted butter, melted

**1.** FOR THE CHICKEN: In a gallon-size zipper-lock plastic bag, dissolve the salt and sugar in 1 quart cold water. Add the chicken, pressing out as much air as possible; seal and refrigerate until fully seasoned, about 1 hour. Remove the chicken from the brine, rinse thoroughly under cold water, and pat dry with paper towels. Refrigerate until ready to use.

**2.** FOR THE BEANS: Bring the beans, whole onion, garlic head, salt, pepper, and 8 cups water to a boil in a stockpot or

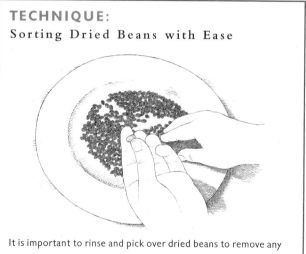

### TECHNIQUE:
### Sorting Dried Beans with Ease

It is important to rinse and pick over dried beans to remove any stones or debris before cooking. To make this task easier, sort dried beans on a white plate or cutting board. The neutral background makes any unwanted matter easy to spot and discard.

Dutch oven over high heat. Cover, reduce the heat to medium-low, and simmer until the beans are almost fully tender, 1¼ to 1½ hours. Drain the beans and discard the onion and garlic.

**3.** While the beans are cooking, fry the bacon in a Dutch oven over medium heat until just beginning to crisp and most of the fat has rendered, 5 to 6 minutes. Using a slotted spoon, add half of the bacon to the pot with the beans; transfer the remaining bacon to a paper towel–lined plate and set aside. Increase the heat to medium-high; when the bacon fat is shimmering, add half of the chicken thighs, fleshy-side down; cook until lightly browned, 4 to 5 minutes. Using tongs, turn the chicken pieces and cook until lightly browned on the second side, 3 to 4 minutes longer. Transfer the chicken to a large plate; repeat with the remaining thighs and set aside. Drain off all but 2 tablespoons fat from the pot. Return the pot to medium heat; add the pork pieces and cook, stirring occasionally, until lightly browned, about 5 minutes. Add the chopped onion and cook, stirring occasionally, until softened, 3 to 4 minutes. Add the minced garlic, tomatoes, tomato paste, thyme, bay leaf, cloves, and pepper to taste; cook until fragrant, about 1 minute. Stir in the chicken broth and wine, scraping up the browned bits off the bottom of the pot with a wooden spoon. Submerge the chicken in the pot, adding any accumulated juices.

Increase the heat to high and bring to a boil, then reduce the heat to low, cover, and simmer about 40 minutes. Remove the cover and continue to simmer until the chicken and pork are fully tender, 20 to 30 minutes more. Using tongs and a slotted spoon, remove and discard the chicken skin.

**4.** FOR THE CROUTONS: While the chicken is simmering, adjust an oven rack to the lower-middle position and heat the oven to 400 degrees. Mix the bread crumbs and butter in a small baking dish. Bake, tossing occasionally, until light golden brown and crisp, 8 to 12 minutes. Cool to room temperature; set aside.

**5.** Gently stir the kielbasa, drained beans, and reserved bacon into the pot with the chicken and pork; remove and discard the thyme and bay leaf and adjust the seasonings with salt and pepper. Sprinkle the croutons evenly over the surface and bake, uncovered, until the flavors have melded and the croutons are deep golden brown, about 15 minutes. Let stand 10 minutes and serve.

VARIATION

### SIMPLIFIED CASSOULET WITH LAMB AND ANDOUILLE SAUSAGE

Lamb, with its robust, earthy flavor, makes an excellent substitute for the pork. Andouille sausage adds a peppery sweetness that tasters loved.

Follow the recipe for Simplified Cassoulet with Pork and Kielbasa, substituting 2 pounds lamb shoulder chops, trimmed, boned, and cut into 1-inch pieces, for the pork, and substituting 8 ounces andouille sausage for the kielbasa.

**GETTING IT RIGHT:**
Blade versus Center Loin Pork

Because the pork is stewed, the blade end of the loin is preferable to the leaner center loin.

BLADE          CENTER LOIN

## TASTING LAB: Canned Diced Tomatoes

IN LATE SUMMER AND EARLY FALL, SUN-RIPENED LOCAL tomatoes abound. But fast-forward to mid-February... what are you going to use in your sauce now? The pale, hard, flavorless orbs that pass for fresh tomatoes during the off season—which is most of the year here in New England—won't get you far in the flavor department, and the handsome "on-the-vine" and deep red hydroponic specimens usually look better than they taste.

The conventional wisdom holds that canned tomatoes surpass fresh for much of the year because they are packaged at the height of ripeness. After side-by-side tests of fresh, off-season tomatoes and canned tomatoes while we were developing recipes for cream of tomato soup, pasta all'Amatriciana (pasta with tomatoes, bacon and onion), and shrimp fra diavolo, among others, we agree. But the many brands of canned tomatoes available beg an obvious question: Which brand tastes best? Having sampled eight brands of canned diced tomatoes, both plain and cooked in a simple sauce, we have the answer.

According to both Bob Graf, president of the California League of Food Processors, and representatives of Small Planet Foods, distributors of Muir Glen tomato products, canned diced tomatoes emerged on the market in the early 1990s. Sales of diced tomatoes have since come to dominate the category of canned processed tomato products, outselling tomato paste, whole and crushed tomatoes, and tomato sauce and puree, all products that have been around for generations.

Depending on the season and growing location, more than 50 varieties of tomatoes are used to makes these products, according to Graf and Dr. Diane Barrett, fruit and vegetable products specialist in the department of food science and technology at the University of California, Davis. Graf said that while tomato varieties are generally not genetically engineered, they are refined for traits that will satisfy growers (yield and harvesting characteristics), processors (ease of skinning and solid-to-liquid ratio), and consumers (color and flavor) alike.

Packers generally reserve the ripest, best-colored specimens for use as whole, crushed, and diced tomatoes, products in which consumers demand vibrant color and fresher flavor. Lower-grade tomatoes are generally used in cooked products, such as paste, puree, and sauce.

Before processing, the tomatoes are peeled by means of either steam—always the choice of Muir Glen, the only organic brand in our lineup—or a hot lye bath, which many processors currently favor. Because temperatures in lye peeling are not as high as those in steaming, many processors believe that lye leaves the layer of flesh just beneath the skin in better condition, giving the peeled tomato a superior appearance. Our tasters, however, could not detect specific flavor characteristics in the canned tomatoes based on this aspect of processing. Two of our three highly recommended products, Muir Glen and S&W, use steam, while the third, Redpack, uses lye.

After peeling, the tomatoes are sorted again for color and the presence of obvious deficiencies, and then they're diced. After the dice is sorted, the cans are filled with the tomatoes and topped off with salt and filler ingredients (usually tomato juice, but sometimes puree—read on). Finally, the lids are attached to the cans and the cans are cooked briefly for sterilization, and then cooled and dried so they can be labeled.

The flavor of a ripe, fresh tomato balances elements of sweetness and tangy acidity. The texture should be somewhere between firm and pliant, and certainly not mushy. Ideally, canned diced tomatoes should reflect the same combination of characteristics. Indeed, tasters indicated that excessive sweetness or saltiness (from the salt added during processing), along with undesirable texture qualities, could make or break a can of diced tomatoes. If the tasters thought that any one of these characteristics was out of whack, they downgraded that sample. In fact, two of the eight brands in the tasting were deemed to have major flaws in both flavor and texture that landed them in the lowest echelon of the ratings.

The downfall of Hunt's, the lowest rated brand of the eight, was saltiness. According to the label on the can, one serving of Hunt's diced tomatoes contains 380 milligrams of sodium; the other brands tested average just over 240 milligrams per serving. That's a good 50% more salt, a characteristic that tasters easily detected and didn't appreciate.

Cento, the only other brand besides Hunt's that tasters relegated to the "Not Recommended" category, suffered from a triple whammy of flavor and texture problems, according to our tasters. First, it was the only product in the bunch that was packed in tomato puree, rather than the more common tomato juice. This led to complaints about the flavor, which some tasters perceived as "way cooked," "like candy," and "ketchupy." By comparison, the thin, watery juice in which the other canned diced tomatoes are packed tasted lighter and more natural. Puree is heavier and pulpier than juice, and must be heated longer to achieve its specified concentration. In short, more cooking equals less freshness. The heavy puree is probably also responsible for tasters' impressions that Cento tomatoes were overly sweet, another significant point against them.

Cento was also the only brand in the lineup that didn't include calcium chloride among its ingredients. According Diane Barrett, the calcium in this compound helps the tomato pieces maintain a firm texture by stabilizing the pectin network in the tomato tissue. Because calcium is divalent, that is, it has an electrical charge of +2, it acts as a bridge between two long chains of pectin, in effect bonding them together. Based on our results, the absence of calcium chloride made a difference, as tasters described the Cento tomatoes as "mealy," "very broken down," and "squishy."

Oddly, no one flavor profile dominated. The three highly recommended brands, Muir Glen, S&W, and Redpack, displayed a range of flavor characteristics. Muir Glen led the ratings with a favorable balance of sweetness and saltiness and a notably "fresh" flavor in the sauce. Redpack also ranked high for its fresh flavor in the sauce. The same group of tasters, however, gave the thumbs up to S&W tomatoes, a brand noted for its bracing acidity and powerful, almost exaggerated, tomato flavor. What link these three brands, then? Well, it's more about what characteristics they don't have than what they do. None of them exhibited major flavor flaws, the likes of which landed some other brands down in the ratings. The three winners were neither too sweet, like Cento, nor too salty, like Hunt's. Likewise, they tasted neither bitter nor metallic.

On the topic of winning texture, however, tasters were in accord. Both Muir Glen and S&W placed in the middle of pack in terms of firmness, while Redpack was rated firmest of all. Clearly, our tasters frowned on mushy canned tomatoes.

## TASTING LAB: Petite Diced Tomatoes

WHILE WE WERE SHOPPING FOR CANNED DICED tomatoes for the tasting, we noticed a new product on the shelves: petite diced canned tomatoes. Was this just a tweak by manufacturers' marketing departments to boost sales or a genuinely useful product? Because we often find pieces of regular diced tomatoes to be too large for certain recipes and are forced to break them up with our fingers or a knife, we wanted to see if petite tomatoes could save us the trouble.

We picked a widely available recommended brand, Del Monte (the only other brand we saw at press time was Hunt's), and made quick tomato sauces with both regular and petite diced tomatoes. (The regular dice measured 7/8 inch, the petite dice 3/8 inch.) The result? We were surprised to find that we unanimously preferred the sauce made with the petite diced tomatoes. The differences between the sauces resided not in their flavor but in their texture: Small, uniformly cut pieces of tomato created a cohesive sauce that clung to the strands of pasta. The regular diced tomato sauce was separated and watery, and the large firm chunks of tomatoes easily evaded our forks. That is not to say the petite diced tomatoes are always preferable to regular. For quick preparations, such as this tomato sauce, the petite diced worked very well, but for recipes that call for longer cooking times, such as chili or stew, you may want beefier chunks of tomato.

# Rating Canned Diced Tomatoes

TWENTY MEMBERS OF THE *COOK'S ILLUSTRATED* STAFF TASTED EIGHT DIFFERENT BRANDS OF CANNED DICED TOMATOES. The tomatoes were tasted two ways; plain, to get opinions of overall flavor, texture, and size, and cooked, in a simple sauce with garlic, olive oil, sugar, and salt. The tomatoes are listed in order of preference based on the combined results of both tastings.

### RECOMMENDED
### Muir Glen Organic Diced Tomatoes
**$1.99 for 28 ounces**

A few tasters thought these tomatoes were "bland" and "mellow" when tasted plain, but for these same reasons this brand rated number one in the sauce tasting. "Sweet," "fresh tasting," and "most like fresh tomatoes" were some of the comments that explained why this brand received high marks.

### RECOMMENDED WITH RESERVATIONS
### Contadina "Recipe Ready" Diced Tomatoes
**$1.39 for 28 ounces**

While some tasters thought these tomatoes tasted "bright and fresh," the overall consensus was that they were too "soft and fleshy." The sauce had a "nice balance of sweet/salty," but was "very broken down" and looked as if "it had cooked for a very long time." These tomatoes tasted "very, very sweet."

### RECOMMENDED
### S&W "Ready Cut" Premium Peeled Tomatoes
**$2.46 for 28 ounces**

This West Coast brand was liked for its "tangy," "vibrant" flavor. It was rated as "very acidic" in both the plain and the sauce tasting, and made one of the saltiest sauces. Tasters also commented on the "concentrated" flavor, which was "like tomato paste."

### RECOMMENDED WITH RESERVATIONS
### Furmano's Diced Tomatoes
**$1.39 for 28 ounces**

This highly acidic and salty brand secured a decent rating in the sauce tasting because the "tomatoes retained their texture" and "bright flavor" when cooked. When tasted raw, however, they were viewed as "bitter," "with the taste of a tin can."

### RECOMMENDED
### Redpack "Ready Cut" Diced Tomatoes
### (Known as Redgold on the West Coast)
**$1.19 for 28 ounces**

These tomatoes did not score very high in the plain tasting and were considered "bland" by some. But they were also judged the firmest tomatoes, which may have contributed to their jump to second place in the sauce tasting, where they exhibited a "fresh tomato-y taste," and a texture that "did not break down at all."

### NOT RECOMMENDED
### Cento "Chef's Cut" Tomatoes
**$1.59 for 28 ounces**

The only brand without calcium chloride in the ingredient list was very mushy. Tasters commented on the addition of basil only in the raw tasting; some welcomed it, others thought it tasted of "stale herbs." The sauce was described as too sweet, "like ketchup."

### RECOMMENDED WITH RESERVATIONS
### Del Monte Diced Tomatoes
**$1.79 for 28 ounces**

The flavor of these tomatoes was slightly "musty" and "sweet" to some and "bright and balanced" to others when eaten raw but became "like stewed tomatoes" in sauce. This brand may be better suited for raw sauces; when cooked, the tomatoes turned "mushy."

### NOT RECOMMENDED
### Hunt's Diced Tomatoes
**$1.59 for 28 ounces**

The word "hypersalty" sums up these tomatoes. Eaten raw, they tasted like V-8, with an unpleasant metallic aftertaste. And things only got worse in the sauce, which tasted "like soy sauce" to several people, with a "fermented," "burnt" flavor. To top it off, tasters found the texture "mealy" and "mushy."

# TARTE TATIN

**WHAT WE WANTED:** Caramelized apples resting in a buttery, flaky pastry—but without the usual hassles.

Making a true tarte Tatin is a labor of love. First, you need to make the puff pastry, a multi-hour endeavor requiring dexterity with a rolling pin and a no-fear attitude of incorporating hundreds of layers of butter within a single sheet of dough. Once the pastry is made, the apples go into a heavy-bottomed hot pan to caramelize. The pastry tops the browned apples, and the entire pan goes into the oven where the apples will caramelize further, their juices bubbling into the dough as the pastry puffs like an inflatable pillow. With a pot holder in one hand and a plate in the other, fearless Tatin-makers invert the tart onto the plate. In a perfect world, the apples fall from the pan and perfectly nestle into the pastry.

If this process sounds stressful, you're right, it is. Not only do you have to worry about making puff pastry and caramelizing the apples in a pretty concentric circle (so that when they're inverted onto the pastry, they retain an orderly look), but the entire inverting process can spawn a rational fear of spitting hot caramel dripping from the pan and down your arm.

Our goal was to whittle the Tatin process down to a manageable affair. We still wanted to retain the flavor of sticky-sweet caramelized apples and the flakiness of buttery puff pastry, but didn't want to be chained to the kitchen for hours to do so. So we came up with an idea—could the apples and puff pastry be made separately and then married together just before serving? It was definitely worth a try.

We started by simplifying the puff pastry—rather than making it from scratch, we bought pre-made puff pastry from the grocery store. We popped it in the oven for about 12 minutes and took it out when it was golden and inflated. Easy enough.

We then focused on the apples, melting butter in a large pan, sprinkling in some sugar, and laying quartered apples on top of it all. We allowed the apples to caramelize for about 10 minutes, flipped them over, and browned the other side. We then removed the apples, piece by piece with tongs, and arranged them in pretty overlapping rows on the baked puff pastry square.

We spooned about ¾ of the leftover caramelized juices in the pan over the tart. To the remaining juices, we added a few tablespoons of the whipped sour cream topping that gets served alongside the tart. This makes an instant caramel sauce that provides a nice tangy contrast to the sweet, syrupy juices of the tart. In just 30 minutes, we created a faux Tatin that even Francophiles will like.

**WHAT WE LEARNED:** Cook the apples and caramel separately on top of the stove. Bake the crust in the oven (using store-bought puff pastry), and then assemble the tart just before serving.

## 30-MINUTE TARTE TATIN Serves 6 to 8

To get this dessert on the table in 30 minutes, peel the apples while the oven preheats and the pastry thaws, and then bake the pastry while the apples are caramelizing. If the pastry rises unevenly in the oven, press it flat immediately after removing it from the oven. Some of the whipped sour cream topping is stirred into the caramelized apple juices left in the pan to make a caramel sauce. The remaining whipped sour cream topping is dolloped over individual portions of the tart.

### puff pastry

- 1 sheet (9 by 9½ inches) frozen commercial puff pastry, thawed on the counter for 10 minutes

### caramelized apples

- 8 tablespoons unsalted butter
- ¾ cup (5¼ ounces) sugar
- 2 pounds Granny Smith apples (6 medium or 4 large), peeled, quartered, and cored

### whipped sour cream topping

- ½ cup sour cream
- 1 cup heavy cream
- 2 tablespoons liqueur, optional (spiced rum, Calvados apple liqueur, or Grand Marnier orange liqueur)

**1.** FOR THE PASTRY: Adjust an oven rack to the middle position and heat the oven to 400 degrees. Line a rimmed baking sheet with parchment paper. Place the puff pastry on the parchment, prick all over with a fork, and bake until golden brown and puffed, 10 to 12 minutes. Using a wide metal spatula, transfer the baked pastry shell to a cutting board or to a flat serving platter.

**2.** FOR THE APPLES: Meanwhile, melt the butter in a 12-inch heavy-bottomed skillet. Remove the pan from the heat and sprinkle evenly with the sugar. Place the apples in the skillet so they are all resting flat side down. Return the

skillet to high heat and cook until the juices in the pan turn a rich amber color, 10 to 12 minutes. Using tongs, turn the apples over to the other flat side. Continue to caramelize the apples for an additional 5 minutes.

**3.** FOR THE TOPPING: Whip the sour cream and heavy cream to soft peaks in the bowl of a standing mixer. Add the liqueur (if desired) and continue to whip to medium-stiff peaks.

**4.** TO ASSEMBLE: Using tongs, remove the apple slices from the pan one at a time and place in 3 overlapping horizontal rows on the baked pastry square. Spoon about three-quarters of the pan juices over the top of the apples (you can use a pastry brush to dab some of the liquid onto the edges of the pastry). To the leftover liquid in the pan whisk in 2 tablespoons whipped sour cream topping.

**5.** TO SERVE: Cut the tart in half vertically down the center, and then horizontally into 3 or 4 rows (to serve 6 or 8, respectively). Transfer portions to individual plates and top each with a dollop of whipped sour cream and a drizzle of caramel sauce from pan. Serve immediately.

### VARIATION

### TARTE TATIN WITH PEARS

Follow the recipe for 30-Minute Tarte Tatin, substituting 2 pounds Anjou or Bartlett pears (6 to 8 medium) for the apples. You may need to increase the caramelization time in step 2 to 15 minutes for the first side, and to 8 minutes for the second side. Poire William is best liqueur to use in the whipped sour cream.

Weeknight Bolognese Sauce **page 77**

Green Beans with Orange Essence and Toasted Maple Pecans **page 109**

228

Pasta with Sautéed Mushrooms and Thyme **page 66**

Sesame Noodles with Shredded Chicken **page 199**

230

Charcoal-Grilled Chicken Alla Diavola **page 210**

Corn and Apricot Muffins with Orange Essence **page 262**

Oatmeal Scones **page 245**

German Apple Pancake **page 278**

234

Blueberry Pancakes **page 272**

Simple Carrot Cake with Cream Cheese Frosting **page 306**

Summer Berry Pie **page 295**

Thin, Crispy Chocolate Chip Cookies **page 284**

Chocolate-Dipped Triple-Coconut Macaroons **page 289**

Lemon Cheesecake **page 315**

Chocolate Sheet Cake with Creamy Milk Chocolate Frosting **page 309**

Lemon Pound Cake with Lemon Glaze **page 249**

242

# TEATIME

CHAPTER 19

IN THIS CHAPTER

**THE RECIPES**

Oatmeal Scones
Cinnamon-Raisin Oatmeal
    Scones
Apricot-Almond Oatmeal Scones
Oatmeal Scones with Dried
    Cherries and Hazelnuts
Glazed Maple-Pecan Oatmeal
    Scones

Lemon Pound Cake
Lemon Glaze
Lemon-Poppy Seed Pound Cake

**EQUIPMENT CORNER**

Citrus Juicers and Reamers

**TASTING LAB**

Supermarket Teas

In the test kitchen, we think afternoon (or morning) tea is an excellent excuse to whip up a batch of scones or a golden loaf of lemon pound cake. Making these simple baked goods at home certainly yields better results than what you can buy.

Most American scones have strayed far from the British original and are either much too sweet (scones are not cookies or muffins) or oversized, dense, and heavy (scones are biscuits and should be light in texture and small in size).

Pound cake dates back several centuries and was originally made from 1 pound each of eggs, butter, sugar, and flour. This recipe may be easy to remember, but we found that it yields a leaden cake that does not suit modern palates. On the other hand, contemporary pound cakes, especially store-bought versions that come in foil containers, are often gummy and riddled with artificial ingredients and flavors. Could we make this classic cake appeal to modern tastes and still keep the process simple?

# OATMEAL SCONES

**WHAT WE WANTED:** The dry, fat-free triangles passed off as scones at coffeehouses would make better paperweights. Is it possible to bake a rich, toasty oatmeal scone that's tender and flaky?

Scones in America—unlike their diminutive English counterparts—have the reputation of being thick, heavy, dry bricks. To enhance their appeal, they are often disguised under a sugary shellac of achingly sweet glaze or filled with chopped ginger, chopped fruit, or chocolate chips. Despite these feeble attempts to dress them up, it is no secret that today's coffeehouse confections are a far cry from what a scone should be: tender and flaky, like a slightly sweetened biscuit.

Still, creating the perfect scone didn't seem like enough of a challenge. We were up for revamping the heaviest, densest, driest variation of them all: the oatmeal scone. The first few recipes we tried confirmed our worst fears about scones. There was the lean, mean whole-wheat flour oatmeal scone, which was gritty and dense, and the dried fruit–laden scone, which was like a thick cookie. Luscious cream scones were liked for their rich flavor but ultimately rejected for their gummy texture. And while scones made from a melted butter batter were tender, they were too cakey and delicate. Although tasters had different preferences when it came to texture, all agreed on the need for a stronger oat flavor. Our goal, then, was to pack the chewy nuttiness of oats into a moist and tender breakfast pastry, one that wouldn't require a fire hose to wash down the crumbs.

The first hurdle was deciding what type of oat to use. Because they take at least 30 minutes to cook, steel-cut oats were quickly ruled out—the baking time of the scones would not be long enough to cook these crunchy oats through. Instant oats turned out soft and gooey scones, which left us with two choices: rolled (or old-fashioned) and quick. This was not an easy decision, as each had qualities to recommend it. The whole rolled oats gave the scones a deeper, nuttier flavor (a few tasters even asked if there was peanut butter in the scones), whereas the smaller flaked quick oats gave the scones a softer texture, which was considered more palatable by some. We finally decided that either would do.

Next we had to figure out how to pack in the most oat flavor without sacrificing texture. We were sure we could achieve this by simply processing the oats into the flour. But this made for a horrible texture, very gluey and dense. Leaving the oats intact, we found that equal parts oats and flour combined good flavor with a decent texture. (Most of the recipes we tested called for much smaller proportions of oats, thus their wimpy oat flavor.) But we were still yearning for a nuttier taste, so we toasted the oats before mixing them with the flour. We tried toasting them in butter on the stovetop and on a baking sheet in the oven and found that while both methods worked well, throwing oats into the preheated oven required much less effort.

Wary of scones that were too sweet, we tried to keep the sugar content to a minimum—just enough to tenderize the scones while enhancing the oat flavor. We wanted to use a minimal amount of leavener to avoid the off flavors detected in many of the preliminary tests. We settled on just 2 teaspoons of baking powder, a much smaller amount than the tablespoon or more called for in the test recipes.

Moving on to the butter, we quickly realized why so many scones are so dry: They don't have nearly enough fat. A lean scone, we decided, is simply not worth eating, so we used 10 tablespoons of butter, which added flavor as well as making the scones tender. As for how to add the butter to the dough, we tried cutting cold butter into the dry ingredients (a standard biscuit-making technique), and we tried stirring in melted butter. Tasters preferred the lightness of the former to the cakiness of the latter.

We knew that heavy cream alone would create gummy scones, while milk alone would give us lean scones. The solution? Use a mixture of milk and heavy cream (or half-and-half) for a rich oatmeal scone that doesn't double as a paperweight. As with biscuits, we found it important not to overwork the dough. It should be mixed just until the ingredients come together. Overmixing will yield tough, flat scones.

In keeping with the recommendations of the test recipes, we baked scones at temperatures ranging from 350 degrees all the way up to 425 degrees—and every 25-degree increment in between. The best of the lot were those baked at 425 degrees, but they were not ideal. We tried pushing the oven temperature to 450 degrees (a bit of a gamble, as the sugar in the recipe might burn) and were rewarded. These scones had a dramatic rise and a deep, golden brown crust. And this is what sold tasters on them. In such high heat, the cold butter melted quickly and produced steam, which created the light texture we were looking for. The intensity of the rise also gave the scones a cracked, craggy, rustic look. This higher temperature also meant that the scones spent less time in the oven, depriving them of the opportunity to dry out.

Until this point, our tests had shown that good scones follow the three basic rules of biscuit making: plenty of cold fat, a light hand when mixing, and a high oven temperature. Would we spoil our good luck by adding an egg, something rarely included in biscuit recipes? Perhaps scones are not exactly biscuits after all. We added one egg to our recipe, and this version won hands down for its richness. Finally, we had a scone that was hearty and flavorful from toasty whole oats, yet light enough to be consumed in one sitting without having to wash it down with a giant-size latte.

---

WHAT WE LEARNED: Use old-fashioned or quick oats (not instant) and toast them for a nutty oat flavor. Use a lot of butter (scones with too little butter are not worth eating) and a blend of milk and cream for richness without gumminess. Finally, bake the scones in a very hot oven to achieve maximum rise and deep browning.

## OATMEAL SCONES Makes 8 scones

This recipe was developed using Gold Medal unbleached all-purpose flour; best results will be achieved if you use the same or a similar flour, such as Pillsbury unbleached. King Arthur flour has more protein; if you use it, add an extra 1 to 2 tablespoons milk. Half-and-half is a suitable substitute for the milk/cream combination.

1½ cups (4½ ounces) old-fashioned rolled oats or quick oats
¼ cup whole milk
¼ cup heavy cream
1 large egg
1½ cups (7½ ounces) unbleached all-purpose flour
⅓ cup (2¼ ounces) sugar, plus 1 tablespoon for sprinkling
2 teaspoons baking powder
½ teaspoon salt
10 tablespoons cold unsalted butter, cut into ½-inch cubes

**1.** Adjust an oven rack to the middle position and heat the oven to 375 degrees. Spread the oats evenly on a baking sheet and toast in the oven until fragrant and lightly browned, 7 to 9 minutes; cool on a wire rack. Increase the oven temperature to 450 degrees. Line a second baking sheet with parchment paper. When the oats are cooled, measure out 2 tablespoons (for dusting the work surface and the dough) and set aside.

**2.** Whisk the milk, cream, and egg in a large measuring cup until incorporated; remove 1 tablespoon to a small bowl and reserve for glazing.

**3.** Pulse the flour, ⅓ cup sugar, baking powder, and salt in a food processor until combined, about four 1-second pulses.

Scatter the cold butter evenly over the dry ingredients and pulse until the mixture resembles coarse cornmeal, twelve to fourteen 1-second pulses. Transfer the mixture to a medium bowl; stir in the cooled oats. Using a rubber spatula, fold in the liquid ingredients until large clumps form. Mix the dough by hand in the bowl until the dough forms a cohesive mass.

**4.** Dust the work surface with half of the reserved oats, turn the dough out onto the work surface, and dust the top with the remaining oats. Gently pat into a 7-inch circle about 1 inch thick. Using a bench scraper or chef's knife, cut the dough into 8 wedges and set on the parchment-lined baking sheet, spacing them about 2 inches apart. Brush the surfaces with the reserved egg mixture and sprinkle with 1 tablespoon sugar. Bake until golden brown, 12 to 14 minutes; cool the scones on the baking sheet on a wire rack for 5 minutes, then remove the scones to a rack and cool to room temperature, about 30 minutes. Serve.

VARIATIONS
### CINNAMON-RAISIN OATMEAL SCONES
Follow the recipe for Oatmeal Scones, adding ¼ teaspoon ground cinnamon to the dry ingredients and ½ cup raisins to the flour/butter mixture along with the toasted oats.

### APRICOT-ALMOND OATMEAL SCONES
Follow the recipe for Oatmeal Scones, reducing the oats to 1 cup, toasting ½ cup slivered almonds with the oats, and adding ½ cup chopped dried apricots to the flour/butter mixture along with the toasted oats and nuts.

### OATMEAL SCONES WITH DRIED CHERRIES AND HAZELNUTS
Follow the recipe for Oatmeal Scones, reducing the oats to 1¼ cups, toasting ¼ cup coarsely chopped skinned hazelnuts with the oats, and adding ½ cup chopped dried sour cherries to the flour/butter mixture along with the toasted oats and nuts.

### GLAZED MAPLE-PECAN OATMEAL SCONES
Follow the recipe for Oatmeal Scones, toasting ½ cup chopped pecans with the oats, whisking ¼ cup maple syrup into the milk/cream/egg mixture, and omitting the sugar. When the scones are cooled, whisk 3 tablespoons maple syrup and ½ cup confectioners' sugar in a small bowl until combined; drizzle the glaze over the scones.

---

**GETTING IT RIGHT:** Hotter Is Better

The scone on the left was baked in a moderate oven and did not rise as much as the scone on the right, which was baked in a very hot oven. The intense heat quickly turns the moisture in the dough into steam, and the resulting scones rise dramatically and have a craggy, well-browned top.

BAKED AT 350 DEGREES     BAKED AT 450 DEGREES

---

# LEMON POUND CAKE

**WHAT WE WANTED**: Although made from only a handful of ingredients, pound cake can be a finicky, disappointing dessert prone to disaster. We set out to construct a foolproof recipe.

Making a wedding cake is hard. Making a multi-layered Dobos torte out of génoise sponge cake and buttercream is daunting. But lemon pound cake? Well, that's easy, isn't it? After all, it's made only of eggs, butter, sugar, flour, and lemon mixed together and baked in a loaf pan. But if it's so easy, why do pound cakes often turn out spongy, rubbery, heavy, and dry rather than fine-crumbed, rich, moist, and buttery? In addition, most pound cake recipes call for creaming the butter, a tricky method that demands the ingredients be at just the right temperature to achieve a silken cake batter. So our goal was twofold: Produce a superior pound cake while making the process as simple and foolproof as possible.

We started with a pound cake recipe developed in the test kitchen many years ago that was known for being excellent in its results but finicky in its preparation. The cake was top-notch, with a submissive crumb and a golden, buttery interior. In fact, it was everything we wanted from a pound cake, except for one thing—the preparation method was anything but foolproof. The method—calling for the traditional creaming of the butter and sugar until fluffy and pale—was so exacting that even the smallest diversion curdled the batter. To achieve perfection, the ingredients had to be at an unforgiving 67 degrees, the butter and sugar beaten together for exactly five minutes to aerate, and the eggs drizzled into the batter over a period of three to five minutes. All of these precautions were advised to eliminate the danger of "breaking" the batter (a pound cake has so many eggs that keeping them in emulsion can be tricky when using the creaming method), which can make the crust look mottled and leave the cake's interior dense and tough.

We knew there had to be a simpler way to achieve greatness. First we tried cutting softened butter into flour using a standing mixer. Once the butter and flour resembled knobby crumbs, we added some of the eggs, beat the mixture until cohesive, then added the rest of the eggs and beat the batter further until thick, fluffy, and lush. We often favor this method for cakes because it produces a velvety texture and a superfine crumb. Although the pound cake batter assembled in this way looked great, the baked cake was too open-grained and tender. It looked more like a yellow cake than it did a pound cake.

Next we tried melting the butter, a method often used in making quick breads. The liquids are combined and the dry ingredients then mixed into the wet by hand. This method was quick and easy. Melting the butter eliminated all of the temperature issues associated with creaming. Best of all, the batter could be pulled together and put into the oven in five minutes.

With a tight grain, a perfect swell and split in its center, and a nice, browned exterior, this cake showed promise. When we made it a second time, however, it sagged in the center. Additional tests yielded varying results. The problem may have been in the mixing method; perhaps inconsistent mixing produced inconsistent cakes. The solution? A food processor would do a better job of emulsification and also standardize the process. We added the eggs, sugar, and vanilla to the food processor bowl, combining them enough to integrate the sugar and eggs, and then drizzled the melted butter in through the feed tube. We transferred the watery base to a large bowl and sifted in flour and salt, then whisking in these ingredients by hand.

This method was a success. The cake had a split dome that afforded a peek inside at the marvelously yellow color of its interior. Just to be sure, we made the cake again and again, with the same results. Recognizing that some home cooks don't have a food processor, we tried the method in a blender. Although the cake was a bit more dense, the differences were so minimal that we can recommend either approach. With the method determined, we focused on the cake's texture and flavor.

Our objective was to make the cake just a bit lighter—but not so light as to resemble a yellow cake. (Pound cakes are by definition heavier and more dense than layer cakes.) When we tested cake flour against all-purpose, the former was superior, making the cake more tender. But the cake still needed more lift and less sponginess.

We were at this point using two sticks of melted butter. Thinking that more butter might improve the texture, we increased the amount, but the cake turned out greasy. Next we turned to the eggs. The original test kitchen recipe called for three eggs plus three yolks, so we tried four whole eggs instead (an equivalent liquid amount), thinking that the additional white might add some lift. The cake was better but still on the dense side. Without success, we tried adding cream (this cake turned out heavy) and reducing the flour (this one was greasy). Four whole eggs had gotten us close, but the texture was still not ideal.

In the oldest of recipes (from the 1700s), eggs were the only ingredient in pound cake that gave it lift. In the 1850s, however, many cooks began adding the new wonder ingredient—baking powder—to achieve a lighter texture and a higher rise. Although traditionalists might scoff at the addition of chemical leavening, we were willing to give it a try. With just 1 teaspoon, we instilled enough breath into the cake to produce a consistent, perfect crumb. Now that we had simplified the method and achieved the right texture, it was time to concentrate on lemon flavor.

In all of our prior tests, we had experienced difficulty keeping the lemon zest afloat. In cake after cake, the zest came together in large yellow clumps. The solution turned out to be simple. When the lemon zest was pulsed with the sugar before the eggs were added to the food processor bowl, the baked cake came out evenly dotted throughout with perfect specks of zest. We also added lemon juice to the batter to boost flavor.

While some prefer their lemon pound cake plain, or with only a simple shower of confectioners' sugar, we like a blast of lemon flavor. A quick glaze—made by bringing sugar and lemon juice to a boil—tasted great in the pan but failed to migrate into the nooks and crannies of the cake's crumb when simply brushed on top. We used an old trick to help the glaze on its way, poking small holes in the cake's top crust and sides with a toothpick. The glaze now penetrated to the interior of the cake, distributing plenty of lemon flavor. Finally, we had a quick, foolproof recipe that delivered a great crumb and great lemon flavor. Pound for pound, this cake's a winner.

---

WHAT WE LEARNED: Melt the butter instead of creaming to foolproof the recipe. Assemble the batter in the food processor to make sure the melted butter is evenly incorporated. Use cake flour for maximum tenderness and a bit of baking powder for lift. Grind the lemon zest with the sugar so it remains evenly distributed in the cake, and brush the cake with lemon glaze as it cools.

## LEMON POUND CAKE

*Makes one 9 by 5-inch cake, serving 8*

You can use a blender instead of a food processor to mix the batter. To add the butter, remove the center cap of the lid so it can be drizzled into the whirling blender with minimal splattering. This batter looks almost like a thick pancake batter and is very fluid. The Lemon Glaze (recipe follows) makes the pound cake especially moist and flavorful.

| | |
|---|---|
| 16 | tablespoons (2 sticks) unsalted butter, plus 1 tablespoon, softened, for greasing pan |
| 1½ | cups (6 ounces) cake flour, plus 1 tablespoon for dusting pan |
| 1 | teaspoon baking powder |
| ½ | teaspoon salt |
| 1¼ | cups (8¾ ounces) sugar |
| 2 | tablespoons grated zest plus 2 teaspoons juice from 2 medium lemons |
| 4 | large eggs |
| 1½ | teaspoons vanilla extract |

**1.** Adjust an oven rack to the middle position and heat the oven to 350 degrees. Grease a 9 by 5-inch loaf pan with 1 tablespoon softened butter; dust with 1 tablespoon flour, tapping out the excess. In a medium bowl, whisk together the flour, baking powder, and salt; set aside.

**2.** In a glass measuring cup or microwave-safe bowl, microwave the butter, covered with plastic wrap, at full power until melted, 1 to 2 minutes. (Alternatively, melt the butter in a small saucepan over medium heat.) Whisk the melted butter thoroughly to reincorporate any separated milk solids.

**3.** In a food processor, process the sugar and zest until combined, about five 1-second pulses. Add the lemon juice, eggs, and vanilla; process until combined, about 5 seconds. With the machine running, add the melted butter through the feed tube in a steady stream (this should take about 20

seconds). Transfer the mixture to a large bowl. Sift the flour mixture over the eggs in three steps, whisking gently after each addition until just combined.

**4.** Pour the batter into the prepared pan and bake 15 minutes. Reduce the oven temperature to 325 degrees and continue to bake until deep golden brown and a skewer inserted in the center comes out clean, about 35 minutes, rotating the pan halfway through the baking time. Cool in the pan for 10 minutes, then turn onto a wire rack and brush on the Lemon Glaze, if desired. Cool to room temperature, at least 1 hour. (The cooled cake can be wrapped tightly in plastic wrap and stored at room temperature for up to 5 days.)

**LEMON GLAZE** Enough to glaze one 9 by 5-inch cake
Brush this glaze onto the warm cake to give it a fresh, sweet-tart lemon kick.

½  cup (3½ ounces) sugar
¼  cup juice from 1 or 2 medium lemons

While the cake is cooling, bring the sugar and lemon juice to a boil in a small nonreactive saucepan, stirring occasionally to dissolve the sugar. Reduce the heat to low and simmer until thickened slightly, about 2 minutes. After removing the cake from the pan, poke the top and sides of the cake throughout with a skewer or long toothpick. Brush the top and sides of the cake with the glaze and cool to room temperature.

### VARIATION
**LEMON–POPPY SEED POUND CAKE**
Follow the recipe for Lemon Pound Cake through step 1. Toss 1 tablespoon flour mixture with ⅓ cup poppy seeds in a small bowl; set aside. Continue with the recipe from step 2, folding the poppy seed mixture into the batter after the flour is incorporated.

## EQUIPMENT CORNER:
### Citrus Juicers and Reamers

CITRUS JUICERS AND REAMERS OFFER A QUICK, SIMPLE way to juice a lemon or two, with a modicum of fuss. The working part of both of these tools is a ridged, conical head. In the case of the reamer, the tool is turned; with the juicer, the lemon is turned. Are all juicers and reamers created alike? Of course not. After testing nine models, we found that the better models have a pointed tip, which effectively pierces the flesh of the lemon and grabs hold. Without the pointed tip, the lemon slips right off the head. The second important feature is the sharpness of the ridges. Those models with sharp, pointed ridges "gripped" the lemon well, making it easy to extract maximum juice with minimum effort, while those with rounded ridges allowed the lemon to slide around, making for difficult juicing.

The two winners were the plastic Oxo Good Grips Citrus Juicer and the Fox Run Wood Lemon Reamer. They both juiced the lemons quickly and efficiently. The Oxo Citrus Juicer features a unique design with two open ridged heads (for both larger and smaller citrus fruit) and a nonskid bowl for juice collection. The Fox Run reamer has a classic design and an especially comfortable handle.

The remaining reamers and juicers tested were less successful. Two models of Oxo Good Grips Citrus Reamers (one featuring a black plastic head, the other an aluminum head) and the Harold Stainless Steel Citrus Reamer featured relatively sharp tips, but their dull ridges caused lemons to slip. The other models all failed to pierce or grab lemons effectively owing to rounded heads and dull ridges.

# Rating Citrus Juicers and Reamers

WE TESTED NINE JUICERS AND REAMERS BY JUICING HALVED LEMONS WITH EACH DEVICE. THE JUICERS AND REAMERS are listed in order of preference based on their effectiveness (that is, the amount of juice they extracted) and their ease of use. See www.americastestkitchen.com for up-to-date prices and mail-order sources for top-rated products.

### RECOMMENDED—BEST JUICER
**Oxo Good Grips Citrus Juicer**
**$11.99**
The pointed tip and sharp ridges make for maximum juice extraction. A unique design accommodates lemons and oranges equally well.

### RECOMMENDED—BEST REAMER
**Fox Run Wood Lemon Reamer**
**$2.99**
A pointed tip, sharp ridges, comfortable handle, and low price—what more could you ask for?

### RECOMMENDED WITH RESERVATIONS
**Oxo Good Grips Lemon Reamer**
**$4.99**
The tip on this plastic reamer with a comfortable black plastic handle is pointed, but the ridges are rounded, so the lemons tend to slip and slide.

### RECOMMENDED WITH RESERVATIONS
**Oxo Silver Lemon Reamer**
**$8.50**
The tip on this aluminum reamer with a comfortable black plastic handle is pointed, but the ridges are rounded and dull. The lemons tended to slip and slide on this model.

### RECOMMENDED WITH RESERVATIONS
**Harold Stainless Steel Lemon Reamer**
**$10.00**
The pointed tip pierces lemons, but the rounded ridges allow too much slippage.

### NOT RECOMMENDED
**Mason Cash Vitrified Ceramic Reamer**
**$6.95**
This ceramic reamer did a poor job at both piercing and holding onto lemons.

### NOT RECOMMENDED
**Endurance Citrus Juicer**
**$12.99**
This stainless steel juicer has two strikes against it—a rounded tip and rounded ridges.

### NOT RECOMMENDED
**SCI Cuisine Internationale Citrus Juicer**
**$8.95**
This glass juicer has a rounded head and ridges that we didn't like, although the pour spout is a nice touch.

### NOT RECOMMENDED
**Zyliss Fruit Juicer**
**$11.95**
This plastic juicer has a rounded head and dull ridges and doesn't juice very effectively.

## TASTING LAB: Supermarket Teas

TEA IN THE UNITED STATES HAS BEEN RUNNER UP IN THE hot beverage pageant ever since our founding fathers turned Boston Harbor into the world's largest cup of tea more than 200 years ago. Today, tea is making a bit of a comeback. While nowhere near as ubiquitous as coffee shops, tea shops have sprouted, with menus featuring dozens (and sometimes hundreds) of different teas and blends.

But what about the old standby, traditional supermarket tea? With most around 3 cents per bag, there's no beating the price or the convenience.

Unless otherwise labeled, supermarket offerings contain black tea. There are three basic types of tea: green, black,

and oolong. (Herbal teas are not actually teas at all but rather a blend of leaves, flowers, and/or herbs.) Green teas contain leaves that have been steamed and dried, black teas contain fermented leaves, and oolong teas fall right in the middle, fermented for a shorter period of time than black teas. The two major categories of black teas are leaf and broken, and each category is then further broken down by size. Of the leaf category, orange pekoe refers to the largest leaf size.

If you look closely at a box of supermarket tea, you'll likely see the words "Orange Pekoe and Pekoe Cut Teas." That means that the tea bags contain large and small pieces of tea. Most supermarket teas are a blend of black teas. While all teas come from the same basic plant, regional variances in climate and soil make for more than 3,000 varieties of tea.

We tasted five popular national brands of supermarket

# Rating Supermarket Teas

TWELVE MEMBERS OF THE *COOK'S ILLUSTRATED* STAFF TASTED FIVE NATIONAL BRANDS OF TEA BAGS AS WELL AS A generic store brand. All tea bags were steeped in boiled water for four minutes and tasted plain. The teas are listed in order of preference based on scores from the tasting. With the exception of the Stop & Shop tea, all brands are sold in supermarkets nationwide.

### HIGHLY RECOMMENDED
**Lipton Tea** **$2.99 for 100 individually wrapped bags**
Tasters described this familiar brand as "well bodied," "smoky," and "rich." The clear winner.

### RECOMMENDED
**Salada Tea Bags** **$3.19 for 100 bags**
The runner-up received generally favorably comments, such as "full, smooth flavor," but a few tasters complained about a "dusty" flavor.

### RECOMMENDED
**Tetley Classic Blend** **$3.19 for 100 bags**
Depending on the taster, this popular brand was described as "mellow and smooth" or "weak" and "watery."

### NOT RECOMMENDED
**Twinings Ceylon Orange Pekoe Tea** **$2.99 for 25 individually wrapped bags**
This "premium" brand was roundly dismissed by tasters as "fishy" and "slightly bitter."

### NOT RECOMMENDED
**Red Rose Tea** **$3.19 for 100 bags**
This tea was described as "thin and bitter" as well as "soapy and harsh."

### NOT RECOMMENDED
**Stop & Shop Original Tea Bags** **$1.49 for 48 individually wrapped bags**
This supermarket brand received the lowest scores and harshest assessment from tasters, with comments like "sour" and "absolutely heinous."

tea, as well as the generic store brand from our local supermarket. Directions on the packages called for the tea to steep for three to five minutes in boiled water. We held a quick preliminary test to determine the best steeping time. At three minutes teas were deemed too flat, while at five minutes they were too strong. Tea steeped for four minutes had just the right balance. Most of the teas cost just above 3 cents per bag; the cheapest tea (at less than 3 cents per bag) ranked higher than our lone double-digit tea (at less than 12 cents per bag).

A significant range of scores separated our first- and last-place finishers. Lipton was the favorite, praised for its "smooth" and "slightly musty" flavor and "complexity." Fans of our second-place finisher, Salada, called it "earthy," "musty," and "floral," while detractors deemed it "nasty," "bitter," and "very average." At the bottom of the ranking were a generic store brand and Red Rose. One taster said of the generic brand, "It tastes like brown recycled paper towels." Though one taster described Red Rose as "light, with a good round flavor," most agreed with the two tasters who wrote, "Yuck."

Keith and Erin examine the long
prep list in the back kitchen.

# SUNDAY brunch

## CHAPTER 20

**IN THIS CHAPTER**

**THE RECIPES**
Denver Omelet

Corn Muffins
Corn and Apricot Muffins with
    Orange Essence
Bacon-Scallion Corn Muffins with
    Cheddar Cheese

**EQUIPMENT CORNER**
Rubber Spatulas
Spoonulas

**TASTING LAB**
Eggs
Baking Powder

Sunday brunch sounds so civilized. Every other day of the week breakfast happens in seconds. You eat a bowl of cereal as you dress, or you grab a bagel on the way to work. But one day a week you spend the morning preparing eggs, baking muffins, and squeezing fresh juice. All that extra work better be worth the time and effort.

But all too often that Denver omelet is rubbery, with raw chunks of vegetable poking holes in its surface, and the corn muffins turn out like the sticky-sweet cakes or dry hockey pucks you get in bad coffee shops. You wonder why you should bother. Cold cereal looks pretty good compared with such disappointing fare.

We figure that if you're going to make a real breakfast, it better be really good. Our recipes for Denver omelets and corn muffins are special enough to make you long for Sunday mornings.

# DENVER OMELET

WHAT WE WANTED : A hearty American omelet with properly cooked vegetables and tender eggs.

While we love soft, delicately flavored French omelets, we also have a weakness for lightly browned diner-style omelets bursting at the seams with filling. And our favorite is the Denver omelet, a mixture of sautéed bell peppers, onions, and ham with a generous handful of melted Monterey Jack cheese. Unfortunately, like too much diner food, Denver omelets are often ill-prepared and lacking in flavor. We set out to remedy this problem and make a refined Denver omelet worthy of cooking at home.

As we see it, the two biggest problems facing Denver omelets are undercooked filling and overcooked eggs. And the two together can be quite off-putting: crunchy, vegetal-tasting peppers sandwiched between layers of tough eggs. The filling proved the easiest place to start. We wanted a well-cooked, slightly browned filling that brought out the natural sweetness in the peppers. And we wanted the ham's smokiness to cut through the rich creaminess of the eggs and cheese. To emphasize the peppers' sweetness and build complexity of flavor, we used both red and green peppers, which also made for a more attractive filling. We first tried julienning the vegetables, as done in many diners do, but

tasters complained that the vegetables were hard to eat and the peppers' skins added an unpleasant, fibrous quality to the filling. So we switched to a dice, which was easier to eat, and the peppers' thick skins no longer marred the texture. To keep the cooking time short, we diced everything fairly small. The vegetables softened and lightly browned with about six minutes of cooking over medium-high heat.

After trying several different kinds of ham, including ham steaks, canned ham, and sliced deli ham, we found they all worked fine, but ham steaks proved the easiest to dice and provided the deepest, smokiest flavor. We first tried adding the ham to the vegetables long enough to just warm through but found that the filling did not take on the ham's potent flavor. When the ham was added midway through cooking, however, the smokiness infused the vegetables and the diced ham browned at the edges.

Although we had overcome the hurdle of under-cooked vegetables, the filling tasted one-dimensional. Borrowing from the classic Basque dish of piperade—a mixture of ham, peppers, and onions from which the Denver filling is clearly derived—we added a hint of garlic and parsley. The garlic sharpened the robust flavors, and the parsley added some freshness. The final touch was a dash of hot pepper sauce, which accented the flavors without necessarily tasting spicy.

With our filling perfected, we moved on to the eggs. There are probably more techniques for cooking omelets than for any other dish under the sun. We tested a variety and came up with a relatively foolproof method. First off, a good-quality, nonstick pan is crucial; otherwise you are guaranteed to produce scrambled eggs instead of an omelet. For these big, overstuffed omelets, we found that a 10-inch pan worked best, allowing the eggs to spread out to provide plenty of surface area for the filling. After experimenting with different heat levels, medium-high seemed to work the best because the eggs set quickly. At

## FOOD FACT: Eggs

Annual per capita consumption of eggs in the shell has dropped from 283 eggs in 1966 to 177 today. During that same period, annual per capita consumption of processed eggs (in baked good, cookies, etc.) has risen from 30 eggs to 73. Although we are eating fewer eggs in total per year (313 in 1966 versus 250 today), the numbers are less dramatic when you look at the total egg picture, not just consumption of whole eggs purchased in supermarkets.

lower heat, they tended to get rubbery. The sizzling point of the butter added to the pan proved a good indicator of when the pan was hot enough to receive the eggs (the butter added great flavor as well).

With the eggs in the pan, we quickly stirred them with a heat-safe rubber spatula until they just began to set, a matter of a few seconds. Then, gingerly, we lifted up the edges of the set eggs with the spatula and tilted the pan, allowing the uncooked eggs to run underneath and cook. When the eggs were almost fully set—just a little runny on top—we added the cheese. We discovered that once the cheese was almost melted, the bottom had lightly browned and was ready to come out of the pan. We quickly covered half the omelet with the warm pepper filling, slid the omelet onto a plate, filled-side first, and, with a slight twist of the wrist, flipped the empty half over the filled half. (We tried folding the omelet in the pan with the spatula, but this method occasionally ripped the omelet.)

We were pleased with the technique and the egg's light browning, but the omelet itself was a little dense and tough. Because the omelet cooked longer than a French-style omelet, the eggs were robbed of moisture. To increase the moisture, we tried adding milk, cream, and water to the beaten eggs. Milk and cream worked equally well, but water diluted the omelet's subtle flavor. As little as 1 tablespoon of cream or milk to 3 eggs was just right. The interior stayed fluffy and moist, while the exterior was lightly browned.

---

WHAT WE LEARNED: Dice the pepper and onion so they cook quickly and don't poke through the eggs. Add diced ham steak, garlic, parsley, and hot sauce to enliven the vegetable filling. Add milk or cream to keep the eggs moist as they cook and make sure to use a nonstick pan set over medium–high heat.

## DENVER OMELET Serves 1

Prepare the filling (recipe follows) and then begin making the omelet. The filling recipe makes enough for two omelets and can be doubled. See the illustrations on page 259 for tips on folding an omelet. You can make one omelet after another in the same pan, although you may need to reduce the heat. For the best results, serve all omelets, including this one, on warmed plates.

3 large eggs
1 tablespoon cream or milk
  Salt and ground black pepper
½ tablespoon unsalted butter
2 ounces Monterey Jack cheese, shredded (about ½ cup)

**1.** Beat the eggs, cream or milk, and salt and pepper to taste with a fork in a small bowl until thoroughly combined.

**2.** Heat the butter in a 10-inch nonstick skillet over medium-high heat. When the foaming subsides and the butter just begins to turn color, pour in the eggs. Cook until the edges begin to set, about 2 to 3 seconds, then, with a rubber spatula, stir in a circular motion until slightly thickened, about 10 seconds. Use the spatula to pull the cooked edges in to the center, then tilt the pan to one side so that the uncooked egg runs to the edge of the pan. Repeat until the omelet is just set but still moist on the surface, 1 to 2 minutes.

**3.** Sprinkle the cheese evenly across the surface of the omelet and allow to partially melt, 15 to 20 seconds. With the handle of the pan facing you, spoon the filling over the left side of the omelet. Slide the omelet onto a warmed plate, filled-side first, and, with a slight twist of the wrist, invert the pan so that the other side of the omelet folds over the filling. Serve immediately.

## FILLING FOR DENVER OMELET

**Makes enough to fill 2 omelets**

A ham steak is our top choice for this recipe, although canned ham and sliced deli ham will work. (If using sliced deli ham, add it with the garlic, parsley, and hot sauce.) If you can find them, Cook's brand ham steaks are our favorite.

|      |                                                               |
| ---- | ------------------------------------------------------------- |
| 1    | tablespoon unsalted butter                                    |
| ½    | medium red bell pepper, stemmed, seeded, and diced            |
| ½    | medium green bell pepper, stemmed, seeded, and diced          |
| 1    | small onion, diced                                            |
| ¼    | teaspoon salt                                                 |
| 4    | ounces ham steak, diced (about 1 cup)                         |
| 1    | tablespoon minced fresh parsley leaves                        |
| ½    | teaspoon hot pepper sauce, such as Tabasco                    |

Heat the butter in a medium nonstick skillet over medium-high heat. When the foaming subsides, add the peppers, onions, and salt. Cook, stirring occasionally, until the onions begin to soften, about 4 minutes. Add the ham and cook until the peppers begin to brown lightly, about 2 minutes. Add the garlic, parsley, and hot sauce and cook for 30 seconds. Transfer to a small bowl and cover to keep warm.

## TASTING LAB: Eggs

WE WERE CURIOUS HOW EGGS FROM DIFFERENT sources might stack up when tasted side-by-side. Despite marketing hype to the contrary, a kitchen taste-test proved that shell color has no effect on flavor. Brown eggs and white eggs from similar sources taste the same.

But what about organic or farm-fresh eggs? To find out, we put the following four varieties to the test by cooking each sunny-side up: farm-fresh eggs (less than a week old), Egg Innovations organic eggs ("free roaming"), Eggland's Best brand eggs from hens raised on vegetarian feed (the labels says these eggs are guaranteed to possess "25% less saturated fat than regular eggs" and "100 mg of omega 3 fatty acids"), and standard supermarket eggs. The farm-fresh eggs were standouts from the get-go. The large yolks were shockingly orange and sat very high above the comparatively small white. Their flavor was exceptionally rich and complex. The organic eggs followed in second place, with eggs from hens raised on a vegetarian diet in third and the standard supermarket eggs last.

Our conclusion? If you have access to eggs fresh from the farm, by all means buy them; they are a special treat. Otherwise, organic eggs are worth the premium—about a dollar more than standard supermarket eggs—especially if you frequently eat them on their own or in simple recipes such as an omelet.

We also wondered how freshness affected flavor. Egg cartons are marked with both sell-by and "pack dates" (the

---

### GETTING IT RIGHT: Egg Sizes

Eggs come in six sizes—jumbo, extra-large, large, medium, small, and peewee. Most markets carry only the top four sizes—small and peewee are generally reserved for commercial use. There's little mystery about size—the bigger the chicken, the bigger the egg. All of our recipes are tested with large eggs, but substitutions are possible when large quantities of eggs are used. See the chart for help in making accurate calculations. For example, four jumbo eggs are equivalent to five large eggs because their weight (10 ounces) is the same.

### EGG SIZES AND WEIGHTS

| Size        | Weight      |
| ----------- | ----------- |
| Medium      | 1.75 ounces |
| Large       | 2.00 ounces |
| Extra-Large | 2.25 ounces |
| Jumbo       | 2.50 ounces |

latter is a three number code printed just below the sell-by date and it runs consecutively from 001, for January 1, to 365, for December 31). The sell-by date is the legal limit to which eggs may be sold and is within 30 days of the pack date. The pack date is the day the eggs were graded and packed, which is generally within a week of being laid but, legally, may be as much as 30 days. In short, a carton of eggs may be up two months old by the end of the sell-by date. Even so, according to the U.S. Department of Agriculture, they are still fit for consumption three to five weeks past the sell-by date. The dates, then, are by no means an exact measure of an egg's freshness; they provide vague guidance at best.

So how old is too old? We tasted two- and three-month-old eggs that were perfectly palatable, though at four months, the white was very loose and the yolk "tasted faintly of the refrigerator"—though it was still edible. Our advice? Use your discretion: if the egg smells odd or displays discoloration, pitch it. Older eggs also lack the structure-lending properties of fresh eggs, so beware when baking. Both the white and yolk becomes looser. We whipped four-month old eggs and found they rapidly deflated.

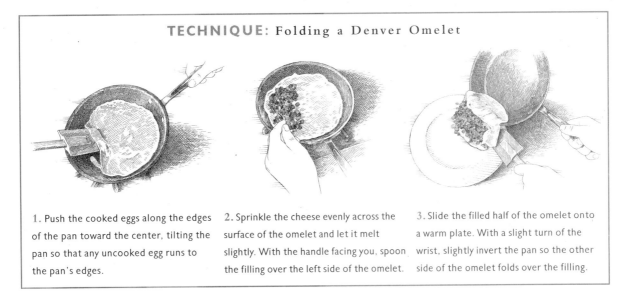

**TECHNIQUE:** Folding a Denver Omelet

**1.** Push the cooked eggs along the edges of the pan toward the center, tilting the pan so that any uncooked egg runs to the pan's edges.

**2.** Sprinkle the cheese evenly across the surface of the omelet and let it melt slightly. With the handle facing you, spoon the filling over the left side of the omelet.

**3.** Slide the filled half of the omelet onto a warm plate. With a slight turn of the wrist, slightly invert the pan so the other side of the omelet folds over the filling.

# CORN MUFFINS

WHAT WE WANTED: A muffin that won't set off sucrose alarms, a pronounced but not overwhelming cornmeal flavor, and a moist and tender crumb. And all of this goodness has to be capped off with a crunchy, golden, craggy muffin top.

We have a love/hate relationship with corn muffins, and it seems to be getting harder to find any to love. Whether too coarse, dry, and crumbly, too sticky and sweet, or just too fluffy and cupcake-like, the majority of corn muffins on the market today just don't make the cut. What do we want? To find out, we started by testing an assortment of recipes (see "Corn Muffins," page 262) from various cookbooks. Although their ingredient lists were similar, the end results were not. Some were too chewy, too short, and too puck-shaped, while others had too little corn flavor or were just plain too sweet or savory. Two recipes, however, stood out. One produced muffins that were tall and rustic; the other made muffins with a pleasant, wholesome cornmeal flavor. Working with these recipes as a starting point, we began to test variables.

There are two basic methods used to mix muffins. The creaming method calls for beating softened butter and sugar together, adding eggs one at a time, then adding dry and wet ingredients alternately to complete the batter. In the quick-bread (or straight) method, the dry and wet ingredients are combined separately and then mixed together. First, we tried creaming, which produced a high-rise muffin, but the crumb was too light and fluffy, much like a layer cake. (Air is whipped into the butter and sugar during creaming.) We then tried the quick-bread method, which turned out a muffin with not only good height but also a more substantial crumb. The quick-bread method, in its use of melted rather than creamed butter, apparently introduced less air to the batter, and the resulting muffin was less cupcake-like.

Because we wanted a sturdy muffin, not an airy confection, this suited us just fine. As an added bonus, the quick-bread method was also both easier and quicker than creaming: Just melt the butter, pour, and stir.

With our mixing method down, it was now time to focus on the choice of cornmeal. We tested three brands: Quaker, Arrowhead Mills, and Hodgson Mill. Quaker cornmeal, the most common brand in supermarkets, is degerminated. During processing, the dried corn is steel-rolled, which removes most of the germ and husk. Because the germ contains most of the flavor and natural oils, this process results in a drier, less flavorful cornmeal. When baked into a corn muffin, Quaker offered an unremarkable corn flavor and, because of its dryness, an unpleasant "crunch."

Arrowhead Mills and Hodgson Mill are similar in that both are whole-grain cornmeals, made from the whole corn kernel. Hodgson Mill, which is stone-ground (the dried corn is ground between two stones), has a coarse, inconsistent texture, while Arrowhead Mills, which is hammer-milled (pulverized with hammers), has a consistent, fine texture. Both brands delivered a more wholesome and complex corn flavor than Quaker. However, the Hodgson Mill cornmeal made the muffins coarse, dry, and difficult to chew. Arrowhead Mills produced by far the best corn muffin, with a consistently fine texture and real cornmeal flavor. The conclusion? Use a whole-grain cornmeal in a fine grind, such as Arrowhead Mills.

At this point, our muffins had the right texture and good flavor, but they were too dry. Some recipes suggest mixing the

---

**FOOD FACT: Corn Muffins**

We knew there was a reason why America's Test Kitchen was based in Massachusetts. The corn muffin was designated the official state muffin in 1986. But what about other local favorites, such as blueberry and cranberry muffins?

buttermilk, sour cream, and yogurt. We tried them all, using different amounts of each. Our initial thought was "butter, butter, butter," with enough milk added to hit the right consistency. When tested, however, these muffins were lacking in moisture. We then tried using buttermilk in place of the milk. This muffin packed more flavor into each bite, but it was still on the dry side. What finally produced a superior muffin was sour cream paired with butter and milk. These muffins were rich, light, moist, and tender, but they were no dainty cupcakes, either. We were curious to see how a muffin made with whole milk yogurt would stand up to the muffin made with sour cream. The difference was slight. The muffin made with whole milk yogurt was leaner but still moist and delicious. Muffins made with low-fat yogurt, on the other hand, were too lean and dry. Based on these tests, we concluded that a moist muffin requires fat and the tenderizing effect of acidity, both of which are found in sour cream.

The leavener used in most muffins is baking powder and/or baking soda, and we found that a combination of 1½ teaspoons baking powder and 1 teaspoon baking soda delivered the ideal height. We tested temperatures from 325 to 425 degrees and found that 400 degrees delivered the crunchy, crispy, golden crust we were looking for.

So, with the right cornmeal and the addition of sour cream, butter, and milk, it is possible to bake a tender, moist, and delicious corn muffin. By decreasing the amount of sugar and adding a few savory ingredients, you can serve these muffins with dinner as well as for breakfast. Either way, they beat the coffee-shop variety by a country mile.

cornmeal with a hot liquid before adding it to the batter. This method allows the cornmeal to absorb the liquid while expanding and softening the grain. The other wet ingredients are then added to the mush and combined with the dry ingredients. This seemed like a good way to make a moister muffin—or so we thought. Unfortunately, tasters found these muffins too dense and strong-tasting, more like cornbread than corn muffins, which should be lighter.

Back to square one. We made a list of the ingredients that might help produce a moist muffin: butter, milk,

WHAT WE LEARNED: Use the quick-bread method rather than the creaming method to assemble the batter. Use whole-grain cornmeal that has been finely ground for the best flavor and texture. Butter and sour cream make the crumb tender and moist, and baking at 400 degrees delivers a crunchy top.

**CORN MUFFINS** Makes 12 muffins

Whole-grain cornmeal has a fuller flavor than regular corn-meal milled from degerminated corn. To determine what kind of cornmeal a package contains, look closely at the label. See page 263 for more tips about buying cornmeal.

| | |
|---|---|
| 2 | cups (10 ounces) unbleached all-purpose flour |
| 1 | cup (4½ ounces) fine-ground, whole-grain yellow cornmeal |
| 1½ | teaspoons baking powder |
| 1 | teaspoon baking soda |
| ½ | teaspoon salt |
| 2 | large eggs |
| ¾ | cup (5¼ ounces) sugar |
| 8 | tablespoons (1 stick) unsalted butter, melted |
| ¾ | cup sour cream |
| ½ | cup milk |

**1.** Adjust an oven rack to the middle position and heat the oven to 400 degrees. Spray a standard muffin tin with non-stick cooking spray.

**2.** Whisk the flour, cornmeal, baking powder, baking soda, and salt in a medium bowl to combine; set aside. Whisk the eggs in a second medium bowl until well combined and light-colored, about 20 seconds. Add the sugar to the eggs; whisk vigorously until thick and homogenous, about 30 seconds; add the melted butter in 3 additions, whisking to combine after each addition. Add half the sour cream and half the milk and whisk to combine; whisk in the remaining sour cream and milk until combined. Add the wet ingredients to the dry ingredients; mix gently with a rubber spatula until the batter is just combined and evenly moistened. Do not over-mix. Using an ice cream scoop or large spoon, divide the batter evenly among muffin cups, dropping it to form mounds. Do not level or flatten the surface of the mounds.

**3.** Bake until the muffins are light golden brown and a skewer inserted into the center of the muffins comes out clean, about 18 minutes, rotating the muffin tin from front to back halfway through the baking time. Cool the muffins in the tin for 5 minutes; invert the muffins onto a wire rack, stand the muffins upright, cool 5 minutes longer, and serve warm.

VARIATIONS

**CORN AND APRICOT MUFFINS WITH ORANGE ESSENCE**

Apricots in the batter and a dusting of orange sugar makes these muffins are our favorites in the test kitchen.

---

**GETTING IT RIGHT:** Corn Muffins

Despite the simplicity of corn muffins, a lot can wrong when making them. Here are some of the worst muffins we encountered in our testing, from left to right: (A) This flat muffin contains too much cornmeal and tastes like cornbread. (B) This pale muffin contains no butter and relies on egg whites as the leavener. (C) This hockey puck-like muffin starts with cornmeal mixed with hot water. (D) This cupcake-like muffin resembles many store-bought muffins and is made with too much sugar and leavener.

A. Squat and Corny    B. Dense and Tough    C. Small and Wet    D. Fluffy and Cakey

**1.** In a food processor, process ⅔ cup granulated sugar and 1½ teaspoons grated orange zest until pale orange, about 10 seconds. Transfer to a small bowl and set aside.

**2.** In a food processor, pulse 1½ cups (10 ounces) dried apricots for ten 2-second pulses, until chopped fine. Transfer to a medium microwave-safe bowl; add ⅔ cup orange juice to the apricots, cover the bowl tightly with plastic wrap, and microwave on high until simmering, about 1 minute. Let the apricots stand, covered, until softened and plump, about 5 minutes. Strain the apricots; discard the juice.

**3.** Follow the recipe for Corn Muffins, substituting ¼ cup packed dark brown sugar for an equal amount granulated sugar and stirring ½ teaspoon grated orange zest and strained apricots into the wet ingredients before adding to the dry ingredients. Before baking, sprinkle a portion of the orange sugar over each mound of batter. Do not invert the baked muffins; use a paring knife to lift the muffins from the tin one at a time and transfer to a wire rack. Cool muffins 5 minutes longer; serve warm.

## BACON-SCALLION CORN MUFFINS WITH CHEDDAR CHEESE

Because these muffins contain bacon, store leftovers in the refrigerator wrapped in plastic. Bring them to room temperature or re-warm the muffins before serving.

**1.** Grate 8 ounces cheddar cheese (you should have 2 cups); set aside. Fry 3 slices bacon (about 3 ounces), cut into ½-inch pieces, in a small skillet over medium heat until crisp and golden brown, about 5 minutes. Add 10 to 12 medium scallions, sliced thin (about 1¼ cups), ¼ teaspoon salt, and ⅛ teaspoon ground black pepper; cook to heat through, about 1 minute. Transfer the mixture to a plate to cool while making the muffins.

**2.** Follow the recipe for Corn Muffins, reducing the sugar to ½ cup. Stir 1½ cups grated cheddar cheese and bacon/scallion mixture into the wet ingredients, then add to the dry ingredients and combine. Before baking, sprinkle a portion of additional ½ cup cheddar over each mound of batter.

---

### GETTING IT RIGHT: Buying Cornmeal

Cornmeal can vary greatly in texture (depending on how the corn kernels are ground) and flavor (depending on whether the kernels are whole grain or degerminated). We found that whole-grain Arrowhead Mills cornmeal (left) makes the best corn muffins. Its texture resembles slightly damp fine sand. Whole-grain Hodgson Mills cornmeal (middle) has great flavor, but the texture is coarser (akin to kosher salt), making corn muffins that are too coarse. Degerminated Quaker cornmeal (right) has a fine texture (similar to table salt) and makes muffins that are bland and dry.

---

### TASTING LAB: Baking Powder

DOUBLE-ACTING BAKING POWDER IS COMPRISED OF BAKING soda (the single acting ingredient), another rise ingredient (such as sodium aluminum sulfate and/or calcium phosphate), and cornstarch (a buffer to keep the ingredients separate in the can). Baking powder goes to work immediately when mixed with a liquid, and then gets its second lift when it hits the heat of an oven. You do have a choice of baking powders at the supermarket, so we put four nationally available brands to the test.

Two brands, Davis and Clabber Girl, contain both sodium aluminum sulfate and calcium phosphate. Calumet contains both of these ingredients along with calcium sulfate, which according to the label "maintains leavening," while Rumford has just calcium phosphate. We wondered if these leaveners would perform differently. Also, some experts say baking powders with aluminum can give baked goods an off flavor. Is this true? To find out, we tested each brand in carrot cake (with lots of sugar and spices) and in plain biscuits (made with just flour, salt, baking powder, and cream).

Well, when it comes to cake, you've got one less thing to worry about. All four baking powders lifted the cake to nearly equal heights (the cake made with Clabber Girl had a slight depression on top, but it was not big enough to affect the texture of the cake). Also, tasters could not detect any off flavors in any of the cakes. We wondered if the spices in the cake were hindering the tasting process, so we baked up four batches of cream biscuits. The biscuits were nearly identical in appearance. A couple of sensitive tasters did notice a very faint chemical taste in the biscuits made with Clabber Girl, but admitted that if they hadn't been looking for it, they wouldn't have noticed it at all. Our conclusion is to forget about brand when choosing baking powder, but do make sure your powder is fresh.

## EQUIPMENT CORNER:
### Rubber Spatulas

GOOD RUBBER SPATULAS AND PLACID, WELL-ADJUSTED people have two things in common. Both are firm enough to stay the course, yet flexible enough to hug the curves and contours (of the mixing bowl and of life). We all know that it takes years of experience for people to achieve that delicate balance, but you can buy a spatula with those traits this afternoon. While a rubber spatula is not a particularly costly kitchen purchase, the few dollars you spend should get you a comfortable, efficient utensil. To that end, we identified

four design factors—two each for the blade and the handle—that make for a great spatula.

The group of 10 spatulas displayed blades of different shape, size, and flexibility. Given that the two most important tests were folding whipped egg whites into pastry cream to make soufflé batter and scraping down the sides of a mixing bowl as we prepared cookie dough, size and flexibility proved most important.

When folding whipped egg whites, the idea is to work gently and efficiently to avoid bursting the bubbles that constitute the foam. Larger spatula blades moved more of the mixture at once, thereby decreasing the number of strokes necessary to integrate the beaten whites and reducing the risk of deflating the foam. The Rubbermaid, Le Creuset, KitchenAid, Oxo, and Rösle spatulas had the largest blades. It's worth noting, however, that a smaller spatula is also useful for scraping the last bits of something out of a small- or narrow-mouthed jar or for reaching crevices that a large blade can't touch. That said, if you buy only one spatula, make it a large one.

Blending chocolate chips into stiff cookie dough and scraping the mixture down the sides of the bowl illustrated the importance of the relative flexibility and stiffness of the blade. Every spatula but one was flexible enough to conform to the curve of the mixing bowl. That one was the Farberware, which was so soft that the blade bent over on itself when we pushed it against the dough, rendering it nearly useless. In a related observation, we noticed that the blades with relatively thin, sharp edges, like those of the Rubbermaid, KitchenAid, Pyrex, Cuisipro, and Oneida, cut through the mixture a little more efficiently and left the bowl walls slightly cleaner. In our minds, then, stiffer blades with thinner edges make better spatulas.

Among the 10 spatulas tested, only two, the Henckels and the Farberware, are made of rubber. The other eight blades are made of silicone, a polymer that is similar to rubber. Silicone is supposed to be more heat-resistant than rubber, making silicone spatulas the choice when cooking. To find out if this is true, we tested the heat resistance of all

# Rating Rubber Spatulas

WE TESTED 10 RUBBER OR SILICONE SPATULAS IN FOUR APPLICATIONS—FOLDING, HEAVY SCRAPING, LIGHT SCRAPING, and simmering tomato sauce (the latter was designed to judge heat damage, staining, and odor absorption). Spatulas are listed in order of preference based on their overall performance in these tests as well as their design. See www.americastestkitchen.com for up-to-date prices and mail-order sources for the top-rated product.

**HIGHLY RECOMMENDED**
## Rubbermaid 13.5-inch High Heat Scraper
**$13.95**
Long, rigid handle is great for leverage and firm, thin-edged blade is great for scraping. Just don't leave it in the sauce.

**HIGHLY RECOMMENDED**
## Le Creuset Heatproof 13-inch (Large) Spatula
**$12.50**
Wooden handle is rigid but slightly less comfortable than thicker, more rounded plastic handles. Also, blade edge is slightly thicker and more blunt than is ideal. The abuse champ of the group.

**HIGHLY RECOMMENDED**
## KitchenAid Silicone Mixing Spatula
**$9.99**
Handle was fine for many testers, but too bulky for some. Long blade reached into deep bowls, but motivated some staffers to refer to this spatula as "the oar."

**HIGHLY RECOMMENDED**
## Oxo Good Grips Silicone Turner Spatula
**$8.99**
Performed well, but the handle grip aroused controversy. Some testers felt it forced their hand into the wrong position; others were not bothered by it.

**RECOMMENDED WITH RESERVATIONS**
## Pyrex Professional All Purpose Spatula–Silicone Head
**$5.99**
This would be a great spatula if it weren't for the sharp, midhandle protrusion Pyrex calls a bowl rest. It's possible, though, to place fingers around it and march on.

**RECOMMENDED WITH RESERVATIONS**
## J.A. Henckels Rubber Spatula
**$5.99**
Not quite as efficient for folding as those spatulas with large blades, but otherwise fine. No real advantage to the deeply curved shape of the blade.

**NOT RECOMMENDED**
## Cuisipro Silicone Spatula
**$13.95**
Pointed blade gets into the corners of a saucepan but is too small to fold very efficiently. Stainless steel handle looks and feels good, but don't tap it too hard the rim of a ceramic or glass mixing bowl.

**NOT RECOMMENDED**
## Rösle 12.5-Inch Silicone Spatula
**$19.00**
Large blade would be great if it weren't rendered almost useless by a torturous handle, which is an example of how high style can fail no-nonsense cooks.

**NOT RECOMMENDED**
## Oneida Silicone Head Spatula
**$1.99**
Flexible handle offers no leverage against stiff mixtures. Forget about most heavy-duty tasks with the Gumby-handle.

**NOT RECOMMENDED**
## Farberware Classic Series 2 Piece Spoon Spatula Set
**$5.99**
Blade is much too flexible to scrape nearly any type of mixture very efficiently. Short handle can lead to sticky hands.

10 models by leaving them in a pan of tomato sauce cooking over medium-high heat for an hour. None of them showed significant heat damage. The silicone may be more heat resistant, but in normal, everyday cooking, rubber spatulas are unlikely to melt.

The tomato sauce test pointed out another problem with spatulas—staining and odor absorption. On this front, we have bad news to report. Even after multiple trips through the dishwasher, every spatula—whether made from rubber or silicone—was still stained and smelled of tomato.

A poorly designed handle turned out to be the Achilles heel of several otherwise good spatulas. In fact, several of the handles were so bad as to be considered fatal flaws—reason enough not to buy the spatula.

When testing was complete, the two traits we came to prize in spatula handles were rigidity and comfort. Handles that were too flexible, like those on the Oneida and Farberware models, bent when we dug into a batch of cookie dough, thus pushing our patience more than the dough. Stiff handles provided more leverage, which translates into much more efficient scraping, folding, and stirring.

No matter what the task, it was always more pleasant to use a spatula with a comfortable handle. The key here was simplicity of design. The Rubbermaid and Le Creuset spatulas, for example, had straight handles with rounded edges that were comfortable for all testers. Handles with sharp bowl rests, odd grips, or uncomfortable shapes (such as those made from stainless steel wire) were downgraded.

Which spatula, then, do you want in your kitchen? If you are going to buy only one spatula, go for one with a large, relatively stiff blade (preferably with a thin edge) and a rigid, rounded handle. Taken together, these factors can make your next trip through a batch of egg white foam or down the sides of a mixing bowl filled with chocolate chip cookie dough as efficient and comfortable as can be.

## EQUIPMENT CORNER: Spoonulas

TRULY A FUSION UTENSIL IF EVER THERE WAS ONE, THE spoonula, as some manufacturers call it, is a spoon/spatula hybrid that marries the concave shape of a spoon with the material and overall form of a spatula. But to what effect, we wondered? The answer, it turned out, depends on whom you ask. Every day in the test kitchen we use both spatulas and spoonulas by the dozen, and we tested four spoonulas (Pyrex, Oneida, Le Creuset, and Farberware) along with our lineup of spatulas for this article.

Spoonula detractors make two main claims. The first is that the mixture you are stirring, scraping, or folding sticks in the shallow bowl of the blade and is difficult to remove. Others among us do not find that to be the case. Sticky mixtures show no preference for one utensil over the other; they stick to spatulas and spoonulas equally. The second claim is that spoonulas do not fold as well as spatulas, again because the mixture sticks in the depression of the blade, thereby creating drag. Although many tests cooks were unable to detect excess drag during the folding tests, several test cooks were adamant that a thinner, flatter blade is better suited to gliding through a delicate mixture—to their minds, a spoonula is a blunt instrument.

Several test cooks noted that they use the two utensils differently, choosing a regular spatula for folding and scraping batters and egg whites and using a spoonula in place of a wooden spoon to stir simmering sauces, soups, and stews. Most spoonula blades are broader than the heads of many wooden spoons, so they are more efficient at moving the mixture being stirred.

Our recommendation is simple. A spoonula is really a replacement for a wooden spoon. For folding, we feel that a spatula is the better instrument.

With eager anticipation, Chris watches Julia as she puts the finishing touch—a light dusting of confectioners' sugar—on her German apple pancake.

# THE PANCAKE show

## CHAPTER 21

**IN THIS CHAPTER**

**THE RECIPES**
Blueberry Pancakes
Lemon-Cornmeal Blueberry
    Pancakes

German Apple Pancake
Caramel Sauce

**EQUIPMENT CORNER**
Electric Griddles

**SCIENCE DESK**
Why Does Lumpy Pancake
    Batter Produce Fluffier
    Pancakes?
Why Are Some Apples Mushy
    When Cooked?

**TASTING LAB**
Blueberries

Few recipes deliver so much pleasure for so little work as pancakes. The batter comes together in minutes, and the cooking time is brief. Why, then, do most Americans never make pancakes from scratch? Frozen pancakes, with their cardboard-like texture and dull flavor to match, are the standard offering in most homes. Pancake mixes yield slightly better results than frozen products, but it hardly takes more time to measure your own flour, salt, and leavener.

The test kitchen decided to develop two great recipes that would tempt even die-hard microwavers to make pancakes from scratch. Our recipes for blueberry pancakes and German apple pancake rely on ingredients you likely already have on hand. Once you've tasted the real thing, we doubt you'll ever buy frozen pancakes or packaged mixes again.

# BLUEBERRY PANCAKES

**WHAT WE WANTED:** Fluffy, flavorful pancakes that were easy to make at any time of the year.

Plain old pancakes may be a dime a dozen, but when it comes to blueberry pancakes, we say stack 'em high and bring on the maple syrup. When perfect, they're light and fluffy, sweet and tangy, and studded with juicy bursts of summer's best berry. Unfortunately, most blueberry pancakes are either are so tough and rubbery that they snap back and smack you in the face or are so cottony and tasteless that they must be accompanied by a very tall glass of milk. As for the blueberries—well, those sweet little berries leak into the batter without fail. The result? A gray, marbled pancake.

We decided to remedy this problem once and for all and began by cooking up a big stack of pancake recipes. The test kitchen came to a few conclusions. One: We like our pancakes tender and fluffy. Two: A good blueberry pancake starts with a great pancake. Three: Even though we were after the best blueberry pancake, we wanted to avoid any nonsensical techniques or ingredients that required a jaunt to the grocery store, especially given that we would likely be making these pancakes early in the morning, with only one eye open and one cup of coffee running through our veins.

Before we even thought about blueberries, we wanted to get the pancake part out of the way. First up was flour, and because this no-nonsense recipe would not put up with a blend of flours, we pitted cake flour, bleached all-purpose flour, and unbleached all-purpose flour against one another. The pancake made with cake flour lacked structure, and the flour gave the pancake a strange, chemical taste. The pancake made with bleached all-purpose flour had a similar "off" flavor, so unbleached flour—usually the test kitchen standard—was the winner.

Sugar was next, and the question was not whether to add but how much. We like pancakes on the sweet side. Starting at 1 teaspoon of sugar, we worked our way up until tasters cried "enough" at 2 tablespoons. As for leavener, we were hoping to use just baking powder, but, sure enough, tasters preferred the golden brown color that baking soda provided, so in the end we had to use them both. Two teaspoons of baking powder and ½ teaspoon of baking soda did the job. Finally, a little salt went in to make everything taste better.

In most pancake recipes, the dry ingredients are measured out, and the wet ingredients, such as eggs, melted butter, and dairy (usually milk or buttermilk), are added to the dry ingredients. Most recipes call for 2 eggs per 2 cups of flour, but tasters unanimously found these cakes to be too eggy. Using an egg and a fraction thereof (one whole egg plus one egg yolk) was too fussy for our recipe, so we simply used one egg. What about butter—was it truly necessary? One quick test later we found the answer to be an emphatic yes. Without butter, the pancakes were more evenly colored (no spots of scorched butter), but they had the cottony interior that we just couldn't stomach. In went 3 tablespoons of melted butter, and everyone was happy.

As for the dairy, we tested milk and buttermilk and also threw half-and-half into the mix to see what would happen. To no one's surprise, buttermilk took first place. This tangy, thick liquid produced a pancake with great flavor and beat-all fluffiness. But to be true to our "rule number three," we couldn't pretend that buttermilk would be found on most people's lists of basic pantry ingredients. We needed a substitute.

A quick search on the Internet led us to a few buttermilk impostors, usually a little white distilled vinegar, cream of tartar, or lemon juice stirred into regular milk, then left to sit for a few minutes to thicken. This faux buttermilk method mimics the effects of the modern process of making buttermilk, which is produced by injecting milk with acidic bacterial cultures. The cultures not only give buttermilk that characteristic tang, but they also thicken it. When we compared the buttermilk pancakes with pancakes made

with the lemon and milk mixture, we were surprised to find that those made with lemon juice had a tang that was similar to that provided by the buttermilk ("sour" was the word for those made with vinegar or cream of tartar). Even more surprising was that tasters preferred the pancakes made with lemon juice and whole milk over those made with buttermilk. One tablespoon of lemon juice per 2 cups of milk was the right amount. After allowing the mixture to sit for a few minutes, it thickened to a consistency much like that of buttermilk. (If you have buttermilk on hand, however, go ahead and use it.)

We had a good idea that overmixing was likely to produce a tough, rubbery pancake. Boy, were we right. When we whisked the batter until no lumps of flour were detectable, the pancakes were tough. We cannot emphasize enough that a less thorough mixing is needed here, just until

the ingredients are blended. A few lumps or streaks of flour here and there, and you know that you've done it correctly.

OK. We had a great pancake recipe. But what about those berries? We found that the size of the berry really mattered. If possible, choose small, fresh, wild blueberries; they are much sweeter than their bigger blueberry cousins. We also found that if you can't find good blueberries in the produce section, you should head right for the frozen foods. One particular brand of frozen blueberries, Wyman's, tasted nearly as good as (and in some cases better than) fresh berries. If you keep a stash of frozen blueberries on hand, you're always ready to make these pancakes.

Now, how to avoid those mottled berry pancakes. Stirring the berries into the batter proved unsuccessful for two reasons. One, no matter how carefully we stirred, a few berries would invariably break and produce blue-gray pancakes. Two, extra stirring was a no-no; the more we stirred, the tougher the pancake. The best method was simply to ladle out some batter onto the hot skillet, then scatter a handful of berries on top.

And speaking of skillet, we wasted a couple of cups of batter using a regular skillet. No matter how well we oiled the pan (butter scorched every time), the pancakes would stick and the blueberries would rip open. Do yourself a favor and use a nonstick skillet.

So there they were. Fluffy, tender, flavorful, and very simple blueberry pancakes, without a broken berry in sight. Good enough to eat without maple syrup, you ask? Sure, but why on earth would you want to do that?

WHAT WE LEARNED: Use a mixture of lemon juice and milk to create that buttermilk tang without having to run out to the store. Leave a few streaks of flour in the batter; if you mix more, the pancakes will be tough. Add small wild berries directly to the pancakes in the skillet, not to the batter, to keep them from dying everything blue.

## BLUEBERRY PANCAKES

Makes about sixteen 4-inch pancakes, serving 4 to 6

When local blueberries are not in season, frozen blueberries are a better alternative (see the Tasting Lab on page 274). To make sure that frozen berries do not bleed, rinse them under cool water in a mesh strainer until the water runs clear, and then spread them on a paper towel–lined plate to dry. If you have buttermilk on hand, use 2 cups instead of the milk and lemon juice. To keep pancakes warm while cooking the remaining batter, see the tip at right.

| | |
|---|---|
| 1 | tablespoon juice from 1 lemon |
| 2 | cups milk |
| 2 | cups (10 ounces) unbleached all-purpose flour |
| 2 | tablespoons sugar |
| 2 | teaspoons baking powder |
| ½ | teaspoon baking soda |
| ½ | teaspoon salt |
| 1 | large egg |
| 3 | tablespoons unsalted butter, melted and cooled slightly |
| 1–2 | teaspoons vegetable oil |
| 1 | cup fresh or frozen blueberries, preferably wild, rinsed and dried (see note) |

**1.** Whisk the lemon juice and milk in a medium bowl or large measuring cup; set aside to thicken while preparing the other ingredients. Whisk the flour, sugar, baking powder, baking soda, and salt in a medium bowl to combine.

**2.** Whisk the egg and melted butter into the milk until combined. Make a well in the center of the dry ingredients in the bowl; pour in the milk mixture and whisk very gently until just combined (a few lumps should remain). Do not overmix.

**3.** Heat a 12-inch nonstick skillet over medium heat for 3 to 5 minutes (see the photos on page 273 for tips on gauging when the pan is properly heated); add 1 teaspoon oil and brush to coat the skillet bottom evenly. Pour ¼ cup batter onto 3 spots on the skillet; sprinkle 1 tablespoon blueberries over each pancake. Cook the pancakes until large bubbles begin to appear, 1½ to 2 minutes. Using a thin, wide spatula, flip the pancakes and cook until golden brown on second side, 1 to 1½ minutes longer. Serve immediately, and repeat with the remaining batter, using the remaining vegetable oil only if necessary.

VARIATION

## LEMON-CORNMEAL BLUEBERRY PANCAKES

Follow the recipe for Blueberry Pancakes, adding 2 teaspoons grated lemon zest to the milk along with the lemon juice and substituting 1½ cups stone-ground yellow cornmeal for 1 cup flour.

---

### GETTING IT RIGHT:
Keeping Pancakes Warm

A large skillet can turn out only three pancakes at a time, so if you want everyone to eat at the same time, you must keep the first few batches warm. After testing various methods in cookbooks (most of which suggest covering the pancakes, causing them to become steamed and rubbery), we discovered that pancakes will hold for 20 minutes when placed on a greased rack set on a baking sheet in a 200-degree oven. The warm oven keeps the pancakes hot enough to melt a pat of butter, and leaving the pancakes uncovered prevents them from becoming soggy.

## Electric Griddles

WITH COUNTERTOP REAL ESTATE SO VALUABLE, WE'RE wary about buying "extra" appliances, such as an electric griddle. But after standing in front of what must have been our 40th batch of blueberry pancakes, we gave electric griddles a second thought. Many electric griddles have a bigger cooking surface than even a large 12-inch skillet (which will fit only three pancakes at a time comfortably). The possible payoff—less time cooking—was too good to resist.

We bought the four largest models we could find. They were seemingly identical: All had an electric probe with an indicator light that turned off when the selected temperature was reached, all were fully immersible or dishwasher-safe (except for the electric probe control), all were made of cast aluminum with a nonstick coating, all had a hole or channel so that excess fat would drain into a removable grease tray. After heating each griddle to 350 degrees, we poured on the batter (each griddle fit eight pancakes at a

time) and checked the pancakes for even browning. We also cooked bacon on each griddle.

The BroilKing Extra Large Griddle ($49.99), which measured a whopping 21 inches by 12 inches and was the only griddle that could comfortably hold a full pound of bacon (16 strips), was the clear winner. Good thing that it also had one of the largest grease trays. Its only downfall was the excruciating 12½ minutes it took to heat up to 350 degrees. But this could be due to the thickness of the aluminum griddle. After it reached the proper temperature, there was very little temperature fluctuation. As a result, pancakes were evenly cooked every time.

The West Bend Cool Touch Electric Griddle ($39.99) was the runner-up. The cooking surface measured 20½ inches by 10½ inches and could hold 12 strips of bacon. The West Bend heated up to 350 degrees in 6½ minutes and cooked pancakes very evenly. One minor drawback: The grease channel was slightly cumbersome to wash.

The remaining two models, the Rival Electric Griddle ($29.99) and the Presto Cool Touch Electric Griddle ($38.99), were the same size as the West Bend, and both heated up to 350 degrees in 5½ minutes. The cooking surfaces on both models heated unevenly, however, and some pancakes were lighter in color than others. Also, some of the pancakes spread out very thin because of cool spots.

Are electric griddles worth the counter space? If you find yourself making stacks of pancakes and pounds of bacon every weekend, you can't beat the speedy delivery they provide.

**BEST ELECTRIC GRIDDLE**
The BroilKing griddle took top honors in our testing, in part because it is so big. It also demonstrated even browning, without any of the cool spots that plagued two other models.

---

## GETTING IT RIGHT: Is the Pan Ready?

The only way to know when the pan is ready is to make a test pancake about the size of a half-dollar (use 1 tablespoon of batter). If after 1 minute the pancake is blond in color (left), the pan is not hot enough. If after 1 minute the pancake is golden brown, the pan is heated correctly. Speeding up the process by heating the pan at a higher temperature will result in a dark, unevenly cooked pancake (right).

soda. Gluten is a mix of very long proteins that are disorganized in structure. Once gluten is dissolved in water, these proteins can more easily rearrange their structure. Kneading or mixing gluten elongates the proteins and somewhat organizes them, an action similar to combing the strands of your hair. As the proteins start to lie more or less parallel to each other, the dough becomes elastic and less tender. By reducing the mixing time of your batter, you give the gluten less opportunity to organize.

Baking soda (either on its own or as part of the baking powder formula) creates the bubbles that make pancakes rise. When baking soda encounters an acid, carbon dioxide is formed to produce the bubbles in the batter. The stirring of the pancake batter speeds bubble formation by moving the baking soda and acid together. Unfortunately, stirring also causes the release of carbon dioxide gas by bringing formed bubbles to the surface of the mixture. Just a little too much stirring and the bubble-forming capacity of the baking soda will be quickly exhausted. To make the fluffiest pancakes possible, then, you should stir the batter until the ingredients are just incorporated—and not one stir more!

## SCIENCE DESK:
### Why Does Lumpy Pancake Batter Produce Fluffier Pancakes?

THERE ARE TWO FACTORS THAT PROMOTE FLUFFINESS IN pancake batter, underdeveloped gluten and dissolved baking

## TASTING LAB: Blueberries

WHEN LOCAL BERRIES ARE NOT IN SEASON, WHAT KIND of blueberries should you buy? Should you rely on fresh berries imported from South America (often at a cost of $5 for a dry half-pint container) or frozen berries? If you choose the latter, should you pick cultivated or wild frozen berries? And what about price? A January cobbler that costs $25 seems, well, silly. Likewise, spending $5 on berries for pancakes seems excessive.

During the winter, the test kitchen tried fresh berries from Chile as well as five frozen brands. Easily beating the fresh imported berries as well as the other frozen contenders were Wyman's frozen wild berries. (Compared with cultivated berries, wild berries are smaller, more intense in color, firmer in texture, and more sweet and tangy in flavor.) The

# Rating Blueberries

NINE MEMBERS OF THE *COOK'S ILLUSTRATED* STAFF TRIED FIVE KINDS OF BLUEBERRIES COOKED IN A SIMPLE COMPOTE to compare their flavor. (Because many of these berries were frozen, we were not concerned with texture, although juiciness was a consideration.) The brands are listed below in order of preference. All brands are available in supermarkets nationwide.

### HIGHLY RECOMMENDED
#### Wyman's Frozen Wild Blueberries

**$2.19 for 12 ounces**

These small blueberries were intense in color and flavor, with a pleasing balance of sweetness and tang and a clean, fresh berry finish.

### RECOMMENDED
#### Fresh (South American) Blueberries

**$5.00 for 4 ounces**

Nice, plump berries lacked that "picked at peak ripeness" sweet flavor you get with local fresh berries. However, these out-of-season berries were still sweet and juicy, with a nice level of tartness. But look at the price.

### RECOMMENDED
#### Cascadian Farms 100% Organic Frozen Blueberries

**$3.79 for 10 ounces**

This mix of berries contains several varieties, including one that is "wild." The berries had the tart punch characteristic of wild berries and a pleasant "jammy" sweetness.

### RECOMMENDED WITH RESERVATIONS
#### 365 Grade A Fancy Frozen Blueberries

**$2.99 for 16 ounces**

These cultivated berries were very sweet, with just a hint of tartness. Compared with the other brands of frozen berries, they lacked complexity.

### NOT RECOMMENDED
#### Shaw's Individually Quick Frozen Whole Blueberries

**$2.59 for 16 ounces**

Of all the frozen berries tasted, this supermarket brand was the most disappointing. The berries were watery, bland, and flat tasting, with a mushy consistency.

---

fresh imported berries tied for second place with Cascadian Farms frozen berries, which includes a mix of cultivated and wild berries. Frozen cultivated berries trailed in the tasting.

Flavor aside, the average cost of these frozen berries is $8 for a small cobbler versus the above-mentioned $25 for the fresh South American berries. You could make three cobblers using the frozen berries for that price, and the money would also buy you better quality.

Why did the frozen wild blueberries beat the fresh imported berries? Well, the imported berries are picked before they have a chance to fully ripen to help them survive the long trip north. As a result, they are often tart and not so flavorful. Frozen blueberries have been picked at the peak time—when perfectly ripe—and are then put through a cleaning and sanitation process before being sent to the freezer tunnel, where they are individually quick frozen (IQF) at a temperature of minus 20 degrees. The quick freezing preserves their sweetness, making it possible to enjoy them year-round—and at a price that even a humble test cook can afford.

# GERMAN APPLE PANCAKE

**WHAT WE WANTED:** This Old World classic combines the best qualities of a popover and a pancake. Could we make a version that had both great apple flavor and perfect puff-pancake texture?

Started on the stove and finished in the oven, German apple pancakes (similar to puff pancakes, Panaküchen, and Dutch babies) bear little resemblance to their American cousin, fluffy flapjacks. Unlike the American version, which owes its cakelike texture to baking powder or baking soda, the German pancake has more in common with a popover, getting its dramatic rise from eggs and a hot oven. A German apple pancake is also prone to the same pitfalls as a popover: insufficient rise, leaden texture, and too much egg flavor. The perfect German apple pancake should have crisp, lighter-than-air edges and a custard-like center, with buttery sautéed apples baked right into the batter.

We started our research by going to a local diner chain known for its German apple pancake. The dinner plate–sized version arrived at the table sparsely scattered with pale pieces of apple and dusted with confectioners' sugar. We tasted it. The pancake had little flavor, and the apples were soggy, blond, and bland. We knew that the test kitchen could do better.

German pancake batter is composed of three main ingredients: flour, eggs, and liquid (usually milk). We began by experimenting with different types of liquid, making pancakes with half-and-half, heavy cream, and a combination of sour cream and milk. The pancake made with heavy cream was leaden and flat, while the sour cream/milk version had a strange, tart flavor. Half-and-half turned out to be the perfect solution. It has just enough butterfat to give the pancake a rich flavor without sacrificing the texture. After trying various ratios of half-and-half, eggs, and flour, we found that a combination of two eggs, ⅔ cup half-and-half,

and ½ cup all-purpose flour made a nicely puffed pancake. The addition of a little sugar, salt, and vanilla gave it just the right balance of flavors.

The next step was to find the perfect oven temperature. Like a popover, this pancake relies on steam (instead of chemical leavening) for its explosive rise. Because the batter is poured into a preheated pan and placed immediately into a hot oven, the surfaces of the batter set first. While in the oven, the liquid in the batter turns to steam, creating pockets of air that cause the pancake to rise, much like an inflating balloon. We tried baking the pancake at 400, 425, and 450 degrees. The pancake baked at 400 degrees never rose high enough, and even at 450 degrees the airy texture we were looking for was lacking. In desperation, we cranked up the temperature to 500 degrees. It puffed spectacularly, but both the bottom and top of the pancake were charred. We tried preheating the oven to 500 degrees and lowering it to a more moderate 425 degrees when the pancake went into the oven. The initial high heat gave the batter the quick rise it needed, and the more moderate heat cooked the pancake to perfection.

Now that the pancake was rising so dramatically, the expanding batter was pushing some of the apples out of the pan and onto the oven floor. To solve this problem, we poured the batter around the perimeter of the pan first, then over the apples. This ring of batter along the edge of the pan, which added a cushion between the apple slices and the pan, kept the apples from jumping ship.

Our next task was to figure out how to cook the apples. Apples cooked with granulated sugar were sweet but flat tasting, while those cooked with either light or dark brown sugar were fabulous. When the light brown sugar combined with the butter and apples, it made a great sauce that enhanced the apples' clean flavor. Dark brown sugar did the same, producing a slightly smokier caramel with molasses highlights. Adding a little cinnamon and some

lemon juice made the apples at once earthy and bright. We tried other apple-friendly spices (nutmeg, allspice, and cloves), but they all made the apple pancake taste like apple pie. Not bad, but not what we were going for. As for the size of the apple slices, we found that cutting the apples into ½-inch-thick pieces kept them from getting mushy during cooking.

Our last task was to figure out which kind of apple to use. We chose 10 widely available varieties and made pancakes with each. The pancake made with Golden Delicious—the first choice of many bakers—was liked for its simple fruity character, though some tasters found it cloyingly sweet. Empires, Southern Roses, and Royal Galas didn't have enough apple flavor to stand up to the brown sugar, and both McIntosh and Red Delicious became too soft when sautéed. Fujis were sweet but tasted more like pears than apples. Tasters unanimously disliked the pancake made with Red Romes; these apples were bitter and dry and had a texture that reminded one taster of cardboard. With their perfect balance of sweetness and tartness, Granny Smith apples were the favorite. Braeburns were also liked; they were more sugary-sweet, with just the slightest hint of lemony brightness.

Inverted onto a serving platter and covered with a snowy dusting of confectioners' sugar (and a generous drizzle of maple syrup or caramel sauce), this German apple pancake was ideal.

WHAT WE LEARNED: Use half-and-half in the batter for a rich flavor and a light texture. For maximum rise without burning the edges, preheat the pan in a 500-degree oven, add the batter to the hot pan, and then reduce the oven temperature to 425 degrees. As for the apples, use Granny Smiths and cook them with brown sugar for the best flavor.

## GERMAN APPLE PANCAKE Serves 4

A 10-inch ovenproof skillet is necessary for this recipe; we highly recommend using a nonstick skillet for the sake of easy cleanup, but a regular skillet will work. You can also use a cast-iron pan; if you do, set the oven temperature to 425 degrees in step 1, and when cooking the apples in step 3, cook them only until just barely golden, about 6 minutes. Cast iron retains heat better than stainless steel, making the higher oven temperature unnecessary. If you prefer tart apples, use Granny Smiths; if you prefer sweet ones, use Braeburns. For serving, dust the apple pancake with confectioners' sugar and pass warm maple syrup or Caramel Sauce (recipe follows) separately, if desired.

| | |
|---|---|
| ½ | cup (2½ ounces) unbleached all-purpose flour |
| 1 | tablespoon granulated sugar |
| ½ | teaspoon salt |
| 2 | large eggs |
| ⅔ | cup half-and-half |
| 1 | teaspoon vanilla extract |
| 2 | tablespoons unsalted butter |
| 1¼ | pounds Granny Smith or Braeburn apples (3 to 4 large apples), peeled, quartered, cored, and cut into ½-inch-thick slices |
| ¼ | cup packed light or dark brown sugar |
| ¼ | teaspoon ground cinnamon |
| 1 | teaspoon lemon juice from 1 lemon |
| | Confectioners' sugar for dusting |
| | Maple syrup or Caramel Sauce for serving |

**1.** Adjust an oven rack to the upper-middle position and heat the oven to 500 degrees.

**2.** Whisk to combine the flour, granulated sugar, and salt in a medium bowl. In a second medium bowl, whisk the eggs, half-and-half, and vanilla until combined. Add the liquid ingredients to the dry ingredients and whisk until no lumps remain, about 20 seconds; set the batter aside.

**3.** Heat the butter in a 10-inch ovenproof nonstick skillet over medium-high heat until sizzling. Add the apples, brown sugar, and cinnamon; cook, stirring frequently with a heatproof rubber spatula, until the apples are golden brown, about 10 minutes. Off heat, stir in the lemon juice.

**4.** Working quickly, pour the batter around the edge of the pan and then over the apples. Place the skillet in the oven and immediately reduce the oven temperature to 425 degrees. Bake until the pancake edges are brown and puffy and have risen above the edges of the skillet, about 18 minutes.

**5.** Using oven mitts to protect your hands, remove the hot skillet from the oven and loosen the pancake edges with a

---

### GETTING IT RIGHT:
#### Choosing the Right Apple

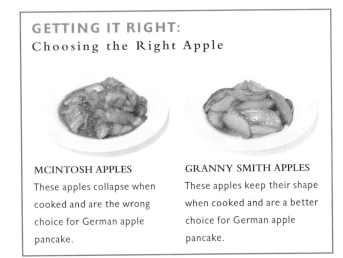

**McINTOSH APPLES**
These apples collapse when cooked and are the wrong choice for German apple pancake.

**GRANNY SMITH APPLES**
These apples keep their shape when cooked and are a better choice for German apple pancake.

---

heatproof rubber spatula; invert the pancake onto a serving platter. Dust with confectioners' sugar, cut into wedges, and serve with syrup or Caramel Sauce.

## CARAMEL SAUCE Makes about 1 1/2 cups

To prevent undissolved sugar crystals from marring the sauce, we prefer to cook the sugar with some water in a covered pot. The trapped moisture ensures that the sugar will dissolve. Make sure to remove the cover during the final minute or two so you can monitor the progress of the sugar syrup. When the hot cream mixture is added in step 3, the hot sugar syrup will bubble vigorously (and dangerously), so don't use a smaller saucepan. If you make the caramel sauce ahead, reheat it in the microwave or a small saucepan over low heat until warm and fluid.

½   cup water
1   cup (7 ounces) granulated sugar
1   cup heavy cream
⅛   teaspoon salt
½   teaspoon vanilla extract
½   teaspoon lemon juice from
    1 lemon

**1.** Place the water in a heavy-bottomed 2-quart saucepan; pour the sugar in the center of the pan, taking care not to let the sugar crystals adhere to the sides of the pan. Cover and bring the mixture to a boil over high heat; once boiling, uncover and continue to boil until the sugar syrup is thick and straw-colored (it should register 300 degrees on a candy thermometer), about 7 minutes. Reduce the heat to medium and continue to cook until the syrup is deep amber (it should register 350 degrees on a candy thermometer), about 1 to 2 minutes.

**2.** Meanwhile, bring the cream and salt to a simmer in a small saucepan over high heat (if the cream boils before the sugar syrup reaches a deep amber color, remove the cream from the heat and cover to keep warm).

**3.** Remove the pan with the sugar syrup from the heat; very carefully pour about one quarter of hot cream into it (the mixture will bubble vigorously), and let the bubbling subside. Add the remaining cream, vanilla, and lemon juice; whisk until the sauce is smooth. (The sauce can be cooled and refrigerated in an airtight container for up to 2 weeks.)

## SCIENCE DESK: Why Are Some Apples Mushy When Cooked?

AS ANYONE WHO HAS MADE APPLESAUCE OR AN APPLE PIE knows, some apple varieties are ideal for cooking while others are best eaten raw. When testing different types of apples in the German apple pancake, we found that some turned to mush in the pan while others remained toothsome, maintaining their shape and texture.

So why does this happen? The texture of an apple depends on three things: the thickness and composition of the cell walls, the amount of acid in the apple, and the amount of air between the apple cells.

The first factor is the composition of the cell walls, which are made of cellulose and are held together with pectin. The crunchier, crispier varieties (such as Granny Smith) contain more cellulose. Even before cooking, you can clearly see the difference between crunchy Granny Smith apples and softer McIntoshes. As an apple is cooked, the pectin melts and the cells fall apart. The varieties with more cellulose will remain more firm, while those with less cellulose will become softer.

The next factor is acid. Acid strengthens pectin and keeps it from dissolving so readily when heated. Naturally acidic apples, such as Granny Smiths, are thus more likely to hold their shape than other varieties.

Finally, the air. Apples have lots of air pockets between their cells (25 percent or more of their volume may consist of air), which is why they float. When apples are cooked, the air escapes and the air pockets collapse. As a result, there is a loss of firmness and volume. The less air an apple has to begin with, the firmer it will be, both before and after cooking.

Can store-bought cookie dough compare to homemade? We baked up piles of cookies to find out.

# COOKIE JAR favorites

CHAPTER 22

IN THIS CHAPTER

**THE RECIPES**

Thin, Crispy Chocolate Chip
Cookies

Triple-Coconut Macaroons
Chocolate-Dipped Triple-
Coconut Macaroons

**EQUIPMENT CORNER**

Potholders

**TASTING LAB**

Refrigerator Cookie Dough
Coconut Milk, Coconut Cream,
and Cream of Coconut

Good cookies don't really require any more work than bad cookies. Unless, of course, you are willing to consider dry, crumbly, tasteless packaged cookies from the supermarket—but we aren't. Although easy to prepare, most cookie recipes are notoriously fickle. A minor ingredient change or fluctuation in oven temperature can yield unexpected results. Our goal was simple: Take two favorite cookies and develop reliable recipes that taste great.

We love the buttery crunch of thin, crisp chocolate chip cookies. These aren't the soft, chewy cookies that have become all the rage in malls. These are the kind of cookies our grandmothers might have kept in a tin above the refrigerator. Almost delicate, these cookies are a study in restraint.

Macaroons may seem a bit old-fashioned, but we think few cookies can rival a well-made coconut macaroon. We wanted something that would be both rich with coconut flavor and chewy. Our macaroons would not be dry or crumbly, our macaroons would be easy to shape (no pastry bags, please), and they would be sturdy enough to withstand a partial dip in melted chocolate.

# CRISP CHOCOLATE CHIP COOKIES

WHAT WE WANTED: A flat, almost praline-like cookie with plenty of crunch and packed with the flavors of butter, caramelized sugar, and chocolate.

Rich and buttery, with their soft, tender cores and crispy edges, Toll House cookies are the American cookie-jar standard. As such, they serve as the springboard for all other versions of the chocolate chip cookie. A popular variation, thin and crispy, embodies one of the Toll House cookie's textural extremes.

We could see the thin, crisp cookies clearly. They would be very flat, almost praline in appearance, and they would pack a big crunch without either breaking teeth or shattering into a million pieces when eaten. They'd have the simple, gratifying flavors of deeply caramelized sugar and rich butter, along with agreeable amounts of salt and vanilla. The chips—always tender and super-chocolatey—would not overwhelm but leave plenty of room for enjoyment of the surrounding cookie. Finally, these cookies would be resilient enough for pantry storage and worthy of five consecutive appearances in a school lunchbox.

To get our bearings, we first surveyed a handful of recipes for thin and crispy chocolate chip cookies, taking inventory of the ingredient lists and ratios. We were hoping to find the key to what might make these cookies thinner and crispier than the classic Toll House. Our collection of test recipes featured the same basic ingredients—butter, flour, sugar, flavorings, and chocolate chips—but widely varying ratios and yields. As a result, the cookies were all quite different when baked. While all of the cookies tasted good, tasters were dissatisfied with the various textures, which they found too brittle, too crumbly, too dense, or too greasy. Believe it or not, we were pleased with the mixed reactions. The ingredients we had to work with held promise; we just needed to understand the role of each one and tweak the proportions to arrive at a cookie with the texture we wanted.

Whether chewy or crispy, nearly all chocolate chip cookies contain a mixture of granulated and brown sugars. Aside from contributing sweetness, sugar also affects the texture, flavor, and color of the cookies. Doughs high in granulated sugar yield crispy cookies. As the cookies cool, the sugar crystallizes and the cookies harden. Brown sugar is quite different from granulated. It contains 35 percent more moisture and is also more hygroscopic (that is, it more readily absorbs moisture from the atmosphere). Consequently, cookies made with brown sugar come out of the oven tender and pliable and often soften further as they stand. These characteristics were the opposite of what we were looking for. Nevertheless, we knew the recipe had to include some brown sugar, because it alone is responsible for the irresistible butterscotch flavor we associate with chocolate chip cookies.

With this understanding, we went on to test various proportions of sugar. Too much granulated sugar produced cookies with no butterscotch flavor. Too much brown sugar produced cookies that were delicious but too soft. Desperate to retain the flavor of the brown sugar, we shifted from dark brown to light brown. Light brown sugar, we knew, had the potential to crisp the cookies because it contains half the molasses—and therefore less moisture—than dark brown sugar does. But we were skeptical because its flavor is weaker. We needn't have worried; the cookies were much improved, producing a flavor that fully satisfied tasters. After a little more tinkering, we settled on ⅓ cup light brown sugar and ½ cup granulated sugar, yielding cookies with a notable butterscotch flavor and sufficient crunch.

Satisfied with the crispness of the cookies, we turned our attention to their thickness. Throughout earlier testing, we hadn't been totally happy with the way the cookies spread in the oven. They were never as thin as we wanted them to be. This was important not just for appearance' sake

but because we had noticed that the flatter the cookies were, the more delicate and tender they became; we wanted them crisp, without being tough.

After some research, we returned to the kitchen armed with the understanding that a cookie's spread is determined largely by the type, treatment, and melting properties of fat in the dough. Butter, which is key in this recipe, has both a low melting point and outstanding flavor. Initial test recipes advised creaming butter and sugar, but we noticed that cookies made with this technique came out of the oven with a slight lift. We were certain that creaming was the culprit.

When butter and sugar are creamed, rigid sugar crystals cut into the butterfat and create air cells. As the remaining ingredients are incorporated into the airy mixture, the air cells get locked up in the dough and capture moisture from the butter (and other ingredients) as it vaporizes in the oven. The cells expand, and the cookies rise. Our other option, melting the butter, was much more successful. Because melted butter, unlike creamed, does not accommodate air cells, the moisture from various ingredients has nowhere to go except out. Working our way down from 12 tablespoons, we found that the cookies spread evenly and effortlessly at 8 tablespoons (one stick) of melted butter. To get them thinner still, we added a couple of tablespoons of

milk to the dough. The cookies were flatter than pancakes.

Having spent all of our time thus far perfecting the cookies' texture and spread, we were surprised to notice that they were looking slightly pallid and dull. The light brown sugar we had introduced to the recipe was the problem: It has less browning power than dark brown sugar. Knowing that corn syrup browns at a lower temperature than sugar, we tried adding a few tablespoons. As it happened, the corn syrup made the surface of the cookies shiny and crackly. Despite their new spiffy, dressed-up look, though, they remained a little pale. We rectified the situation by adding a bit of baking soda, which enhances browning reactions in doughs. With only a few tests at various amounts, the cookies went from washed out to a beautiful deep golden brown.

Finally, after a few last-minute adjustments to the amount of salt and vanilla, we turned a full recipe of the finished dough onto two parchment-lined baking sheets and tested baking times and temperatures. Much to our disappointment, these cookies did not spread properly and were slightly chewy. After a few batches, we found that these cookies, like Greta Garbo, wanted to be alone, baked one sheet at a time. In 12 uninterrupted minutes at 375 degrees, they spread, flattened, caramelized, and cooled into thin, crispy, and delicious chocolate chip cookies.

Now we just had to find out if these cookies had staying power. We stored a batch in an airtight container for a week to test their longevity. After the wait, tasters gathered to give them a final critique. The cookies were still a hit, as crisp and flavorful as they had been on day one. In fact, some commented that the crunch had improved with time.

WHAT WE LEARNED: Use melted butter and milk to make a batter that will spread in the oven. Add a bit of corn syrup for a nice sheen and baking soda for better browning. Finally, bake the cookies one sheet at time to achieve maximum crispness.

## THIN, CRISPY CHOCOLATE CHIP COOKIES

**Makes about forty 2-inch cookies**

The dough, en masse or shaped into balls and wrapped well, can be refrigerated up to 2 days or frozen up to 1 month. Be sure to bring it to room temperature before baking.

| | |
|---|---|
| 1½ | cups (7½ ounces) unbleached all-purpose flour |
| ¾ | teaspoon baking soda |
| ¼ | teaspoon salt |
| 8 | tablespoons (1 stick) unsalted butter, melted and cooled |
| ½ | cup (3½ ounces) granulated sugar |
| ⅓ | cup packed (2¾ ounces) light brown sugar |
| 2 | tablespoons light corn syrup |
| 1 | large egg yolk |
| 2 | tablespoons milk |
| 1 | tablespoon vanilla extract |
| ¾ | cup (4½ ounces) semisweet chocolate chips |

**1.** Adjust an oven rack to the middle position and heat the oven to 375 degrees. Line two baking sheets with parchment paper.

**2.** Whisk the flour, baking soda, and salt in a medium bowl until thoroughly combined; set aside.

**3.** In the bowl of a standing mixer fitted with the paddle attachment, beat the melted butter, granulated sugar, light brown sugar, and corn syrup at low speed until thoroughly blended, about 1 minute. Add the yolk, milk, and vanilla; mix until fully incorporated and smooth, about 1 minute, scraping the bottom and sides of the bowl with a rubber spatula as necessary. With the mixer running on low speed, slowly add the dry ingredients and mix until just combined. Do not overbeat. Add the chips and mix on low speed until distributed evenly throughout the batter, about 5 seconds.

**4.** Leaving about 2 inches between each ball, scoop the dough onto the parchment-lined baking sheets with a 1¼-inch (1 tablespoon capacity) ice cream scoop. Bake, one sheet at a time, until the cookies are deep golden brown and flat, about 12 minutes.

**5.** Cool the cookies on the baking sheet for 3 minutes. Using a wide metal spatula, transfer the cookies to a wire rack and let sit until crisped and cooled to room temperature.

## TASTING LAB:
### Refrigerator Cookie Dough

TAKE A WALK DOWN THE REFRIGERATOR AISLE OF YOUR local supermarket and you'll be amazed at the plethora of options for cookie lovers. Ready-to-bake cookie dough comes in a variety of shapes and sizes, dotted with everything from traditional chocolate chips to pink and purple flowers. The commercials for these products promise just-like-homemade cookies with almost no effort—just slice and bake, or, with many of the newer cookies, just break and

---

### TECHNIQUE: Softening Brown Sugar

To bring hardened brown sugar back to life, place a cup or so of it in a glass pie plate or bowl, cover with a small piece of waxed paper, then top with a slice of bread to provide a bit of moisture. Loosely cover the pie plate or bowl with plastic wrap and microwave until softened, about 30 seconds.

---

# Rating Refrigerator Cookie Dough

FIFTEEN MEMBERS OF THE *COOK'S ILLUSTRATED* STAFF TASTED EIGHT BRANDS OF READY-TO-BAKE CHOCOLATE CHIP cookie dough sold in supermarket refrigerator cases. All of the cookies were baked according to the package instructions. The cookie doughs are listed in order of preference based on scores in this test. All brands are sold in supermarkets.

### RECOMMENDED WITH RESERVATIONS
**Nestlé Toll House Break & Bake Chocolate Chip Cookies** **$3.19 for 18 ounces**
Though the most processed of the bunch, these cookies were praised for their "good flavor and texture" and for being "not too sweet." Long list of unrecognizable ingredients, plus molasses, eggs, margarine, and cornstarch.

### RECOMMENDED WITH RESERVATIONS
**600-Lb. Gorillas Chocolate Chip Cookie Dough Balls** **$3.99 for 18 ounces**
This brand, available only in the Northeast, was deemed "deliciously chocolatey," though some thought it had a "weird aftertaste." Made with just flour, chocolate, butter, brown sugar, oil, water, eggs, salt, and baking soda.

### RECOMMENDED WITH RESERVATIONS
**Mrs. Fields Semi-Sweet Chocolate Chip Cookie Dough** **$5.19 for 16 ounces**
Many tasters praised these cookies because they were "not overly sweet." Though this cookie is ubiquitous in malls, distribution of the frozen dough is limited. Made with chocolate chips, flour, butter, sugar, brown sugar, eggs, vanilla, salt, and baking soda.

### RECOMMENDED WITH RESERVATIONS
**Tom's Chocolate Chip Cookie Dough** **$3.69 for 16 ounces**
Many tasters liked these "buttery" cookies, noting that the "flavor tastes almost homemade." Others, however, found them "dry and ugly." Made with wheat flour, chocolate chips, brown sugar, sugar, butter, eggs, whole oats, baking powder, vanilla, and salt.

### NOT RECOMMENDED
**Pillsbury Ready-to-Bake Chocolate Chip Cookies** **$2.50 for 18 ounces**
Most tasters rejected these processed, preformed cookies as "artificial tasting" and "too sweet." Among their long list of mostly unrecognizable ingredients were partially hydrogenated vegetable oil, molasses, eggs, sodium aluminum phosphate, and nut flours (peanut, walnut, and macadamia nut).

### NOT RECOMMENDED
**Pillsbury Chocolate Chip Cookies (log)** **$2.99 for 18 ounces**
There were few fans of this popular brand, which was deemed "too oily" and "bland." Another long list of unrecognizable ingredients, plus partially hydrogenated vegetable oil, molasses, and eggs.

### NOT RECOMMENDED
**Nestlé Toll House Chocolate Chip Cookie Dough (log)** **$2.99 for 18 ounces**
Although the preformed version of this brand won the tasting, the traditional log was found to be "too greasy," with a "chemical taste." A long list of unrecognizable ingredients, plus molasses, eggs, and margarine.

### NOT RECOMMENDED
**Maury's Chocolate Chip Cookie Dough** **$4.99 for 18 ounces**
Despite the short list of organic ingredients (just organic flour, sugar, chocolate, butter, eggs, and baking soda), this cookie from a well-known New York bakery was rejected as tasting "fake" and having an off-putting "butterscotch flavor."

bake. Do any of these cookies really deliver homemade flavor? We gathered eight popular brands of ready-to-bake chocolate chip cookies to find out.

Our selection included the traditional (Pillsbury and Nestlé Toll House logs of dough), the newfangled (Pillsbury and Nestlé Toll House portioned blocks of dough—just break and bake), the classic (Mrs. Fields), the all-natural (Maury's and Tom's), and the local start-up (600-Lb. Gorillas). Most of the cookies sampled are available nationwide, with the exception of 600-Lb. Gorillas, a brand available only in the Northeast, and Mrs. Fields, available in some, but not all, areas of the country.

Nestlé Toll House portioned cookies won the tasting, with comments ranging from "tastes sort of homemade" to "not homemade tasting at all, but good." Our last-place finisher, Maury's, which came from the local Whole Foods Market, was deemed "not very chocolatey," "way too crisp," and "greasy." So was this a matter of choosing the lesser of all evils, or can Nestlé Toll House cookies really hold a candle to homemade? Well, both.

Our *Cook's* tasters, who have eaten much more than their fair share of good and bad chocolate chip cookies (and, sadly, have the waistlines to prove it), weren't thrilled with any of the prefab cookies. Most agreed with the taster among them who picked the Toll House block cookies as his favorite but wrote, "None of them are good, though."

We realized, however, that these ready-to-bake chocolate chip cookies aren't really marketed to us, they're marketed to kids. So we brought in a dozen fifth- and sixth-graders from the Atrium School in Watertown, Mass., and asked them to taste our homemade cookie alongside the winner and loser of our ready-to-bake cookies (we didn't tell them that any of the three were homemade). Maury's again suffered a landslide loss. Toll House block cookies managed to hold their own against our homemade cookies, with votes evenly split between the two. "This cookie is not sweet enough," wrote one young taster of the Toll House block cookies, while another found them "very good in one part, OK in the other." Of our homemade cookies, one

taster (who may be looking ahead to career in food writing) wrote, "My taste buds went to heaven with a side trip to paradise." We couldn't agree more.

Why did Toll House Break & Bake cookies top our tasting? We don't know. We would have bet our money on one of the all-natural brands (the only cookies with a completely recognizable list of ingredients: flour, butter, sugar, etc.). In our mayonnaise tasting (see page 49), we discovered that taste preferences are predisposed toward the familiar, which explained why most tasters chose Hellmann's or Kraft—in short, the brand they grew up with. That could explain the results of this tasting. No matter how active our parents were in the kitchen, we probably all grew up with Nestlé Toll House morsels, either in homemade cookies or the ready-to-bake dough. Perhaps our tasters chose what was most familiar to them. Though why tasters chose Nestlé Break & Bake, which includes stabilizers like cornstarch, over the company's traditional log of dough, is a mystery.

Of course, for the top chocolate chip cookie, we recommend our own: They're easy to make and delicious to boot. But if you absolutely, positively must buy ready-to-bake cookies, go with the one that tasters young and not-so-young agree is the best of the lot: Nestlé Toll House Break & Bake cookies. After all, 6 out of 12 fifth- and sixth-graders can't be wrong.

# COCONUT MACAROONS

**WHAT WE WANTED:** Most coconut macaroons are achingly sweet, sticky mounds of semicooked dough that don't taste much like coconut. We set out to make something better—much better.

Coconut macaroons are a bit like broughams. In the age of horse-pulled transport, a brougham was a light closed carriage with seating for either two or four. When Detroit got hold of this term, realizing that nobody had a clue as to what a real brougham was, they appropriated it, transforming the brougham from an elegant 19th-century conveyance into a rather pedestrian, motor-powered two-door sedan. Macaroons have undergone a similar transformation. Hundreds of years ago they were baked almond paste, and by the 19th century they had become quite elegant (and very popular) cone-shaped cookies flavored with real coconut. But today they have deteriorated into lackluster mounds of beaten egg whites and coconut shreds or, at their worst, nothing more than a baked mixture of condensed milk and sweetened coconut.

When we began looking at recipes for modern coconut macaroons, we found that they varied widely. In addition to different kinds of coconut and sweeteners, they often called for one or more of a wide range of ingredients, including extracts such as vanilla or almond, salt, flour, sugar, sweetened condensed milk, and even an egg or two (in extreme variations).

We were sure that somewhere among these second-rate cookies was a great coconut macaroon waiting to be found, with a pleasing texture and real, honest coconut flavor. We decided to find it.

The initial recipe testing included five recipes. What came out of the oven that day ranged from dense, wet cookies to light, if not dry, mounds of coconut. In the former category were recipes that used unbeaten egg whites mixed with sweetened coconut and sugar. (One of them, a Brazilian macaroon, even included whole eggs and produced a gooey, cavity-inducing cookie with a strong caramel flavor but nary a hint of coconut.) A recipe calling for beaten egg whites resulted in a light, airy, meringue-style cookie, pleasantly delicate but totally lacking in coconut flavor or chew. The test winners were simple enough: unbeaten egg whites mixed with sugar, unsweetened coconut, salt, and vanilla. But even these lacked coconut flavor and were a bit on the dry side, not sufficiently chewy or moist. We set out to find a happy medium among our test recipes.

Our tests had shown us that the use of sweetened versus unsweetened coconut has a major effect on texture. The unsweetened variety resulted in a less sticky, more appealing texture, but it made the cookies just a bit too dry. Flour—we tried both cake and all-purpose—was helpful in eliminating the stickiness of cookies made entirely with sweetened coconut, but it also made the cookies a bit too dense. Looking for a way past this roadblock, we decided to test a combination of sweetened and unsweetened coconut. This worked very well, giving the cookies a more luxurious texture without making them wet or heavy.

We also found, to our surprise, that the sweetened coconut had more flavor than unsweetened, so the coconut flavor was turned up a notch. A scientist who works with the Baker's brand of coconut, which is sweetened and flaked, explained this phenomenon. He said that fresh coconut is 53 percent moisture; unsweetened, which is dried, is 3 to 5 percent moisture; and sweetened and flaked coconut (which is dried before being flaked and then rehydrated) is 9 to 25 percent moisture. Unlike most fruits that are quite sweet, coconut is mostly fat and, when dried, is rather tasteless, unlike, say, dried apples or apricots. Hydrating dried coconut therefore adds flavor, as does the addition of sugar. Although one could add more moisture and more sweetness to a macaroon batter and then use dried, unsweetened coconut, the coconut itself would still be less flavorful than sweetened coconut flakes.

Another key issue was the ratio of coconut to unbeaten egg whites. Testing showed that cookies made with 3½ cups of coconut and only one egg white were dense and heavy; 3 cups of coconut to 4 egg whites, however, seemed like a better ratio.

To add still more moisture to the cookies, we tried using corn syrup instead of sugar as a sweetener and found that the cookies were slightly more moist, held together a bit better, and were pleasantly chewy. Melted butter was tried but discarded because it masked the flavor of the coconut, as did sweetened condensed milk.

We still felt that the cookies were a bit light in coconut flavor. To remedy this, we tried adding cream of coconut, and we hit the jackpot. The coconut flavor was superior to any of the cookies we had made to date. Finally, a coconut macaroon with real coconut flavor. (Because cream of coconut is sweetened, we did have to decrease the amount of corn syrup. For more information on this and similar products, see the Tasting Lab on page 289.)

Putting these cookies together is easy. There is no need to even whip the egg whites. The liquid ingredients are whisked together, the dry ingredients are mixed, and then the two are combined. We found it best to refrigerate this dough for 15 minutes to make it easier to work with, but in a pinch you can skip this step. In an effort to produce a nicely browned, crisp exterior, we experimented with oven temperatures and finally settled on 375 degrees; the bottoms tended to overcook at 400 degrees, and lower temperatures never produced the sort of browning we were after.

We also found that these cookies are great when the bottom third is dipped in chocolate. Because the cookie is not overly sweet, the chocolate is a nice complement.

WHAT WE LEARNED: For the best flavor, use three kinds of coconut—unsweetened, sweetened, and cream of coconut. Corn syrup adds more moisture to the batter than granulated sugar and is preferred.

FOOD FACT: Macaroons

Macaroons were first developed in Italy during the Renaissance. They originally were biscuits made of marzipan and served at banquets. During the 18th and 19th centuries, macaroons became especially popular in Britain at teatime.

## TRIPLE-COCONUT MACAROONS
Makes about 4 dozen 1-inch cookies

Cream of coconut, available canned, is a very sweet product commonly used in piña colada cocktails. Be sure to mix the can's contents thoroughly before using, as the mixture separates upon standing. Unsweetened desiccated coconut is commonly sold in natural food stores and Asian markets. If you are unable to find any, use all sweetened flaked or shredded coconut, but reduce the amount of cream of coconut to ½ cup, omit the corn syrup, and toss 2 tablespoons cake flour with the coconut before adding the liquid ingredients. For larger macaroons, shape haystacks from a generous ¼ cup of batter and increase the baking time to 20 minutes.

1    cup cream of coconut
2    tablespoons light corn syrup
4    large egg whites
2    teaspoons vanilla extract
½    teaspoon salt
3    cups (8 ounces) unsweetened, shredded, desiccated (dried) coconut
3    cups (8 ounces) sweetened flaked or shredded coconut

**1.** Adjust the oven racks to the upper-middle and lower-middle positions and heat the oven to 375 degrees. Line two baking sheets with parchment paper and lightly spray the parchment with nonstick vegetable cooking spray.

**2.** Whisk together the cream of coconut, corn syrup, egg whites, vanilla, and salt in a small bowl; set aside. Combine the unsweetened and sweetened coconuts in a large bowl;

for beauty

toss together, breaking up clumps with your fingertips. Pour the liquid ingredients into the coconut and mix with a rubber spatula until evenly moistened. Chill for 15 minutes.

**3.** Drop heaping tablespoons of batter onto the parchment-lined baking sheets, spacing them about 1 inch apart. With moistened fingertips, form the cookies into loose haystacks. Bake until light golden brown, about 15 minutes, turning the baking sheets from front to back and switching from the top to bottom racks halfway through baking.

**4.** Cool the cookies on the baking sheets until slightly set, about 2 minutes; remove to a wire rack with a metal spatula.

### VARIATION

### CHOCOLATE-DIPPED TRIPLE-COCONUT MACAROONS

Using the two-stage melting process for the chocolate helps ensure that it will be at the proper consistency for dipping the cookies.

Follow the recipe for Triple-Coconut Macaroons. Cool the baked macaroons to room temperature, about 30 minutes. Line two baking sheets with parchment paper. Chop 10 ounces semisweet chocolate; melt 8 ounces in a small heat-proof bowl set over a pan of almost-simmering water, stirring once or twice, until smooth. (To melt the chocolate in a microwave, heat at 50 percent power for 3 minutes and stir. If the chocolate is not yet entirely melted, heat an additional 30 seconds at 50 percent power.) Remove from the heat; stir in the remaining 2 ounces of chocolate until smooth. Holding the macaroon by its pointed top, dip the bottom and ½ inch up the sides in the chocolate, scrape off the excess with your finger, and place the macaroon on the prepared baking sheet. Repeat with the remaining macaroons. Refrigerate until the chocolate sets, about 15 minutes.

### TASTING LAB: Coconut Milk, Coconut Cream, and Cream of Coconut

COCONUT MILK IS NOT THE THIN LIQUID FOUND INSIDE the coconut itself—that is called coconut water. Coconut milk is a product made by steeping equal parts shredded coconut meat and either warm milk or water. The meat is pressed or mashed to release as much liquid as possible, the mixture is strained, and the result is coconut milk. The same method is used to make coconut cream, but the ratio of coconut meat to liquid is higher, about 4 to 1. (The cream that rises to the top of coconut milk after it sits a while is also referred to as coconut cream.) Finally, cream of coconut—not to be confused with coconut cream—is a sweetened product based on coconut milk that also contains thickeners and emulsifiers. Cream of coconut and coconut cream are not interchangeable in recipes, as the former is heavily sweetened and the latter is not.

To find out firsthand how coconut milk, coconut cream, and cream of coconut stack up, we made coconut milk and cream in the test kitchen and compared them with commercial products. For the first test batch, we made coconut milk with water. (One cup of fresh coconut meat was ground in a food processor with 1 cup of warm water. The mixture steeped for one hour and then was strained.) Next we made a batch with milk, using the same method. The coconut cream was made using the same method, but with a higher ratio of meat to water: 2 cups of fresh coconut meat to ½ cup of water. We then did a blind taste test, pitting our homemade products against canned cream of coconut and canned coconut milk.

Both the canned and the homemade coconut milks were very thin, with only a modest amount of coconut flavor (although the coconut milk made with cow's milk rather than water was superior). The homemade coconut cream, though made with water, was quite good: thicker, creamier, and somewhat more flavorful than the coconut milk. The canned cream of coconut was very sweet and syrupy, really inedible right out of the can, with sugar being the predominant flavor. However, we found that it can be used in baking with good results.

## EQUIPMENT CORNER: Potholders

IN PROFESSIONAL KITCHENS, A TRUSTY, ALBEIT FLIMSY, side towel folded over a few times offers protection from things hot. Home cooks, however, whose hands are not as hardened as the vocational cook's, prefer to protect their paws with potholders. And, lucky for them, there is a panoply of potholders from which to choose, from simple terry-cloth swatches to high-tech silicone to plush leather squares. We selected six different potholders (we purchased two of each type) and used them when handling the handles on a tea kettle, stockpot, and heavy skillet (which had been in a 450-degree oven for 15 minutes), when removing a soufflé from the oven, and when manipulating hot pie plates and cake pans in the oven.

All potholders were adequately heat-resistant. The attributes of a winning potholder were softness, thinness, and suppleness, all of which allow a potholder to conform to the shape of the hand, making it comfortable to use and easy to grasp a hot object, whatever its shape.

The three best were the LamsonSharp Leather Handiholder ($12.95 each), a very basic potholder made by Ritz ($2.99 each), and the Ritz Sterling Pocket Mitt ($4.95 each). The washable suede Handiholder was uniquely soft and supple and afforded the user a very good, secure grip, but at 9½ inches square it seemed excessively large, which was a minor annoyance given its tendency to flop around. Both Ritz potholders were made of terry cloth and had a comfortable, broken-in feel from the get-go, but we slightly preferred the plain potholder over the Pocket Mitt because of its compact size (about 8½ inches square before washing, about 8 inches square after three washes) and its thinner, more svelte feel. But the Pocket Mitt was good as well, just a bit bulkier.

We recommend Pyro Guard potholders ($3.95 each) with reservations. They were decent, not exceptional, performers whose shiny metallic side felt slippery in some tasks and whose overall feel was on the stiff side of acceptable. Of greater concern, however, was the fact that these potholders are not machine-washable. The label says to wipe clean with a damp sponge or cloth. Knowing how grungy potholders can become with use, we wondered about the life expectancy of these potholders.

Two potholders fell into the "not recommended" category. The Kitchensafe potholders ($9.99 each), made of a washable, flame-resistant fabric and dotted on one side with "hot dots" that offer a no-slip surface, were far too rigid,

# Rating Potholders

WE TESTED SIX SETS OF POTHOLDERS IN VARIOUS KITCHEN APPLICATIONS, INCLUDING PICKING UP HANDLES ON A HOT tea kettle, stockpot, and heavy skillet; removing a soufflé dish from the oven; and turning pie plates and cake pans in the oven. The potholders are listed in order of preference based on their performance in these tests. See www.americastestkitchen.com for up-to-date prices and mail-order sources for top-rated products.

**RECOMMENDED**
### LamsonSharp Leather Handiholder
**$12.95 each**
This washable suede potholder is soft and supple and so conforms to any shape handle or pot. Very secure in testers' hands.

**RECOMMENDED**
### Ritz Potholder
**$2.99 each**
This terry-cloth potholder is reliable if not terribly sexy. Compact size is a plus.

**RECOMMENDED**
### Ritz Sterling Pocket Mitt
**$4.95 each**
This terry-cloth mitt has a nice, broken-in feel and performed well in tests. A bit bulkier than we like, though.

**RECOMMENDED WITH RESERVATIONS**
### Pyro Guard Potholders
**$3.95 each**
The shiny metallic side is somewhat slippery and a bit too stiff. Not machine-washable, which is a big drawback given how dirty potholders get.

**NOT RECOMMENDED**
### Kitchensafe Potholders
**$9.99 each**
The washable, flame-resistant fabric is far too rigid, making it difficult to grasp small handles or rims.

**NOT RECOMMENDED**
### HotSpot Silicone Potholders
**$7.95 each**
The material on these high-tech potholders is too springy, and it became very slippery when coated with even a drop of fat.

even after three washes. They did not conform easily to the movements and shape of the hand, which made grasping the small rims on pie plates and cake pans difficult; securing a good grasp on the narrow girth of a skillet handle was nearly impossible. The look of the newfangled HotSpot silicone potholders ($7.95 each) elicited wows, but they failed to impress when pressed into service. Though bendable, these potholders possessed a springy nature that made them awkward to use. On most surfaces, the HotSpot silicone potholders afforded the user a firm, no-slip grip. But even a small drop of fat on the potholders or the item being grasped can render them slick and slippery, as one test cook discovered when using one to grasp a skillet whose handle had been lightly splattered with grease.

Garth and Adam have the scoop on the latest high-tech ice cream machines.

# SUMMER BERRY
## desserts

CHAPTER 23

IN THIS CHAPTER

### THE RECIPES
Summer Berry Pie

Berry Gratin with Lemon
  Sabayon

### EQUIPMENT CORNER
Ice Cream Machines

### SCIENCE DESK
Why Do Egg Yolk Foams Require
  Heat?

When local berries are in season, we like to showcase them in simple desserts. While berries and ice cream make a fine dessert, on occasion we like to attempt something a bit more challenging. But an all-day battle with pastry isn't our idea of summer fun.

We especially like to use summer berries in a no-bake pie. Unfortunately, most recipes are nothing more than berries suspended in gelatin, with a can of "whipped cream" as garnish. We wanted a no-bake pie that was every bit as appealing as a traditional double-crust pie—but without all of the work.

Sabayon is a frothy dessert sauce made with egg yolks, sugar, and flavorings. It takes just minutes to prepare and can transform a bowl of berries into a real dessert. Like many custards, however, sabayon can be fickle. We wanted to figure out the dos and don'ts when making this classic sauce.

# SUMMER BERRY PIE

**WHAT WE WANTED:** No-bake pies can be soupy, chewy, or tasteless. Could we make a pie with great texture and flavor—and still keep it simple?

We love summer fruit pies, but the prospect of wrestling with buttery pie dough in a 90-degree kitchen is not especially appealing. We also find that berries are spectacular when not baked at all. But the alternatives to baked pies hardly inspired us. Most quick "no-bake" pies consist mainly of rubbery Jell-O or viscous pudding garnished with Cool Whip. Our idea for this summer dessert was closer to the bright flavors of a berry tart; we just wanted it in the more substantial form of a pie.

Our first round of tests with no-bake pies was disheartening. The first recipe called for "red" flavored gelatin and a cornstarch-thickened syrup that were poured over fresh berries in a premade crust. It had only one redeeming quality: neat slices. Other attempts to use cornstarch as a thickener left us with a soupy, cinnamon-laden blueberry "icebox" pie and an overly sweet mixed-berry mash in soggy pastry dough. The best recipe called for merely tossing the mixed berries in melted raspberry jam and then pouring them into a prebaked graham cracker crust. The problem with this method became readily apparent: Once the pie was sliced, the berries spilled out, making it impossible to serve neatly and difficult to eat. Exasperated, we set out to find a technique for making a fresh, flavorful pie with good texture and neat slices.

We did learn one thing from these initial tests: A graham cracker crust is not only easy to make but pairs nicely with tangy sweet berries. Our first thought was to give store-bought graham cracker pie crusts a chance. It quickly became apparent that this was not going to be an option (see the Tasting Lab on page 129), so we decided to make our own.

Some recipes call for simply pressing the crumbs in place and chilling the crust before filling it, but we found that prebaking dramatically improved the flavor of the crust and gave it more structure by melting the butter and sugar together. As we continued testing, it became clear that a careful balance of the three ingredients—crumbs, butter, and sugar—would also be crucial to texture and flavor. If we added too much butter, the sides of the crust slid down as it baked, causing the crust to pool in the center of the pan. If we added too much sugar, the crust became too hard and exceedingly sweet. The right proportions were 5 tablespoons of butter and 2 tablespoons of sugar to 1 cup of crumbs. We found that it was much easier to press the crumbs into the pan when the butter was very warm.

The biggest issue now before us was figuring out how to hold the berries together. We needed a binder that would give the pie enough structure to stand up to slicing without interfering with the pure flavor of the fruit.

Early on we found that combining a berry puree with whole berries was best for optimal flavor; using Jell-O or some other commercial filler resulted in poor flavor and less than ideal texture. But we still needed to thicken the puree somehow. An early test recipe called for cornstarch, which seemed like a good idea, but that recipe also added orange juice, which made the pie soupy. Our plan was simple: Lose the juice but keep the cornstarch (or another thickener). We would briefly cook the puree with the thickener, sugar, and salt, and then season with lemon juice at the end. After

---

## FOOD FACT: Graham Crackers

Graham crackers were created by dietary reformer Sylvester Graham in 1829 and originally made with whole-wheat flour (sometimes called graham flour in older cookbooks). Today's graham crackers are often made with bleached white flour, something that would surely distress Graham, who regarded refined flour as one of the world's great dietary evils. He also believed that mustard and ketchup caused insanity. Go figure.

cooling this mixture slightly, we would pour it over the whole berries in the prebaked crust. The pie would then go into the refrigerator to set up.

But which thickener would be best? We started our tests with tapioca, which, because of the short stovetop cooking time, turned out an unpleasantly grainy filling. (We wanted to keep the cooking time as short as possible to retain the fresh berry flavor.) Potato starch produced a gummy filling. In the end, cornstarch worked just fine, producing a good texture without adding any off flavors. But we still had some kinks to work out—namely, the seeds that kept sticking between our teeth. The obvious solution was to strain the filling before cooking, a step that took only a couple of minutes and made a huge difference.

So far, so good, but now that it was time to assemble the pie, we found that pouring the puree over sun-sweetened whole berries made the filling dark and murky looking. And merely tossing the berries on top of the thickened puree was no way to turn heads either. This pie needed some gloss. So we borrowed a trick from tart making: glazing the fresh whole berries with a thin layer of melted seedless jam. Because we weren't interested in a precise arrangement of berries (we wanted a fast and unfussy pie), gently tossing them with the glaze (rather than painting them with it, as is often done when making tarts) was a quick solution. We had managed to gussy them up and enhance their flavor at the same time. When we poured the glazed berries over the puree, the result was a truly attractive berry pie. Better yet, it tasted fresh, sliced well, and was a whole lot easier to make than a traditional American pie.

**WHAT WE LEARNED**: Skip the Jell-O and the Cool Whip, make a berry puree thickened with cornstarch to hold the whole berries together, toss the whole berries with warm jam for a glossy finish, and pour the puree and then the berries into a freshly made graham cracker crust.

## SUMMER BERRY PIE

Makes one 9-inch pie, serving 8 to 10

Berries are not sold in standard half-pint containers. When shopping for ingredients, use the weights on the containers as a guideline but make sure to measure out the berries (gently, to avoid bruising). If you wind up short on one type of berry but have extras of another type, make up the difference with the extras. If blackberries are not available, use 3 cups each of raspberries and blueberries. When pureeing the berries, be sure to process them for a full minute; otherwise, the yield on the puree may be too small. Apple jelly can be substituted if red currant jelly is unavailable. If you have a salad spinner, line the basket with paper towels, add the berries, and spin until dry.

### graham cracker crust
- 9   graham crackers, broken into rough pieces
- 2   tablespoons sugar
- 5   tablespoons unsalted butter, melted and warm

### berry filling
- 2   cups (about 9 ounces) raspberries
- 2   cups (about 11 ounces) blackberries
- 2   cups (about 10 ounces) blueberries
- ½   cup (3½ ounces) granulated sugar
- 3   tablespoons cornstarch
- ⅛   teaspoon salt
- 1   tablespoon juice from 1 lemon
- 2   tablespoons red currant jelly

### whipped cream
- 1   cup cold heavy cream
- 1   tablespoon sugar
- 1   teaspoon vanilla extract

**1.** FOR THE CRUST: Adjust an oven rack to the middle position and heat the oven to 325 degrees.

**2.** In a food processor, process the graham crackers until evenly fine, about 30 seconds (you should have 1 cup crumbs). Add the sugar and pulse to combine. Continue to pulse while adding the warm melted butter in a steady stream; pulse until the mixture resembles wet sand. Transfer the crumbs to a 9-inch glass pie plate. Using a ½-cup dry measuring cup, press the crumb mixture into the place. Use your thumb to square off the top of the crust. Bake the crust until fragrant and beginning to brown, 15 to 18 minutes; transfer to a wire rack and cool completely while making the filling.

**3.** FOR THE FILLING: Combine the berries in a large colander and gently rinse (taking care not to bruise them); spread the berries on a paper towel–lined rimmed baking sheet and gently pat dry with additional paper towels.

**4.** In a food processor, puree 2½ cups mixed berries until smooth and fully pureed, about 1 minute. Strain the puree through a mesh strainer into a small nonreactive saucepan, scraping and pressing on the seeds to extract as much puree as possible (you should have 1¼ to 1½ cups). Whisk the sugar, cornstarch, and salt in a small bowl to combine, then whisk the mixture into the puree. Bring the puree to a boil over medium heat, stirring constantly with a wooden spoon; when the mixture reaches a boil and is thickened to the consistency of pudding, remove from the heat, stir in the lemon juice, and set aside to cool slightly.

**5.** While the puree is cooling, place the remaining berries in a medium bowl. Heat the jelly in a second small saucepan over low heat until fully melted. Drizzle the melted jelly over the berries and toss gently with a rubber spatula to coat. Pour the slightly cooled puree into the cooled pie shell and smooth the top with a spatula. Distribute the glazed berries evenly over the puree and gently press them into the puree. Loosely cover the pie with plastic wrap; refrigerate until chilled and the puree has set, about 3 hours or up to 1 day.

**6.** FOR THE WHIPPED CREAM: Just before serving, beat the cream, sugar, and vanilla with an electric mixer on low speed until small bubbles form, about 30 seconds. Increase the speed to medium; continue beating until the beaters leave a trail, about 30 seconds longer. Increase the speed to high; continue beating until the cream is smooth, thick, nearly doubled in volume, and forms soft peaks, about 30 to 60 seconds.

**7.** Cut the pie into wedges and serve with whipped cream.

## EQUIPMENT CORNER:
### Ice Cream Machines

FRUIT DESSERTS AND HOMEMADE ICE CREAMS ARE natural pairings. If you're in the market for an ice cream maker, you've got several options. We tested seven models, ranging in price from a fairly modest $50 to a whopping $600. They fell into three basic categories: expensive machines that don't require the use of a freezer, midpriced machines with an electric motor and a removable canister that must be frozen in advance, and midpriced machines with a hand crank and a removable canister that must be frozen in advance.

The two canister-free models were also the most expensive, and they produced smooth, creamy ice cream. They have two distinct advantages over the other models tested (some of which also produced high-quality ice cream): volume and ready-to-serve ice cream (it was frozen fully and could be eaten right from the machine). The Lussino Dessert Maker from Musso ($594.95, 1½-quart capacity) contains a built-in refrigerator unit and is the Cadillac of ice cream makers. It lets you make endless batches of ice cream without having to wait 12 hours for a freezer canister to get back down to the proper temperature. The White Mountain Ice Cream Maker ($199.95, 4-quart capacity) produces a whole gallon of great ice cream in one shot, but it requires 10 pounds of ice as well as rock salt. This

# Rating Ice Cream Machines

WE TESTED SEVEN ICE CREAM MACHINES, EVALUATING THE QUALITY OF THE ICE CREAM THAT EACH PRODUCED AS WELL as ease of use. The ice cream machines are listed in order of preference based on these tests. See www.americastestkitchen.com for up-to-date prices and mail-order sources for top-rated products.

### HIGHLY RECOMMENDED
### Lussino Dessert Maker from Musso

**$594.95**

This quiet 1 1/2 quart-machine makes top-notch ice cream, and there's no need to freeze a canister in advance—it contains a built-in refrigerator. But you have to pay dearly for these conveniences.

### RECOMMENDED
### Krups La Glacière

**$59.95**

This electric machine is pretty quiet and turns out really good ice cream. Although you need to freeze the canister overnight before making ice cream and the churned ice cream will require further hardening in the freezer, this machine offers the best value.

### RECOMMENDED
### Cuisinart Flavor Duo Frozen Yogurt/Ice Cream/Sorbet Maker

**$99.95**

This machine comes with two 1-quart canisters so you can make vanilla and chocolate ice cream on the same day. Otherwise, it's similar to the other Cuisinart model tested.

### RECOMMENDED
### Cuisinart Automatic Frozen Yogurt and Ice Cream Maker

**$49.95**

This machine is similar to the Krups (both come with 1 1/2 quart-canisters) but is a bit noisier. The ice cream, however, is very good.

### RECOMMENDED WITH RESERVATIONS
### White Mountain Ice Cream Maker

**$199.95**

The huge 4-quart capacity is a plus, as is the superior quality of the ice cream, but this electric machine requires 10 pounds of ice and rock salt, and it's extremely noisy. Great as a weekend project on the back porch.

### NOT RECOMMENDED
### Donvier Ice Cream Maker

**$49.95**

Although this hand-cranked machine turns out ice cream quickly, the quality is only so-so. Given the price tag, the ice cream should be better.

### NOT RECOMMENDED
### Chilly by William Bounds

**$69.99**

The machine makes grainy, icy, dense ice cream. For the money, you can do much better.

## TECHNIQUE:
## Chilling the Bowl for Whipping Cream

For the best results, you should chill a bowl before whipping cream in it. If your freezer is too small or too full to accommodate a large bowl, here's how to accomplish this task.

1. At least 15 minutes before whipping the cream, fill the bowl with ice cubes and cold water, place the whisk (or mixer beaters) in the ice water and put the bowl in the refrigerator.

2. When ready to whip the cream, dump out the ice water, dry the bowl and whisk (or beaters), and add the cream. The bowl will stay cold as you work, and the cream whips up beautifully.

machine is unbearably loud to boot, better suited to a back porch than a kitchen.

The three electric models with canisters that must go in the freezer overnight made delectably smooth, creamy ice cream in less than 30 minutes. The ice cream was quite soft, however, and benefited from a few hours in the freezer to firm it up before eating. The Krups La Glacière ($59.95, 1½-quart capacity) was quieter than both the Cuisinart one-canister machine ($49.95, 1½-quart capacity) and the Cuisinart two-canister machine ($99.95, 2-quart capacity). Given its modest price and size (and immodestly good ice cream), the Krups machine is an excellent choice.

The two manual models tested—the Donvier ($49.95, 1-quart capacity) and the Chilly by William Bounds ($69.99, 1-quart capacity)—made ice cream in just 15 to 20 minutes (once the canisters had been chilled overnight). While it seemed miraculous that ice cream could be made so quietly and so quickly with so little hand churning, the ice cream was grainy, icy, and dense. If you can buy a model with a built-in motor for about the same price, why settle for hand-cranked, inferior ice cream?

# BERRY GRATIN WITH SABAYON

**WHAT WE WANTED:** A medley of summer fruit warmed slightly and topped with frothy sabayon and a delicate, caramelized sugar crust.

Fruit and egg yolk foam (called *sabayon* in French or *zabaglione* in Italian) are simple summertime pleasures. Most recipes start with a mixture of sugared berries, which are then topped with chilled sabayon and served in goblets. We wanted something a bit different—warming the fruit in a gratin dish so that the juices would run. The sabayon would be spooned over the fruit and then sprinkled with sugar, which we would caramelize with a torch. Although still simple, this dish is far more elegant than the typical frothy zabaglione and berries served in old-fashioned Italian restaurants.

We started with the fruit. Tasters liked a mixture of raspberries, blackberries, and blueberries. We tried sugaring the berries as well as flavoring them with liqueur or vanilla, but tasters objected. They wanted pure berry flavor. In any case, a brief stay in the oven heated the berries and released their juices, so the sugar was not needed for this purpose.

Sabayon is a thick, slightly frothy, and creamy dessert sauce made of nothing but whipped egg yolks, sugar, and wine (often Marsala) or lemon juice. We began by testing the various flavoring options. Tasters quickly chose lemon as the best complement to the fruit; alcohol seemed to overpower the delicate berries. A mixture of zest and juice was best, providing the most complex lemon flavor.

Next we focused on the ratio of egg yolks to lemon juice. Three egg yolks and a scant half cup of lemon juice produced a sauce with the correct consistency—light and frothy, not loose and watery—but the lemon flavor was overwhelming. We solved this problem by cutting the lemon juice with water.

As for the sugar, we began with ½ cup (an amount that seemed typical in most research recipes), but tasters thought the sauce was too sweet. We reduced the sugar tablespoon by tablespoon, ultimately deciding that ⅓ cup was enough to sweeten the sauce without overwhelming it. (Remember, we wanted to add a crunchy layer of caramelized sugar to finish this dessert.) A pinch of salt rounded the flavors in the sabayon.

With the ingredients chosen, it was time to refine our technique. There are two main goals when heating sabayon ingredients: to dissolve the sugar fully and to whip enough air into the sauce to create the desired frothy texture. Whisking the egg yolks and sugar together in a bowl, off heat, dissolved most of the sugar. Setting the bowl over a pan of simmering water for a minute while continuing to whisk dissolved the rest of the sugar.

At this point, we added the lemon juice, lemon zest, water, and salt and continued whisking. We found that five to seven minutes of constant whisking yielded a threefold increase in volume. We tried whisking occasionally but ended up with scrambled eggs. If the mixture is not in constant motion, the yolks in direct contact with the bowl (where the heat is most intense) will overcook and curdle (see the Science Desk on page 300 for more details). For this reason, it is necessary to whisk the mixture constantly while it is on the stovetop. Once the sabayon thickens properly, it should be removed from the heat immediately. We found it best to continue whisking for 30 seconds to cool off the sabayon.

With the sabayon made and the berries warmed, the dessert came together very quickly. We simply spooned the sabayon over the warmed fruit and then added a sprinkling of sugar, which we quickly caramelized with a kitchen torch.

**WHAT WE LEARNED:** Warm the berries—without sugar or flavorings—to release their juices. Use lemon juice and zest to brighten the flavor of the sabayon, and whisk constantly to prevent the sauce from curdling.

## BERRY GRATIN WITH LEMON SABAYON

Serves 6

When making the sabayon, make sure the heat under the simmering water is not set too high. If the egg yolks overheat, they will scramble. Constant whisking is also required. Although we prefer to make this recipe with a mix of raspberries, blackberries, and blueberries, you can use three cups of just one berry if that's what you have on hand.

### lemon sabayon

¼ cup water
½ teaspoon grated zest and 3 tablespoons juice from 1 large lemon
    Pinch salt
3 large egg yolks
⅓ cup (2⅓ ounces) sugar

### berries

1 cup raspberries
1 cup blackberries
1 cup blueberries

3 tablespoons sugar for caramelized crust

**1.** FOR THE SABAYON: Adjust an oven rack to the upper-middle position and heat the oven to 400 degrees.

**2.** Combine the water, lemon zest, lemon juice, and salt in a small bowl and set aside.

**3.** Whisk the egg yolks and sugar in a medium bowl until frothy, about 1 minute. Set the bowl over a pan of simmering water. Continue whisking until the mixture begins to thicken, about 1 minute. Gradually whisk in the lemon mixture and continue cooking, whisking constantly, until the mixture is thick, light yellow, and tripled in volume, 5 to 7 minutes. Remove the bowl from the saucepan, whisk constantly for about 30 seconds to cool, then set aside while preparing the berries, occasionally whisking the mixture.

**4.** FOR THE BERRIES: Combine the berries in a wide, shallow 2-quart broiler-safe gratin dish or divide among 6 ramekins or individual gratin dishes set on a rimmed baking sheet. Bake the berries until the fruit is warm and just beginning to release its juices, about 8 minutes. Remove the berries from the oven. Spoon the lemon sabayon over the berries and sprinkle with the sugar. Ignite a kitchen torch and caramelize the sugar. Serve immediately.

---

### SCIENCE DESK:
### Why Do Egg Yolk Foams Require Heat?

ACCORDING TO LEGEND, THE FROTHY SAUCE KNOWN AS *zabaglione* in Italian and *sabayon* in French was created in the Medici court in Florence in the 16th century. It is one of the few recipes still prepared in the modern kitchen that makes use of egg yolk foam. Foams made from egg whites are routine: just place the whites in a bowl and beat in air (see the Science Desk on page 334 for more information). If this method is attempted with egg yolks, however, very little air will be incorporated. In fact, if even a small amount of egg yolk contaminates egg whites, the whites will not foam. Why?

While egg whites are essentially protein and water, egg yolks are about 34 percent fat, and it is the fat that spells disaster for egg white foam. Foams are the result of egg proteins denaturing, or unfolding, and associating with adjacent proteins to form a web; this web stabilizes the foam structure. In the case of egg white foam, your arm (and a whisk) or a mixer can provide enough energy to reorganize the protein structure, but with egg yolks this is not the case. Instead, a significant amount of heat is required to encourage the yolk proteins to form a sturdy matrix. Specifically, the yolk must be heated above 140 degrees to get good foam formation. Caution must be taken, however. If the temperature of the foam rises above 160 degrees, the proteins will begin to coagulate, an irreversible process wherein the proteins tighten, leaving the cook with a serving of sweet scrambled eggs.

Rows and rows of cakes are ready
to be frosted and filmed.

# EASY sheet cakes

## CHAPTER 24

**IN THIS CHAPTER**

**THE RECIPES**

Simple Carrot Cake with Cream
Cheese Frosting
Spiced Carrot Cake with Vanilla
Bean–Cream Cheese Frosting
Ginger-Orange Carrot Cake with
Orange–Cream Cheese
Frosting

Chocolate Sheet Cake
Creamy Milk Chocolate Frosting

**SCIENCE DESK**
To Sift or Not to Sift?

**TASTING LAB**
Milk Chocolate

A sheet cake is like a two-layer cake with training
wheels—it's hard to fall off. Unlike regular cakes, which often require
trimming and decorating skills to ensure that the cake doesn't turn out
lopsided, domed, or altogether amateurish, sheet cakes are single-story
and easy to frost. These are the sorts of cakes made for church suppers,
old home days, bake sales, and Fourth of July picnics, decorated with
red, white, and blue frosting.

But sheet cakes are still cakes. They can still turn out dry, sticky, or
flavorless and, on occasion, can even sink in the middle. The test kitchen
decided to tackle two popular sheet cakes—carrot and chocolate—and
produce simple recipes (a complicated sheet cake makes no sense) that
would deliver superior results. We think we've succeeded.

# CARROT CAKE

**WHAT WE WANTED:** A streamlined recipe that was moist (but not soggy) and rich (but not oily).

A relic of the health food craze, carrot cake was once heralded for its use of vegetable oil in place of butter and carrots as a natural sweetener. But healthy or not (and we doubt that it ever was), we have never been a fan of this cake. Sure, the carrots add some sweetness, but they also add a lot of moisture, which is why carrot cake is invariably soggy. And oil? It makes this cake dense and, well, oily. Save for the mercifully thick coating of cream cheese frosting, many of us in the test kitchen think carrot cake is nothing but a good spice cake gone bad.

But other colleagues spun stories about the ultimate carrot cake. They spoke of moist (not soggy) cakes that were rich (not greasy). The crumb should be relatively tight and tender, while the spices should be nicely balanced. And what about the cake's namesake? They admitted that it was not all that important to taste the carrots, but they did want to know on first glance that what they were eating was carrot cake. As a group, we reasoned that if we were going to make this cake, it had better be simple—from ingredient list to mixing method.

Our initial research turned up numerous recipes, and we chose several that seemed promising. Some of these recipes were not in our desired sheet-cake form, but at this point we figured it was worth testing all kinds of recipes. To our dismay, all of these initial test cakes were, with the exception of one, very bad (see Getting It Right, page 307). But the test wasn't a complete wash, as we learned two very important things.

First, shape mattered. Layer cakes could hardly be considered part of our "simple" plan. Loaf-shaped was easy but looked more like quick bread than cake. A Bundt-shaped cake was easy as well as attractive but difficult to ice with a thick coating of cream cheese frosting (a must, if you

remember). No, for our purposes, there was nothing easier than a sheet cake baked in a standard 13 by 9-inch pan, and this round of testing had confirmed our opinion.

Second, there are carrot cakes out there made with just about anything and everything. Canned crushed pineapple, toasted coconut, wheat germ, raisins, and nuts all made appearances in the cakes. The first three were unanimously voted out, but the raisins and nuts were liked well enough to make them an option.

All-purpose flour worked better than cake flour (the latter proved too delicate for this sturdy American classic), and we used 2½ cups as the base for our tests. We quickly found that this cake would need healthy amounts of baking soda and baking powder—1 and 1¼ teaspoons, respectively (nearly twice the amount found in many recipes)—to give it sufficient lift and a beautiful brown color. Four eggs gave the cake a slight spring and a tender crumb. As for sugar, this cake clearly benefited from both granulated and light brown sugar, the former giving the cake clean sweetness, the latter bringing out the warmth of the spices. While many recipes use handfuls of every baking spice in the pantry, we found that a conservative touch with cinnamon, along with a little help from nutmeg and cloves, won the approval of tasters.

Now that we had a reasonably simple working recipe, we introduced carrots to the mix. We rejected any idea of first boiling, steaming, or pureeing the carrots, as called for in some recipes. It was just too much work. Grating the carrots was clearly the way to go, but it took a few failed efforts before we realized that just the right amount of carrots was paramount, as their high moisture content could determine whether a cake was moist or soggy. After baking cakes with as few cups of grated carrots as 1 (no carrot presence) and as many as 5 (soaking-wet cake), we found that 3 cups gave the cake a pleasantly moist texture. To hasten the grating (as well as to spare ourselves a few grazed knuckles), we put away the box grater and plugged in the food processor.

About 99 percent of carrot cake recipes use oil instead of softened butter in the batter, and while the idea of not having to wait on softened butter fit into our simple approach, the thought of using oil gave us some pause. As a compromise, we tested melted butter versus oil. We were shocked to find that tasters preferred the cleaner taste of the cake made with oil. Any more than 1½ cups of oil and the cake was too dense and greasy; any less and tasters found the cake too lean.

Just as we would with a butter-based cake, we beat the oil with the sugar and the eggs in a standing mixer before adding the dry ingredients and the carrots. This cake was good, but we still weren't happy about two things. First, the bottom of the cake was too dense. Second, we weren't thrilled with the idea of pulling out both the food processor and standing mixer to bake a "simple" cake. Deciding to work with the easier problem first, we examined our mixing method. Because we were using the food processor to grate the carrots, we wondered if we could use it to mix the cake. We processed the eggs and oil together with sugar,

then added the dry ingredients and finally the carrots. This cake was tough from the beating of the flour and jack-o'-lantern orange from the processing of the carrots. Next time around we again processed the eggs, oil, and sugar but then transferred the mixture to another bowl, into which we could stir the carrots and dry ingredients. This was much better, but we still had to deal with that annoyingly dense bottom.

On a whim, we wondered if gradually adding the oil to the sugar and eggs while the machine was running (much like making a mayonnaise) would have any impact on the cake. You bet it did. By first creating this stable emulsion of eggs and oil, we were breaking up the oil into tiny particles that were less likely to sink to the bottom, instead dispersing themselves evenly throughout the cake. No more soggy bottom, no more heavy texture. This cake was light, tender, and pleasantly moist.

Our cake was now good enough to eat on its own, but there was no way we were going to pass up the frosting. Made with cream cheese, butter, and confectioners' sugar, cream cheese frosting is one of those things that even when it's bad, it's still good. So we made (and happily ate) several frostings made with various proportions of each ingredient. We added vanilla for depth of flavor, but it wasn't until we added a little sour cream that the frosting really shone on top of the cake.

---

**WHAT WE LEARNED:** This cake is best made with all-purpose flour and plenty of leavener to give it lift. Neutral-tasting oil works better than butter with the flavor of the carrots. For the best texture, beat the sugar and eggs in a food processor (which is also used to grate the carrots) and then add the oil in a steady stream. By using the same method to mix the cake that you would to mix mayonnaise, the oil gets broken into tiny droplets, and the texture of cake is moist throughout but neither soggy nor heavy.

## SIMPLE CARROT CAKE WITH CREAM
## CHEESE FROSTING Makes one 13 by 9-inch cake

If you like nuts in your cake, stir 1 1/2 cups toasted chopped pecans or walnuts into the batter along with the carrots. Raisins are also a good addition; 1 cup can be added along with the carrots. If you add both nuts and raisins, the cake will need an additional 10 to 12 minutes in the oven.

### carrot cake

| | |
|---|---|
| 2½ | cups (12½ ounces) unbleached all-purpose flour |
| 1¼ | teaspoons baking powder |
| 1 | teaspoon baking soda |
| 1¼ | teaspoons ground cinnamon |
| ½ | teaspoon ground nutmeg |
| ⅛ | teaspoon ground cloves |
| ½ | teaspoon salt |
| 1 | pound (6 to 7 medium) carrots, peeled |
| 1½ | cups (10½ ounces) granulated sugar |
| ½ | cup (3½ ounces) packed light brown sugar |
| 4 | large eggs |
| ½ | cups safflower, canola, or vegetable oil |

### cream cheese frosting

| | |
|---|---|
| 8 | ounces cream cheese, softened but still cool |
| 5 | tablespoons unsalted butter, softened but still cool |
| 1 | tablespoon sour cream |
| ½ | teaspoon vanilla extract |
| 1¼ | cups (4½ ounces) confectioners' sugar |

**1.** FOR THE CAKE: Adjust an oven rack to the middle position and heat the oven to 350 degrees. Spray a 13 by 9-inch baking pan with nonstick cooking spray. Line the bottom of the pan with parchment and spray the parchment.

**2.** Whisk together the flour, baking powder, baking soda, cinnamon, nutmeg, cloves, and salt in a large bowl; set aside.

**3.** In a food processor fitted with a large shredding disk, shred the carrots (you should have about 3 cups); transfer

the carrots to a bowl and set aside. Wipe out the food processor workbowl and fit with the metal blade. Process the granulated and brown sugars and eggs until frothy and thoroughly combined, about 20 seconds. With the machine running, add the oil through the feed tube in a steady

---

### TECHNIQUE:
### Transporting a Frosted Cake

The common method for keeping plastic wrap from touching gooey frosting or glaze is to stick the cake with toothpicks and place the wrap over the toothpicks. Occasionally, though, the sharp points of the toothpicks puncture the wrap, which can then slide down and stick to the frosting. To keep the wrap securely above the frosting, try this method.

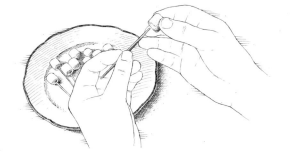

1. Place a miniature marshmallow over the end of each toothpick.

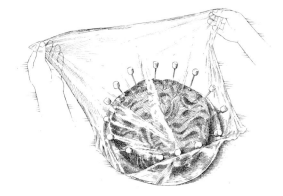

2. Insert the toothpicks into the cake with the marshmallows facing up. Lay the plastic wrap over the marshmallows.

stream. Process until the mixture is light in color and well emulsified, about 20 seconds longer. Scrape the mixture into a medium bowl. Stir in the carrots and the dry ingredients until incorporated and no streaks of flour remain. Pour into the prepared pan and bake until a toothpick or skewer inserted into the center of the cake comes out clean, 35 to 40 minutes, rotating the pan halfway through the baking time. Cool the cake to room temperature in the pan on a wire rack, about 2 hours.

**4.** FOR THE FROSTING: When the cake is cool, process the cream cheese, butter, sour cream, and vanilla in a clean food processor workbowl until combined, about 5 seconds, scraping down the bowl with a rubber spatula as needed. Add the confectioners' sugar and process until smooth, about 10 seconds.

**5.** Run a paring knife around the edge of the cake to loosen from the pan. Invert the cake onto a wire rack, peel off the parchment, then invert again onto a serving platter. Using an icing spatula, spread the frosting evenly over the surface of the cake. Cut into squares and serve. (Cover leftovers and refrigerate for up to 3 days.)

VARIATIONS

## SPICED CARROT CAKE WITH VANILLA BEAN–CREAM CHEESE FROSTING

The Indian tea called chai inspired this variation.

Follow the recipe for Simple Carrot Cake with Cream Cheese Frosting, substituting an equal amount ground black pepper for the nutmeg, increasing the cloves to ¼ teaspoon, and adding 1 tablespoon ground cardamom along with the spices. For the frosting, using a paring knife, halve and scrape the seeds from 2 vanilla beans and add the seeds to the food processor along with the vanilla extract.

## GINGER-ORANGE CARROT CAKE WITH ORANGE–CREAM CHEESE FROSTING

Follow the recipe for Simple Carrot Cake with Cream Cheese Frosting, reducing the cinnamon to ½ teaspoon, adding 1½ teaspoons ground ginger along with the spices, adding ½ cup finely chopped crystallized ginger along with the carrots, and processing 1 tablespoon grated orange zest along with the sugar and eggs. For the frosting, substitute an equal amount orange juice for the sour cream and 1 tablespoon grated orange zest for the vanilla.

---

### GETTING IT RIGHT: Some Failed Carrot Cakes

We uncovered a number of problems in our initial round of testing. Pureed carrots gave one cake (left) an odd texture. The curved Bundt shape (center) was hard to ice, and the cake was bland. One layer cake (right) was so delicate that we had to slice it cold.

TOO SOGGY

TOO BLAND

TOO DELICATE

# CHOCOLATE SHEET CAKE

**WHAT WE WANTED:** The simplest, most dependable recipe for a chocolate sheet cake—one that was moist yet also light and chocolatey.

A basic chocolate sheet cake is used as the foundation for Mississippi mud cake (just add a layer of marshmallow cream and chocolate frosting) and is also referred to as Texas sheet cake. It's arguably America's most popular sheet cake, served at birthday parties, picnics, and potluck suppers.

We started our kitchen work by preparing a test batch of five different recipes that required a variety of mixing techniques, everything from creaming butter to beating yolks, whipping whites, and gently folding everything together at the end. The best of the lot was the most complicated to make. But we were taken with another recipe that simply whisked together the ingredients without beating, creaming, or whipping. Although the recipe needed work, its approach was clearly a good match for the simple, all-purpose nature of a sheet cake.

The recipe called for 2 sticks of butter, 4 eggs, 1½ cups flour, 2 cups sugar, ½ cup cocoa, 1 teaspoon vanilla, and ⅛ teaspoon salt. Our first change was to add buttermilk, baking powder, and baking soda to lighten the batter, as the cake had been dense and chewy in its original form. To increase the chocolate flavor, we reduced the sugar and flour, increased the cocoa, and decreased the butter. To further deepen the chocolate taste, we decided to use semisweet chocolate in addition to the cocoa.

With this revised recipe and our simple mixing method, we actually had a cake that was superior to those whose recipes called for creaming butter or whipping eggs.

The only significant problem came when we tested natural versus Dutch-processed cocoa and discovered that the cake fell a bit in the center when we used the former. A few tests later, we eliminated the baking powder entirely, relying instead on baking soda alone, and the problem was fixed. (Natural cocoa is more acidic than Dutch-processed, and when it was combined with baking powder, which also contains acid, it produced an excess of carbon dioxide gas. This in turn caused the cake to rise very fast and then fall like a deflated balloon.)

Also of note is the low oven temperature—325 degrees—which, combined with a relatively long baking time of 40 minutes, produced a perfectly baked cake with a lovely flat top. Using a microwave oven rather than a double boiler to melt the chocolate and butter also saved time and hassle.

This cake can be frosted with almost anything—a buttercream, an Italian meringue, a sour cream or whipped cream frosting—but we developed a classic American milk chocolate frosting that pairs well with the darker flavor of the cake. Unlike a regular two-layer cake, this cake is a snap to frost.

**WHAT WE LEARNED:** Use both semisweet chocolate and cocoa powder for depth of flavor and buttermilk to give the cake a tender crumb. Bake at a low oven temperature so the cake rises slowly and finishes up with a nice flat top that is easy to frost.

## CHOCOLATE SHEET CAKE Serves 10 to 12

Melting the chocolate and butter in the microwave is quick and neat, but it can also be done in a heatproof bowl set over a saucepan containing 2 inches of simmering water. We prefer Dutch-processed cocoa for the deeper chocolate flavor it gives the cake. The baked and cooled cake can be served simply with lightly sweetened whipped cream or topped with any frosting you like. We particularly like Creamy Milk Chocolate Frosting (recipe follows).

| | |
|---|---|
| 12 | tablespoons (1½ sticks) unsalted butter, plus 1 tablespoon for greasing the baking pan |
| ¾ | cup cocoa, preferably Dutch-processed |
| 1¼ | cups (6¼ ounces) unbleached all-purpose flour |
| ½ | teaspoon baking soda |
| ¼ | teaspoon salt |
| 8 | ounces semisweet chocolate, chopped |
| 4 | large eggs |
| 1½ | cups sugar |
| 1 | teaspoon vanilla extract |
| 1 | cup buttermilk |

**1.** Adjust an oven rack to the middle position and heat the oven to 325 degrees. Grease the bottom and sides of a 13 by 9-inch baking pan with 1 tablespoon butter.

**2.** Sift together the cocoa, flour, baking soda, and salt in a medium bowl; set aside. Heat the chocolate and remaining 12 tablespoons butter in a microwave-safe bowl covered with plastic wrap for 2 minutes at 50 percent power; stir until smooth. (If not fully melted, heat 1 minute longer at 50 percent power.) Whisk together the eggs, sugar, and vanilla in a medium bowl. Whisk in the buttermilk until smooth.

**3.** Whisk the chocolate into the egg mixture until combined. Whisk in the dry ingredients until the batter is smooth and glossy. Pour the batter into the prepared pan; bake until firm in the center when lightly pressed and a

toothpick inserted in the center comes out clean, about 40 minutes. Let the cake cool on a wire rack to room temperature, at least 1 hour; serve, or ice with frosting, if desired. (The cake can be wrapped in plastic and stored at room temperature for up to 2 days.)

## CREAMY MILK CHOCOLATE FROSTING

Makes about 2 cups, enough to ice one 13 by 9-inch cake

This frosting needs about an hour to cool before it can be used, so begin making it when the cake comes out of the oven. Use the best-quality milk chocolate you can find—it will make a big difference in this recipe. See the Tasting Lab on page 310 for specific recommendations.

| | |
|---|---|
| ½ | cup heavy cream |
| | Pinch salt |
| 1 | tablespoon light or dark corn syrup |
| 10 | ounces milk chocolate, chopped |
| ½ | cup (2 ounces) confectioners' sugar |
| 8 | tablespoons (1 stick) cold unsalted butter, cut into 8 pieces |

**1.** Heat the cream, salt, and corn syrup in a microwave-safe measuring cup on high until simmering, about 1 minute, or bring to a simmer in a small saucepan over medium heat.

**2.** Place the chocolate in the workbowl of a food processor fitted with the steel blade. With the machine running, gradually add the hot cream mixture through the feed tube; process 1 minute after the cream has been added. Stop the machine; add the confectioners' sugar to the workbowl and process to combine, about 30 seconds. With the machine running, add the butter through the feed tube one piece at a time; process until incorporated and smooth, about 20 seconds longer.

**3.** Transfer the frosting to a medium bowl and cool at room temperature, stirring frequently, until thick and spreadable, about 1 hour.

## SCIENCE DESK: To Sift or Not to Sift?

SIFTING FLOUR IS A CHORE. THIS IS ESPECIALLY TRUE when sifting into a measuring cup because you inevitably end up sifting twice as much as you need to fill the cup. Many bakers skip this step, thinking it insignificant. Here's why you shouldn't, especially when the recipe says to do so.

Sifting reduces the overall amount of flour (in weight) that goes into the recipe. Because sifting aerates the flour, 1 cup of sifted cake flour weighs in at about 3 ounces, whereas 1 cup of cake flour measured straight from the bin using the dip-and-sweep method (the test kitchen's standard, in which you dip the measure into the flour and then level it by sweeping with a straight-edged spatula) weighs around 4 ounces. To see what effect this difference in amount of flour has on the finished product, we baked two cakes—one with sifted flour, one with unsifted. The cake made with sifted flour baked up perfectly flat, a dream to frost and layer because it required no trimming or leveling. The cake made with unsifted flour, however, mounded in the center and, though still very tasty, was also a bit drier.

Recipes with cocoa powder, such as our chocolate cake, often call for sifting. In this case, sifting breaks up small clumps of cocoa that form as the powder sits in the package. Sifted cocoa can be evenly distributed throughout a cake batter; with unsifted cocoa this isn't always the case.

## TASTING LAB: Milk Chocolate

IF LIFE IS LIKE A BOX OF CHOCOLATES, THEN THE MILK chocolates are childhood. Sweet and simple, milk chocolate is the first choice for a kid in a candy store but rarely sought after as an ingredient in grown-up chocolate desserts. In 10 years at *Cook's Illustrated*, we have developed only one recipe using milk chocolate. That recipe, Milk Chocolate Frosting, doesn't specify a brand of chocolate, so we wondered if we could detect any significant differences in the widely available brands. And, to be perfectly honest, some of us really like to eat milk chocolate. When we reach for a bar of milk chocolate in a candy store, we want to be sure we grab the best one.

We gathered nine brands of milk chocolate, ranging from supermarket favorites, such as Hershey's and Nestlé, to boutique brands, such as Valrhona and Callebaut. We tasted them plain and in our Milk Chocolate Frosting (there was no shortage of tasters for these tests).

In the straight chocolate tasting, Lindt took first place, its flavor described as "very rich" and "just about perfect." Close behind was Perugina (a European brand owned by Nestlé), which won points for its "creamy, firm texture," though one taster described it as "waxy." Falling at the bottom of our tasting was boutique brand Valrhona, which was deemed "bitter," "chalky," and "weird." Valrhona has strong fruit and floral notes that many tasters found disagreeable.

There was some shuffling in our Milk Chocolate Frosting tasting, which again saw Perugina and Lindt among the top three (first and third, respectively) but also saw Nestlé jump from fourth to second place. Nestlé was praised for its "deep chocolate flavor" and "smooth texture," though some found the flavor "slightly fake." Valrhona again took the bottom berth (by a wide margin), with its "slightly rancid flavor" that led one taster to wonder, "Is this from one of those tubs?"

If you're looking for an eating chocolate, we recommend splurging on Lindt or Perugina. For baking, when the subtle nuances are much more difficult to detect, save your money. At less than half the price of the top finishers, and with a much wider availability (both Lindt and Perugina could be found only at specialty food stores), Nestlé is a good choice.

# Rating Milk Chocolates

TWENTY-TWO MEMBERS OF THE *COOK'S ILLUSTRATED* STAFF TASTED NINE BRANDS OF MILK CHOCOLATE IN TWO WAYS— plain and in a simple frosting. The chocolates are listed below in order of preference based on their combined scores in both tastings. Most brands are sold in supermarkets. A few are available only in gourmet shops with good chocolate selections or in candy stores.

---

**HIGHLY RECOMMENDED**
Perugina Milk Chocolate **$2.49 for 3.5 ounces ($11.38/pound)**

This "well-rounded" chocolate was the overall winner. Several tasters called it "honey-like."

---

**HIGHLY RECOMMENDED**
Lindt Excellence Extra Creamy Milk Chocolate **$2.49 for 3.5 ounces ($11.38/pound)**

A close second, this chocolate was described as "super soft and creamy" and "deep and rich."

---

**HIGHLY RECOMMENDED**
Nestlé Superior Quality Milk Chocolate **$1.50 for 5 ounces ($4.80/pound)**

This chocolate offers an excellent value and is readily available. "Nice balance" was the general consensus, although a few tasters thought it "too sweet."

---

**RECOMMENDED**
Callebaut Milk Chocolate **$6.99 for 1 pound**

This premium Belgian chocolate was deemed "really milky" and "somewhat flat."

---

**RECOMMENDED WITH RESERVATIONS**
Hershey's Milk Chocolate **$1.19 for 5 ounces ($3.81/pound)**

Many tasters thought this American favorite had a "rich chocolate flavor," but others disagreed and found it "kind of boring."

---

**RECOMMENDED WITH RESERVATIONS**
Ghirardelli Milk Chocolate Premium Baking Bar **$2.10 for 4 ounces ($8.76/pound)**

This supermarket brand was described as "sweet" and "harmless," but several tasters complained that it had "no depth."

---

**RECOMMENDED WITH RESERVATIONS**
Newman's Own Organics Milk Chocolate **$1.89 for 2.8 ounces ($10.80/pound)**

Tasters were neither wowed nor disappointed by this natural foods store brand. "Buttery" and "not too bad" were typical comments.

---

**RECOMMENDED WITH RESERVATIONS**
Cadbury Dairy Milk Milk Chocolate **$1.39 for 4.5 ounces ($4.94/pound)**

This chocolate has a "nice sweet flavor," but tasters also found it "very chewy."

---

**NOT RECOMMENDED**
Valrhona Jivara Lactee Milk Chocolate **$10.99 for 1 pound**

Most tasters derided the "gummy" texture and "odd," "fruity" flavors in this premium French chocolate, although it did have a few defenders.

Lemon zest is a key ingredient in our cheesecake recipe. To keep the zest's fibrous texture from marring the smooth cheesecake, it is ground fine with some sugar.

# LEMON
CHAPTER 25
## cheesecake

IN THIS CHAPTER

**THE RECIPE**
Lemon Cheesecake

**EQUIPMENT CORNER**
Springform Pans

**SCIENCE DESK**
Why Bother with a Water Bath?

**TASTING LAB**
Cookies for Crumb Crusts
Lemon Substitutes

Although some would never dare to adulterate plain cheesecake, there are plenty of variations out there: some good, some bad, some ugly. Standing out against a Ben & Jerry's–style menu of flavors such as chocolate chip and cappuccino (and many more deplorable variations), lemon is the one version that serves a function by cutting through the cloying nature of this rich dessert.

During our initial recipe testing, we discovered a host of different lemon cheesecake styles. One was a towering soufflé made by separating the eggs, whipping the whites, and folding them in at the end. Another had a pasty texture owing to the addition of sweetened condensed milk. And in all cases the lemon flavor was either too fleeting or too harsh. What we wanted was a light, creamy-textured cheesecake, a style that everyone in the test kitchen felt would be a good partner with the flavor of lemon.

# LEMON CHEESECAKE

**WHAT WE WANTED:** A light, creamy cheesecake with a bracing but not overpowering lemon flavor.

We began our kitchen testing with the foundation of the cheesecake: the crust. Most cheesecakes have a sweet and spicy graham cracker crust that remains crunchy under the weight of the heavy filling. But after our first few attempts, we realized that the strong molasses flavor of the graham crackers overpowered the lemon. We experimented with several types of crumb crusts and ended up preferring one made with biscuit-type cookies. Of all the brands that we tried, Nabisco's Barnum's Animals Crackers were the surprise favorite (see the Tasting Lab on page 317).

We based our filling on our favorite creamy cheesecake recipe, which, although a bit heavy, came closest to our ideal. Our first move was to lighten it by reducing the amount of cream cheese from 2 pounds to 1½. Next we eliminated the sour cream because the addition of lemon provided a tangy counterpoint to the cream cheese. To our surprise, a bit more heavy cream was a good thing, producing a luscious texture.

As for the lemon flavor, we discovered that one can have too much of a good thing by using too much lemon

juice. Zest provided a balanced lemon flavor, but it came with a hitch: The fibrous texture of the zest marred the creamy smoothness of the filling. To solve this problem, we tried processing the zest and sugar together before adding them to the cream cheese. This produced a wonderfully potent lemon flavor by breaking down the zest and releasing its oils, but it also caused the cheesecake to become strangely dense. After many trials, we realized that the food processor was wreaking havoc with the sugar, breaking down its crystalline structure (necessary for the aeration of the cream cheese) as well as melding it with the oils from the lemon zest. By processing only ¼ cup of the sugar with the zest and then stirring in the remaining sugar by hand, we solved the problem.

Baking this cheesecake in a water bath at a low oven temperature of 325 degrees was also key to achieving a creamy texture. We were surprised to find that when we used hot tap water instead of boiling water (we like shortcuts), the result was a more evenly baked cheesecake (and about 10 minutes of extra baking time). We also discovered that an additional hour in the oven, with the heat off and the door ajar, was crucial to a consistent texture. When we tried to skip this step, the cheesecake set up on the edges but remained gooey in the center.

Our cheesecake was certainly lemony, but we wanted more pizzazz. We found it by revisiting a test recipe that had included a topping of lemon curd. We found we could make a curd in just five minutes and let it set up in the refrigerator while the cheesecake was baking and cooling.

Based on previous work done in the test kitchen for a lemon tart recipe, we knew three things about lemon curd: There must be enough acid to denature the proteins in the eggs and thereby form the curd; sugar helps to prevent the eggs from overcooking; and butter helps to emulsify the ingredients, creating a smoother product. Many recipes called for only yolks in the curd, but these were too rich. Curd made

---

## FOOD FACT: Animal Crackers

In the late 1800s these animal-shaped cookies were first imported to the United States from England, answering a demand for fancy baked goods. In 1902, Nabisco designed a box that looked just like a circus wagon cage and even attached a string so the box could be hung from the Christmas tree. Called Barnum's Animals, these crackers have remained popular for a century. Today the company bakes 19 animals into cracker likenesses. The newest animal to join the collection is the koala, which beat out the penguin, walrus, and cobra in recent voting by consumers.

with just two whole eggs was pale in color and lacked depth of flavor. Just one extra yolk gave the curd the right color and amount of richness. The only problem remaining was the curd's slightly acidic edge. To curb it, we mixed in 1 tablespoon of heavy cream at the end of cooking, along with a dash of vanilla. Cold cubed butter, also added at the end, served both to cool the curd (and prevent overcooking) and to form a smoother emulsion. The curd now complemented the cheesecake perfectly, adding a bit of easy showmanship to this otherwise plain dessert.

---

WHAT WE LEARNED: Use biscuit-type cookies, such as animal crackers, to create a mild-tasting crust that will let the lemon flavor of the cheesecake shine. Grind the zest with some of the sugar to release its flavor and improve its texture. Add heavy cream for richness, and bake the cake in a water bath for ultimate creaminess. Finally, top off the cake with lemon curd for another layer of lemon flavor.

## LEMON CHEESECAKE  Serves 12 to 16

While this recipe takes several hours from start to finish, the actual preparation is simple, and baking and cooling proceed practically unattended. Chill the finished cheesecake at least 4 hours before attempting to slice it. The cheesecake can be made up to a day in advance; leftovers can be refrigerated for up to 4 days, although the crust will become soggy.

### cookie-crumb crust

|   |   |
|---|---|
| 5 | ounces Nabisco's Barnum's Animals Crackers or Social Tea Biscuits |
| 3 | tablespoons sugar |
| 4 | tablespoons unsalted butter, melted and kept warm |

### filling

|   |   |
|---|---|
| 1¼ | cups (8¾ ounces) sugar |
| 1 | tablespoon grated zest plus ¼ cup juice from 1 or 2 lemons |
| 1½ | pounds (three 8-ounce packages) cream cheese, cut into rough 1-inch chunks and left to stand at room temperature 30 to 45 minutes |
| 4 | large eggs, room temperature |
| 2 | teaspoons vanilla extract |
| ¼ | teaspoon salt |
| ½ | cup heavy cream |

### lemon curd

|   |   |
|---|---|
| ⅓ | cup juice from 2 lemons |
| 2 | large eggs plus 1 large egg yolk |
| ½ | cup (3½ ounces) sugar |
| 2 | tablespoons unsalted butter, cut into ½-inch cubes and chilled |
| 1 | tablespoon heavy cream |
| ¼ | teaspoon vanilla extract |
|   | Pinch salt |

**1.** FOR THE CRUST: Adjust an oven rack to the lower-middle position and heat the oven to 325 degrees. In a food processor, process the cookies to fine, even crumbs, about 30 seconds (you should have about 1 cup). Add the sugar and pulse 2 or 3 times to incorporate. Add the warm melted butter in a slow, steady stream while pulsing; pulse until the mixture is evenly moistened and resembles wet sand, about ten 1-second pulses. Transfer the mixture to 9-inch springform pan; using the bottom of a ramekin or a dry measuring cup, press the crumbs firmly and evenly into the pan bottom, keeping the sides as clean as possible. Bake until fragrant and golden brown, 15 to 18 minutes. Cool on a wire rack to room temperature, about 30 minutes. When cool, wrap the outside of the pan with two 18-inch-square pieces of heavy-duty foil; set the springform pan in the roasting pan.

**2.** FOR THE FILLING: While the crust is cooling, process ¼ cup sugar and lemon zest in a food processor until the sugar is yellow and the zest is broken down, about 15 seconds, scraping down the bowl if necessary. Transfer the lemon sugar to a small bowl; stir in the remaining 1 cup sugar.

**3.** In a standing mixer fitted with the paddle attachment, beat the cream cheese on low to break up and soften slightly, about 5 seconds. With the machine running, add the sugar mixture in a slow steady stream; increase the speed to medium and continue to beat until the mixture is creamy and smooth, about 3 minutes, scraping down the bowl with a rubber spatula as needed. Reduce the speed to medium-low and add the eggs 2 at a time; beat until incorporated, about 30 seconds, scraping the sides and bottom of the bowl well after each addition. Add the lemon juice, vanilla, and salt and mix until just incorporated, about 5 seconds; add the heavy cream and mix until just incorporated, about 5 seconds longer. Give the batter a final scrape, stir with a rubber spatula, and pour into the prepared springform pan; fill the roasting pan with enough hot tap water to come halfway up the sides of the springform pan. Bake until the center jiggles slightly, the sides just start to puff, the surface is no longer shiny, and an instant-read thermometer inserted in the center of the cake registers 150 degrees, 55 to 60 minutes. Turn off the oven and prop open the oven door with a potholder or wooden spoon handle; allow the cake to cool in the water bath in the oven for 1 hour. Transfer the springform pan without the foil to a wire rack; run a small paring knife around the inside edge of the pan to loosen the sides of the cake, and cool the cake to room temperature, about 2 hours.

---

### GETTING IT RIGHT: Judging When the Curd Is Done

At first, the curd will appear thin and soupy, as shown at left. When the spatula leaves a clear trail in the bottom of the saucepan (which quickly disappears), the curd is ready to come off the heat (center). If the curd continues to cook, it will become too thick and pasty, and a spatula will leave a wide clear trail (right).

**4.** FOR THE LEMON CURD: While the cheesecake bakes, heat the lemon juice in a small nonreactive saucepan over medium heat until hot but not boiling. Whisk the eggs and yolk in a medium nonreactive bowl; gradually whisk in the sugar. Whisking constantly, slowly pour the hot lemon juice into the eggs, then return the mixture to the saucepan and cook over medium heat, stirring constantly with a wooden spoon, until the mixture registers 170 degrees on an instant-read thermometer and is thick enough to cling to a spoon, about 3 minutes (see the photos on page 316 to gauge doneness). Immediately remove the pan from the heat and stir in the cold butter until incorporated; stir in the cream, vanilla, and salt, then pour the curd through a fine-mesh strainer into a small nonreactive bowl. Cover the surface of the curd directly with plastic wrap; refrigerate until needed.

**5.** TO FINISH THE CAKE: When the cheesecake is cool, scrape the lemon curd onto the cheesecake still in the springform pan; using an offset icing spatula, spread the curd evenly over the top of the cheesecake. Cover tightly with plastic wrap and refrigerate for at least 4 hours or up to 24 hours. To serve, remove the sides of the springform pan and cut the cake into wedges.

---

### GETTING IT RIGHT: Chill Thoroughly

If the cheesecake is not thoroughly chilled, it will not hold its shape when sliced (left). After four hours in the refrigerator (preferably longer), the cheesecake has set up and can be sliced neatly (right).

---

### TASTING LAB: Cookies for Crumb Crusts

AFTER REJECTING GRAHAM CRACKERS IN FAVOR OF something more delicate, we decided to try shortbread cookies in the crust for our lemon cheesecake. Walkers Shortbread, Nabisco's Lorna Doones, and Keebler Sandies all produced crusts that were dense and chewy, with a toffee-like flavor that was too rich and sweet. Next we used digestive biscuits to make the crust. Although this crust was too sweet and a little gritty (these biscuits contain whole-wheat flour), the dryness of the biscuit produced the best-textured crust to complement the creamy cheesecake; it also let us add more butter to the crust, which resulted in a better flavor. After testing all of the biscuit-type cookies we could find, the surprising favorite was Barnum's Animals Crackers from Nabisco. Nabisco's Social Tea Biscuits were a close second.

**BEST COOKIES FOR CRUMB CRUST**
Biscuit-type cookies, especially Barnum's Animals Crackers from Nabisco, beat out shortbread cookies, digestive biscuits, and graham crackers in our tasting of 10 cookies for the crumb crust.

---

### TASTING LAB: Lemon Substitutes

FACED WITH THE TASK OF SQUEEZING LEMONS FOR BAKED goods, we wondered if there was an easier alternative. We found several possible timesaving products at the grocery store: Minute Maid frozen lemon juice made from concentrate and bottled reconstituted lemon juice made by ReaLemon and Concord Foods; both of the latter two products contain preservatives and lemon oil as well as lemon juice from concentrate. Would it be possible to make decent baked goods with these products, or would they result in cookies that tasted as plastic as the lemon-shaped squeeze bottle?

To give all three products a thorough testing, we tasted them two different ways: in lemonade and in glazed lemon cookies—intense, lemony cookies. The results of the lemonade tasting were no surprise. Tasters overwhelmingly preferred lemonade made with the freshly squeezed lemons. The lemonade made with frozen juice wasn't bad but "tasted like store-bought lemonade," and the reconstituted

juices tasted artificial and weak. When baked into cookies and made into a glaze, the differences were smaller but still noticeable. Tasters thought the cookies made with reconstituted juices were "acidic but not very lemony" and had the least amount of flavor. The frozen juice fared slightly better—the cookies had more lemon flavor. No surprise—the

---

**TECHNIQUE:** Juicing Lemons

Everyone has a trick for juicing lemons. After testing dozens of methods, we think this one extracts the most juice from lemons as well as limes.

1. Start by rolling the lemon on a hard surface, pressing down firmly with the palm of your hand to break the membranes inside the fruit.

2. Cut the lemon in half. Use a reamer with a pointed tip (see the Equipment Corner on page 250) to extract the juice. To catch the seeds, place a mesh strainer over the bowl.

---

**TECHNIQUE:** Cleaning the Food Processor Workbowl

The easiest way to clean bowls is to soak them with sudsy water before washing. However, the hole in the center of a food processor workbowl makes this impossible, unless you plug up that hole. Here's how we do it in the test kitchen.

1. Remove the bowl cover and blade. Set an empty 35mm film canister upside down over the hole in the workbowl.

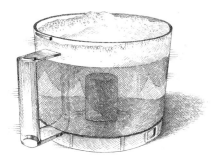

2. Now you can fill the bowl with warm, soapy water and allow it to soak.

---

cookies made with fresh lemon juice were "nice and tangy" and "tasted the most like lemons."

The verdict? Get out your cutting board and lemon reamer. It's best to squeeze your own lemon juice, even for baked goods.

## SCIENCE DESK:
### Why Bother with a Water Bath?

A WATER BATH IS COMMONLY CALLED FOR WHEN BAKING cheesecakes and custards. The theory is that the water bath moderates the temperature around the perimeter of the pan, preventing overcooking at the edges. To figure out exactly what's happening, we prepared two identical cheesecakes; one was placed in an oven alone while the other was placed in a water bath before baking. Both were taken from the oven when their centers reached 147 degrees. The cake that had

been baked in a water bath was even-colored and smooth, while the other had browned and cracked. A quick comparison of the temperature at the edges of the cakes confirmed what we suspected. The cake that had had the benefit of a water bath was 184 degrees at the edge, while the cake baked without the water bath had climbed to 213 degrees.

Why was the cheesecake baked in a water bath 30 degrees cooler at the edges than the cake baked without the water bath? Although the oven had been set to 325 degrees, a water bath can never exceed 212 degrees, as this is the temperature at which water converts to steam. In fact, more than half of the water in the bath had indeed evaporated, resulting in quite a humid oven. The increased water content of the air in the oven served to keep the top of the cake moist and to prevent cracking. For five minutes of work, then, our water bath protected the edges of the cake by keeping the temperature low and protected the top of the cake through added humidity.

## EQUIPMENT CORNER: Springform Pans

ALTHOUGH SELDOM USED IN MOST HOME KITCHENS, A springform pan is essential if you want to make cheesecake, chocolate mousse cake, or any other cake that would be impossible to release intact from a standard cake pan. We baked cheesecake and chocolate mousse cake in six (9-inch) springform pans, ranging in price from $9 to $38, to see if more money bought a better pan.

An ideal pan, we thought, would release the cakes from the sides and bottom of the pan effortlessly. All six pans tested had acceptable side release, but dislodging a cake from the pan bottom was trickier. Here, the top-performing pans were the Kaiser Bakeware Noblesse and the Frieling Glass Bottom, each of which has a rimless bottom; the other four pans tested have a ridge around the outside edge that can get in the way of cake removal. We also found that pans with rimless bottoms are much easier to clean.

Another valuable quality in a springform pan is its resistance to leakage when placed in a water bath. To test leakage, we baked cheesecakes in a water bath tinted with green food coloring, our theory being that the less secure the seal of the pan, the more water would seep through and the greener the cheesecake. This was a tough test. Even the best-performing pan in this test, the Kaiser Noblesse, showed an edge of green that traveled in a ring around one third of the cake. The worst performers here were the Kaiser Bakeware Tinplate and the Cuisipro Tall Tinned pan, in which the green made a complete circle around the outside edge of the cake. Of all the pans tested, these two also had the most flimsy construction and were the cheapest, priced at $8.99 and $9.99, respectively. The Frieling pan as well as the Roscho Commercial ($12.99) and the Exeter Non-Stick ($11.49) showed decent performance in this test. Because no pan demonstrated a perfect seal, we recommend wrapping the bottom of a springform pan with foil when baking in a water bath.

The good news is that we found two pans we like quite a lot. The bad news is that they were the priciest pans tested.

# Rating Springform Pans

WE TESTED SIX 9-INCH SPRINGFORM PANS BY BAKING A CHEESECAKE AND A CHOCOLATE MOUSSE CAKE (SEE RECIPE ON page 326) in each pan. We rated the pans for ease of release (from the sides as well as the bottom), leakage (we dyed a water bath green to see how much water was getting into each pan), and design (including their overall construction). The pans are listed in order of preference based on scores from these tests. See www.americastestkitchen.com for up-to-date prices and mail-order sources for top-rated products.

---

**RECOMMENDED**
### Kaiser Bakeware Noblesse Springform Pan
**$19.80**
This well-made pan won the leak test. It is well constructed and well designed. The rimless bottom means removing cakes is especially easy.

---

**RECOMMENDED**
### Frieling Handle-It Glass Bottom Springform Pan
**$31.95**
The handles come in handy when lifting this pricey pan out of a water bath. The rimless bottom means removing cakes is especially easy.

---

**RECOMMENDED WITH RESERVATIONS**
### Roscho Commercial Springform Pan
**$12.99**
Decent performance in the leak test, but the rimmed bottom gets in the way when trying to remove cakes at serving time.

---

**RECOMMENDED WITH RESERVATIONS**
### Exeter Non-Stick Springform Pan
**$11.49**
Minimal leaking, but the rimmed bottom makes removal of neat slices somewhat tricky. The rim also makes cleanup more tedious than is necessary.

---

**NOT RECOMMENDED**
### Kaiser Bakeware Tinplate Springform Pan
**$8.99**
This pan performed poorly in the leak test (the green food dye made a complete circle around the edge of the cake), and it does not seem well constructed.

---

**NOT RECOMMENDED**
### Cuisipro Tall Tinned Springform Pan
**$9.99**
Flimsy construction and serious leaking sunk this pan to the bottom of the ratings. Again, the rimmed bottom made it difficult to remove neat slices from this pan.

Foil collars are attached to ceramic ramekins so that individual chilled lemon soufflés can rise high above the rims of the dishes.

# SHOWSTOPPER
## desserts

CHAPTER 26

IN THIS CHAPTER

**THE RECIPES**

Bittersweet Chocolate Mousse
    Cake
Chocolate-Orange Mousse Cake

Chilled Lemon Soufflé
Chilled Lemon Soufflé with
    White Chocolate
Individual Chilled Lemon Soufflés

**SCIENCE DESK**

Why Add Cream of Tartar When
    Beating Egg Whites?

**TASTING LAB**

Unsweetened Chocolate

In the test kitchen, we tend to favor simple, homespun desserts. Most of us would rather make a batch of really good cookies than a fancy cake or tart. That said, we all recognize the need for showy desserts, especially when entertaining. A plate of chocolate chip cookies just won't do after some meals.

On these occasions, we like desserts that look more complicated to prepare than they really are. A chocolate mousse cake requires a minimum of ingredients and comes together in minutes, but it is sure to elicit the proper oohs and aahs from guests. A chilled lemon soufflé is made from ingredients that probably are in your kitchen right now—eggs, milk, lemon, sugar, and cream. Even better, this soufflé must be prepared in advance, making it far more suitable for entertaining than the more familiar baked soufflés that must go straight from oven to table. We hope these two easy but special desserts will become favorites in your home.

# CHOCOLATE MOUSSE CAKE

**WHAT WE WANTED:** Chocolate mousse cake runs the gamut from fluffy, insubstantial layer cake to dense-as-a-brick, fudge-like slab. Could we make one that maintained the qualities of a perfect chocolate mousse—rich, creamy, and full of chocolate flavor?

Chocolate mousse is comfort food dressed up for company, like pudding for grownups. Less familiar to most home cooks is the chocolate mousse cake. After investigating local bakeries, we discovered that this dessert has two distinct styles. One was a fancy, fluffy chocolate sponge layer cake, brushed with syrup, with mousse sandwiched between the layers. The other was essentially chocolate mousse baked in a cake pan, almost cheesecake-like in density. Before deciding on one style, we'd have to make both.

The sponge cake/mousse combination was incredibly time-consuming (make the cake, cool the cake, cut the cake, make the syrup, soak the cake, make the mousse, assemble the cake, chill the cake—whew). An enormous sinkful of dishes and several grueling hours later, we tasted the cake. Its elegant appearance couldn't make up for its lack of chocolate flavor. This cake was a dud—all show and no substance. Although we could work on improving the flavor, we decided not to try. This cake was simply too much work for the home cook.

The baked mousse was much simpler—a major benefit—but it came out of the oven a dense, homely mess. Texture and appearance aside, however, this ugly duckling showed promise. The flavor was excellent: fudgy, chocolatey, and very, very rich. With a more mousse-like texture and a bit of a facelift, this cake could be a winner.

The ingredient list for chocolate mousse cake is short: chocolate, sugar, butter, eggs, vanilla, and salt. We tackled the most important ingredient first: the chocolate. We tried grocery-store brands as well as a few high-end boutique chocolates and determined that Hershey's Special Dark made a great cake with nicely balanced chocolate flavor. Baker's Bittersweet Chocolate was less successful, having an artificial aftertaste that tasters rejected. Other, more expensive brands worked, but we decided to stick to the more widely available Hershey's, which had also done well in a previous tasting of bittersweet chocolates.

But bittersweet chocolate alone didn't bring the intensity we were looking for. We tried cocoa, but it gave the cake a sour flavor. After some experimentation, we found that adding a mere ounce of unsweetened chocolate to 12 ounces of bittersweet provided a deep, chocolatey taste and a darker, slightly more sophisticated quality. (See the Tasting Lab on page 327 for information about buying unsweetened chocolate.)

Butter and egg yolks are the ingredients that give this cake its melt-in-your-mouth texture. Twelve tablespoons was the perfect amount of butter. Any more made the cake unpalatably greasy; less made it dry. As for egg yolks, we made cakes using as few as four and as many as 10. The 10-yolk version remained a little too damp in the middle, even when thoroughly baked. Eight was the magic number. Some vanilla and a pinch of salt heightened the chocolate flavor even more. The vanilla does double duty: It rounds out the smokiness of the chocolate, giving the cake slightly fruity overtones, while taming the egginess of the yolks.

The final ingredient in this cake is beaten egg whites, which are folded into the batter just before it goes into the oven. But folding the beaten egg whites into the chocolate mixture was proving problematic. The delicate whites collapsed under the weight of the chocolate, giving the cake a dense, bricklike texture. Was there anything we could do to make the whites sturdier? We tried beating the egg whites further, until they were almost rigid. That wasn't the answer; it just made the cake unappealingly dry. Maybe beating the whites less rigorously was the answer. No such luck. That

made the cake even more dense. We looked again at the mousse cake recipes we had found in our initial research. All of them called for the sugar to be added to the yolks and chocolate. We decided to add the sugar, along with a pinch of cream of tartar, to the whites instead. (Sugar creates a thicker, more stable egg foam, and acids, such as cream of tartar, help prevent egg foams from collapsing.) Finally, we had uncovered the secret to the perfect texture. This method produced a creamy meringue that held up well when folded into the chocolate mixture and produced a baked mousse cake that was moist, rich, and creamy.

We tried baking the cake at 350 degrees, the standard temperature for most cakes. Not for this one. It turned into a giant mushroom that collapsed after cooling. A more gentle heat was clearly necessary. We tried lowering the temperature, but even at 300 degrees the outside of the cake was overdone while the center remained raw. Baking the mousse cake in a water bath—an extra complication we had hoped to avoid—might do the trick. We placed the mousse-filled springform pan in a roasting pan, filled the roasting pan with hot water, and put it all in the oven. Once again, we tried baking the cake at 350, 325, and 300 degrees. The cake baked at 325 degrees was perfect. It rose evenly and had a velvety, creamy texture throughout. That extra step was definitely worth the effort.

Now we had a cake with great texture, but there was still something missing. The chocolate flavor was intense but still a little too sweet and one-dimensional. Perhaps reducing the sugar was the answer. Not so. It only made the cake slightly bitter. On a whim, we tried using light brown sugar instead of granulated white sugar. The flavor was fabulous, with just the right amount of sweetness and a tiny hint of smokiness from the molasses. Brown sugar offered an additional bonus. The molasses in brown sugar is slightly acidic, eliminating the need for cream of tartar (another acid) to stabilize the egg whites. When beaten together, the whites and brown sugar turned into a glossy, perfect meringue.

Our chocolate mousse cake was rich and creamy, with tremendous chocolate flavor, and it was also pretty easy to make. What more could a chocoholic ask?

**WHAT WE LEARNED:** For the best chocolate punch, use bittersweet chocolate mixed with a bit of unsweetened chocolate. Beat the egg whites with brown sugar for hint of smoky molasses flavor. The acidity in the brown sugar also stabilizes the beaten whites, so they can folded into the heavy batter without collapsing. Finally, bake the cake in a water bath for a velvety, creamy texture.

## BITTERSWEET CHOCOLATE MOUSSE CAKE

Makes one 9-inch cake, serving 12 to 16

Because it is available in most supermarkets and has scored highly in past tastings, Hershey's Special Dark is the chocolate of choice in this recipe. Other bittersweet chocolates will work, but because the amounts of sugar and cocoa butter differ from brand to brand, they will produce cakes with slightly different textures and flavors. When crumbling the brown sugar to remove lumps, make sure that your fingers are clean and grease-free; any residual fat from butter or chocolate might hinder the whipping of the whites. If you like, dust the cake with confectioners' sugar just before serving or top slices with a dollop of lightly sweetened whipped cream. To make slicing easier, freeze the cake for 30 minutes just before serving.

12   tablespoons (1½ sticks) unsalted butter, cut into 12 pieces, plus 1 teaspoon softened butter for greasing pan
     Flour for dusting pan
12   ounces bittersweet chocolate (such as Hershey's Special Dark), chopped
1    ounce unsweetened chocolate, chopped
1    tablespoon vanilla extract
8    large eggs, separated
⅛    teaspoon salt
⅔    cup (4½ ounces) packed light brown sugar, crumbled with fingers to remove lumps (see note)

**1.** Adjust an oven rack to the lower-middle position and heat the oven to 325 degrees. Butter the sides of a 9-inch springform pan; flour the sides and tap out the excess. Line the bottom of the pan with a parchment or waxed paper round. Wrap the bottom and sides of the pan with a large sheet of foil.

**2.** Melt 12 tablespoons butter and the chocolates in a large bowl over a large saucepan containing about 2 quarts barely simmering water, stirring occasionally, until the chocolate

mixture is smooth. Cool the mixture slightly, then whisk in the vanilla and egg yolks. Set the chocolate mixture aside, reserving the hot water, covered, in the saucepan.

**3.** In the clean bowl of a standing mixer fitted with the whisk attachment, beat the egg whites and salt at medium speed until frothy, about 30 seconds; add half of the crumbled brown sugar, beat at high speed until combined, about 30 seconds, then add the remaining brown sugar and continue to beat at high speed until soft peaks form when the whisk is lifted (see photo on page 334), about 2 minutes longer. Using a whisk, stir about one third of the beaten egg whites into the chocolate mixture to lighten it, then fold in the remaining egg whites in 2 additions, using the whisk. Gently scrape the batter into the prepared springform pan, set the springform pan in a large roasting pan, then pour the hot water from the saucepan into the roasting pan to a depth of 1 inch. Carefully slide the roasting pan into the oven; bake until the cake has risen, is firm around the edges, the center has just set, and an instant-read thermometer inserted into the center registers about 170 degrees, 45 to 55 minutes.

**4.** Remove the springform pan from the water bath, discard the foil, and cool on a wire rack 10 minutes. Run a thin-bladed paring knife between the sides of the pan and cake to loosen; cool the cake in the springform pan on a wire rack until barely warm, about 3 hours, then wrap the pan in plastic wrap and refrigerate until thoroughly chilled, at least 8 hours. (The cake can be refrigerated for up to 2 days.)

**5.** To unmold the cake, remove the sides of the pan. Slide a thin metal spatula between the cake and pan bottom to loosen, then invert the cake onto a large plate, peel off the parchment, and re-invert onto a serving platter. To serve, use a sharp, thin-bladed knife, dipping the knife in a pitcher of hot water and wiping the blade before each cut.

### VARIATION
### CHOCOLATE-ORANGE MOUSSE CAKE
Follow the recipe for Bittersweet Chocolate Mousse Cake, reducing the vanilla extract to 1 teaspoon and adding 1 tablespoon orange liqueur and 1 tablespoon finely grated orange zest to the chocolate mixture along with the vanilla and egg yolks.

---

## TASTING LAB: Unsweetened Chocolate

LIKE HOLLYWOOD, THE WORLD OF CHOCOLATE HAS celebrities, some of whom earn their fame through stellar performances, while others simply coast on favorable publicity. We wanted to see if all of the fuss over premium chocolates was based on quality or hype. We selected unsweetened chocolate (rather than semi- or bittersweet) because it is a building-block ingredient in countless desserts, most notably brownies and chocolate cake. Not for nibbling, it is pure, unadulterated chocolate, or solidified chocolate liquor, produced without added sugar or flavorings (see "Chocolate Glossary" on page 329 for more definitions). Seven brands were rated: the four American supermarket standbys—Baker's, Ghirardelli, Hershey's, and Nestlé; the premium American brand, Scharffen Berger; and two brands used largely by candy makers and pastry chefs, Callebaut from Belgium and Valrhona from France. We

---

> **FOOD FACT: Chocolate**
>
> Although Americans love chocolate, our affair with this heavenly foodstuff pales in comparison with the passions of citizens of other countries around the world. The average American consumes more than 11 pounds of chocolate a year, putting us 11th in per capita consumption. The Swiss take top honors, devouring more than 22 pounds of chocolate per person every year. Austria, Ireland, Germany, and Norway round out the top five leading consumers of chocolate.

conducted a blind tasting, sampling a classic American brownie and a chocolate sauce.

Our assumption going into this tasting (based on prior taste tests) was that, in general, the more expensive brands would prevail. In fact, this was the outcome. However, we found a surprising range of taste differences from one brand to the next. If unsweetened chocolate is pure chocolate, how could one brand be so different from another? We spent weeks searching for the answer to this question, encountering red herrings, unhelpful company representatives, and conflicting stories along the way.

The first thing we learned was that most chocolate companies don't like to talk about their product in detail. With the exception of Scharffen Berger, the companies we contacted were distinctly vague. The response from Marie Olson of Nestlé said it all: "Most of what we do is proprietary. Nestlé has established a certain flavor profile, and we blend beans from various sources based on availability and cost to match our profile."

We turned to outside experts to uncover the trade secrets of chocolate manufacturers. One was Maricel Presilla, author of *The New Taste of Chocolate: A Cultural and Natural History of Cacao with Recipes* (Ten Speed Press, 2001). "Normally," she told us, "companies use a lower-priced bulk bean—from Malaysia, Indonesia, the Dominican Republic, or the Ivory Coast—for their unsweetened. I would not use a company's unsweetened as a barometer for the quality of any brand. With a few notable exceptions, that is not where a company uses their best beans." A cacao trader who sells to most of the major chocolate companies and wished to remain unnamed agreed. "They don't use their best beans for unsweetened. After all, you don't put your best burgundy in a coq au vin." The irony of this practice is that there is more chocolate in unsweetened than in any other type, so the quality of the beans may matter more, not less.

Every expert we contacted told us that the flavor of unsweetened chocolate is largely determined before it gets to the chocolate processor. Country of origin and specific bean blend are the most critical factors. In fact, the above-mentioned cacao trader said, "If you gave Scharffen Berger Nestlé's beans and they put it through their process, the chocolate would taste like Nestlé." Scharffen Berger cofounder Robert Steinberg concurred, adding, "A processor can ruin a good bean but cannot make good chocolate from an inferior one." Both comments underscore a simple fact: When it comes to making chocolate, you have to start with good ingredients. If this is the case, however, then why don't all companies purchase the highest quality beans?

Cacao beans come mainly from West Africa, Indonesia, Brazil, and Malaysia, with smaller amounts coming from other South American countries and the Caribbean. Each region has diverse outputs and characteristics. If a flavor profile includes, say, the taste of coffee, a company would select West African beans; for floral notes, Ecuadorian arriba; for fruity flavor, beans from Venezuela and Trinidad; and for citrus flavor, beans from Madagascar.

Scharffen Berger's Steinberg allows that taste is his company's priority when it comes to buying beans, and he is willing to pay more to secure that taste. "Without exception," he said "we are paying above-market prices for our beans." But some companies can't afford the luxury of buying the best-flavored beans, and it's not necessarily because of the price. Large companies may use 10,000 tons of beans per year, so what is most important to them is supply. They need to buy chocolate from a region that consistently produces a large amount, such as West Africa. They cannot risk a short supply from Venezuela, for instance, which produces a tiny amount of some of the best beans.

We concluded that the really big players in the unsweetened chocolate business use a more limited mix of beans because their volume demands exclude smaller suppliers. This in turn may make the flavor profile of their product less interesting.

If the quality of a bean is one important determinant of flavor, the blend of beans selected is another. "One great bean can give you a flat taste, whereas a blend of many can give you more depth," said the cacao trader. Greg Ziegler, associate professor of food science at Penn State University, agreed, pointing out that roasting is yet another key step in the process. Of most interest, according to Ziegler, is whether a company roasts bean types individually or together.

Other experts agree that roasting varieties of beans separately allows the roaster to be more selective and to both preserve and concentrate flavor. Beans vary in size, moisture content, and acidity, and as a result they require different roasting temperatures and times. "If you mix everything

together," said Presilla, "you're not doing justice to any bean; you destroy the nuances. Beans should be roasted independently." Of the companies whose chocolate we tasted, Scharffen Berger is the only one that would confirm that it roasts beans separately by type. Although many experts vouch for roasting independently, our tasting results suggest it's not the only way to produce a high-quality chocolate. In fact, a spokesperson for third-place Ghirardelli noted that the company roasts all types of beans together.

One final production issue is conching, which aerates and homogenizes the chocolate, thereby mellowing the flavor and making its texture smooth and creamy. While eating chocolates are always conched, only Scharffen Berger and Valrhona conch their unsweetened chocolate, and these chocolates finished first and third in our chocolate sauce tasting, where smooth texture was an important consideration.

What do we recommend? The more expensive chocolates—Scharffen Berger, Callebaut, Ghirardelli, and Valrhona—were all well liked and received similar scores. If you are willing to buy in bulk by mail, Callebaut turns out to be a best buy. Of the three mass-market brands (Nestlé, Baker's, and Hershey's), Nestlé received more positive comments and significantly higher scores. In fact, there were so many negative comments about Baker's and Hershey's that we cannot recommend either chocolate. It's important to remember, though, that chocolate, much like coffee, is a matter of personal preference, so consider each brand to find a chocolate that suits your palate. The gamut of flavors runs from "nutty" and "cherry" to "smoky," "earthy," and "spicy."

## CHOCOLATE GLOSSARY

HERE ARE DEFINITIONS FOR VARIOUS KINDS OF CHOCOLATE as well as the products that are precursors in the process of making eating chocolates.

Cacao Beans: Seeds harvested from fleshy yellow pods that grow on cacao trees.

Nibs: The meats of cacao beans, which get ground into chocolate liquor.

Chocolate Liquor: The thick, nonalcoholic liquid that results when the roasted, hulled beans (nibs, see above) are ground.

Cocoa Butter: The fat that can be extracted from chocolate liquor. It is not a dairy product.

Cocoa Powder: The solids that remain after the cocoa butter is extracted. When the solids are dried, they are processed and then either "Dutched" (treated with alkali) or left as is.

Unsweetened Chocolate: Solidified pure chocolate liquor that contains between 50 percent and 60 percent cocoa butter.

Bittersweet/Semisweet Chocolate: Chocolate that contains at least 35 percent chocolate liquor. The remainder is sugar, vanilla and/or lecithin.

Milk Chocolate: Chocolate made primarily from sugar, at least 10 percent chocolate liquor, milk solids, vanilla and/or lecithin.

# Rating Unsweetened Chocolates

TWENTY MEMBERS OF THE *COOK'S ILLUSTRATED* STAFF AND FOUR PASTRY CHEFS TASTED THE CHOCOLATES IN TWO applications. Because unsweetened chocolate, which does not contain sugar or milk solids, is an ingredient that is not eaten in its raw form, we tested it in brownies and in chocolate sauce. The chocolates are listed in order of preference based on the combined scores from these two tests. These chocolates are sold in gourmet shops or supermarkets.

**RECOMMENDED**

### Scharffen Berger Unsweetened Pure Dark Chocolate $8.95 for 275 grams ($14.78/pound)

Scharffen Berger chocolate is made in small batches from high-quality beans from small producers with refurbished vintage equipment from Europe. Tasters described this American chocolate as "fruity" and "nutty," with a "deep, caramelized flavor."

**RECOMMENDED**

### Callebaut Unsweetened Chocolate $11.95 for 1 kilogram ($5.43/pound)

Belgian Callebaut is the number one chocolate manufacturer in the world and a favorite of pastry chefs. In both tests, our tasters ranked this chocolate second and described it as "nutty," with hints of "cinnamon" and "cherry." One devotee called it "spicy," while another said it had "deep, chocolate flavor."

**RECOMMENDED**

### Ghirardelli Unsweetened Chocolate Baking Bar $2.19 for 4 ounces ($8.76/pound)

Testers regularly used the adjectives "coffee," "rich," and "earthy" when commenting on this sample. One panelist described the Ghirardelli brownie as "normal," which may explain its top finish in that test.

**RECOMMENDED**

### Valrhona Cacao Pâte Extra $25.00 for 1 kilogram ($11.36/pound)

A French chocolate available in unsweetened only in bulk, it often elicited the words "cherry," "fruity," "wine," and "rich." One detractor said that it "tasted more like flowers than chocolate," while another found it "dull."

**RECOMMENDED**

### Nestlé Unsweetened Baking Chocolate Bars $1.99 for 8 ounces ($3.98/pound)

The only chocolate in our group processed with alkali; our lab found it significantly higher in pH (or lower in acidity). Its fat content was the highest at 58.42%. A basic chocolate that fans called "earthy" and "nutty" and detractors described as "smoky," "scorched," or "dull."

**NOT RECOMMENDED**

### Baker's Unsweetened Baking Chocolate Squares $2.39 for 8 ounces ($4.78/pound)

The unsweetened chocolate we all have in our kitchens was considered "smoky," "acidic," and "bitter," but a few fans found it "rich" and "earthy." One taster described it as "dry and mealy," while another said it "didn't have much chocolate flavor."

**NOT RECOMMENDED**

### Hershey's Unsweetened Baking Chocolate $2.19 for 8 ounces ($4.38/pound)

Hershey's adds cocoa to its unsweetened chocolate, which came in last in both tastings. Tasters found it "acidic," "muted," and "chemical-y." One described its flavor as having a "hint of anchovy," while another said it was "plain and dull."

# CHILLED LEMON SOUFFLÉ

**WHAT WE WANTED:** An ethereal, creamy dessert that dissolves on the tongue and satisfies with a complex lemon flavor.

Based on a classic Bavarian cream, chilled lemon soufflé is most often a mixture of a custard base, gelatin, whipped cream, beaten egg whites, sugar, and lemon flavorings. But like any good mongrel American classic, "chilled lemon soufflé" covers a wide range of recipes, from baked pudding cakes, which are cooled and served at room temperature, to nothing more than lemon juice, sugar, and beaten whites, with no egg yolks and no whipped cream.

Given these various guises, it's hard to know exactly how this dessert should taste. For us, a chilled lemon soufflé is an unusual marriage of cream and foam, of sweet and sour, of high lemony notes and lingering, rich custard. It starts at the tip of the tongue with the sharp tingle of lemon zest and then slides slowly down the throat, filling the mouth with cream and pudding and a soft, long finish. At least that's what it is supposed to do. The question is, how can a home cook make this delicate balance of ingredients and technique turn out just right? We set out to test as many recipes as possible to find out.

After testing several recipes, we discovered that there are five basic approaches to this dessert. The most elaborate begins with a custard base that is then combined with gelatin, whipped cream, and beaten egg whites. Many recipes, however, leave out the custard, using only beaten egg yolks and sugar as the base, while some classic French versions of this dish also leave out the egg whites. Other recipes omit the egg yolks altogether, using just sugar, lemon juice, whipped cream, and beaten egg whites. If the whipped cream is eliminated in a further act of reductionism, you have what is known as a lemon snow pudding. We also looked up recipes for lemon mousse and found that mousse is usually made without gelatin, the key ingredient in chilled lemon soufflé.

We began our testing with the simplest approach, just beaten egg whites, gelatin, sugar, and lemon juice. The result was a foamy confection, much like being served a mound of beaten egg whites. This dessert needed some fat for texture and flavor. We then thought we would try a recipe with whipped cream as well. This was quite good, rated number one by some tasters. It had lots of lemon punch but a somewhat airy, foamy texture that called for a bit more fat. Next, we added beaten egg yolks to the mixture, perhaps the most common approach to chilled lemon soufflé, but the texture of this version of the dessert was tough. We tried a second variation on this theme and were still unsatisfied with the texture. We then left out the egg whites and produced a dense, rubbery lemon dome, the sort of dessert that might hold up nicely in Death Valley in July. Finally, we started with a custard base made with sugar, egg yolks, milk, lemon juice, and gelatin and then added this to the whipped cream and beaten whites. This was highly rated, but the lemon flavor was a bit muted by the fat in the milk and egg yolks.

Upon reviewing the test results, we decided that a compromise might be reached between the two test

winners. The lemon juice/whipped cream/beaten egg-white dessert was light and lemony but too foamy; the custard base dessert had a better finish and mouthfeel but was lacking the bright, clear flavor of lemon. We worked up a new master recipe that called for softening one package of gelatin in a half cup of lemon juice. (We tried two packages of gelatin and ended up with a rubbery orb.) Next, a cup of milk was heated with sugar while we beat two egg yolks with an extra 2 tablespoons of sugar. The milk and the beaten yolks were combined on top of the stove and heated until the mixture began to steam. Finally, the cooled custard was folded into ¾ cup of whipped heavy cream, and six beaten egg whites were folded into the result. This was the best variation to date, but it still needed a few refinements.

First, we cut back the whites from six to five to give the dessert less air and more substance. Next, we added just ¼ teaspoon of cornstarch to the custard mixture to prevent the yolks from curdling too easily, and we added grated lemon zest to the custard mixture to pump up the lemon flavor. We also discovered that to maintain a more consistent texture it

was better to whisk a small part of the beaten egg whites into the custard base before folding the mixture together.

Although many recipes call for individual ramekins, we decided to make one large and impressive soufflé and save the individual portions for a variation. To make this chilled dessert look even more like its baked cousin, we added a simple collar of aluminum foil and increased the recipe to the point where the mixture would rise above the rim of the dish, much like a real soufflé. We were also curious about how well this dessert would hold up in the refrigerator. After one day, it was still good but slightly foamy, losing the creamy, tender undercurrent that is the hallmark of this dessert when well made. After two and three days, it quickly deteriorated. This is one dessert that is best served the day it is made.

WHAT WE LEARNED: Start with a silky custard base (milk, egg yolks, sugar, and lemon juice) and lighten it with whipped cream and beaten egg whites. Stabilize the mixture with gelatin and use grated lemon zest for an extra citrus punch.

## CHILLED LEMON SOUFFLÉ  Serves 4 to 6

To make this lemon soufflé "soufflé" over the rim of the dish, use a 1-quart soufflé dish and make a foil collar for it as follows: Cut a piece of foil 3 inches longer than the circumference of the soufflé dish and fold it lengthwise into fourths. Wrap the foil strip around the upper half of the soufflé dish and secure the overlap with tape. Tape the collar to the soufflé dish as necessary to prevent it from slipping. Spray the inside of the foil collar with vegetable cooking spray. When ready to serve, carefully remove the collar.

For those less concerned with appearance, this dessert can be served from any 1½-quart serving bowl. For best texture, serve the soufflé after 1½ hours of chilling. It may be chilled up to 6 hours; though the texture will stiffen slightly because of the gelatin, it will taste just as good.

½  cup lemon juice from 2 or 3 lemons, plus 2½ teaspoons grated zest
1  packet (¼ ounce) unflavored gelatin
1  cup whole milk
¾  cup sugar
5  large egg whites, plus 2 yolks, at room temperature
¼  teaspoon cornstarch
   Pinch cream of tartar
¾  cup heavy cream
   Mint, raspberries, confectioners' sugar, or finely chopped pistachios for garnish (optional)

**1.** Place the lemon juice in a small nonreactive bowl; sprinkle the gelatin over. Set aside.

**2.** Heat the milk and ½ cup sugar in a medium saucepan over medium-low heat, stirring occasionally, until steaming and the sugar is dissolved, about 5 minutes. Meanwhile, whisk together the yolks, 2 tablespoons sugar, and cornstarch in a medium bowl until pale yellow and thickened. Whisking constantly, gradually add the hot milk to the yolks. Return the milk-egg mixture to the saucepan and cook, stirring constantly, over medium-low heat until the foam has dissipated to a thin layer and the mixture thickens to the consistency of heavy cream and registers 185 degrees on an instant-read thermometer, about 4 minutes. Pour the mixture through a mesh sieve and into a medium bowl; stir in the lemon juice mixture and zest. Set the bowl with the custard in a large bowl of ice water; stir occasionally to cool.

**3.** While the custard mixture is chilling, in the bowl of a standing mixer fitted with the whisk attachment, beat the egg whites and cream of tartar on medium speed until foamy, about 1 minute. Increase the speed to medium-high; gradually add the remaining 2 tablespoons sugar and continue to beat until glossy and the whites hold soft peaks when the beater is lifted, about 2 minutes longer. Do not overbeat. Remove the bowl containing the custard mixture from the ice water bath; gently whisk in about one third of the egg whites, then fold in the remaining whites with a large rubber spatula until almost no white streaks remain.

**4.** In the same mixer bowl (washing is not necessary), using the whisk attachment, beat the cream on medium-high speed until soft peaks form when the beater is lifted, 2 to 3 minutes. Fold the cream into the custard and egg-white mixture until no white streaks remain.

**5.** Pour into the prepared soufflé dish (see note) or bowl. Chill until set but not stiff, about 1½ hours; remove the foil collar, if using, and serve, garnishing if desired.

VARIATIONS

### CHILLED LEMON SOUFFLÉ WITH WHITE CHOCOLATE

The white chocolate in this variation subdues the lemony kick. The difference is subtle, but the sweeter, richer flavor and texture was popular among tasters.

Follow the recipe for Chilled Lemon Soufflé, adding 2 ounces chopped white chocolate to the warm custard before adding the lemon juice mixture and the zest. Stir until melted and fully incorporated.

### INDIVIDUAL CHILLED LEMON SOUFFLÉS

Follow the recipe for Chilled Lemon Soufflé, dividing the batter equally among eight ¾-cup ramekins (filled to the rim) or six ¾-cup ramekins with foil collars.

---

SCIENCE DESK: **Why Add Cream of Tartar When Beating Egg Whites?**

---

IN MOST KITCHENS, IN THE BACK OF THE SPICE CUPBOARD, you will find an aged tin of cream of tartar covered with some dust. We obediently add it when whipping egg whites, but otherwise leave this curious white powder alone.

What is cream of tartar and how does it work? Its technical name is acid potassium tartrate, and it is derived from a crystalline acid deposited on the inside of wine barrels as the wine ferments. It is known as an acid salt, that

is, an acid that has been partially neutralized to leave a weakly acidic salt.

Egg whites have the miraculous ability to increase their volume over eight-fold when provided with enough energy by means of a strong arm or a good mixer. Mechanical energy causes strands of the protein albumin to partially unfold and connect with one another. These interconnected albumin strands can wrap around air bubbles and lead to foam development.

As anyone who has made egg foams can tell you, it is an imperfect art ripe with opportunities for collapse. Cream of tartar, because of its acidic nature, gives the cook a leg up by lowering the alkaline pH of the egg whites from about 9 to 8. This change in pH helps neutralize certain proteins that tend to repel each other and encourages their association. The result is easier development of a more stable foam.

Our kitchen tests have confirmed that egg whites beaten with cream of tartar achieve greater volume than egg whites beaten on their own. In addition, egg whites beaten with cream of tartar will not collapse as quickly as egg whites beaten on their own. When it comes time to beat egg whites, we suggest that you dust off that tin of cream of tartar.

---

**GETTING IT RIGHT:** Beating Egg Whites

The egg whites should be beaten until they appear smooth and creamy. When the beater is lifted out of the bowl, the egg whites should hold a soft peak (left). If the egg whites are beaten too long, they will look dry and grainy and will begin to separate (right).

---

# INDEX

## A

Ale and Onion Sauce, Pan-Roasted Chicken
    Breasts with, 134
Almond:
    Apricot Oatmeal Scones, 246
    -Crusted Chicken Cutlets with Wilted
        Spinach–Orange Salad, 138–39
Andouille sausage:
    Cassoulet with Lamb and, Simplified, 221
    Chicken and Shrimp Jambalaya, 54–56,
        *86*
    tasting of, 56–57
Animal crackers, history of, 314
Appetizers and first courses:
    Frico, 206–7
    Gazpacho, 14–17
        Classic (Master Recipe), 16, *83*
        Garlic Croutons for, 17
        origins of, 16
        Quick Food Processor, 16
        Spicy, with Chipotle Chiles and
            Lime, 16–17
        texture of, 17
    Spinach Salad, Wilted, with Warm
        Bacon Dressing, 10–11, *87*
Apple(s):
    Pancake, German, *234*, 276–79
        Caramel Sauce for, 278–79
        choosing right apple for, 279
    Tarte Tatin, 30-Minute, 225–26
    texture of, when cooked, 279
Apricot:
    Almond Oatmeal Scones, 246
    and Corn Muffins with Orange Essence,
        *232*, 262–63
Asiago cheese, in Frico, 206–7
Asian (cuisines), 179–200
    Pad Thai, *90*, 192–95
        soaking noodles for, 194
    see also Chinese; Stir-fry(ied)(ies)
Asparagus, Spicy Stir-Fried Pork, Onions
    and, with Lemon Grass, 187

## B

Bacon:
    Beef Chili with Black Beans and, 32
    Dressing, Warm, Wilted Spinach Salad
        with, 10–11, *87*

Bacon: *(cont.)*
    pancetta, 79
        Pasta with Mushrooms, Sage and,
            67
    Scallion Corn Muffins with Cheddar
        Cheese, 263
Baked goods:
    corn muffins, 260–63
        Apricot, with Orange Essence,
            *232*, 262–63
        Bacon-Scallion, with Cheddar
            Cheese, 263
        best cornmeal for, 263
        food fact about, 260
        Master Recipe for, 262
        problems with, 262
    oatmeal scones, 244–46
        Apricot-Almond, 246
        Cinnamon-Raisin, 246
        with Dried Cherries and Hazelnuts,
            246
        Glazed Maple-Pecan, 246
        Master Recipe for, *233*, 245–46
        oven temperature for, 246
    sifting flour for, 310
    see also Cakes; Cookie(s)
Baking powder, tasting of, 263–64
Baking soda, fluffiness of pancakes and, 274
Balsamic vinegar:
    Strawberries with, 212–13
    tasting of, 213–15
Bananas:
    consumption of, 60
    Foster, 60–61
Basil:
    Baked Four-Cheese Pasta with
        Tomatoes and, 82
    Chicken Provençal with Saffron,
        Orange and, 153
Beans:
    cassoulet, simplified, 218–21
        with Lamb and Andouille Sausage,
            221
        with Pork and Kielbasa (Master
            Recipe), 220–21
    chili, 30–32
        Beef, with Bacon and Black Beans,
            32

Beans: *(cont.)*
        Beef, with Kidney Beans (Master
            Recipe), 32, *89*
        rating of slow cookers for, 32–33
        tasting of tomato purees for, 33–34
    dried, sorting, 220
    see also Green Bean(s)
Beef:
    chili, 30–32
        with Bacon and Black Beans, 32
        with Kidney Beans (Master
            Recipe), 32, *89*
        rating of slow cookers for, 32–33
        tasting of tomato purees for, 33–34
    chuck roasts, 104
    collagen in, 104, 105
    consumption of, 32
    eight primal cuts of, 158
    infusing with moisture and flavor, 173
    pot roast, 100–103
        chuck roasts for, 104
        with Mushrooms, Tomatoes, and
            Red Wine, 103
        with Root Vegetables, *98*, 102–3
        Simple (Master Recipe), 102
        tying top-blade roast for, 105
    science of braising and, 103–5
    stir-fried broccoli and, 180–83
        with Oyster Sauce, *97*, 182–83
        slicing flank steak for, 182
        stir-frying technique for, 183
        tasting of broccoli relations for,
            184
        tasting of oyster sauce for, 184
    tenderness of
        cooking in milk and, 79
        juiciness and, 160
    see also Meat; Steak(s)
Berry(ies), 293–300
    Gratin with Lemon Sabayon, 299–300
    Pie, Summer, *237*, 294–96
    see also specific berries
Black Beans, Beef Chili with Bacon and,
    32
Blackberries, in Summer Berry Pie, *237*,
    294–96
Blueberry(ies):
    frozen, tasting of, 274–75

Blueberry(ies): (cont.)
  pancakes, 270–72
    Lemon-Cornmeal, 272
    Master Recipe for, 235, 272
  Summer Berry Pie, 237, 294–96
Blue Cheese, Mashed Potatoes with Port-
  Caramelized Onions and, 163–64
Bolognese Sauce, Weeknight, 76–78, 227
  braising meat in milk for, 77, 79
  choosing right pan for, 79
  tasting of tomato pastes for, 79–80
Braising:
  roasting versus, 103
  science of, 103–5
Bread:
  Croutons, 220–21
    Garlic, 17
  crumbs, panko, 137
  see also Baked goods
Breakfast. See Brunch dishes
Brining, 173
Broccoli:
  Chinese and baby, tasting of, 184
  stir-fried beef and, 180–83
    with Oyster Sauce, 97, 182–83
    slicing flank steak for, 182
    stir-frying technique for, 183
    tasting of broccoli relations for,
      184
    tasting of oyster sauce for, 184
Broccoli rabe:
  Orecchiette with Sausage and, 70–71
  preparing, 71
  tasting of, 184
Broth, vegetable, tasting of, 57–59
Brown sugar, softening, 284
Brunch dishes, 255–63
  Apple Pancake, German, 234,
    276–79
    Caramel Sauce for, 278–79
    choosing right apple for, 279
  blueberry pancakes, 270–72
    Lemon-Cornmeal, 272
    Master Recipe for, 235, 272
  corn muffins, 260–63
    Apricot, with Orange Essence,
      232, 262–63
    Bacon-Scallion, with Cheddar
      Cheese, 263
    best cornmeal for, 263
    Master Recipe for, 262
    problems with, 262

Brunch dishes (cont.)
  Denver Omelet, 256–58
    filling for, 258
    folding, 259
  oatmeal scones, 244–46
    Apricot-Almond, 246
    Cinnamon-Raisin, 246
    with Dried Cherries and Hazelnuts,
      246
    Glazed Maple-Pecan, 246
    Master Recipe for, 233, 245–46
    oven temperature for, 246
Brushes, grill, rating of, 174–75
Butterflying chicken, 210
Butters:
  Lemon, Garlic, and Parsley, 91, 159
  Roasted Red Pepper and Smoked
    Paprika, 159

C

Cajun. See New Orleans menu
Cakes, 303–27
  carrot, 304–7
    Ginger-Orange, with Orange–
      Cream Cheese Frosting, 307
    problems with, 307
    Simple, with Cream Cheese
      Frosting (Master Recipe), 236,
      306–7
    Spiced, with Vanilla Bean–Cream
      Cheese Frosting, 307
  chocolate mousse, 324–27
    Bittersweet (Master Recipe),
      326–27
    Orange, 327
  Chocolate Sheet, 241, 308–9
  frosted, transporting, 306
  lemon cheesecake, 313–21
    chilling thoroughly, 317
    judging when curd is done for, 316
    Master Recipe for, 240, 315–17
    rating of springform pans for,
      320–21
    water bath for, 319
  lemon pound, 247–50
    Lemon Glaze for, 250
    Master Recipe for, 242, 249–50
    mixing methods for, 249
    Poppy Seed, 250
  Camembert, Pasta with Mushrooms, Peas
    and, 67
  Caramel Sauce, 278–79

Carrot(s):
  cake, 304–7
    Ginger-Orange, with Orange–
      Cream Cheese Frosting, 307
    problems with, 307
    Simple, with Cream Cheese
      Frosting (Master Recipe), 236,
      306–7
    Spiced, with Vanilla Bean–Cream
      Cheese Frosting, 307
  Pot Roast with Root Vegetables, 98,
    102–3
Casseroles:
  four-cheese pasta, creamy baked, 81–82
    Master Recipe for, 82
    with Prosciutto and Peas, 82
    with Tomatoes and Basil, 82
  Green Bean "Casserole," Quick, 108–9
Cassoulet, simplified, 218–21
  with Lamb and Andouille Sausage, 221
  with Pork and Kielbasa (Master
    Recipe), 220–21
Cheddar:
  Bacon-Scallion Corn Muffins with, 263
  shredding neatly, 23
  Smoked, Mashed Potatoes with Grainy
    Mustard and, 164
Cheese:
  Blue, Mashed Potatoes with Port-
    Caramelized Onions and, 163–64
  Camembert, Pasta with Mushrooms,
    Peas and, 67
  cheddar
    Bacon-Scallion Corn Muffins with,
      263
    Smoked, Mashed Potatoes with
      Grainy Mustard and, 164
  Cream, Frosting, 236, 306–7
    Orange, 307
    Vanilla Bean, 307
  feta, in Greek salad, 4–5
    Country-Style, 5
    Master Recipe for, 5
  four-, pasta, creamy baked, 81–82
    Master Recipe for, 82
    with Prosciutto and Peas, 82
    with Tomatoes and Basil, 82
  Frico, 206–7
  Monterey Jack, in Denver Omelet,
    256–58
  semisoft, shredding neatly, 23
  see also specific cheeses

Cheesecake, lemon, 313–21
    chilling thoroughly, 317
    judging when curd is done for, 316
    Master Recipe for, *240,* 315–17
    rating of springform pans for, 320–21
    water bath for, 319
Cherries, Dried, Oatmeal Scones with
    Hazelnuts and, 246
Chicken, 131–53
    breasts, pan-roasted, 132–34
        with Garlic-Sherry Sauce, 133
        with Onion and Ale Sauce, 134
        with Sage-Vermouth Sauce (Master
            Recipe), *88,* 133
        with Sweet-Tart Red Wine Sauce,
            133–34
    butterflying, 210
    cassoulet, simplified, 218–21
        with Lamb and Andouille Sausage,
            221
        with Pork and Kielbasa (Master
            Recipe), 220–21
    cutlets
        Almond-Crusted, with Wilted
            Spinach–Orange Salad (Master
            Recipe), 138–39
        freezing small portions of, 139
        Macadamia Nut–Crusted, with
            Wilted Spinach–Pineapple Salad,
            139
        nut-crusted, 137–39
        trimming, 139
    cutting up, 145
        rating of kitchen shears for, 145–47
    alla diavola, 208–11
        Charcoal-Grilled (Master Recipe),
            210–11, *231*
        Gas-Grilled, 211
    with 40 Cloves of Garlic, *96,* 142–45
        cutting up chicken for, 145
        developing flavor of garlic for, 144
    Provençal, 150–53
        Master Recipe for, *84,* 152–53
        with Saffron, Orange, and Basil,
            153
    Shredded, Sesame Noodles with, 199,
        *230*
    shredding, 56
    and Shrimp Jambalaya, 54–56, *86*
        chopping vegetables in food pro-
            cessor for, 58
        tasting of pork products for, 56–57

Chicken-Fried Steak, 122–24
Chile(s), chipotle. *See* Chipotle chile(s)
Chili, beef, 30–32
    with Bacon and Black Beans, 32
    with Kidney Beans (Master Recipe),
        32, *89*
    rating of slow cookers for, 32–33
    tasting of tomato purees for, 33–34
Chilling mixing bowls, 298
Chinese (cuisine):
    beef and broccoli, stir-fried, 180–83
        with Oyster Sauce, *97,* 182–83
        slicing flank steak for, 182
        stir-frying technique for, 183
        tasting of broccoli relations for, 184
        tasting of oyster sauce for, 184
    pork and vegetable stir-fries, 185–87
        with Eggplant, Onions, Garlic, and
            Black Pepper, 186
        with Green Beans, Red Bell
            Pepper, and Gingery Oyster
            Sauce, *92,* 186–87
        slicing pork tenderloin for, 188
        Spicy, with Asparagus, Onions, and
            Lemon Grass, 187
    sesame noodles, cold, 198–200
        with Shredded Chicken (Master
            Recipe), 199, *230*
        with Sweet Peppers and
            Cucumbers, 200
Chipotle chile(s):
    Sauce, Creamy, 49
    Spicy Gazpacho with Lime and, 16–17
Chocolate(s):
    chip cookies, 282–86
        tasting of refrigerator doughs for,
            284–86
        Thin, Crispy, *238,* 282–84
    consumption of, 327
    -Dipped Triple-Coconut Macaroons,
        *239,* 289
    glossary for, 329
    milk
        Frosting, Creamy, *241,* 309
        tasting of, 310–11
    mousse cake, 324–27
        Bittersweet (Master Recipe), 326–27
        Orange, 327
    Sheet Cake, *241,* 308–9
    unsweetened
        food analysis of, 328
        tasting of, 327–30

Chocolate(s): *(cont.)*
    White, Chilled Lemon Soufflé with,
        334
Chowders:
    clam, New England, 40–43
        Master Recipe for, 42
        Quick Pantry, 42–43
        scrubbing clams for, 42
        steaming clams for, 43
    use of term, 44
Chuck roasts, 104
Cinnamon-Raisin Oatmeal Scones, 246
Citrus juicers and reamers, rating of,
    250–51
Clam(s):
    chowder, New England, 40–43
        Master Recipe for, 42
        Quick Pantry, 42–43
        scrubbing clams for, 42
        steaming clams for, 43
    hard- versus soft-shell, 43
    Indoor Clambake, 35–37
    sandiness of, 43–44
    scrubbing, 42
Clambake, Indoor, 35–37
Coconut:
    Cream Pie, 126–29
    Graham Cracker Crust, 128–29
    macaroons, 287–90
        Chocolate-Dipped Triple-Coconut,
            *239,* 289
        food fact about, 288
        Triple-Coconut (Master Recipe),
            288–89
    milk, coconut cream, and
        cream of coconut, tasting
        of, 289–90
Cold food, seasoning, 17–18
Collagen, 104, 105
Cookie(s), 281–91
    chocolate chip, 282–86
        tasting of refrigerator doughs for,
            284–86
        Thin, Crispy, *238,* 282–84
    coconut macaroons, 287–90
        Chocolate-Dipped Triple-Coconut,
            *239,* 289
        food fact about, 288
        Triple-Coconut (Master Recipe),
            288–89
    Crumb Crust, 315–16
        tasting of cookies for, 317

Corn:
    Indoor Clambake, 35–37
    muffins, 260–63
        Apricot, with Orange Essence,
            *232,* 262–63
        Bacon-Scallion, with Cheddar
            Cheese, 263
        best cornmeal for, 263
        food fact about, 260
        Master Recipe for, 262
        problems with, 262
Cornmeal:
    Lemon Blueberry Pancakes, 272
    tasting of, 263
Crab Cakes, Maryland, 47–48
    Creamy Chipotle Sauce for, 48
    Tartar Sauce for, 47
Cranberries, Dried, Wild Rice Pilaf with
    Pecans and, *95,* 116–17
Cream:
    Coconut, Pie, 126–29
    Gravy, 124
    whipped
        chilling bowl for, 298
        Topping, 128
        Topping, Sour Cream, 226
Cream Cheese Frosting, *236,* 306–7
    Orange, 307
    Vanilla Bean, 307
Creaming method, 249
Cream of tartar, egg whites and, 334
Creole. *See* New Orleans menu
Crock-Pots (slow cookers), rating of,
    32–33
Croutons, 220–21
    Garlic, 17
Crusts:
    Cookie-Crumb, 315–16
        tasting of cookies for, 317
    Graham Cracker, 295–96
        Coconut, 128–29
        store-bought, tasting of, 129
Cucumbers:
    cutting into perfect dice, 19
    gazpacho, 14–17
        Classic (Master Recipe), 16, *83*
        Garlic Croutons for, 17
        origins of, 16
        Quick Food Processor, 16
        Spicy, with Chipotle Chiles and
            Lime, 16–17
        texture of, 17

Cucumbers: *(cont.)*
    Greek salad, 4–5
        Country-Style, 5
        Master Recipe for, 5
    seeding, 5
    Sesame Noodles with Sweet Peppers
        and, 200
Curd, Lemon, 315–16
Cutting boards, keeping stable, 18

D
Denver Omelet, 256–58
    Filling for, 258
    folding, 259
Desserts, 281–335
    Apple Pancake, German, *234,* 276–79
        Caramel Sauce for, 278–79
        choosing right apple for, 279
    Bananas Foster, 60–61
    Berry Gratin with Lemon Sabayon,
        299–300
    Berry Pie, Summer, *237,* 294–96
    Coconut Cream Pie, 126–29
    lemon cheesecake, 313–21
        chilling thoroughly, 317
        judging when curd is done for,
            316
        Master Recipe for, *240,* 315–17
        rating of springform pans for,
            320–21
        water bath for, 319
    lemon soufflé(s), chilled, 331–34
        Individual, 334
        Master Recipe for, 333–34
        with White Chocolate, 334
    Strawberries with Balsamic Vinegar,
        212–13
    Tarte Tatin, 225–26
        with Pears, 226
        30-Minute (Master Recipe), 226
    Whipped Cream Topping, 128
        chilling bowl for, 298
        Sour Cream, 226
    *see also* Cakes; Cookie(s); Frostings
Dicing vegetables, 19
Diners, food facts about, 129
Dressings:
    Bacon, Warm, 10–11, *87*
    vinaigrettes, 3
        for Greek Salad, 5
Dutch ovens, simmering sauces in skillets
    versus, 79

E
Egg(s):
    consumption of, 256
    Denver Omelet, 256–58
        Filling for, 258
        folding, 259
    Hard-Cooked, Foolproof, 11
    sizes and weights of, 258
    tasting of, 258–59
    whites, beating
        with cream of tartar, 334
        getting it right, 334
    yolk foams, science of, 300
Eggplant, Stir-Fried Pork, Onions and, with
    Garlic and Black Pepper, 186
Equipment:
    cutting boards, keeping stable, 18
    food processors
        chopping vegetables in, 58
        cleaning workbowl of, 318
        mixing pound cake batter in,
            249
    microwave, softening brown sugar in,
        284
    pans, determining when hot enough
        for browning meat, 134
        for pancakes, 273
    pans, for simmering sauces, skillets
        versus Dutch ovens, 79
    ratings of
        citrus juicers and reamers,
            250–51
        food storage containers, 118–19
        griddles, electric, 273
        grill brushes, 174–75
        herb choppers, 67–69
        ice cream machines, 296–98
        ice cream scoops, 61
        meat pounders, 125
        oyster knives, 44–46
        potholders, 290–91
        saucepans, large, 165–67
        shears, kitchen, 145–47
        skillets, traditional, 134–36
        slow cookers, 32–33
        spatulas, rubber, 264–66
        spoonulas, 266
        springform pans, 320–21
        vegetable choppers, 106–7
        woks, electric, 188–89
        woks, flat-bottom, 196–97
    trivets, extra-large, improvising, 145

## F

Feta, in Greek salad, 4–5
Country-Style, 5
Master Recipe for, 5
Filets mignons, grilled, 156–57
butters for
Lemon, Garlic, and Parsley, *91,*
159
Roasted Red Pepper and Smoked
Paprika, 159
Charcoal- (Master Recipe), *91,*
158–59
Gas-, 159
Flank steak, slicing for stir-fries, 182
Flour, sifting, 310
Fontina, in creamy baked four-cheese pasta,
81–82
Master Recipe for, 82
with Prosciutto and Peas, 82
with Tomatoes and Basil, 82
Food processors:
chopping vegetables in, 58
cleaning workbowl of, 318
mixing pound cake batter in, 249
Food storage containers, rating of, 118–19
Four-cheese pasta, creamy baked, 81–82
Master Recipe for, 82
with Prosciutto and Peas, 82
with Tomatoes and Basil, 82
Freezing small portions, 139
French (cuisine), 217–26
Berry Gratin with Lemon Sabayon,
299–300
cassoulet, simplified, 218–21
with Lamb and Andouille Sausage,
221
with Pork and Kielbasa (Master
Recipe), 220–21
chicken Provençal, 150–53
Master Recipe for, *84,* 152–53
with Saffron, Orange, and Basil,
153
Chicken with 40 Cloves of Garlic, *96,*
142–45
cutting up chicken for, 145
developing flavor of garlic for,
144
tarte Tatin, 225–26
with Pears, 226
30-Minute (Master Recipe), 226
Frico, 206–7
Fries, Steak, 176–77

Frostings:
Cream Cheese, *236,* 306–7
Orange, 307
Vanilla Bean, 307
Milk Chocolate, Creamy, *241,* 309

## G

Garlic:
Chicken with 40 Cloves of, *96,* 142–45
cutting up chicken for, 145
Croutons, 17
developing flavor of, 144
Ginger, and Soy Marinade, 173
hardneck versus softneck, 148
Lemon, and Parsley Butter, *91,* 159
Lemon Green Beans with Toasted
Bread Crumbs, 109
Pepper Oil, 210
Sherry Sauce, Pan-Roasted Chicken
Breasts with, 133
Stir-Fried Pork, Eggplant, and Onions
with Black Pepper and, 186
tasting of, 148
Toasted, Mashed Potatoes with Smoked
Paprika and, 165
Gazpacho, 14–17
Classic (Master Recipe), 16, *83*
Garlic Croutons for, 17
origins of, 16
Quick Food Processor, 16
Spicy, with Chipotle Chiles and Lime,
16–17
texture of, 17
German Apple Pancake, *234,* 276–79
Caramel Sauce for, 278–79
choosing right apple for, 279
Ginger:
Garlic, and Soy Marinade, 173
Orange Carrot Cake with Orange–
Cream Cheese Frosting, 307
Glaze, Lemon, 250
Gorgonzola, in creamy baked four-cheese
pasta, 81–82
Master Recipe for, 82
with Prosciutto and Peas, 82
with Tomatoes and Basil, 82
Graham cracker(s):
Crust, 295–96
Coconut, 128–29
store-bought, tasting of, 129
food fact about, 294
Gravy, Cream, 124

Greek salad, 4–5
Country-Style, 5
Master Recipe for, 5
Green Bean(s), 108–9
"Casserole," Quick, 108–9
Garlic-Lemon, with Toasted Bread
Crumbs, 109
with Orange Essence and Toasted
Maple Pecans, 109, *228*
Stir-Fried Pork, Red Bell Pepper and,
with Gingery Oyster Sauce, *92,*
186–87
Griddles, electric, rating of, 273
Grill brushes, rating of, 174–75
Grilled:
chicken alla diavola, 208–11
butterflying chicken for, 210
Charcoal- (Master Recipe), 210–
11, *231*
Gas-, 211
filets mignons, 156–57
Charcoal- (Master Recipe), *91,*
158–59
Gas-, 159
Lemon, Garlic, and Parsley Butter
for, *91,* 159
Roasted Red Pepper and Smoked
Paprika Butter for, 159
steak tips, 170–73
Charcoal- (Master Recipe), *93,* 172
Garlic, Ginger, and Soy Marinade
for, 173
Gas-, 172
Southwestern Marinade for, 173
strip or rib steaks, 156–59
Charcoal- (Master Recipe), 157–58
Gas-, 158

## H

Ham:
Denver Omelet, 256–58
Filling for, 258
prosciutto
Baked Four-Cheese Pasta with Peas
and, 82
Tomato and Mozzarella Tart with,
23
Hazelnuts, Oatmeal Scones with Dried
Cherries and, 246
Herb choppers, rating of, 67–69
Horseradish, Mashed Potatoes with Scallions
and, 164

# I

Ice cream, in Bananas Foster, 60–61
Ice cream machines, rating of, 296–98
Ice cream scoops, rating of, 61
Ingredients, tastings of. *See* Tastings
Italian (cuisine), 205–15
    Chicken Breasts, Pan-Roasted, with
        Sweet-Tart Red Wine Sauce, 133–34
    chicken alla diavola, 208–11
        butterflying chicken for, 210
        Charcoal-Grilled (Master Recipe),
            210–11, *231*
        Gas-Grilled, 211
    Frico, 206–7
    Pot Roast with Mushrooms, Tomatoes,
        and Red Wine, 103
    Strawberries with Balsamic Vinegar,
        212–13
    tastings for
        balsamic vinegar, 213–15
        canned diced tomatoes, 222–24
        extra-virgin olive oil, 71–73
        mozzarella, 23–27
        tomato pastes, 79–80
        tomato purees, 33–34
    *see also* Pasta

# J

Jambalaya, Chicken and Shrimp, 54–56, *86*
    chopping vegetables in food processor
        for, 58
    shredding chicken for, 56
    tasting of pork products for, 56–57
Juicers, rating of, 250–51
Juicing lemons, 318

# K

Kidney Beans, Beef Chili with, 32, *89*
Kielbasa:
    Cassoulet with Pork and, Simplified,
        220–21
    Indoor Clambake, 35–37
Knives, oyster, rating of, 44–46

# L

Lamb, Simplified Cassoulet with Andouille
    Sausage and, 221
Lemon(s):
    cheesecake, 313–21
        chilling thoroughly, 317
        judging when curd is done for, 316
        Master Recipe for, *240,* 315–17

Lemon(s): *(cont.)*
        rating of springform pans for,
            320–21
        water bath for, 319
    Cornmeal Blueberry Pancakes, 272
    Garlic, and Parsley Butter, *91,* 159
    Garlic Green Beans with Toasted Bread
        Crumbs, 109
    Glaze, 250
    juicers and reamers for, rating of,
        250–51
    juicing, 318
    pound cake, 247–50
        Lemon Glaze for, 250
        Master Recipe for, *242,* 249–50
        mixing methods for, 249
        Poppy Seed, 250
    Sabayon, Berry Gratin with, 299–300
    soufflé(s), chilled, 331–34
        Individual, 334
        Master Recipe for, 333–34
        with White Chocolate, 334
    substitutes, tasting of, 317–19
Lemon Grass, Spicy Stir-Fried Pork,
    Asparagus, and Onions with, 187
Lime, Spicy Gazpacho with Chipotle Chiles
    and, 16–17
Lobsters, in Indoor Clambake, 35–37

# M

Macadamia Nut–Crusted Chicken Cutlets
    with Wilted Spinach–Pineapple Salad,
    139
Macaroons, 287–90
    Chocolate-Dipped Triple-Coconut,
        *239,* 289
    food fact about, 288
    Triple-Coconut (Master Recipe),
        288–89
Main dishes:
    beef and broccoli, stir-fried, 180–83
        with Oyster Sauce, *97,* 182–83
        slicing flank steak for, 182
        stir-frying technique for, 183
        tasting of broccoli relations for,
            184
        tasting of oyster sauce for, 184
    Bolognese Sauce, Weeknight, 76–78,
        *227*
        braising meat in milk for, 77, 79
        choosing right pan for, 79
        tasting of tomato pastes for, 79–80

Main dishes: *(cont.)*
    cassoulet, simplified, 218–21
        with Lamb and Andouille Sausage,
            221
        with Pork and Kielbasa (Master
            Recipe), 220–21
    chicken alla diavola, 208–11
        butterflying chicken for, 210
        Charcoal-Grilled (Master Recipe),
            210–11, *231*
        Gas-Grilled, 211
    Chicken and Shrimp Jambalaya, 54–56,
        *86*
        chopping vegetables in food
            processor for, 58
        shredding chicken for, 56
        tasting of pork products for, 56–57
    chicken breasts, pan-roasted, 132–34
        with Garlic-Sherry Sauce, 133
        with Onion and Ale Sauce, 134
        with Sage-Vermouth Sauce (Master
            Recipe), *88,* 133
        with Sweet-Tart Red Wine Sauce,
            133–34
    chicken cutlets, nut-crusted, 137–39
        Almond-Crusted, with Wilted
            Spinach–Orange Salad (Master
            Recipe), 138–39
        Macadamia Nut–Crusted, with
            Wilted Spinach–Pineapple Salad,
            139
    chicken Provençal, 150–53
        Master Recipe for, *84,* 152–53
        with Saffron, Orange, and Basil,
            153
    Chicken with 40 Cloves of Garlic, *96,*
        142–45
        cutting up chicken for, 145
        developing flavor of garlic for, 144
    chili, 30–32
        Beef, with Bacon and Black Beans,
            32
        Beef, with Kidney Beans (Master
            Recipe), 32, *89*
        rating of slow cookers for, 32–33
        tasting of tomato purees for, 33–34
    Clambake, Indoor, 35–37
    clam chowder, New England, 40–43
        Master Recipe for, 42
        Quick Pantry, 42–43
        scrubbing clams for, 42
        steaming clams for, 43

Main dishes: (cont.)
    Crab Cakes, Maryland, 47–48
        Creamy Chipotle Sauce for, 48
        Tartar Sauce for, 47
    filets mignons, grilled, 156–57
        Charcoal- (Master Recipe), 91,
            158–59
        Gas-, 159
        Lemon, Garlic, and Parsley Butter
            for, 91, 159
        Roasted Red Pepper and Smoked
            Paprika Butter for, 159
    four-cheese pasta, creamy baked, 81–82
        Master Recipe for, 82
        with Prosciutto and Peas, 82
        with Tomatoes and Basil, 82
    Orecchiette with Broccoli Rabe and
        Sausage, 70–71
    Pad Thai, 90, 192–95
        soaking noodles for, 194
    pasta with sautéed mushrooms, 64–67
        with Pancetta and Sage, 67
        with Peas and Camembert, 67
        and Thyme (Master Recipe),
            66–67, 229
    pork and vegetable stir-fries, 185–87
        with Eggplant, Onions, Garlic, and
            Black Pepper, 186
        with Green Beans, Red Bell
            Pepper, and Gingery Oyster
            Sauce, 92, 186–87
        Spicy, with Asparagus, Onions, and
            Lemon Grass, 187
    pork roast, maple-glazed, 112–15
        Master Recipe for, 94, 114
        with Orange Essence, 115
        with Rosemary, 115
        with Smoked Paprika, 115
        with Star Anise, 115
    pot roast, 100–103
        chuck roasts for, 104
        with Mushrooms, Tomatoes, and
            Red Wine, 103
        with Root Vegetables, 98, 102–3
        Simple (Master Recipe), 102
        tying top-blade roast for, 105
    sesame noodles, cold, 198–200
        with Shredded Chicken (Master
            Recipe), 199, 230
        with Sweet Peppers and
            Cucumbers, 200
    Steak, Chicken-Fried, 122–24

Main dishes: (cont.)
    steak tips, 170–73
        buying, 172
        Charcoal-Grilled (Master Recipe),
            93, 172
        Garlic, Ginger, and Soy Marinade
            for, 173
        Gas-Grilled, 172
        Southwestern Marinade for, 173
        tasting of, 173
    strip or rib steaks, grilled, 156–59
        Charcoal- (Master Recipe), 157–58
        Gas-, 158
    tomato and mozzarella tart, 20–23
        assembling tart shell for, 24
        Master Recipe for, 22, 85
        preventing soggy crust in, 20–21, 22
        with Prosciutto, 23
        with Smoked Mozzarella, 23
        tasting of mozzarella for, 23–27
        tasting of puff pastry for, 23
Maple:
    -glazed pork roast, 112–15
        Master Recipe for, 94, 114
        with Orange Essence, 115
        with Rosemary, 115
        with Smoked Paprika, 115
        with Star Anise, 115
    pancake syrups and, 114
    Pecan Oatmeal Scones, Glazed, 246
    Pecans, Toasted, Green Beans with
        Orange Essence and, 109, 228
Marinades:
    Garlic, Ginger, and Soy, 173
    prying flavor out of spices for, 211
    science of flavor development and, 173
    Southwestern, 173
Maryland Crab Cakes, 47–48
    Creamy Chipotle Sauce for, 48
    Tartar Sauce for, 48
Mashed potatoes, 163–65
    with Blue Cheese and Port-Caramelized
        Onions, 163–64
    with Scallions and Horseradish, 164
    with Smoked Cheddar and Grainy
        Mustard, 164
    with Smoked Paprika and Toasted
        Garlic, 165
Mayonnaise:
    food analysis of, 49
    Tartar Sauce, 48
    tasting of, 49–51

Meat:
    Bolognese Sauce, Weeknight, 76–78,
        227
        braising meat in milk for, 77, 79
        choosing right pan for, 79
        tasting of tomato pastes for, 79–80
    collagen in, 104, 105
    infusing with moisture and flavor, 173
    science of braising and, 103–5
    tenderness of
        cooking in milk and, 79
        juiciness and, 160
    see also Beef; Pork; Steak(s)
Meat pounders, rating of, 125
Mezzalunas, rating of, for cutting herbs, 68,
    69
Microwave, softening brown sugar in, 284
Milk, meat tenderness and, 79
Mixing bowls, chilling, 298
Montasio cheese, in Frico, 206–7
Monterey Jack cheese, in Denver Omelet,
    256–58
Mousse cake, chocolate, 324–27
    Bittersweet (Master Recipe), 326–27
    Orange, 327
Mozzarella:
    shredding neatly, 23
    tastings of
        fresh, 27
        supermarket, 23–27
    and tomato tart, 20–23
        assembling tart shell for, 24
        Master Recipe for, 22, 85
        preventing soggy crust in, 20–21, 22
        with Prosciutto, 23
        with Smoked Mozzarella, 23
        tasting of puff pastry for, 23
Muffins, corn, 260–63
    Apricot, with Orange Essence, 232,
        262–63
    Bacon-Scallion, with Cheddar Cheese,
        263
    best cornmeal for, 263
    food fact about, 260
    Master Recipe for, 262
    problems with, 262
Mushrooms:
    cooking, 66
    Green Bean "Casserole," Quick, 108–9
    poisonous, 67
    Pot Roast with Tomatoes, Red Wine
        and, 103

Mushrooms: *(cont.)*
    sautéed, pasta with, 64–67
        with Pancetta and Sage, 67
        with Peas and Camembert, 67
        and Thyme (Master Recipe),
           66–67, *229*
    shiitake, tough stems of, 67
Mussels:
    debearding, 36
    Indoor Clambake, 35–37
Mustard, Grainy, Mashed Potatoes with
    Smoked Cheddar and, 164

**N**

New England (cooking):
    clam chowder, 40–43
        Master Recipe for, 42
        Quick Pantry, 42–43
        scrubbing clams for, 42
        steaming clams for, 43
    maple-glazed pork roast, 112–15
        Master Recipe for, *94,* 114
        with Orange Essence, 115
        with Rosemary, 115
        with Smoked Paprika, 115
        with Star Anise, 115
New Orleans menu, 53–61
    Bananas Foster, 60–61
    Chicken and Shrimp Jambalaya, 54–56,
        *86*
        chopping vegetables in food pro-
           cessor for, 58
        shredding chicken for, 56
        tasting of pork products for, 56–57
Noodles:
    Pad Thai, *90,* 192–95
        soaking noodles for, 194
    sesame, cold, 198–200
        with Shredded Chicken (Master
           Recipe), 199, *230*
        with Sweet Peppers and
           Cucumbers, 200
    *see also* Pasta
Nut(s):
    -crusted chicken cutlets, 137–39
        Almond-Crusted, with Wilted
           Spinach–Orange Salad (Master
           Recipe), 138–39
        Macadamia Nut–Crusted, with
           Wilted Spinach–Pineapple Salad,
           139
    *see also specific nuts*

**O**

Oatmeal scones, 244–46
    Apricot-Almond, 246
    Cinnamon-Raisin, 246
    with Dried Cherries and Hazelnuts,
        246
    Glazed Maple-Pecan, 246
    Master Recipe for, *233,* 245–46
    oven temperature for, 246
Oils:
    Garlic-Pepper, 210
    olive, boutique extra-virgin, tasting of,
        71–73
    smoking point of, 134
Olive oil, boutique extra-virgin, tasting of,
    71–73
Olives, Niçoise, pitting, 152
Omelet, Denver, 256–58
    Filling for, 258
    folding, 256–58
Onion(s):
    and Ale Sauce, Pan-Roasted Chicken
        Breasts with, 134
    crying from, science of, 44
    Denver Omelet, 256–58
        Filling for, 258
    Port-Caramelized, Mashed
        Potatoes with Blue Cheese
        and, 163–64
    Spicy Stir-Fried Pork, Asparagus and,
        with Lemon Grass, 187
    Stir-Fried Pork, Eggplant
        and, with Garlic and
        Black Pepper, 186
Orange(s):
    Chicken Provençal with Saffron, Basil
        and, 153
    Chocolate Mousse Cake, 327
    essence
        Corn and Apricot Muffins with,
           *232,* 262–63
        Green Beans with Toasted Maple
           Pecans and, 109, *228*
        Maple-Glazed Pork Roast with,
           115
    –Cream Cheese Frosting, Ginger Carrot
        Cake with, 307
    removing peel and pith from, 138
    Wilted Spinach Salad, 138–39
Orecchiette with Broccoli Rabe and
    Sausage, 70–71
Oyster knives, rating of, 44–46

Oyster sauce:
    Gingery, Stir-Fried Pork, Green Beans,
        and Red Bell Pepper with, *92,*
        186–87
    Stir-Fried Beef and Broccoli with, *97,*
        182–83
    tasting of, 184
Oysters, shucking, 45

**P**

Pad Thai, *90,* 192–95
    soaking noodles for, 194
Pancake(s), 269–79
    Apple, German, *234,* 276–79
        Caramel Sauce for, 278–79
        choosing right apple for, 279
    blueberry, 270–72
        Lemon-Cornmeal, 272
        Master Recipe for, *235,* 272
    keeping warm, 272
    knowing when pan is ready for, 273
    promoting fluffiness in, 274
    rating of electric griddles for, 273
Pancake syrups, 114
Pancetta, 79
    Pasta with Mushrooms, Sage and, 67
Panko, 137
Pans:
    determining when hot enough
        for browning meat, 134
        for pancakes, 273
    for simmering sauces, Dutch ovens
        versus skillets, 79
Paprika, smoked:
    Maple-Glazed Pork Roast with, 115
    Mashed Potatoes with Toasted Garlic
        and, 165
    and Roasted Red Pepper Butter, 159
Parmesan, in creamy baked four-cheese
    pasta, 81–82
    Master Recipe for, 82
    with Prosciutto and Peas, 82
    with Tomatoes and Basil, 82
Parsley, Lemon, and Garlic Butter, *91,* 159
Parsnips, in Pot Roast with Root Vegetables,
    *98,* 102–3
Pasta, 63–82
    Bolognese Sauce, Weeknight, 76–78,
        *227*
        braising meat in milk for, 77, 79
        choosing right pan for, 79
        tasting of tomato pastes for, 79–80

Pasta (cont.)
consumption of, 70
four-cheese, creamy baked, 81–82
Master Recipe for, 82
with Prosciutto and Peas, 82
with Tomatoes and Basil, 82
Orecchiette with Broccoli Rabe and
Sausage, 70–71
with sautéed mushrooms, 64–67
mushroom cooking and, 66
with Pancetta and Sage, 67
with Peas and Camembert, 67
and Thyme (Master Recipe),
66–67, 229
see also Noodles
Pastry:
puff
assembling tart shell with, 24
food fact about, 226
tasting of, 23
Tarte Tatin, 225–26
with Pears, 226
30-Minute (Master Recipe),
226
tomato and mozzarella tart, 20–23
assembling tart shell for, 24
Master Recipe for, 22, 85
preventing soggy crust in, 20–21,
22
with Prosciutto, 23
with Smoked Mozzarella, 23
tasting of mozzarella for, 23–27
tasting of puff pastry for, 23
Peanut(s):
butter
separation of, 200
tasting of, 200–202
food fact about, 198
Pears, Tarte Tatin with, 226
Peas:
Baked Four-Cheese Pasta with
Prosciutto and, 82
Pasta with Mushrooms, Camembert
and, 67
Pecan(s):
Maple Oatmeal Scones, Glazed,
246
Toasted Maple, Green Beans
with Orange Essence and,
109, 228
Wild Rice Pilaf with Dried Cranberries
and, 95, 116–17

Pecorino Romano, in creamy baked four-
cheese pasta, 81–82
Master Recipe for, 82
with Prosciutto and Peas, 82
with Tomatoes and Basil, 82
Pepper (black):
Garlic Oil, 210
Stir-Fried Pork, Eggplant, and Onions
with Garlic and, 186
Pepper(s), bell:
cutting into perfect dice, 19
Denver Omelet, 256–58
Filling for, 258
Pepper(s), red bell:
gazpacho, 14–17
Classic (Master Recipe), 16, 83
Garlic Croutons for, 17
origins of, 16
Quick Food Processor, 16
Spicy, with Chipotle Chiles and
Lime, 16–17
texture of, 17
Greek salad, 4–5
Country-Style, 5
Master Recipe for, 5
roasted
jarred, tasting of, 6
and Smoked Paprika
Butter, 159
Sesame Noodles with Cucumbers
and, 200
Stir-Fried Pork, Green Beans
and, with Gingery Oyster
Sauce, 92, 186–87
Pie(s):
Berry, Summer, 237, 294–96
Coconut Cream, 126–29
crusts, graham cracker, 295–96
Coconut, 128–29
store-bought, tasting of, 129
Pigs, food fact about, 221
Pilaf, Wild Rice, with Pecans and Dried
Cranberries, 95, 116–17
Pineapple–Wilted Spinach Salad,
138–39
Poppy Seed–Lemon Pound Cake, 250
Pork:
blade versus center loin, 221
Cassoulet with Kielbasa and, Simplified,
220–21
ham, in Denver Omelet, 256–58
Filling for, 258

Pork: (cont.)
roast, maple-glazed, 112–15
Master Recipe for, 94, 114
with Orange Essence, 115
with Rosemary, 115
with Smoked Paprika, 115
with Star Anise, 115
roasts
browning and glazing, 115
enhanced versus regular, 115
loin, tying, 115
and vegetable stir-fries, 185–87
with Eggplant, Onions, Garlic, and
Black Pepper, 186
with Green Beans, Red Bell
Pepper, and Gingery Oyster
Sauce, 92, 186–87
slicing pork tenderlon for, 188
Spicy, with Asparagus, Onions, and
Lemon Grass, 187
see also Bacon; Sausage
Port-Caramelized Onions, Mashed Potatoes
with Blue Cheese and, 163–64
Potatoes:
consumption of, 176
Indoor Clambake, 35–37
mashed, 163–65
with Blue Cheese and Port-
Caramelized Onions, 163–64
with Scallions and Horseradish,
164
with Smoked Cheddar and
Grainy Mustard, 164
with Smoked Paprika and
Toasted Garlic, 165
New England clam chowder,
40–43
Master Recipe for, 42
Quick Pantry, 42–43
scrubbing clams for, 42
steaming clams for, 43
Pot Roast with Root Vegetables, 98,
102–3
Steak Fries, 176–77
Potholders, rating of, 290–91
Pot roast, 100–103
chuck roasts for, 104
with Mushrooms, Tomatoes, and Red
Wine, 103
with Root Vegetables, 98, 102–3
Simple (Master Recipe), 102
tying top-blade roast for, 105

Pound cake:
  lemon, 247–50
    Lemon Glaze for, 250
    Master Recipe for, *242*, 249–50
    Poppy Seed, 250
  mixing methods for, 249
Prosciutto:
  Baked Four-Cheese Pasta with Peas
    and, 82
  Tomato and Mozzarella Tart with, 23
Provençal (cuisine):
  chicken, 150–53
    Master Recipe for, *84*, 152–53
    with Saffron, Orange, and Basil, 153
  Chicken with 40 Cloves of Garlic, *96*,
    142–45
    cutting up chicken for, 145
    developing flavor of garlic for, 144
  use of term, 150
Puff pastry:
  assembling tart shell with, 24
  food fact about, 226
  Tarte Tatin, 225–26
    with Pears, 226
    30-Minute (Master Recipe), 226
  tasting of, 23

## R

Raisin-Cinnamon Oatmeal Scones, 246
Raspberries, in Summer Berry Pie, *237*, 294–96
Ratings. *See* Equipment—ratings of; Tastings
Reamers, rating of, 250–51
Red wine:
  Pot Roast with Mushrooms, Tomatoes
    and, 103
  Sauce, Sweet-Tart, Pan-Roasted
    Chicken Breasts with, 133–34
Red wine vinegars:
  food analysis of, 7
  tastings of
    gourmet, 9
    supermarket, 7–9
Rib steaks, grilled, 156–59
  Charcoal- (Master Recipe), 157–58
  Gas-, 158
Rice:
  Chicken and Shrimp Jambalaya, 54–56, *86*
    chopping vegetables in food pro-
     cessor for, 58
    shredding chicken for, 56
    tasting of pork products for, 56–57
  consumption of, 185

Rice stick noodles, in Pad Thai, *90*, 192–95
  soaking noodles for, 194
Roasting, braising versus, 103
Root Vegetables, Pot Roast with, *98*, 102–3
Rosemary, Maple-Glazed Pork Roast with,
  115

## S

Sabayon, Lemon, Berry Gratin with, 299–300
Saffron, Chicken Provençal with Orange,
  Basil and, 153
Sage:
  Pasta with Mushrooms, Pancetta and, 67
  Vermouth Sauce, Pan-Roasted Chicken
    Breasts with, *88*, 133
Salad dressings:
  Bacon, Warm, 10–11, *87*
  vinaigrettes, 3
    for Greek Salad, 5
Salads, 3–11
  Greek, 4–5
    Country-Style, 5
    Master Recipe for, 5
  leafy green, with vinaigrette, 3
  spinach, wilted
    Orange, 138–39
    Pineapple, 139
    problems with, 11
    with Warm Bacon Dressing,
     10–11, *87*
Salt, seasoning cold food with, 18
Saucepans, large, rating of, 165–67
Sauces:
  Bolognese, Weeknight, 76–78, *227*
    braising meat in milk for, 77, 79
    choosing right pan for, 79
    tasting of tomato pastes for, 79–80
  Caramel, 278–79
  for chicken (pan)
    Garlic-Sherry, 133
    Onion and Ale, 134
    Red Wine, Sweet-Tart, 133–34
    Sage-Vermouth, *88*, 133
  Chipotle Chile, Creamy, 49
  Tartar, 48
Sausage:
  andouille
    Cassoulet with Lamb and,
     Simplified, 221
    Chicken and Shrimp Jambalaya,
     54–56, *86*
    tasting of, 56–57

Sausage: *(cont.)*
  kielbasa
    Cassoulet with Pork and,
     Simplified, 220–21
    Indoor Clambake, 35–37
    Orecchiette with Broccoli Rabe and,
     70–71
Scallion(s):
  Bacon Corn Muffins with Cheddar
    Cheese, 263
  Mashed Potatoes with Horseradish and,
    164
Science of cooking:
  apples, cooking and texture of, 279
  braising, 103–5
  cold food, seasoning, 17–18
  collagen, 105
  cream of tartar, beating egg whites with,
    334
  egg yolk foams, 300
  flour, sifting, 310
  meat, infusing with moisture and flavor,
    173
  meat tenderness
    cooking in milk and, 79
    juiciness and, 160
  onions, crying from, 44
  pancakes, promoting fluffiness in, 274
  pans, determining when hot enough to
    begin searing, 134
  peanut butters, separation of, 200
  pork roasts, browning and glazing, 115
  spices, prying flavor out of, 211
  water baths, 319
Scones, oatmeal, 244–46
  Apricot-Almond, 246
  Cinnamon-Raisin, 246
  with Dried Cherries and Hazelnuts, 246
  Glazed Maple-Pecan, 246
  Master Recipe for, *233*, 245–46
  oven temperature for, 246
Seafood, 39–49
  Crab Cakes, Maryland, 47–48
    Creamy Chipotle Sauce for, 48
    Tartar Sauce for, 47
  Indoor Clambake, 35–37
  oysters, shucking, 45
    rating of oyster knives for, 44–46
  sauces for
    Creamy Chipotle Chile, 49
    Tartar, 48
  *see also* Clam(s); Shrimp

Seasoning cold food, 17–18
Sesame noodles, cold, 198–200
    with Shredded Chicken (Master
      Recipe), 199, *230*
    with Sweet Peppers and Cucumbers,
      200
Seven-bone pot roasts or steaks, 104
Shears, kitchen, rating of, 145–47
Sherry-Garlic Sauce, Pan-Roasted Chicken
    Breasts with, 133
Shiitake mushrooms:
    pasta with sautéed mushrooms, 64–67
      with Pancetta and Sage, 67
      with Peas and Camembert, 67
      and Thyme (Master Recipe),
        66–67, *229*
    tough stems of, 67
Shrimp:
    and Chicken Jambalaya, 54–56, *86*
      chopping vegetables in food pro-
        cessor for, 58
      shredding chicken for, 56
      tasting of pork products for, 56–57
    Pad Thai, *90,* 192–95
      soaking noodles for, 194
Side dishes:
    four-cheese pasta, creamy baked, 81–82
      Master Recipe for, 82
      with Prosciutto and Peas, 82
      with Tomatoes and Basil, 82
    Greek salad, 4–5
      Country-Style, 5
      Master Recipe for, 5
    green bean(s), 108–9
      "Casserole," Quick, 108–9
      Garlic-Lemon, with Toasted Bread
        Crumbs, 109
      with Orange Essence and Toasted
        Maple Pecans, 109, *228*
    pasta with sautéed mushrooms, 64–67
      with Pancetta and Sage, 67
      with Peas and Camembert, 67
      and Thyme (Master Recipe),
        66–67, *229*
    potatoes, mashed, 163–65
      with Blue Cheese and Port-
        Caramelized Onions, 163–64
      with Scallions and Horseradish, 164
      with Smoked Cheddar and Grainy
        Mustard, 164
      with Smoked Paprika and Toasted
        Garlic, 165

Side dishes: *(cont.)*
    spinach salads, wilted
      Orange, 138–39
      Pineapple, 139
      Steak Fries, 176–77
      Wild Rice Pilaf with Pecans and
        Dried Cranberries, *95,* 116–17
Skillets:
    simmering sauces in, 79
    traditional, rating of, 134–36
Slow cookers, rating of, 32–33
Soufflé(s), lemon, chilled, 331–34
    Individual, 334
    Master Recipe for, 333–34
    with White Chocolate, 334
Soups:
    chowders, use of term, 44
    clam chowder, New England, 40–43
      Master Recipe for, 42
      Quick Pantry, 42–43
      scrubbing clams for, 42
      steaming clams for, 43
    gazpacho, 14–17
      Classic (Master Recipe), 16,
        *83*
      Garlic Croutons for, 17
      origins of, 16
      Quick Food Processor, 16
      Spicy, with Chipotle Chiles
        and Lime, 16–17
      texture of, 17
Sour Cream Topping, Whipped, 226
Southwestern Marinade, 173
Soy, Garlic, and Ginger Marinade,
    173
Spanish gazpacho, 14–17
    Classic (Master Recipe), 16, *83*
    Garlic Croutons for, 17
    origins of, 16
    Quick Food Processor, 16
    Spicy, with Chipotle Chiles and
      Lime, 16–17
    texture of, 17
Spatula/spoon hybrids (spoonulas), rating
    of, 266
Spatulas, rubber, rating of, 264–66
Spice(d)(s):
    Carrot Cake with Vanilla
      Bean–Cream Cheese
      Frosting, 307
    prying flavor out of, 211
    *see also specific spices*

Spinach salad, wilted:
    Orange, 138–39
    Pineapple, 139
    problems with, 11
    with Warm Bacon Dressing, 11, *87*
Spoonulas, rating of, 266
Springform pans, rating of, 320–21
Star Anise, Maple-Glazed Pork Roast with, 115
Steak(s), 155–62
    Chicken-Fried, 122–24
    cuts of beef for, 158
    filets mignons, grilled, 156–57
      Charcoal- (Master Recipe), *91,* 158–59
      Gas-, 159
      Lemon, Garlic, and Parsley Butter
        for, *91,* 159
      Roasted Red Pepper and Smoked
        Paprika Butter for, 159
    flank, slicing for stir-fries, 182
    judging doneness of, 159
    mail-order, tasting of, 160–62
    origins of names for, 156
    strip or rib, grilled, 156–59
      Charcoal- (Master Recipe), 157–58
      Gas-, 158
    tips, 170–73
      buying, 172
      Charcoal-Grilled (Master Recipe),
        *93,* 172
      Garlic, Ginger, and Soy Marinade
        for, 173
      Gas-Grilled, 172
      Southwestern Marinade for, 173
      tasting of, 173
Steak Fries, 176–77
Stir-fry(ied)(ies), 179–89
    beef and broccoli, 180–83
      with Oyster Sauce, *97,* 182–83
      slicing flank steak for, 182
      tasting of broccoli relations for, 184
      tasting of oyster sauce for, 184
    Pad Thai, *90,* 192–95
      soaking noodles for, 194
    pork and vegetable, 185–87
      with Eggplant, Onions, Garlic, and
        Black Pepper, 186
      with Green Beans, Red Bell
        Pepper, and Gingery Oyster
        Sauce, *92,* 186–87
      slicing pork tenderloin for, 188
      Spicy, with Asparagus, Onions, and
        Lemon Grass, 187

Stir-fry(ied)(ies) (cont.)
    technique for, 183
    woks for
        electric, rating of, 188–89
        flat-bottom, rating of, 196–97
Strawberries with Balsamic Vinegar,
    212–13
Strip steaks, grilled, 156–59
    Charcoal- (Master Recipe), 157–58
    Gas-, 158
Sugar:
    brown, softening, 284
    seasoning cold food with, 18
Summer Berry Pie, *237*, 294–96
Sunday brunch. *See* Brunch dishes

## T
Tamarind, 195
    tasting of options for, 195
Tartar Sauce, 48
Tarts:
    Tarte Tatin, 225–26
        with Pears, 226
        30-Minute (Master Recipe), 226
    tomato and mozzarella, 20–23
        assembling tart shell for, 24
        Master Recipe for, 22, *85*
        preventing soggy crust in, 20–21,
            22
        with Prosciutto, 23
        with Smoked Mozzarella, 23
        tasting of mozzarella for, 23–27
        tasting of puff pastry for, 23
Tasso, in jambalaya, 57
Tastings:
    andouille sausage, 56–57
    baking powder, 263–64
    balsamic vinegar, 213–15
    blueberries, frozen, 274–75
    broccoli relations, 184
    chocolates
        milk, 310–11
        unsweetened, 327–30
    coconut milk, coconut cream, and
        cream of coconut, 289–90
    cookie(s)
        for crumb crusts, 317
        dough, refrigerator, 284–86
    cornmeal, 263
    eggs, 258–59
    garlic, 148

Tastings: *(cont.)*
    graham cracker crusts, store-bought,
        129
    lemon substitutes, 317–19
    mayonnaise, 49–51
    mozzarella
        fresh, 27
        supermarket, 23–27
    olive oil, boutique extra-virgin,
        71–73
    oyster sauce, 184
    peanut butter, 200–202
    puff pastry, 23
    red peppers, jarred roasted, 6
    red wine vinegars
        gourmet, 9
        supermarket, 7–9
    steak(s)
        mail-order, 160–62
        tips, 173
    tamarind options, 195
    teas, supermarket, 252–53
    tomato(es)
        canned diced, 222–24
        paste, 79–80
        petite canned diced, 223
        puree, 33–34
    vegetable broth, 57–59
    vermouth, dry, 148–49
Teas, supermarket, tasting of, 252–53
Thai Pad Thai, *90*, 192–95
    soaking noodles for, 194
Thyme, Pasta with Sautéed Mushrooms
    and, 66–67, *229*
Tomato(es), 13–23
    Baked Four-Cheese Pasta with Basil
        and, 82
    canned diced, tasting of, 222–24
        petite, 223
    cutting into perfect dice, 19
    gazpacho, 14–17
        Classic (Master Recipe), 16, *83*
        Garlic Croutons for, 17
        origins of, 16
        Quick Food Processor, 16
        Spicy, with Chipotle Chiles and
            Lime, 16–17
        texture of, 17
    Greek salad, 4–5
        Country-Style, 5
        Master Recipe for, 4–5

Tomato(es) *(cont.)*
    and mozzarella tart, 20–23
        assembling tart shell for, 24
        Master Recipe for, 22, *85*
        preventing soggy crust in, 20–21,
            22
        with Prosciutto, 23
        with Smoked Mozzarella, 23
        tasting of mozzarella for, 23–27
        tasting of puff pastry for, 23
    paste, tasting of, 79–80
    Pot Roast with Mushrooms, Red Wine
        and, 103
    puree, tasting of, 33–34
Top-blade roasts, 104
    tying, 105
Trivets, extra-large, improvising, 145
Tupperware, rating of, 118–19

## V
Vanilla Bean–Cream Cheese Frosting, 307
Vegetable(s):
    broth, tasting of, 57–59
    chopping in food processor, 58
    cutting into perfect dice, 19
    *see also specific vegetables*
Vegetable choppers, rating of, 106–7
Vermouth:
    dry, tasting of, 148–49
    Sage Sauce, Pan-Roasted Chicken
        Breasts with, *88*, 133
Vinaigrettes, 3
    for Greek Salad, 5
Vinegars:
    balsamic
        Strawberries with, 212–13
        tasting of, 213–15
    red wine
        food analysis of, 7
        gourmet, tasting of, 9
        supermarket, tasting of, 7–9
    seasoning cold food with, 18

## W
Water baths, science of, 319
Whipped cream:
    chilling bowl for, 298
    Topping, 128
        Sour Cream, 226
White Chocolate, Chilled Lemon Soufflé
    with, 334

Wild rice:
  food facts about, 116
  getting right texture of, 117
  Pilaf with Pecans and Dried Cranberries,
    *95,* 116–17
Wine:
  Port-Caramelized Onions, Mashed
    Potatoes with Blue Cheese and,
    163–64
  red
    Pot Roast with Mushrooms,
      Tomatoes and, 103
    Sauce, Sweet-Tart, Pan-Roasted
      Chicken Breasts with, 133–34

Wine: *(cont.)*
  Sherry-Garlic Sauce,
    Pan-Roasted Chicken
    Breasts with, 133
  vermouth
    dry, tasting of, 148–49
    Sage Sauce, Pan-Roasted
      Chicken Breasts with,
      *88,* 133
Wine vinegars, red:
  food analysis of, 7
  tastings of
    gourmet, 9
    supermarket, 7–9

Woks, ratings of:
  electric, 188–89
  flat-bottom, 196–97